LEADERS
and
LIBERALS
in
20th Century America

LEADERS

and

LIBERALS

in

20th Century America

CHARLES A. MADISON

FREDERICK UNGAR PUBLISHING CO.
NEW YORK

TO ALL AMERICANS
WHO CHERISH DEMOCRACY
AND SEEK TO MAKE IT WORK

PREFACE

I N THIS BOOK I have sought to delineate the personalities and events that have helped to change the United States from the almost classic *laissez-faire* economy of 1900 to the relatively well-regulated industrial society of the 1960's. Emphasis is given to the idea that the democratic welfare state is the product of large-scale corporate enterprise; that the very bigness of modern business, making most men wholly dependent on it for their livelihood, makes government regulation of economic practices an unavoidable necessity.

It has always seemed to me that historic events assume realistic vividness when fleshed with the life stories of their chief participants. With this in mind I have chosen for detailed and dramatic study the outstanding liberals in office during the first half of this century, men who have made the largest impact upon the nation's development into a democratic world power. The cumulative effect of their colorful careers—their struggles and aspirations, their achievements and limitations, as well as the cross-currents, enmeshing incidents, and the acute crises of economic depression and world war—provides concrete evidence of how the concept of dynamic democracy has ceased to be associated with the rugged individualism of the Gilded Age and has become synonymous with the goal of the welfare state.

The introductory chapter surveys the emergence of powerful corporations and the sporadic protests against the abuses of free enterprise. Part One depicts the struggle for social justice during the early years of the present century. The study of Theodore Roosevelt presents the strenuous Colonel making sensational yet spurious attempts to curb monopoly and corruption, acting as protean leader in the formation and failure of the 1912 Progressive party, and ending his last years as an embittered conservative. Woodrow Wilson's meteoric political career is discussed in connection with his espousal of the New Freedom—which began so hopefully only to become a casualty of war and give way to the Palmer raids and President Harding's "Normalcy." The chapter on Senator Robert M. LaFollette depicts his midwestern parochial radicalism and his persistent, if futile, fight against monopoly and privilege. Finally Justice Louis D. Brandeis is shown as the chief critic of industrial bigness and social intolerance as well as the ideological link between the New Freedom and the New Deal.

Part Two treats the significant aspects of the New Deal and its postwar eclipse. The portrayal of Franklin D. Roosevelt seeks to encompass his complex character, to indicate his efforts to rebuild the weakened economy on a democratic foundation, to show how he helped defeat world fascism by making America the arsenal of democracy, and to discuss his exertions to establish world peace on the solid premise of an effective United Nations. The chapter on Senator George W. Norris, reviewing his long and distinguished career as a liberal legislator, lays special stress on his struggle for public power from the early days of Muscle Shoals to the successful development of the Tennessee Valley Authority. The review of Justice Hugo L. Black's active life brings out his remarkable rise from the local lawyer who became a member of the Klan because it was the popular thing to do in Alabama in the early 1920's, to an aggressive liberal Senator, and finally to the stanchest defender of the Bill of Rights in American judicial history. The sudden sharp decline of the New Deal spirit, our involvement in the "cold war," and the McCarthyite attack on our basic freedoms are discussed in the chapter on the Truman Administration. A final brief summation defines the place of the welfare state in our modern industrial society.

PREFACE

I am very grateful to the authors whose writings, for the most part cited in the bibliography, have helped me more than I can acknowledge in a mere listing. Professors David M. Potter and Arthur S. Link have kindly read all of the chapters and given me the benefit of their searching criticism; although we differ sharply on questions of interpretation in the latter chapters, I feel deeply in their debt. Individual chapters were read by Walter Johnson, Robert M. La Follette, Jr., Thomas R. Amlie, Susan Brandeis, William Seagle, Samuel I. Rosenman, John P. Frank, and Henry A. Wallace—to all of whom I am very grateful. I also want to thank Helen De Vries for her careful editing of the manuscript. My deepest obligation is to my wife, for she has not only strongly encouraged me to write the book but has read every page of it with acute critical discernment and has helped me with the proofreading.

Charles A. Madison

October 10, 1960

CONTENTS

CONTENTS

PART ONE

THE
STRUGGLE FOR SOCIAL JUSTICE

The Revolt Against *Laissez Faire*

AMERICANS IN THE EARLY NINETEENTH CENTURY cherished the philosophy of *laissez faire* as an essential element of their democracy. Cradled in the tradition of the Declaration of Independence, proud of their role as self-reliant frontiersmen, and kept from dire want by the ready availability of game and garden, they considered the freedom of enterprise as the inalienable right of every individual. Their aggressive offspring in the post-Civil War decades hailed this doctrine as a matter of course. For the "great barbecue" had begun. Untold natural wealth was being uncovered and exploited in the oil fields of Pennsylvania and Ohio, in the fertile virgin acres of the prairies, in the rich coal and mineral mines everywhere. The hope of sudden gain and unearned increment stirred in the hearts of tens of thousands—and none wanted to be kept back from this common opportunity.

A spirit of largess was over the land. The general eagerness to populate the continental expanse and to develop the potential resources of the nation placed a premium upon individual enterprise and accelerated the acceptance of "the gospel of wealth." The seeming prevalence of opportunity for all made it easy for Americans to assume that the practical application of Adam Smith's famous dictum—"man's self-love is God's providence"—would bring the United States the combined blessing of liberty and abundance.

The classical economists, the orthodox and affluent Puritans,

3

the traditional Jeffersonians—all proudly coupled the doctrines of democracy and *laissez faire*. In 1776, when Adam Smith first published *The Wealth of Nations*, democracy and the freedom of enterprise indeed went hand in hand. What Smith and his followers did was to validate theoretically the claim long made by independent craftsmen: the right of each man to produce and sell the work of his hands to his best advantage. Because kings and nobles generally refused to accede to this claim, their overthrow served to establish not only political democracy but also the freedom of individual enterprise.

Once the Revolution succeeded, Americans insisted on living under a minimum of government. Tom Paine well expressed this common sentiment:

Every man wishes to pursue his occupation, and to enjoy the fruits of his labors and the produce of his property in peace and safety, and with the least possible expense. When these things are accomplished, all the objects for which government ought to be established are answered.

Thomas Jefferson, having in 1800 defeated the party favoring strong government, boldly proclaimed in his inaugural address the philosophy of the less government the better:

With all these blessings what more is necessary to make us a happy and prosperous people? Still one thing more, fellow citizens, a wise and frugal government which shall restrain men from injuring one another, shall leave them otherwise free to regulate their own pursuit of industry and improvement, and shall not take from the mouth of labor the bread it has earned.

Paine and Jefferson envisioned a nation composed mainly of farmers, craftsmen, and traders. And this was largely true of the United States till the Civil War. Beginning with the 1850's, however, the discovery of coal, iron, copper, oil, and other mineral deposits greatly stimulated the development of large-scale industry. Shrewd and aggressive entrepreneurs soon began to manipulate vast combinations of wealth. The sharp advance of both

4

technology and markets hastened the rise of powerful corporations and imperious monopolies. Successful industrialists and financiers, holding vast economic power and controlling the livelihood of thousands, nevertheless continued to capitalize on the craftsman's "natural right" to further his individual interests without regard to the effect of their actions on the nation as a whole.

For years none questioned their right to exploit the country's natural resources. In their favor were the democratic admiration for the self-made millionaire, the cultural lag favoring the freedom of enterprise long after altered conditions had vitiated its original validity, and the general antipathy to the expansion of government. The orthodox economists, still clinging to the doctrines of *laissez faire*, likewise bolstered the position of the bold entrepreneur. President James McCosh of Princeton was typical in his advocacy of free enterprise:

God has bestowed upon us certain powers and gifts which no one is at liberty to take from us or to interfere with. All attempts to deprive us of them is theft. Under the same head may be placed all purposes to deprive us of the right to earn property or to use it as we see fit.

The Social Darwinists, headed by Professor William Graham Sumner of Yale, also championed the doctrine of *laissez faire*. Ignoring the practical conditions that refuted their theory, they maintained that man was born to struggle for survival, that no man had any claim on anything he did not achieve by his own efforts, and that all prevalent rights were in fact achieved by successful acts of force. Sumner thus justified his belief in free enterprise as a civilizing force:

The enlightened pursuit of wealth is one of the strongest forces in society for elevating the individual and for advancing the civilization of the state. . . . This pursuit is the animus of that sustained industry and energy which creates values and speeds culture and civilization, and promotes peace, and enlightens men as to the meaning of human brotherhood. . . . I therefore maintain that it is at the present time a matter of patriotism and civic duty to resist the extension of state interference.

This ingenious rationalization failed to recognize the emergent gravity of an uncontrolled industrialism. Sharp and unscrupulous businessmen, bent on getting rich quick, were everywhere recklessly exploiting the nation's natural resources, crushing weaker competitors, corrupting public officials, establishing powerful corporations, and accumulating vast fortunes at the expense of a helpless public. "The business man," wrote Herbert Croly, "in seeking to realize his ambitions and purposes was checked neither by government nor social custom. He had nothing to do and nothing to consider except his own business advancement and success."

Flattered by their constructive part in the development of a continental empire, these successful businessmen considered themselves fully entitled to their acquired wealth. They were therefore impatient with those who questioned their methods or their ethics. John D. Rockefeller, the most enterprising industrialist of his day, honestly believed with the Social Darwinists that "the growth of a large business is merely a survival of the fittest." In his view the fittest were those who succeeded in destroying competition most effectively. Thus, while he and others like him insisted on their right to complete freedom of enterprise, they denied this privilege to their weaker competitors.

Conceit and cupidity soon led a number of entrepreneurs to disregard their professed Christian ethics and to debauch public officials in a position to bestow favors. Corporations that depended on propitious franchises for their profitable enterprises were not loath to bribe politicians on a give-and-take basis. The railroads were among the first and largest practitioners of this form of collusion. The Union Pacific paid a total of $400,000 in bribes during the years 1866–1872; and from 1875 to 1885 the Central Pacific spent up to a half million annually in graft. Legislators were bought fairly openly, and political bosses were paid regularly for favors received. In 1870 Senator Grimes of Iowa accused the Republican party under President Grant of being "the most corrupt and debauched political party that ever existed." Six years later Senator Hoar of Massachusetts declared that government corruption was open and widespread—reaching the highest offices.

I have heard in the highest places the shameless doctrine avowed, by men grown old in public office, that the true way by which power should be gained in the Republic is to bribe the people with the offices created for their service, and the true end for which it should be used when gained is the promotion of selfish ambition and the gratification of personal revenge. I have heard that suspicion haunts the footsteps of the trusted companions of the President.

So callous, indeed, had public officials become to their sworn trust, that they readily confused current business practice with the ethics of their office. Thus Congressman Oakes Ames of Massachusetts considered the distribution of a block of Union Pacific stock to influential members of Congress "the same thing as going into a business community and interesting the leading business men by giving them shares."

Nor was graft always necessary to obtain desired privileges and advantages. A spendthrift and complaisant government made it easy for individuals and corporations to evade and violate the law, often with impunity. In the course of time businessmen acquired valuable mining and forest land at nominal cost; they gained higher tariffs on imports without keeping their promises to raise wages above the level of subsistence; they obtained secret rebates from railroads at the expense of weaker competitors. All this was considered good business.

The railroads probably benefited most from this largess at the great barbecue. Because they were essential to the growth of the opened West, they were provided gratuitously not only with millions of acres along the rights of way but also with large sums of credit. And so deeply rooted was the aversion to government interference in private enterprise that the problem of control was not even considered. Nor were the railroad companies called to account when their system of construction was revealed as wasteful and corrupt; or when their stocks and bonds were badly watered and manipulated to the hurt of small investors. More-

7

over, instead of being operated as public highways open to all on an equal basis, the railroads everywhere were permitted to become powerful and oppressive quasi-monopolies. Their arbitrary rulings, their high freight rates, their collusion with favored large customers and affiliates, their aggressive expansion into related fields of business enterprise—these and other high-handed activities soon made them anathema to an aggrieved general public. A Congress report thus criticized the railroads for abusing the powers granted to them—in this instance in connection with the coal industry:

The carrier drives out both operator and owner, obtains the property, works the mine, "disciplines" the miner, lowers wages by the importation of Huns and Italians, restricts the output, and advances the price of coal to the public. It is enabled to commit such wrongs upon individuals and the public by virtue of exercising absolute control of a public highway.

The Jeffersonian dream of relative social and economic equality was rudely shattered by an industrialism motivated primarily by pecuniary gain. A measure of this growing inequality was revealed by the fact that while there were only three millionaires at the outbreak of the Civil War, that number had grown to 3800 by the end of the century—with some of them counting their assets in the hundreds of millions. Certain economists pointed out that nine-tenths of the nation's wealth had come into the possession of one-tenth of the population. This condition caused millions of Americans to suffer want in the richest country in the world. And the recurring economic depressions accentuated this want by depriving many either of steady employment or of adequate markets for their produce. This of course was hardly consonant with the commonly assumed ideals of the Declaration of Independence. Writing in 1894, Henry D. Lloyd was sharply critical:

How is it that we, who profess the religion of the Golden Rule and the political economy of service for service, come to divide our produce into incalculable power and pleasure for the few, and partial existence for the many who are the fountains of these powers and pleasures?

Nearly twenty years later Herbert Croly, evaluating the promise of American life, likewise deplored the economic disparity accompanying our national development: "The net result of the industrial expansion of the United States since the Civil War has been the establishment in the heart of the American economic and social system certain glaring inequalities of condition and power."

Farmers were the first to cry out against this "extrinsic baleful influence." This was understandable. Agricultural prices declined almost steadily from 1870 to 1897, with corn dropping as low as ten cents a bushel. The harder these farmers worked and the more land they cultivated, the further they went into debt. Overextended holdings and high interest on mortgages combined with bad weather, high freight rates, and low prices to drive many of them to the brink of bankruptcy. Disturbed and distressed, they grew angry at the thought of having to pay in freight rates almost as much as they received for the grain they were shipping. Their anger increased on learning that the bushel of corn for which they were paid ten cents sold for as much as a dollar in New York and that middlemen and millers were combining to bring about "cheaper wheat and dearer flour."

Strong individualists, with a deep antipathy toward government control, they were nevertheless soon forced by dire need to clamor for relief. Resenting their increasing dependence upon the railroads, upon unstable world markets, and upon bank loans, they flocked to the newly organized National Grange—the agrarian organization that sought to lower transportation rates and aimed to cut the cost of production and selling by cooperative means. In the 1870's and later these organized farmers succeeded in securing laws regulating railroad rates in Illinois, Minnesota, Iowa, Wisconsin, and other states. The governor of Illinois, in his message to the legislature in 1871, said of the railroads:

They discriminated against persons and places. Citizens protested against these abuses in vain. The railroad corporations, when threatened with the power of the government, indulged in the language of defiance, and attempted to control legislation to their own advantage. At last, public indignation became excited against them. They did not heed it; they believed that the courts would be their refuge from popular fury.

The courts did favor the railroads, and the political activity of the Grange proved of little avail. Yet this effort on the part of the farmers became the turning point in their altered political philosophy. This change of attitude is stressed by Professor Solon J. Buck:

It marks the final abandonment of the *laissez-faire* theory that natural laws alone are sufficient to insure the management of railroads in the interest of the public, and the beginning of definite attempts to solve the railway problem by restrictive legislation.

Although the Grange failed them, most farmers, harassed and aggrieved, felt they must keep trying. When their local branches began to disintegrate, they formed other political organizations. The Farmers' Alliance, uniting numerous regional groups in 1882, became their next means of protest. By this time criticism of social ills had become vociferous and widespread. Editors of rural weeklies began to question the validity of *laissez faire* and to discuss current social problems with frankness and vehemence. The tone and direction of their criticisms are indicated in the following editorial comment of *The Progressive Farmer*, published in Raleigh, North Carolina:

There is something radically wrong in our industrial system. There is a screw loose. The wheels have dropped out of balance. The railroads have never been so prosperous, and yet agriculture languishes. The banks have never done a better or more profitable business, and yet agriculture languishes. Manufacturing enterprises never made more money or were in a more flourishing condition, and yet agriculture languishes. Towns and cities flourish and "boom" and grow and "boom," and yet agriculture languishes.

10

Nor were the farmers alone in reacting forcefully against the new industrialism. Liberals, reformers, labor leaders, preachers, and economists—all those moved by humanitarian impulses were disturbed by the growing inequality and criticized the social excrescences of a radically changing economy. The socialists, antagonized by the callous disregard for human suffering on the part of the leaders of the Gilded Age, proceeded to scrape off the veneer of capitalistic democracy and disclose the deplorable conditions underneath.

One of the first to strike the tocsin was Wendell Phillips. Once the Negroes were emancipated, he turned his attention to what he regarded as the wage slavery of the white workers. On the platform and in his writings he insisted that human rights were superior to property rights and that the welfare of the workers was more important than the profits of their employers. Another friend of the poor and the oppressed was Peter Cooper, a prosperous inventor and manufacturer. He not only used his own wealth to help the New York indigent but petitioned Congress to stop passing laws favoring "the rich, who can take care of themselves," and to legislate for the poor who were exposed to "periodic distress and starvation." He maintained that large-scale industrialism endangered the community, "for monopolizing corporations, whether in the shape of banks or railroads, have no soul."

The three most popular reformers of the 1880's and 1890's were Henry George, Henry D. Lloyd, and Edward Bellamy. George's *Progress and Poverty*, expounding the social nature of poverty and advocating the remedy of the single tax on land, appeared at a time when millions of Americans were hard pressed and yearned for a solution to their economic difficulties. The logic of the single tax appeared to many at once simple and irrefutable. For a while the crusading single taxers believed they would win the confidence of a majority of the people. But they were seeing only a mirage, and their sweeping reform went the way of all panaceas. Bellamy's *Looking Backward* ran a similar course. Its popularity was astounding, and its admirers actually formed the Nationalist party with

11

a view to winning the government for Bellamy's brand of simple socialism.

If the authors of these two best-sellers were utopian dreamers, Lloyd was critically realistic. As early as 1881 his article in *The Atlantic Monthly* on the nefarious practices of the Standard Oil Company shocked the country into a sudden realization of the harm of monopoly power. Thirteen years later he published in his monumental *Wealth Against Commonwealth* an indictment of corporate capitalism based largely on the record of official investigations and hearings by government agencies. Although he devoted most of his space to the aggressive practices of the Standard Oil Company, he also laid bare the illegal and collusive machinations of other large corporations. Throughout the book he showed that the greed for profit caused all types of businesses to mulct the public to the utmost of their ability. Discussing the fight of the gas companies against public ownership, he declared:

The essence of "private enterprise" was that the public should get their gas from Captains of Industry, and pay them for their captaincy two or three times the real cost as profit, just as monarchial countries pay kings for kindly supplying the people with the government which really comes from the people.

His charge that corporate power corroded the foundations of democracy he bolstered with the following comment from a Michigan supreme court ruling in a match trust suit:

It is indeed doubtful if free government can long exist in a country where such enormous amounts of money are allowed to be accumulated in the vaults of corporations, to be used at discretion in controlling the property and business of the country against the interest of the public and that of the people, for the personal gain and aggrandizement of a few individuals.

These books and the agitation of farmer and labor leaders helped to crystallize the increasing dissatisfaction of millions of Americans. Such ideas as the single tax, government control of business, public ownership of basic utilities, fiat money, and socialism became popular topics of discussion. Nor was their advocacy limited to agitators and radicals. Reputable young men, motivated by Christian ethics rather than by pecuniary gain, were equally critical of economic inequality. When young Franklin K. Lane, later a distinguished public official, visited New York for the first time in 1889, he was deeply distressed by the evidences of extreme poverty on the East Side. "There is justification here for a social-economic revolution and it will come, too, if things are not bettered."

Of course, the defenders of the status quo derided this dissatisfaction as the grumblings of fools and failures. The opportunity to get rich was open to everyone, they argued, and those who remained poor had only themselves to blame. Typical of these rugged individualists was James G. Blaine, a leading politician and Republican candidate for the Presidency in 1884. When the clamor against monopolistic corporations became too loud to be ignored and Congress was forced to act in 1888, he contended against such legislation on the ground that "trusts are largely private affairs, with which neither President Cleveland nor any private citizen has any particular right to interfere." When popular demand nevertheless compelled Congress to pass the Interstate Commerce Act, Senator Nelson W. Aldrich, another Republican stalwart, considered it "a delusion and a sham . . . an empty menace to the great interests, made to answer the clamor of the ignorant and the unreasoning." This opinion was later corroborated by Attorney-General Richard Olney in a letter to the president of the Chicago, Burlington and Quincy Railroad. The Interstate Commerce Commission, he wrote, was in fact "of great use to the railroads. It satisfied the popular clamor for government supervision of the railroads at the same time that that supervision is almost entirely nominal."

In the late 1880's organized labor was still too weak and dispirited to act politically on its own. The farmers, more numerous and more vocal, insisted on conditions favoring their economic betterment. The vanishing frontier had made it impossible for them

13

to strike out anew on a free quarter-section of land. Forced to remain on their farms and pay from 8 to 24 percent interest on their bank loans, they were fighting mad. As one Nebraska farmer expressed their plight,

There are three great crops raised in Nebraska. One is a crop of corn, one a crop of freight rates, and one a crop of interest. One is produced by the farmers who by sweat and toil farm the land. The other two are produced by men who sit in their offices and behind their bank counters and farm the farmers.

Less sardonic but more explicit was the statement made by Mary Elizabeth Lease of Kansas: "We want money, land and transportation. We want the abolition of National Banks, and we want the power to make loans direct from the government. We want the accursed foreclosure system wiped out."

To gain influence within the government, they turned the Farmers' Alliance into an active political instrument. Their zeal was soon tangibly rewarded. In the 1890 campaign they succeeded in electing two Senators, eight Congressmen, and scores of state and local officials. This promise of ultimate victory caused them to intensify their political efforts. Their representatives in the South—among them L. L. Polk of North Carolina, Ben Tillman of South Carolina, Tom Watson of Georgia, and C. W. Macune of Texas—forced by the Negro problem to remain in the Democratic party, made sharp inroads into its conservative leadership. The heads of the Alliance in the Middle West—men such as William A. Peffer and Jerry Simpson of Kansas, William V. Allen of Nebraska, and Ignatius Donnelly of Minnesota—followed a different course. Unable to break the control of Big Business over the Republican party and finding the Democrats weak and uncongenial, they decided to form a political party of their own.

On May 19, 1891, Alliance delegates and representatives from several dissident groups met in Cincinnati to discuss the union of forces in the oncoming elections. The reconciliation of their diverse views was no easy task, and the discussions were prolonged and vehement, but agreement was finally reached and a founding convention was scheduled for the following February. On the appointed date twenty-two organizations met in St. Louis. The hall was crowded with zealous delegates insistent on being heard. In addition to the Alliance leaders there were spokesmen for the Knights of Labor (but not for the young American Federation of Labor), the Single Taxers, the Antimonopolists, the Prohibitionists, and other reform organizations. To the right of the stage, brilliantly decorated with the national colors, was stretched a broad poster bearing the slogan: "We do not ask for sympathy or pity. We ask for justice." And the vociferous delegates who participated in the seemingly endless harangues, interrupted by frequent outbursts of joyous singing and exuberant demonstrations, did not merely ask for justice but shouted defiance to the oppressors of the people.

The delegates had come determined to profess their beliefs and formulate their demands. The extremists, in control of the platform committee, soon prepared a document that condemned the capitalistic system and specified social reforms of a radical character.

We meet in the midst of a nation brought to the verge of moral, political and material ruin. Corruption dominates the ballot box, the legislatures, the Congress, and touches even the ermine of the bench. The people are demoralized. . . . The newspapers are subsidized or muzzled; public opinion silenced; business prostrated, our homes covered with mortgages, labor impoverished, and the land concentrating in the hands of capitalists. . . . The fruits of the toil of millions are boldly stolen to build up colossal fortunes, unprecedented in the history of the world, while their possessors despise the republic and endanger liberty. From the same prolific womb of governmental injustice we breed two great classes—paupers and millionaires. . . . If not met and overthrown at once it forbodes terrible social convulsions, the destruction of civilization, or the establishment of an absolute despotism.

Among the platform planks were those demanding the government ownership of the railroads and telegraph and telephone lines, government loans to farmers at low rates of interest, the free coinage of silver at the ratio of 16 to 1, a graduated income tax, lower tariffs, postal savings banks, the popular election of Senators, and the adoption of the initiative and referendum. This program of political and economic reform, more radical than any previous party platform, was hailed by its proponents as a second declaration of independence.

The following Fourth of July the new People's party held its first nominating convention and chose James B. Weaver, former leader of the Greenback party, as its candidate for the Presidency. The campaign was conducted with vigor and vehemence. Both older parties hotly condemned the new rival as representative of revolution and violence. Their speakers concentrated on the radical issue and called upon the voters to save the country from anarchy. But the Populist candidates advocated their reform planks with unflagging zeal. In the farming communities of the Middle West their appeals and expostulations met with wide approval; but their radicalism, magnified and distorted by their opponents, tended to irritate and frighten the urban populace.

When the votes were counted in November, Weaver's share of over a million did not indicate the true strength of the new party. Perhaps another million who sympathized with the aims of the People's party cast their ballots for Grover Cleveland in order to assure the defeat of the Republican candidate. This was especially true in the North, where a large number of workers, antagonized by the harsh repression of the Homestead strike, voted against the party in power. In the South many Populist farmers, bedevilled by the irrepressible Negro problem, had no choice but to vote the Democratic ticket. Very likely, therefore, Grover Cleveland owed his election to the dissident voters. In the Middle West the Populists made a good start—electing three Senators, ten Congressmen, four governors, and hundreds of lesser officials.

For all their radical claims, the Populists were merely seeking, naively and exuberantly, to adjust an increasingly gargantuan

16

industrialism to the simple precepts of Jeffersonian democracy. Their demands appealed to millions of Americans who found themselves in the grip of the gigantic corporations. Governor L. D. Lewelling of Kansas, voicing the sentiment of the frontier democrat, clearly delineated the aspirations of these millions in his 1893 innaugural address:

The Government must make it possible for the citizen to live by his own labor. The Government must make it possible for the citizen to enjoy liberty and the pursuit of happiness. If the Government fails in these things, it fails in its mission. . . . The people are greater than the law or the statutes, and when a nation sets its heart on doing a great or good thing, it can find a legal way to do it.

The People's party appeared well launched. Not a few of its leaders believed that the 1896 election would establish them in the seat of power. Indeed, all political signs seemed highly favorable toward that possibility. Unforeseen circumstances, however, invalidated these portents. The severe economic depression that began in 1893 made its victims anxious for immediate relief. It also served to give undue prominence to the chronic silver issue. Those who favored the free coinage of silver argued persuasively that the depression was caused by an inadequate currency. The millions of workers and farmers then in dire need were readily attracted to this financial panacea. As Henry D. Lloyd stated subsequently, "Free silver is the cow-bird of the reform movement. It waited until the nest had been built by the sacrifices and labor of others, and laid its eggs in it, pushing out the others which lie smashed on the ground." Another cow-bird was William Jennings Bryan, whose beguiling oratory appealed not only to disgruntled Democrats but also to the more timid of the Populists.

When the People's party convened to nominate its candidates for the 1896 election, its leaders were confused and panicky. Eager as they all were to further the progress of the party, they broke into irreconcilable factions on the question of immediate policy.

17

The Democrats had already nominated Bryan. His Cross of Gold speech still resounded sweetly in the minds of many Populists; they were moreover readily persuaded by Democratic proselytizers that an independent Populist candidate would make certain the election of the conservative "Gold" Republican William McKinley. The numerous reform planks in the liberal Democratic platform were emphasized as evidence that Bryan's election would indeed establish Populism in the seat of government.

The debate at the Populist convention, on the platform as well as behind the scene, was fervent and furious. Many of the more radical delegates insisted that the nomination of Bryan would mean the death of the party. But the pragmatists won out. The lure of immediate gains proved irresistible in a time of crisis. Eager to take their stand on the great issue of the day—that "between men and money"—they joined the crusade against the "gold bugs."

The 1896 campaign was fought with great zeal and passion. The Bryan forces—certain that they must win or submit to the crass rule of Big Business—were imbued with fanatical anxiety. Together with their "peerless" leader they worked day and night to rouse their fellow Americans to the danger confronting them and to enroll them under the Democratic banner. The Populists, not fully reconciled to their alliance with Bryan, yet satisfied with his progressive platform, labored indefatigably in his behalf. But the Republicans were also aware of the crucial nature of the election and exerted themselves to the utmost to assure victory at the polls. Mark Hanna collected millions from wealthy Republicans and spent them lavishly. Many employers informed their workers that they would lose their jobs if Bryan won the Presidency. Scores of Republican speakers denounced Bryan and his leading supporters as extreme radicals bent on ruining the country. To the last day of the campaign the charges and countercharges were made so emphatically and so rancorously that they could not but confuse many of the voters. In the end victory was achieved largely by a combination of Hanna's generous spending and the general threat of unemployment.

Bryan's defeat worked havoc with the dedicated Populists. Their erstwhile confidence in the increasing strength of their party was completely shattered. They felt themselves betrayed by their own gullibility, outmaneuvered by beguiling oratory and seductive promises. The moderate and pragmatic faction, largely responsible for the party's acceptance of Bryan as its candidate and increasingly uneasy in its relationship with the aggressively radical group, tended to remain within the Democratic fold. The extreme dissidents, concluding that socialism was the only ultimate solution to the evils of capitalism, turned their attention to the emerging Marxist movement. The remaining Populists, too discouraged to attempt the rebuilding of their party and yet believing as strongly as ever in the urgency of social reform, drifted in a political void.

Meantime the business cycle entered its upward phase. Confidence returned to the marts of trade. Prosperity rose like the benign sun. The brief but triumphant war with Spain served to tap fresh sources of industrial energy. Scores of shrewd men were making their millions and many thousands of workers carried their "full dinner pail" with mild contentment. At least superficially the nineteenth century was passing into history properly appeased.

In 1900 *laissez faire* remained the dominant policy of the government and the cherished myth of democratic individualism permitted the bold entrepreneur free rein in the economic field. Yet the forces of discontent and reform were not destroyed; defeat scattered them, but could not wholly silence their protests. Moreover, conditions favored the emergence of new, and more resourceful, critics of unrestricted enterprise.

Theodore Roosevelt

THE BULLY CRUSADER AT ARMAGEDDON

AT THE OPENING OF THE TWENTIETH CENTURY the United States suddenly emerged as a mighty nation. Out of the brief, brash war with senescent Spain it came forth as a prime world power, bursting with dynamic force, bustling with self-conscious importance. For by that time, almost unnoticed, the seat of the world's greatest energy—the concentration of dominant economic activity and human vigor—had moved from Europe to the United States. American businessmen functioned with a zeal and zest incomprehensible to industrialists in other parts of the world.

American enterprise was assuming gigantic proportions. Billion-dollar corporations were being established in steel, oil, and the railroads. Near-monopolies were functioning in beef, sugar, copper, and other basic commodities. The large banks, and particularly the private financial institutions, expedited industrial mergers that dwarfed similar economic groupings in England and on the Continent. Indeed, large-scale enterprise and great concentration of wealth began to be regarded as characteristically American.

Businessmen by the score were becoming multimillionaires and striding across their fields of activity with the egotism of unrestrained power. Essentially naive and homespun men, thrust into the industrial forefront by virtue of an excess of shrewdness and energy, tempted by the largess of an unexploited continent, and driven by the force of favorable circumstances ever deeper into rivalry in amassing fortunes, they worked hard to increase the profits from their enterprises. Not the social good but their own personal gain became the goal. Louis M. Hacker noted in *The Triumph of American Capitalism*:

Profits were to be made at all costs: by monopoly controls, first and foremost; and also by limiting production, withholding inventions, fixing and keeping inelastic prices, rigging the security markets, manipulating and vulgarizing the judicial processes, and encouraging paid management (itself insecure) to fight labor mercilessly.

This emphasis on profit tended to increase the fluctuations of the business cycle—which in the depressed phase brought suffering to workers deprived of their jobs and to farmers unable to sell their produce at a fair price. At such times millions of men cursed the notorious industrialists and financiers associated with Big Business. But the Morgans and the Vanderbilts and the Rockefellers either ignored or disdained the resentment generated against them. Ready to finance the campaigns of both major parties, accustomed to having legislators and judges seeing their way, they had no fear of government intervention.

With President McKinley's re-election in 1900 Big Business felt safe from the threat of Bryanism. Confidence bred smugness. Successful businessmen tended to assume that, to paraphrase George F. Baer's pious dictum during the 1902 coal strike, God in his infinite wisdom had chosen them as the guardians and governors of the nation's economy. Consequently they arrogated to themselves the right to carry on their enterprises as they thought best. For others to criticize their methods, to place the welfare of the people above profits—to curb the freedom of doing business —struck them as an insidious and unwarranted violation of their established privileges. Owen Wister, the noted author of *The Virginian*, thus commented on this attitude:

Hands off! was what Big Business felt about itself in relation to the entire outside world; whatever it saw fit to do was, in its own eyes, right. It had come to resemble a good deal what a church was in the

21

Middle Ages, a sanctuary in which you were safe from all hostile assault. . . . Not even the Government of the United States must dare to call Big Business to order.

The rise of finance capitalism was making the practice of *laissez faire* more and more untenable. With the extraordinary concentration of power in large-scale industrialism, the unrestrained individualism of businessmen proved too dangerous to the nation's welfare to remain uncontrolled. As a consequence, the concepts of personal freedom and minimum government, the shibboleths of nineteenth-century liberals, began slowly yet irresistibly to yield to the ideal of social justice. Men of good will everywhere came to perceive the fallacy of the Adam Smith doctrine that the interests of the individual automatically coincided with the welfare of the group. They realized that while the free activity of the individual seemed right and natural in the days of the beckoning frontier, when businesses were small, when land was relatively free and every man could be his own master, it assumed a grievous aspect when exercised by powerful industrialists for private gain. With the frontier gone, with farmers and wage-earners equally dependent for their livelihood upon large corporations, the cry for social justice pierced the conscience of many of our eminent citizens.

Theodore Roosevelt, one of these youthful social reformers, was no radical. He believed in property rights, in law and order, in sound capitalism. When Bryan and the Populists combined to advance radical reforms, he attacked them ferociously. Yet he was a moralist in action. He abhorred injustice and despised the selfish and sordid practices of powerful corporations. Dedicated to fight for the right, he spoke out against "the malefactors of great wealth" with such force and feeling as to call forth Vachel Lindsay's sardonic remark that Roosevelt "cursed Bryan and then aped his ways."

Born on October 27, 1858, of a wealthy and socially prominent family and blessed with a father of high morality and a strong sense of civic stewardship, Theodore Roosevelt early developed a broad altruism. In his childhood he suffered severely from asthma. Many a night his father had to hold him in his arms to help him breathe more freely. The attachment between son and parent was strengthened by the latter's warm and sympathetic attentiveness. In time the elder Roosevelt's charities, civic activities, and general concern for the welfare of mankind became the sickly boy's own ideals for action.

When Theodore was nine his father, eager to develop his son's puny body in the hope of reducing his asthma, turned one of the rooms in their home into a gymnasium and prescribed certain daily exercises. The boy needed no prodding. His anxiety to be strong—to rid himself of physical illness and excel in sports—became the passion of his youth and persisted to the end of his life. He exercised long and regularly and indulged in various sports to the utmost of his endurance. At every opportunity he joined his father in riding horseback and in tramping through the woods. As he grew older and stronger he began to take lessons in boxing and practiced this manly sport until the middle of his Presidency, when an accidental blow practically blinded him in one eye.

By the time Theodore entered Harvard College in 1876 he had almost rid himself of his asthma and had built up his body to more than normal strength. Yet he persisted in strenuous physical exercise and preached its great pleasures and advantages. When he married Alice Lee in 1881 and went to Europe on his honeymoon, he made sure to climb the Jungfrau and Matterhorn peaks. Later still, when he went to live on his ranch in the Dakotas, he prided himself on his ability to work as hard as any of the cowboys. By that time he had attained exceptional robustness, and his ideal of the strenuous life was to him both a living reality and a glorious goal.

At Harvard he early manifested the zest for life and the qualities of leadership that later made him famous the world over. He was not very studious, although his researches in connection with

23

his paper on the American Navy in the War of 1812 gave promise of the scholarship and breadth of view he was later to demonstrate in his numerous writings. Of the courses he took he said afterwards, "There was very little in my actual studies which helped me in after life." But if his courses gave him little, he took much pleasure in certain of his classmates and delighted in his social activities as a member of the elite group of students.

Theodore's father died unexpectedly in 1878, leaving him with a comfortable income. In no need to earn his living after his graduation from Harvard two years later, unable to interest himself in the study of law, he decided to enter politics. That path seemed to him most likely to lead to the goal of social usefulness he had set for himself; incidentally, of course, it also promised the satisfaction his ego craved.

In the early 1880's the practice of politics was considered a dubious career for a wealthy and socially prominent young man. Theodore's friends and mentors urged him against it, pointing out that politics was a dirty business and that members of political clubs were "muckers" and not "gentlemen." He did not agree with them. As a member of the educated, aristocratic class he felt it his duty to do his share as a citizen. "The man with a university education," he maintained, "is in honor bound to take an active part in our political life and to do his full duty as a citizen by helping his fellow citizens to the extent of his power in the exercise of the right of self-government." Moreover, if politics were left to "muckers," they would govern him. That he would not permit. Years later he remarked: "I intended to be one of the class that governs, not one of the class that is governed. So I joined the political club in my district. I joined it as I joined the National Guard."

Aggressive and persistent, Roosevelt persuaded the leader of his Republican club to nominate him as state assemblyman from New York City. To everyone's surprise he was elected. It was his idea to serve only a single term—more for the experience than for anything else. To a friend he wrote: "Don't think I'm going into politics after this year, for I am not." Once in the assembly, however, his zeal for honesty and righteousness forced him into the thick of a political fight against spoils and corruption. Though he was only twenty-two years old, his forthright manner and frank speech soon placed him at the head of a small but active minority of dissidents. And his dogged aggressiveness spiked several "deals" and made his name known favorably throughout the state. Loath to quit in the midst of his fight for reform, he ran successfully for re-election during the next two annual terms.

Very early in his legislative career he came face to face with the disagreeable fact that politicians, the "muckers" despised by his rich friends, were in effect the hirelings of these men of wealth— paid in one way or another for such favors as lucrative franchises and other profitable privileges. As he later remarked:

Various men whom I had known socially and had been taught to look up to, prominent business men and lawyers, acted in a way which not only astounded me, but which I was quite unable to reconcile with the theories I had formed as to their high standing.

He therefore refused to play the game of the big businessmen of his acquaintance, the men of outward respectability and assumed virtue who saw nothing wrong in bribing legislators and judges in order to obtain highly advantageous grants at public expense. On the assembly floor he denounced "the infernal thieves and conscienceless swindlers who have had the elevated railroad in charge" and opposed their demands with such firmness that the political bullies failed to intimidate him. He also persisted in his attack on a corrupt judge until the assembly was forced to appoint an investigating committee that had no choice but to expose the jurist's crookedness.

He labored mightily to enact laws favoring the spread of civil service and the improvement of living conditions in the East Side tenements. He was deeply chagrined when the court of appeals invalidated the tenement law on the fatuous ground that it violated the sanctity of the home. The hypocrisy and deception of this decision still rankled in his mind when he was writing his *Autobiography* many years later:

These business men and lawyers were very adroit in using a word with fine and noble associations to cloak their opposition to vitally necessary movements for industrial fair play and decency. They made it evident that they valued the Constitution, not as a help to righteousness, but as a means to thwarting movements against unrighteousness.

In February 1884 his wife and his mother died within 24 hours of each other, leaving him depressed and discouraged. Considering his statewide prominence as a reformer "ephemeral," he decided to quit politics. Before leaving the East for the Dakotas, where he had bought an interest in two ranches the year before, he attended the Republican national convention as the head of the New York delegation. Although he was strongly opposed to James G. Blaine's nomination and fought against it to the last, he refused to bolt the party along with the "Mugwumps" of his acquaintance. He considered himself "a strong party man" and believed it his duty to remain within the organization and seek its liberalization from within. Then and later he had little patience with the idealistic reformers who refused to compromise with reality. He had already learned that men followed a leader not because of his ideals but because of their identification with his own sympathies. As a practical man he knew that his noble proposals were worthless unless he could adapt them to the needs and wishes of the people.

For nearly two years, with interruptions, he worked as a rancher. He enjoyed the strenuousness of the cattle round-up, the primitive hardness of frontier life, the excitement of the hunt, the seclusion from the social amenities of the East. He was also able to do considerable writing. While still at Harvard he had begun his book, *A History of the Naval War of 1812*, and had it published in 1882. While in the Dakotas he wrote political studies of Thomas Hart Benton and Gouverneur Morris and began to collect material for his six-volume work on the West. This propensity for writing he indulged at all times subsequently—even when at his busiest as President of the United States.

In 1886 he was persuaded to accept the Republican nomination for mayor of New York. His opponents were Abram S. Hewett, a mild reformer backed by the strong Tammany machine, and Henry George, then at the height of his popularity and the candidate of the improvised labor-reform party. The campaign was carried on with great energy by all groups. Although Roosevelt was admittedly the weakest of the candidates, he fought to the very end with unrestrained energy; nor did defeat diminish his personal political strength.

In December he went to London to marry Edith Carow, a childhood playmate of his sister Corinne, and together they sojourned on the Continent for the next several months. On their return to the United States they settled in Oyster Bay and soon built a house at Sagamore Hill, their home for the rest of their lives. Roosevelt was a devoted family man and remarkably intimate with those closely related to him. His letters to his children and to his sisters, written during his busy years of the Presidency, reveal an uncommon flow of affection and sympathy.

For the next two years Roosevelt worked on his books, wrote topical and literary articles, made political addresses, and kept close contact with local and national developments. In the 1888 campaign he devoted himself to the election of Benjamin Harrison and made numerous speeches in his behalf. His reward came the following May when he was appointed Civil Service Commissioner. Long interested in advancing the merit system in government service, he accepted his new post as a challenge to make civil service both honest and efficient. At that time favoritism and "spoils" politics were still common and reliance on merit and fitness was a new idea, honored mostly in the breach. Roosevelt surprised and disturbed many people by his vigorous enforcement of the law and by his exposure of graft and fraud wherever he discovered them. In his six years in office he antagonized powerful politicians and even influential Cabinet members, but he stood his ground and let the facts speak for themselves. When he resigned in 1895 to accept the office of New York police commissioner, the merit system was solidly established and considerably extended. Meantime his aggressive and spectacular methods of action had gained him nationwide prominence.

Roosevelt's two years as head of the New York police were similarly noted for his insistence on law enforcement in the face of powerful opposition from politicians and the beneficiaries of graft and crime. He worked prodigiously, persistently, dramatically, with results as astonishing as they were effective—at least while he remained in office. For the first time saloonkeepers, gamblers, and criminals learned that they had to obey the law or suffer the consequences.

When the 1896 campaign began, and Bryan appeared a formidable opponent, Roosevelt joined the Republican strategists with characteristic excitability. Holding impractical "Mugwumps" in contempt and disdaining Populists as cranks and zealots, he attacked their leaders Bryan and Governor John P. Altgeld of Illinois with demagogic ferocity. In numerous speeches he claimed that Bryan wanted to rob the rich of their wealth and that his principles were "sufficiently silly and wicked to make them fit well in the mouth of the anarchist leader." He also charged that Altgeld in particular wanted to replace the established government with "a red welter of lawlessness and dishonesty as fantastic and as vicious as the Paris commune itself." Moreover, he insisted that Altegeld's pardon of the anarchists involved in the Haymarket bombing had made him "the foe of every true American." He considered Altegeld "more dangerous" and "much slyer" than Bryan. "Mr. Altgeld condones and encourages the most infamous of murders and denounces the Federal Government and the Supreme Court for interfering to put a stop to the bloody lawlessness which would result in worse than murder."

William McKinley's victory made an important federal appointment for Roosevelt practically certain. His friend Senator

Henry Cabot Lodge informed him that the President was ready to make him assistant Secretary of the Navy, but that the appointment was being strongly opposed by the New York party politicians. Roosevelt was not surprised, and in a letter to a friend he was equally uncomplimentary:

The really ugly feature in the Republican canvas is that it *does* represent exactly what the Populists say, that is, corrupt wealth. . . . Both Platt and Tracy represent the powerful, unscrupulous politicians who charge heavily for doing the work—sometimes good, sometimes bad—of the bankers, railroad men, insurance men, and the like.

In time the appointment came through, and Roosevelt returned to Washington to help conduct the affairs of the Navy.

Long a big-navy advocate and a strong believer in American preparedness, he plunged into his new duties with an overflow of zeal and enthusiasm. Checked again and again by Secretary John D. Long and President McKinley, he nevertheless succeeded in improving the efficiency of the fleet and in placing it on a fighting basis. For he believed that a war with Spain was unavoidable if Cuba were to be liberated and the United States were to assume its long-postponed leading position among the world powers. When the crisis came with the sinking of the *Maine,* he felt "humiliated and ashamed" that President McKinley did not immediately ask Congress for a declaration of war.

Once hostilities began, Roosevelt resigned his office and engaged with Colonel Leonard Wood in raising the First Regiment of Volunteer Cavalry, popularly known as the Rough Riders. He was determined to participate in actual combat and be killed if need be for the glory of his country. To Major Archie Butt he later confided:

When the chance came for me to go to Cuba with the Rough Riders Mrs. Roosevelt was very ill and so was Teddy. It was a question if either would ultimately get well. You know what my wife and children mean to me; and yet I made up my mind that I would not allow even a death to stand in my way; that it was my one chance to do something

29

for my country and for my family and my one chance to cut my little notch on the stick that stands as a measuring rod in every family.

Exercising all his ingenuity and influence, he succeeded in getting to Cuba with his men and in leading them in two engagements with the enemy. The excitement and danger exhilarated him. When the fighting ended with Spain's inevitable capitulation, he and his friends agreed that it was "a splendid little war." Soon afterwards, eager to return to the United States and apprehensive of the health of the soldiers kept in Cuba, he made a formal plea to the heads of the Army to remove the American regiments from the fever-infested camps without delay. This act of military insubordination, fully publicized, saved hundreds from needless death and added to the popularity of Colonel Roosevelt. When he landed at Montauk Point on Long Island, he was greeted as a national hero.

The liberal independents lost no time in urging him to become their candidate for governor. He knew better, however, than to commit himself to a handful of reformers without a strong party organization. Moreover, he was not unaware of the plight of the Republicans and of how much they would be helped by the prestige of his name. So he waited until Senator Tom C. Platt, absolute boss of the party in New York, swallowed his dislike and offered him the nomination unconditionally. Roosevelt immediately engaged in a whirlwind campaign against the strong Democratic machine and won by a fair margin. For the next two years he served as governor with active devotion to practical reform.

Roosevelt's attitude toward Senator Platt was friendly but firm. As governor he knew that he had to cooperate with the party leaders to carry out his campaign promises. He therefore readily agreed to consult with Platt on appointments and general policy. Out of deference to the Senator's age and feeble health he did not hesitate to go down from Albany to New York City in order to breakfast with Platt on Saturdays, but he more than once rejected recommendations that clashed with his own preference.

30

By the energetic exercise of his powers as governor and by shrewdly publicized statements he succeeded in forcing a conservative and corrupt legislature to pass laws furthering civil service, factory legislation, and similar reforms. His most important measure, the law taxing corporations that held public franchises, he fought through against the stubborn opposition of both parties. The citizenry of New York, as well as the large corporations and the political bosses, soon learned that Governor Roosevelt meant what he said and did what he thought right regardless of the consequences. And the people hailed him as their hero.

Early in 1900 Platt agreed with his business friends that Roosevelt must not be renominated for governor and that the way to prevent it was to relegate him to the Vice-Presidency. At first Roosevelt balked. He did not want to be elevated to obscurity; he much preferred to be governor again. To Senator Lodge he complained:

I have found out one reason why Senator Platt wants me nominated for the Vice-Presidency. . . . All the big moneyed interests that make campaign contributions of large size and feel that they should have favors in return, are extremely anxious to get me out of the State. I find that they have been at Platt for the last two or three months and he has finally begun to yield to them and to take their view.

As late as June 12 Roosevelt insisted: "I will not accept under any circumstances, and that is all there is about it." Nine days later, however, he did accept. Ever the practical man, he decided it was better to do the party's bidding than to fight Platt for the renomination. For his quick mind was already evaluating his chances for the Presidency in 1904 and was finding them better than even.

On his way to Washington early in March 1901 to attend the inauguration, Senator Platt remarked jocosely, "I'm going down to see Theodore Roosevelt take the veil." Those who knew the new Vice-President wondered how passivity would become him—

31

what would happen to his excessive energy. Henry Adams wrote characteristically:

All Roosevelt's friends knew that his restless and combative energy was more than normal. Roosevelt, more than any other living man within the range of notoriety, showed that singular primitive quality that belongs to ultimate matter—the quality that medieval theology assigned to God—he was pure act.

Indeed, during the first spring months as Vice-President, Roosevelt began to feel time so heavy on his hands that he seriously considered studying law on his return to Washington in the fall.

Suddenly, by a freak of fate, he found himself, despite all the efforts of his enemies, invested with the powerful office he had set his heart upon. While attending the Pan-American Exposition in Buffalo early in September President McKinley was shot by a crazed anarchist and died nine days later. Theodore Roosevelt, on vacation in the wilds of the Adirondacks, hurried to Buffalo to be sworn in as President.

Always the practical politician, if also the impetuous preacher, he went out of his way to placate the political leaders who disliked or feared him. He announced his determination to carry on the policies of his predecessor and showed proper deference to Senators Hanna and Platt. To very near the end of his first term he kept an eager eye on the 1904 nomination. From the first, however, it was obvious that his elevation to the Presidency marked a distinct change in the executive direction of the government. Roosevelt was too definitely the political moralist and too delighted with the opportunity to control the reins of the nation not to impress his personality and his philosophy upon everything that emanated from the White House. He refused to compromise or extenuate his demand of high standards from public officials; he also argued for honesty and decency in the relations between capital and labor, producer and consumer, rich and poor. Now that he had the power, he was resolved to tackle the problems confronting a nation in the throes of rapid industrialization—"the tremendous social problems forced upon us by the far-reaching social changes of the last two generations."

No social radical, Roosevelt was a firm believer in the right to property and in the freedom of enterprise. Elihu Root called him "the great conservator of property and of rights." To this end he expounded the virtues of "honesty and decency alike in public and private life." When he found these virtues wanting, the preacher in him took command. Because at the turn of the century the powerful corporation had become the leviathan of the age and too imperious for the nation's good, Roosevelt grappled with it as best he could. In his first message to Congress in December 1901 he stated:

There is a widespread conviction in the minds of the American people that the great corporations known as trusts are in certain of their features and tendencies hurtful to the general welfare. . . . It is based upon sincere conviction that combination and concentration should be, not prohibited, but supervised and within reasonable limits controlled; and in my judgment this is right.

He made certain to explain that his attack on trusts was a *"fundamental fight for morality"* and that he did not seek to deprive honest businessmen of their rights. To him the basic question was whether the corporation or the government was master— and on this issue his answer was unequivocal.

A few men recognized that corporations and combinations had become indispensable in the business world, that it was folly to try to prohibit them, but that it was also folly to leave them without thoroughgoing control. These men realized that the doctrines of the old *laissez-faire* economists, of the believers in unlimited competition, unlimited individualism, were in actual state of affairs false and mischievous. They realized that the Government must now interfere to protect labor, to subordinate the big corporation to the public welfare, and to shackle cunning and fraud exactly as centuries before it had interfered to shackle the physical force which does wrong by violence.

33

His first major act in the effort to gain mastery over the big corporations was the suit against the Northern Securities Company. Around 1900 James J. Hill and E. H. Harriman had been engaged in a titanic struggle for the control of the railroads from Chicago to Seattle. The large private bankers had backed both men to the limit of their vast financial resources. In 1901 the protagonists had compromised by organizing the jointly controlled Northern Securities Company with a capitalization of $400,000,-000. Roosevelt knew that this arrangement was merely a means to circumvent the Sherman Anti-Trust Act and in line with a Supreme Court decision in *U. S.* v. *E. C. Knight Co.* (1895) that the purchase of stock of other similar firms was not an act of interstate commerce and hence did not constitute restraint of trade under the terms of the Sherman Act. Since this ruling in effect deprived the government of control over corporations, he considered it intolerable. To a friend he explained:

The Knight case practically denied the Federal Government power over corporations, because it whittled to nothing the meaning of "commerce between the States." It had to be upset or we could not get any efficient control by the National Government.

Eager for the Court to reverse itself and believing that some of the Justices were in a mood to take a broader view of the Sherman Act, Roosevelt instructed Attorney General Philander C. Knox to bring suit against the Northern Securities Company as a trust under the Act. News of the action on February 19, 1902, struck Wall Street with the force of a bombshell. Big bankers and businessmen were shocked that, contrary to previous custom, they had learned nothing of this beforehand. J. P. Morgan, who was chiefly affected by this action, hurried to Washington to protest in person. He took the position that such interference on the part of the government was bad for business and should be stopped. As President Roosevelt quoted him later, "If we have done anything wrong, send your man [meaning Attorney General Knox] to my man [one of his lawyers] and they can fix it up." This of course was just what Roosevelt did not wish to do, as he aimed to stop monopoly altogether. After the interview he remarked:

That is a most illuminating illustration of the Wall Street point of view. Mr. Morgan could not help regarding me as a big rival speculator, who either intended to ruin all his interests or else could be induced to come to an agreement to ruin none.

When in 1904 the Supreme Court, by a vote of five to four, in effect reversed the Knight decision and ordered the dissolution of the Northern Securities Company, it for the first time established the right of the government to restrain large corporations from acting contrary to the intent of the law. Roosevelt was elated. His victory was a notice to Big Business that the era of unrestrained enterprise had passed. Years later he said:

The Northern Securities suit is one of the great achievements of my administration. I look back upon it with great pride, for through it we emphasized in signal fashion, as in no other way could be emphasized, the fact the most powerful men in this country were held to accountability before the law.

President Roosevelt, the political moralist, advocated honesty in public as well as in private affairs. He believed that "the corruptionists in public life, whether he be bribe-giver or bribe-taker, strikes at the heart of the commonwealth." Yet he was ever careful to steer a middle course, to oppose not the prevalent system but only its individual abuses. Although he had little respect for mere wealth and disdained the selfish arrogance of certain powerful capitalists, he made plain his benevolent neutrality toward the honest corporations. "We are not hostile to them," he insisted, when speaking of business enterprises as such; "we are merely determined that they shall be so handled as to subserve the public good. We draw the line against misconduct, not against wealth." And to Jacob Schiff, the powerful head of Kuhn, Loeb and Company, he complained:

It is difficult for me to understand why there should be this belief in Wall Street that I am a wild-eyed revolutionist. I cannot condone wrong. But I certainly do not intend to do aught save what is beneficial to the man of means who acts fairly and squarely.

His code of ethics, however, forced him throughout his Presidency to clash with moneyed men who were bent on personal gain at the expense of the public good. An early embroilment with such capitalists was occasioned by the 1902 coal strike. The miners were then being grievously exploited. Compelled to work long hours, yet irregularly, under hazardous conditions and at pitifully low wages, they finally struck the mines in a desperate effort to better their working conditions. Under John Mitchell's capable and conservative leadership they bravely faced the attempt of the mine owners to starve them into submission. As the strike persisted through the summer and into the fall, the scarcity of coal caused acute suffering among the urban poor. At this point Roosevelt asked both sides to meet with him in the hope of reaching an agreement to end the strike. Mitchell came in a highly cooperative spirit. Not so the mine owners. They not only scorned his presence but also scolded President Roosevelt for not having acted previously to break the strike. This callous arrogance greatly annoyed him. Years later he revealed his anger against these employers in the statement, "They came down in a most insolent frame of mind, refused to talk of arbitration or other accommodation of any kind, and used language that was insulting to the miners and offensive to me." Indeed he thought Mitchell was the only one to act the gentleman.

Although the mine owners acted as an organized group, they considered a union of their employees inimical to their interests and therefore illegal. Consequently they not only refused to deal with the union but did everything they could to destroy it. Roosevelt, however, saw the logic and need of labor unions in an era of large-scale industrialism, and the behavior of the mine owners only confirmed him in this view:

36

Individually the miners were impotent when they sought to enter a wage contract with the great companies; they could make fair terms only by uniting into trade unions to bargain collectively. The men were forced to cooperate to secure not only their economic, but their simple human rights.

This particular conflict was finally ended when Roosevelt sent Secretary Elihu Root to J. P. Morgan with the plea that he order the adamant mine owners to agree to arbitration. The powerful banker's word brought about a settlement, but by a commission specified by the mine owners. Writing to Senator Lodge, Roosevelt pointed out the novelty of his part in the strike: "I am genuinely independent of the big moneyed men in all matters where I think the interests of the public are concerned, and probably I am the first President of recent times of whom this could truthfully be said."

Roosevelt was genuinely sympathetic to individual workers and favored unionism in principle. Thus he approved of unions seeking peacefully and patiently to enlarge their membership. "I believe that all men who are benefited by the union are morally bound to help to the extent of their power in the common interests advanced by the union." He maintained, however, that no man must be forced to join a union and that his rights as an individual must be fully protected. When a union demanded the dismissal of a government employee who had broken with it, Roosevelt promptly rebuked the labor officials for making the request. He also disregarded the Bill of Grievances submitted to him in 1906 by the American Federation of Labor, and in a letter to Senator Lodge he referred to Samuel Gompers as "a sleek article."

The labor radicals irritated him especially. He considered socialism a subversive doctrine and scorned the theory of the class struggle. "I have never believed, and do not now believe, that such a class war is upon us, or need ever be upon us, nor do I believe that the interests of wage-earners and employers cannot be harmonized, compromised and adjusted." The agitation of the socialists led by Eugene V. Debs and the open warfare between the Western Federation of Miners and the mine owners caused him much provocation and disquiet. To him these radicals were as inimical to the public welfare as the most arrogant industrialists— both groups being to him "undesirable citizens."

The killing of Governor Steunenberg of Idaho by a bomb planted at the gate to his home deeply shocked President Roosevelt. When leading officials of the Western Federation of Miners were kidnapped in Denver and taken to Idaho to be tried for the murder of the governor, he did not question their guilt and condemned them as enemies of society. To Senator Lodge he indicated that the trial in Idaho was to be "distinctly a fight for civilization." And to an eminent jurist he wrote:

I had been reading with great indignation a certain magazine and the news of the way certain labor unions were subscribing for the defense of those Western Federation of Miners people whose organization certainly, if not they themselves personally, were accessories to murder before the fact in the case of Governor Steunenberg.

His reaction in this instance was similar to that of the frontier vigilante: those suspected of criminality must be dealt quick justice. He did not bother to ascertain the probable guilt of the kidnapped defendants or to take into account the likelihood that the state officials were under the influence of the embittered mine owners. Nor did he trouble to examine the underlying factors that impelled the western miners to resist force with force and to violate laws that served their employers as means of coercion and constraint. All that concerned him was that the law had been broken and that crime must be punished. The motives behind the crime and the conditions stimulating it did not impinge upon his moral indignation.

In his desire to advance the nation's welfare Roosevelt early began to advocate the control of the railroads. Although he was strongly opposed to government ownership, he maintained that a large corporation such as the railroad must be regulated "so that it shall be conducted in the interest of the public." In his first message to Congress he urged the strengthening of the Interstate Commerce Commission with a view to eliminating the rebate evil. "The railway is a public servant," he declared. "Its rates should be just and open to all shippers alike." Early in 1903 Congress, following his recommendation, enacted the Elkins Anti-Rebate Bill to stop the unfair competition made possible by secret rebates to powerful corporations.

When investigation verified the foul conditions in the Chicago meat-packing plants, Roosevelt was "revolted" and strove energetically to compel meat-packers to install sanitary safeguards. He was also outraged by the disclosures of fraud and dangerous deceit on the part of certain manufacturers of foods and patent medicines. After many months of persistent effort he succeeded in overcoming the influence of special interests in Congress and in obtaining the passage of the Pure Food and Drug Act. This law, and the important Hepburn Act regulating railway rates, which was enacted about the same time, marked the radical change of government policy from benevolent neutrality to the active regulation of business for the common good. Nor did Roosevelt veer from this position late in 1907, when he permitted the United States Steel Corporation to purchase control of the Tennessee Coal and Iron Company in order to stave off its certain bankruptcy in a falling and jittery market. Despite the insinuations of his critics, he was in this instance seeking to prevent economic panic without either connivance or collusion.

President Roosevelt considered the building of the Panama Canal one of his major achievements, ranking it in national importance with the Louisiana Purchase and the acquisition of Texas. For many years an active advocate of military preparedness, he early saw the need of the Canal for the effective use of our growing two-ocean navy. His foresight and dynamic impetuosity caused him to prod Congress till he was given the power and the appropriations to purchase the right-of-way and to build the gigantic Canal. When the dictator of Colombia tried to renege on his original agreement in order to demand an additional ten million dollars, Roosevelt angrily canceled the negotiations and took quick advantage of the deliberately contrived Panamanian revolt to obtain approval of the treaty from the successful rebels. On a later occasion he defended this action as a patriotic performance:

Yes. I took the Isthmus, and I am in a wholly unrepentant frame of mind in reference thereto. The ethical conception upon which I acted was that I did not intend that Uncle Sam should be held up while he was doing a great work for himself and all mankind.

To the end of his term in office he closely supervised the construction of the Canal. His sagacity in the choice of General Goethals as chief engineer and in the decision favoring the use of locks greatly expedited the successful completion of the tremendous undertaking.

Equally notable were his efforts to conserve the nation's natural resources. Throughout the nineteenth century and particularly during its final quarter, these resources were exploited with reckless prodigality. Land was used wastefully, forests were cut down and abandoned, water was permitted to run off uncontrolled. When Roosevelt assumed the Presidency the problem was one, as he once put it, "of utilizing the natural resources of the nation in a way that will be of the most benefit to the nation as a whole." Tackling it with characteristic energy and enthusiasm, he proceeded to strengthen the several government agencies concerned with the study and utilization of public lands, to add millions of acres to forest preserves, to speak frequently on the virtues of conservation, and to appoint men devoted to the ideal of preserving natural resources and bent on protecting them from illegitimate and reckless exploitation. As a consequence numerous national parks and forest preserves as well as much of the water resources in the West to a large extent owe their existence to his foresight and persistent efforts.

With all his ability, energy, and determination, President Roosevelt could not have achieved his legislative program and administrative reforms without the favorable climate of opinion stimulated by an able and active group of writers who sympathized with his passion for righteousness. Most of them were young, idealistic, devoted democrats. Incensed against the selfish manipulation of wealth, they sought to right egregious wrongs and reveal the unregenerate wrongdoers. Fortunately for them, technical improvements were bringing into being the low-priced periodical with its mass circulation. In search of material that would attract many readers, editors soon discovered that articles of critical exposure in the fields of politics and business served their purposes best.

Writers like Lincoln Steffens, Ida Tarbell, and Ray Stannard Baker, who became leaders of the group soon to be dubbed "muckrakers" by Roosevelt, were not motivated by any particular philosophy or program. They were serious-minded journalists, eager to write well and vividly of things that interested them. What they saw about them, however, irritated their sense of social justice. Acting on idealistic impulse, they began "to expose, arouse, drive people to better social relationships." Their articles—lengthy, rambling, highly detailed—were written with what Ida Tarbell termed "righteous indignation" and had the ring of sincerity and factual authenticity. Baker wrote in retrospect:

We were personally astonished, personally ashamed, personally indignant at what we found, and we wrote earnestly, even hotly. . . . What the early "exposers" did was to look at their world, *really* look at it. They reported honestly, fully, and above all interestingly what they found.

McClure's Magazine was the first periodical to capitalize on this type of article and soon discovered that nearly all writers stressed the universality of law-breaking among powerful businessmen, prominent politicians, aggressive labor leaders—indeed all influential citizens seeking something for nothing. Soon *McClure's* was read by hundreds of thousands. Its astounding success stimulated not only the emulation of rival periodicals but the establishment of new ones. For about six years everything that lent itself to critical exposure became fair game for muckraking journalists. Their articles incensed many people. Americans suddenly became aware of being mulcted, deceived, duped, and poisoned. When the stockyards in Chicago were discovered selling spoiled meat—and Upton Sinclair's *The Jungle* intensified the natural revulsion—the outcry was immediate and effective. In less dramatic instances indignation sputtered and became spent for the lack of proper direction. On the whole, however, these articles of exposure, while not achieving moral resurgence, caused much soul-searching and vocal protest—thereby furthering President Roosevelt's legislative reforms and preparing the way for his later battle at Armageddon.

As was inevitable, certain writers capitalized on this demand for articles of exposure by peppering their pieces with extravagant claims and sensational charges. President Roosevelt, always anxious to be fair to all sides, was annoyed by their shrill tone. In a speech delivered on April 14, 1906, he struck out against all critical journalists and accused them of being "muck-rakers." Although he had worked closely with such men as Lincoln Steffens and Ray Stannard Baker and had been cautioned by them to make his speech with care, he did not trouble to discriminate between the serious writer and the venal sensationalist. He explained that the man with the muckrake concentrated "on carnal instead of on spiritual things. Yet he also typifies the man who refuses to see aught that is lofty, and fixes his eye with solemn intension on that which is vile and debasing." Such a man, he charged, became "one of the most potent forces for evil." To make his point more explicitly, he added:

It is because I feel that there should be no rest in the endless war against the forces of evil that I ask that the war be conducted with sanity as well as with resolution. The men with the muck-rake are often indispensable to the well-being of society; but only if they know when to stop raking the muck, and to look upward to the celestial crown above them, to the crown of worthy endeavor.

Serious writers of social criticism resented this pious preachment from the man whom they were supporting with devoted zeal. They at once accepted the epithet as a term of honor. Nor were they long in apprizing Roosevelt of their aim not so much to expose crime and wrong-doing as to make clear why good men did evil. Steffens, the most sagacious of these writers and intimately familiar with the working of the vicious circle of graft and corruption, wrote to Roosevelt of the larger truth as he saw it:

I am not seeking proof of crime and dishonesty. If I get that I would turn it over to you or to a criminal prosecutor. What I am after is the cause and the purpose and the methods by which our government, city, state, and federal, is made to represent not the common, but the special interests; the reasons why it is so hard to do right in the United States; the secret of the power which makes it necessary for you, Mr. President, to *fight* to give us a "square deal." In brief, I want to be able some day to explain why it is that you have to force the Senate to pass a pure-food bill or one providing for the regulation of the railroads. . . . You seem to me always to have been looking down for the muck, I am looking upward to—an American Democracy. You ask men in office to be honest, I ask them to serve the public.

More than a year later, in another letter to Roosevelt, Steffens put his finger directly on the mainspring of public corruption— with a simplicity too subtle for the crusading President:

And this, "the evil," which so irritates you, is something which is neither new nor unobserved. It is privilege. Trace every case of corruption you know to its source, and you will see, I believe, that somebody was trying to get out of Government some special right; to keep a saloon open after hours; a protective tariff; a ship subsidy; a public service franchise.

Roosevelt's criticism of the muckrakers neither silenced them nor lessened their popularity. The problems they discussed remained explosive issues. More and more people became cynical toward public officials and manifested their dissatisfaction with things as they were. Although Congress remained in firm control of the representatives of Big Business, here and there the aroused voters managed to elect Congressmen who owed their allegiance only to them and who dared defy the entrenched political bosses.

In time influential businessmen, fearful of the effect of muckraking on the public, determined to stop this devastating criticism of their activities. Where they could not exert indirect pressure on the editors, they began to buy up the magazines themselves. Bank loans granted to publishers to finance their growing enterprises became an effective means of forcing compliance. Muckrakers found themselves compelled either to succumb to the subtle blandishments of new editors or turn to other forms of literary endeavor.

After his highly popular election in 1904, President Roosevelt declared that he would not seek another term. "The wise custom," he volunteered, "which limits the President to two terms regards the substance and not the form, and under no circumstances will I be a candidate for or accept another nomination." Three years later, when the 1908 election came up for consideration and a number of his friends urged him to seek re-election, his refusal was resolute and final. Because he was aware of his worldwide eminence and the ease with which he could continue in office, he was all the more eager to strengthen what he considered a sound democratic precedent.

He wanted, however, to choose his successor: a man sympathetic to his "policies" and the "square deal." Although this choice predicated a progressive, he did not wish him to be imbued with "the La Follette type of fool radicalism." After considering carefully the available aspirants, he decided that his Secretary of War William Howard Taft was the man best able to carry on his principles and purposes. To his friend George Otto Trevelyan he wrote:

Taft will carry on the work substantially as I have carried it on. His policies, principles, purposes and ideals are the same as mine. . . .

44

I have the profound satisfaction of knowing that he will do all in his power to further every one of the great causes for which I have fought.

As head of the Republican party he had little difficulty in having Taft nominated; and his enthusiastic backing sufficed for the voters as well. With admirable restraint he permitted the President-elect a completely free hand in the choice of his Cabinet and in the launching of his Administration. Roosevelt now considered himself out of politics and began to busy himself with preparations for a prolonged hunting expedition in the jungles of Africa.

For more than a year he confined himself to hunting and scientific investigations. When he emerged from the wilds of the "dark" continent, he found himself obligated to make what turned out to be a triumphal tour of the leading capitals of Europe. His speeches at outstanding universities sparkled with well-turned truisms of democratic dogma. Eminent Europeans—kings as well as scholars and statesmen—vied to do him honor. All this was of course reported in detail in American newspapers and assured him a hero's welcome on his return to New York in June 1910.

Meantime President Taft's innate conservatism and political ineptness had made him thoroughly unpopular with the progressives who insisted on measuring his actions with the Roosevelt yardstick. His honest efforts to enforce the laws of the land were completely overshadowed by his cordiality toward political bosses, his acquiescence in a high tariff, and his blunder in favoring Secretary R. A. Ballinger over Chief Forester Gifford Pinchot in the conservation controversy. Many of the "insurgent" members of Congress were in open rebellion against him.

Roosevelt's numerous disciples hastened to apprize him of their complaints against President Taft. The more he learned about the turn of affairs the keener was his disappointment. In various speeches over the country he restated his political liberalism and criticized those who opposed his policies.

I stand for the Square Deal. But when I say that I am for the square deal I mean not merely that I stand for fair play under the present rules of the game, but that I stand for having the rules changed so as to work for a more substantial equality of opportunity and of reward for equally good service.

From his mouth these pleasant platitudes issued as a fresh challenge to his conservative opponents. William Allen White spoke for most liberals when he wrote in his *Emporia Gazette*:

We send our greetings to Theodore Roosevelt, the new world's champion of the rights of man in the world-old contest between rising humanity and the encroachments of special privilege. And as Republicans we stand ready to enlist under his banner in the fight for human rights.

Reason and his conservative friends cautioned Roosevelt against becoming too involved in the politics of the day. His role henceforth, some insisted, must be that of the sagacious elder statesman and not of the politician embroiled in the thick of battle. The advice seemed to him perfectly sensible. He knew that in taking a militant stand in political controversy he personally had little to gain and much to lose. Yet he was in no mood to remain merely a passive observer. What mattered most was, first, the conclusion that Taft had proved himself "utterly worthless" and was an "entirely unfit President"; second, the belief that his "policies" were at stake and that he alone was in a position to revive them. "I am interested in these ideas of mine," he explained to friends, "and I want to carry them through, and I feel that I am the one to carry them through." And in his mind "these ideas" had become the application of "the principles of Abraham Lincoln to the conditions of the twentieth century."

Roosevelt's final decision "to throw his hat in the ring" came after Senator La Follette, who was the regular Progressive candidate for the Presidential nomination, had harmed his chances on February 2, 1912, while delivering an address before the Periodical Publishers in Philadelphia. Under great nervous strain owing to overwork and family illness, La Follette talked ramblingly and rancorously till he collapsed. That very night a number of his erstwhile backers jumped at this chance to turn from him to Roosevelt.

Ten days later, while still debating with his conscience, Theodore Roosevelt was driven to a decision by President Taft's angry address in New York. Stung by attacks from "insurgents," Taft bitterly characterized them as malcontents and radicals. "Such extremists," he insisted, "are not progressives; they are political emotionalists and neurotics." Roosevelt took these aspersions as a personal insult. He was then in receipt of a letter signed by seven progressive Republican governors urging him to seek the nomination. Having by this time reason to believe that he was wanted by about two-thirds of the Republicans, he told himself it was his duty to fight for the people against the evils of plutocracy.

He threw himself into the campaign with characteristic enthusiasm. On February 21 he addressed the Ohio constitutional convention and made that speech his clarion call to battle. It was a carefully worded challenge, mild in tone and highlighted with pious generalizations.

We Progressives believe that the people have the right, the power, and the duty to protect themselves and their own welfare; that human rights are supreme over all other rights; that wealth should be the servant, not the master, of the people. . . . We are engaged in one of the great battles of the age-long contest waged against privilege on behalf of the common welfare. We hold it a prime duty of the people to free our government from the control of money in politics. For this purpose we advocate, not as ends in themselves, but as weapons in the hands of the people, all governmental devices which will make the representatives of the people more easily and certainly responsive to the people's will.

Among the reforms he advocated was "the recall of judicial decisions." This phrase, uttered casually and carrying little more than the thought that court decisions are often fallible, became the spark that exploded conservative tempers. Roosevelt was accused of wanting to undermine the foundations of constitutional government and condemned as an irresponsible insurgent. A number of his lifelong friends—men such as Lodge and Root—severed political relations with him and joined the Republican bosses in the fight against his nomination.

The attack angered Roosevelt. He knew that his disloyal friends were using his espousal of judicial reform as an evasive excuse to justify their alliance with conservative Republicanism. "The judges have decided every which way," he pointed out caustically, "and it is foolish to talk of the sanctity of judge-made law which half of the judges strongly denounce." Taking this position before the Massachusetts legislature, he exclaimed: "If that is revolution, make the most of it!"

Roosevelt was too shrewd a politician to underestimate the strength of the men opposed to his candidacy. Nor did he fully relish the rush of the reform "lunatic fringe" to his support. But these drawbacks served only to spice the campaign. As Owen Wister remarked, "I believe that the only thing which kept him going at all was the zest of action in battle which came from the preacher militant." All that spring he toured the states where convention delegates were chosen in the primaries. In speech after speech and in numerous letters he expounded the progressive principles for which he was fighting.

The excitement of battle caused him to speak with extreme frankness. When a critical friend objected to his platform on the ground that it might do away with representative government, he replied that in fact we had no such government. "I can name forty-six Senators who secured their seats and held them by the favor of a Wall Street magnate and his associates, in all parts of the country. Do you call that popular, representative government?" When the New York workmen's compensation law was invalidated, he insisted that it was up to the voters to "determine whether the law which the court set aside shall be valid or not." And in a speech in Louisville, Kentucky, he declared:

We propose to do away with whatever in our government tends to secure to privilege, and to the great sinister special interests, a rampart from behind which they can beat back the forces that strive for social and industrial justice and frustrate the will of the people.

The magic of his zestful personality and the crescent liberalism of the period combined to make him the obvious choice of Republican voters. Where they were given the opportunity they expressed themselves emphatically in his favor. Of the 378 delegates named in the primaries, 278 were definitely for Roosevelt; the rest were divided between Taft and La Follette.

The popular vote, however, meant little to the embattled machine politicians. They were determined to renominate Taft and stopped at nothing to achieve their purpose. Of the 254 contested delegates they awarded 235 to Taft. In the vote for a temporary chairman—the crucial contest for control of the convention—74 of the contested delegates were permitted to cast their ballots despite the strenuous objections of the progressives, thereby electing Elihu Root by 558 to 501. Roosevelt, called to Chicago to direct his forces in person, termed this action "bare-faced and insolent wrong-doing."

Thereafter most of the progressive delegates simply ignored the proceedings. When Taft was nominated they considered their Republican bonds broken and walked out of the convention to organize a party of their own. With the enthusiasm of joyous release they acclaimed Roosevelt as their candidate and arranged to meet again on August 5 in order to launch the Progressive campaign for the oncoming election.

Roosevelt was quite fully aware that his chances of election were extremely dubious and that defeat would of necessity cost him dearly in prestige and popularity. To more than one friend he confided that his candidacy was not a matter of personal choice but a duty he could not shirk. He believed that the campaign, regardless of the outcome, would do a great deal to further progressive government. "If we form a third party and go out and fight for better social conditions in this country, we will accomplish more in three months than could be accomplished under ordinary conditions in a dozen years." Practical reformer that he was, he decided on launching the Progressive party only when the much-needed financial support was volunteered by such friendly men of wealth as George W. Perkins, formerly of J. P. Morgan and Company, the publisher Frank Munsey, and Daniel Willard of the Baltimore and Ohio Railroad.

The hundreds of delegates that attended the founding convention of the new party were an inspired and exalted group. They represented that part of the American people which had been chafing under the rule of large corporations and their political allies for nearly a half century. They, as their fathers before them, were dedicated to the principles of democracy and yearned to see them prevail not only in government but also in industry. Taught by the Populists and muckrakers to look below the surface for the greed and graft that had presumably become the foundation pillars of Big Business and boss-ridden government, they felt the need of a Moses to deliver them from this oppressive corruption. Roosevelt's reappearance in the shining armor of the progressive crusader seemed to them the miraculous answer to their prayer. They therefore exalted him and hailed his policies and promises as political manna. Under his leadership they were ready to destroy the dogma of the superiority of property rights over human rights and to abolish the special privileges that battened the powerful corporations. No wonder they behaved like frenzied revivalists and made "Onward, Christian Soldiers!" the theme song of the conference.

The convention leaders believed that the political destiny of the United States was in their trust. Inspired by the grandeur of their mission, they propounded the loftiest ideals of social justice as planks of their party platform. In his keynote address Senator Albert J. Beveridge declaimed:

We stand for a nobler America. We stand for an undivided nation. We stand for a broader liberty, a fuller justice. We stand for social brotherhood as against savage individualism. We stand for intellectual cooperation instead of a reckless competition. We stand for mutual helpfulness instead of mutual hatred. We stand for equal rights as a fact of life instead of a catchword of politics. We stand for the rule of the people as a practical truth instead of a meaningless pretense. We stand for a representative government that represents the people. We battle for the actual rights of man.

The party platform, correctly called "A Contract with the People," formalized these ideals and aspirations. A lofty restatement of the principles furthered by the Populists, the Bryan liberals, and the moderate socialists, it read almost like a blueprint of the democratic millennium. Its general statement set the tone:

This country belongs to the people who inhabit it. Its resources, its business, its institutions and its laws should be utilized, maintained or altered in whatever manner will best promote the general interest. It is time to set the public welfare in the first place.

To implement this ideal, the platform called for these specific reforms: pervasive direct primaries; the direct election of Senators; the use of the short ballot; the establishment of initiative, referendum, and recall in the states; the control of business for the general welfare; internal improvements where needed; civil-service expansion; limited international armaments; workmen's compensation, social security, minimum wages for women, the eight-hour-day, and better working conditions though, as a sop to Perkins and others, it shied away from a trust plank.

In accepting the nomination for President, Roosevelt reiterated the ideas and ideals he had been preaching since his return from Europe. He spoke with the fire of the enthusiast and the zeal of the crusader. After denouncing the crooked politicians and the self-seeking businessmen, he extolled the new concept of public welfare and called for greater participation of the people themselves as the chief obstacle to corruption.

I believe in a larger use of the Governmental power to help remedy industrial wrongs, because it has been borne in on me by actual experience that without the exercise of such power many of the wrongs will go unremedied. I believe in a larger opportunity for the people themselves directly to participate in government and to control their governmental agents, because long experience has taught me that without such control many of their agents will represent them badly.

Although most liberals idolized Roosevelt and campaigned for his election with explosive ardor, a telling minority was definitely cool toward him. Even while still President he had ceased to appeal to those insurgents who considered his "trust-busting" tactics more effervescent than effective. They questioned the validity of his objectives and his leadership. They also disliked both his weakness for compromise and his moralistic emphasis. Those who sided with Senator La Follette disdained Roosevelt's political "practicality" and his insistence on maintaining a balance between capital and labor that could not but favor the employing group. Ray Stannard Baker spoke for these liberals:

Roosevelt's typical reaction, that of balancing the blame, without going to the root of the matter, and of seeking "the devil in the mess," satisfied me less and less. His actions often seemed to me to be based not upon principles well thought out, but upon moral judgments which were, or seemed to me to be, too hasty. His notion of a square deal was to cuff the radical on one ear and the conservative on the other, without enlightening either.

In the 1912 campaign a small number of insurgents remained loyal to Senator La Follette and did not leave him even when he chose to remain with the Republican party after the Roosevelt faction had split away from it. Another group of dissidents, also distrustful of Roosevelt's progressivism, decided to work for the election of Governor Woodrow Wilson, the Democratic candidate who impressed them as a genuine liberal. Among these men, in addition to Baker, were such liberals as Louis D. Brandeis, Charles R. Crane, and Norman Hapgood. To them Wilson was not only Roosevelt's intellectual superior but the more incisive progressive.

Mention must also be made of the Socialist party. By 1912 it was attracting many men of good will who had come to believe that capitalism was inherently incapable of abolishing poverty and corruption. Thinking that industrialism had reached a stage of development where it must either control the state or be controlled by it, they backed the candidacy of Eugene V. Debs. That fall the Socialist party received nearly a million votes—bringing it to the crest of its popularity.

Despite these defections, the Roosevelt Progressives were bullish and ubiquitous. They campaigned with evangelical vigor and enthusiasm. Their speakers drew large crowds in every part of the country; their pamphlets and songbooks reached millions of voters; their personal zeal nearly made up for the lack of support on the part of most newspapers. Roosevelt himself displayed his magnetic dynamism most effectively. His energy and exhilaration were boundless. He traveled thousands of miles to deliver fighting speeches before overflow audiences; he attacked his opponents and Wilson in particular with a relish and sharpness that kept the campaign at a point of high excitement.

On October 14 he was leaving his hotel in Milwaukee to deliver a major address. A crowd stood alongside his car, cheering him on his way, when a fanatic fired a revolver at him. The assailant was immediately disarmed, and he might have been lynched had not his victim demanded that the man be delivered to the police.

Fortunately for Roosevelt the bullets were deflected by his steel spectacle case and the sheaf of pages of his prepared speech and did not penetrate his lungs. He coughed into his hand several times, found no blood, and knew that the wound was not dangerous. He then insisted that he be driven to the hall to make his speech. "This is my big chance," he asserted, "and I'm going to make that speech if I die doing it." And to the shocked audience he declared, "It takes more than that to kill a bull moose." That night he was taken to Chicago to be hospitalized; soon afterwards he left for New York. His exceptionally strong body stood him in good stead. By October 31 he was fully enough recovered to address a large audience in Madison Square Garden and to imbue it with the elation of righteous battle.

Surely there never was a fight better worth making than this. I believe we shall win, but win or lose I am glad beyond measure that I am one of the many who in this fight have stood ready to spend and be spent, pledged to fight while life lasts the great fight for righteousness and for brotherhood and for the welfare of mankind.

Roosevelt was too egotistical to accept defeat stoically. Outwardly he behaved as if he were delighted with the splendid showing of the Progressive party. "It was a phenomenal thing," he asserted, "to bring the new party into second place and to beat out the Republicans." The implication was that if it proved so strong after several months of effort it would most probably become the dominant party by the next general election.

Inwardly, however, he was deeply disillusioned. He felt that his popularity had shrunken and that the effort had been a tragic waste. The more he reflected over the situation the more convinced he became that the Progressives were too idealistic to gain favor with the majority. Moreover, he feared that the "lunatic fringe" was too prone to turn the party into "a kind of modified I. W. W. movement." He began to view some of his followers with disdain —with something of the disparagement he reserved for socialists and other extremists.

Notwithstanding his erstwhile eagerness to "spend" himself in behalf of the ideals of social justice and honest government, his mind was back in its habitual middle groove. He began to miss terribly the old friends who had spurned him when he left to fight at Armageddon. Now that the heat of the campaign had become dissipated, he felt more benign toward the conservatives who had "robbed" him of the Republican nomination. Although his pride would not permit an immediate reconciliation, he could not keep from looking forward to it with repressed anticipation. Early in 1913 he confided to a friend: "The fight is over. We are beaten. There is only one thing to do and that is to go back to the Republican party. You can't hold a party like the Progressive party together . . . there are no loaves and fishes."

Roosevelt was in this frame of mind when he left for Brazil in the fall of 1913 to explore the River of Doubt, later renamed Reo Teodoro in his honor. The trip was extremely difficult and dangerous. In the heart of the jungle wilderness he contracted a tropical fever that nearly killed him. On his return to the United States he appeared markedly older and only a shadow of his former zestful self. The fever never quite left him, and its recurrence sapped his strength.

Before leaving for Brazil, Roosevelt had entrusted George Perkins with the management of Progressive party affairs. On his return he made no effort to resume his leadership. He was pleased to see his old Progressive friends and to discuss with them future plans, but he refused to involve himself in any way. In 1914 he would not run for office and spoke for some of the Progressive candidates only after persistent urging. When the party polled less than half the votes it had obtained two years earlier, he readily acknowledged its demise. Without realizing that his own apathy was at least in part responsible for this decline, he complained to William Allen White that the campaign had made clear they were "whipping a dead horse." In a long letter to his son Kermit he explained that in 1912 the sordid conniving of political bosses had compelled him to join forces with reformers who could not work together and "who came dangerously near the mark of lunacy." After the campaign, however, he saw no good reason for going along with them. "The Progressive party," he continued, "cannot in all human probability make another fight as a national party, and, if it does, there will be no expectation that I will have to lead. I am through my hard and disagreeable work."

His Progressive lieutenants, however, refused to acquiesce in the defection of their beloved chief. They assumed that he, like themselves, continued to cherish the ideals of progressivism and would again fight with them for a nobler America. Nor could they believe that he would ever agree to a reconciliation with the unrepentant Republican bosses. They therefore persisted in their plans to nominate him at the 1916 convention of the party and to deal with the Republicans only if they would accept his candidacy.

George Perkins had other plans, however. Having, in the words of Harold L. Ickes, "appointed himself receiver of the Progressive party" after the 1912 election, he considered the reunion of the two factions more important than either Roosevelt's candidacy or the social ideals of the Progressive party. Roosevelt's increasing indifference furthered Perkins's strategy. Although he called the party's executive committee to meet with him occasionally, he divulged nothing of his plans. In January 1916 he arranged a meeting of the National Progressive Committee to discuss the oncoming election. There, to the shocked surprise of its members, he blandly stated: "We are all hoping that both the Progressive and the Republican parties will agree on a candidate, and it will not necessarily have to be Colonel Roosevelt." The Progressive leaders refused to accept this statement, a bald notification of the Republicans that they could reject Roosevelt's candidacy without endangering reunion. Instead they countered it with the declaration that conciliation must be preceded by agreement on a liberal candidate and platform. "We will lay aside partisanship and prejudice," they stated formally. "But we will never surrender those principles for which we stand and have stood." At another similar meeting in May Roosevelt was present and strengthened Perkins's hand by stressing the need for a reconciliation in order to win at the polls in November.

Early in June the large majority of the delegates to the convention of the Progressive party, sparked by their alert spokesmen, were determined to nominate Roosevelt before the Republicans had chosen their candidate in order to force them either to accept Roosevelt or risk disunion—and defeat. Perkins fought desperately to forestall this action. He conspired with his small group of followers to keep the convention from voting on a candidate until the Republicans had announced their own choice. He also kept a direct telephone connection with Roosevelt in his private suite and thus prevented his opponents from communicating with their leader. But the delegates swept all obstacles aside and voted for Roosevelt in the belief that they were thereby forcing his candidacy upon the Republicans as well.

Roosevelt confounded his Progressive admirers by refusing to accept the nomination. They could not but wonder why he had permitted the convention to be held if he had no intention of being their candidate. And his statement urging them to return to the Republican fold and vote for Charles Evans Hughes struck them as a shabby betrayal. For they perceived that his rejection meant the death of the Progressive party; that with its dissolution would perish something noble in the hearts of many thousands.

Many Progressives followed Roosevelt's counsel and voted for Hughes; many others turned from him in disgust and voted for President Wilson. But the ideals that had exhilarated them and had exalted American politics for a generation lay blighted in their consciousness. William Allen White, a strong admirer of Roosevelt and no extremist, commented years later: "I have a notion that the healthiest movement in American politics for two generations was the Bull Moose movement, and Perkins plus a Wall Street coterie plus Roosevelt's weariness of the flesh wrecked it."

If Theodore Roosevelt was all his adult life the dynamic moralist in politics, he was at least equally long the zealous patriot, ever ready to die for his country and demanding similar devotion from his fellow citizens. His youthful struggle against physical infirmity had developed in him an extravagant admiration for prowess and pluck. When he had become strong enough to enjoy the rigors of bodily exertion, he indulged in exercise and sports with the impetuosity of the enthusiast. Always the moralist and preacher, he soon rationalized his pleasure in physical activity as a means to patriotic endeavor.

This philosophy of strenuousness he began to expound early in his career. The words "ease" and "peace" he considered synonymous with "timidity" and even "cowardice." He praised "the man who embodies victorious effort . . . who has those virile qualities necessary to win in the stern strife of actual life." This doctrine he expressed in the following famous statement:

I wish to preach, not the doctrine of ignoble ease, but the doctrine of the strenuous life, the life of toil and effort, or labor and strife; to preach that highest form of success which comes, not to the man who desires mere easy peace, but to the man who does not shrink from danger, from hardship, or from bitter toil, and who out of these wins the splendid ultimate triumph.

His participation in the Spanish-American War, consisting of two relatively minor attacks, greatly stimulated his latent militarism. He extolled the idea of national strength. Again and again he asserted that only through strife, provided it was for the greater good, could we "ultimately win the goal of true national greatness." He therefore wanted the United States to be prepared militarily, to become so strong as to be able to respulse the strongest rival power—thus assuming its destined role in world leadership.

When he became President he exerted himself to enhance the position of the United States in world affairs. His strenuous efforts to build the Panama Canal were primarily motivated by a desire to adjust the country's effective defense to new conditions—the need of a two-ocean navy owing to Japan's emergencec as a naval power. Even his mediation of the Russo-Japanese War in 1905 was in his view a demonstration of American potency among nations. And his decision in 1907 to have the American Navy circle the globe was a blunt reminder to the world—and particularly to Japan and Germany—that American fighting power was supreme.

Intimately familiar with the political and economic rivalries among the leading nations, Roosevelt early perceived the danger of large-scale war. He also believed that the United States would not be able to keep out of the fighting. Nor did he wish it to do so. Ever the moralist, the champion of right against wrong, he regarded our participation in the battle against an aggressor as a matter of plain, practical duty. And if war did come, he wanted an active part in it. As early as 1908 he wrote to St. Loe Strachey,

"If a war should occur while I am still physically fit, I should certainly try to raise a brigade, and if possible a division, of cavalry." Three years later he wrote similarly to President Taft.

When war did begin in August 1914 and the Kaiser made a "scrap of paper" out of the treaty protecting Belgian neutrality, Roosevelt wanted us immediately to join the side against Germany. At first, however, he refrained from taking issue with President Wilson's policy of neutrality. He knew to his regret that the majority of Americans approved this position. To Sir Cecil Spring-Rise he wrote apologetically, "It would be worse than folly for me to clamor now about what ought to be done, when it would be mere clamor and nothing more."

As the fighting grew fiercer and Germany's actions became more arrogant and reckless, Roosevelt's patience gave out. He began to regard President Wilson as a cowardly pacifist and vicious hypocrite. In December 1914 he exclaimed to Senator Lodge, with whom he had become reconciled, "Upon my word, Wilson and Bryan are the very worst men we have ever had in their positions." And to his son Kermit he wrote a month later, "I abhor Wilson and Bryan . . . there is always the chance that they will bring the country to real disaster and disgrace."

The more Roosevelt brooded over the war in Europe, the more keenly did he feel the immorality of American aloofness. To him not peace but righteousness was the greatest good. The thought that some of our leading citizens were active pacifists enraged him. Their "iniquitous peace propaganda" struck him as sheer folly. Over and over he insisted that their praise of peace was not only encouraging aggressors but fostering a flabby internationalism that was at once immoral and subversive.

Literally this agitation of the professional pacifists during these ten years has not represented the smallest advance toward securing the peace of righteousness. It has, on the other hand, represented a very considerable and real deterioration in the American character . . . a distinct increase in hysteria and sentimental untruthfulness.

By 1916 Roosevelt had become so engrossed in the agitation for military preparedness that politics as such, and the fate of the Progressive party in particular, became to him relatively unimportant. In his regular contributions to periodicals, in his platform speeches, and in his voluminous correspondence he condemned American neutrality as cowardly and attacked President Wilson as the personification of hypocrisy. Neutrality, he declared, was never moral "and may be a particularly mean and hideous form of immorality." In a letter to Wayne MacVeigh on January 29 he asserted: "No other public man has ventured to tell the truth of Germany, of the pacifists, of the German-Americans, of Wilson. I have told it and shall tell it as strongly as I know how and without regard to its effect on me." A few days later he wrote to Wister that President Wilson was the real enemy of the United States— "the demagogue, adroit, tricky, false, without one spark of loftiness in him, without a touch of the heroic in his cold, selfish and timid soul." And when Wilson was renominated, Roosevelt complained to Senator Lodge: "It is dreadful to think that some millions of Americans will vote for Wilson—including men like ex-President Eliot. They can't so vote without incurring moral degradation."

When Germany's arbitrary and brutal submarine sinkings finally forced the United States to declare war upon her, Roosevelt felt that his long and intensive agitation had at last taken effect. He immediately offered his services to the government. It was his belief that if he were sent to France with the least delay at the head of a division of volunteers, the gesture would greatly strengthen the morale of the Allied soldiers. But President Wilson offered him no encouragement, as he did not feel kindly toward his bitter and abusive critic. More important, however, was the fact that the present conflict excluded voluntary enlistment. War was no longer fought by individual initiative or spontaneous efforts but by mechanized mass armies directed by cold and calculating strategy. The plans of the American General Staff excluded the need of volunteer divisions; the draft was the surer and quicker method of raising a mass army.

Roosevelt was deeply disappointed. His craving for patriotic glory, his lifelong readiness to die on the field of battle in behalf of his country, thwarted and interdicted, caused him much anguish and made him feel a victim of vengeful persecution. He insisted that the Wilson Administration was "playing the dirtiest and smallest politics"; that Wilson himself, selfish and spiteful, was more hostile to him than he was to Germany.

Although Roosevelt did not slacken his fight for the right and continued to exhort his fellow citizens to battle the enemy, he suddenly felt himself to have grown old and superannuated. The thought that his four sons and other youths dear to him were in the thick of the fighting made it all the harder for him to acquiesce in his enforced inaction. "It is very bitter to me," he complained, "that all of you, the young, should be facing death while I sit in ease and safety."

Roosevelt was by this time a sick man. The fever that had nearly killed him in Brazil was again troubling him. Early in 1918 he suffered from an abscess on his thigh and from mastoiditis. When he left the hospital in March he was deaf in his left ear. He at once resumed his interrupted work, and the fire of his youthful vigor continued to splutter till the end of the fighting in Europe.

His progressivism had gradually oozed out of his consciousness, and he associated with men whom he would have scorned a decade earlier. In his patriotic zeal he condemned radical and pacifist workers as traitors and criminals. When the discontented copper miners in Bisbee, Arizona, were brutally kidnapped and left to die in the desert, he attacked them as men "bent on destruction and murder" and praised the vigilante ruffians who had mistreated them as "honest, upright and well-behaved citizens." Commenting on the efforts of a few persistent Progressives to revive the party for the 1918 elections, he claimed that "it is mere folly to keep it alive."

On Armistice Day he was again forced to be hospitalized and remained a patient until Christmas. The next twelve days he

61

seemed relatively well, but during the night of January 6, 1919, a clot of blood in his heart caused him to die in his sleep.

Time has certified Theodore Roosevelt's eminence among American political leaders. He was the most colorful of Presidents. His colossal energy enabled him to perform extremely well not only the complex duties of his office but many other things of interest to him. Although not endowed with exceptional intellectual acuity, he had until his last years the breadth of view to perceive the basic problems of his time and to deal with them energetically and sympathetically. A man of action rather than reflection, he was generally impelled by an excessively strong sense of morality. He demanded honesty of all men and fought evil wherever he found it—in high places no less than among those of low estate. The intensification of industrialism had revealed to him the gross social injustice of uncontrolled economic enterprise and he sought to curb it as best he could. He was proud to have been the first President to insist that the rich and the powerful obey the laws of the land, but he perceived only dimly that privilege was ever the source of lawbreaking and corruption.

For all his dynamic exuberance, he was not the impulsive man his detractors claimed he was. His seemingly hasty actions were in fact the result of a pattern of behavior formulated only after serious deliberation. His quick moral faculty enabled him to distinguish between right and wrong with intuitive readiness—although not always with infallible accuracy. His decisions to act were therefore, despite their seeming rashness, based upon a clear perception of the pertinent facts.

Roosevelt's success in politics came from his ability, first, to dramatize himself and, second, to ride the wave of majority opinion. Senator La Follette, a hostile witness, declared: "Theodore Roosevelt is the ablest living interpreter of what I would call the superficial public sentiment of a given time and he is spontaneous in his reaction to it." Yet Roosevelt did not merely capitalize on his quick perception of majority feeling; he also gave it effective voice. He stressed the common resentment against corruption in politics and iniquity in business practices and attacked both evils with all the force of his explosive personality. William Howard Taft, no blind admirer, wrote of him in this connection: "No one pointed with more humor and telling denunciation to the injustice and outrage of using government office for personal and party political advancement than did he, and no one gave more practical proof of the possibilities of reform in this matter."

Yet Roosevelt was never a genuine progressive. A strong party man, always eager to avoid extremes, and both suspicious and scornful of the idealistic reformer, he embraced liberalism more as a means to an end than as a basic philosophy. Ever attuned to public sentiment he was, on his return from Europe in 1910, immediately influenced by the rising wave of popular radicalism. In one of his first speeches, made at Osawatomie, Kansas, he proclaimed a doctrine he certainly would have shied away from during his Presidency:

The man who wrongly holds that every human right is secondary to his profit must now give way to the advocate of human welfare, who rightly maintains that every man holds his property subject to the general right of the community to regulate its use to whatever degree the public welfare may require it.

It is doubtful if he ever realized the full implications of this and other radical ideals espoused by him during that period. There is no question, however, that his decision to form the Progressive party was made only after the Republican bosses, serving the large corporations rather than the general public, had robbed him of the nomination. In the heat of the campaign he tended to express himself extremely on various social and economic proposals. Once the fight for election was lost, he was quick to shake off his assumed radicalism. The claims of the "lunatic fringe" actually repelled him. He wanted to forget his political aberration, and felt relieved when the Progressive party began to disintegrate. By that time he was an embittered man, suffering from the lingering aftereffects of a tropical fever and deeply resentful of the nation's pacifism in a world endangered by German aggression.

Roosevelt was a great admirer of Abraham Lincoln and tried earnestly to win a place beside him in the nation's esteem. Yet he never measured up to his hero. He lacked Lincoln's spiritual depth. There was little humility in Roosevelt's nature, only apprehension. From early adulthood, despite protestations to the contrary, he strove to attain the country's highest political office. He was therefore aggressive, even arrogant, in his ambitious quest, and nearly always the practical politician. Honest, moralistic, zealous for the public good, he never quite freed himself from the blinders of his class. Lacking Lincoln's breadth of sympathy, he could not help despising a radical such as Tom Paine, scorning an idealist such as Jefferson, condemning men who hated war, stigmatizing a socialist such as Debs as an "undesirable citizen." The social dreams of the "lunatic fringe" were simply beyond his ken—except for the brief Progressive period. Nor should it be overlooked that his contempt for men who concentrated on making money was tempered by his deep respect for private property and capitalistic enterprise. Equally significant was his strong admiration for President Grant; no doubt overlooking his political ineptitude in his admiration of his military genius, Roosevelt placed him beside Washington and Lincoln and above Jefferson and Jackson.

More the patriot and preacher than the intellectual and humanitarian, Roosevelt never quite achieved the noble heights of human endeavor. The eminence that he did attain came from his ability to sense the social changes initiated by industrialization and to make himself the spokesman of the popular will toward a balance between individual enterprise and the public good.

Woodrow Wilson

THE NEW FREEDOM—A WAR CASUALTY

PROGRESSIVE DEMOCRACY had a formidable protagonist in Woodrow Wilson. A scholar-politician who became President by a fortuitous concatenation of circumstances, he had the vision and the will to assume the leadership of an insurgent liberalism. The cataclysm in Europe, however, swamped his program of domestic reform and soon sucked the nation into the military maelstrom. Wilson entered the conflict very reluctantly but pursued it with surprising determination and dogmatism—all the while salving his conscience with the noble aim of making an end to war itself. For a brief period he became the lofty spokesman of a weary mankind yearning for peace. Yet he ended his career in tragic failure. Overzealous in his idealism, confident of the superiority of reason over fear, vain and willful in his dealings with others, blindly underestimating the hard core of selfishness in the hearts of men, he refused to bend before the gusts of greed and chauvinism and was broken and thrust aside.

Thomas Woodrow Wilson prided himself on being "an inbred Calvinist." Born on December 28, 1856, in Staunton, Virginia, he came of a stout line of Scottish and Irish strict Presbyterians. The families of both of his parents were intellectually vigorous, firm in their faith, and active in the pursuit of a life of righteousness. The Woodrows, first-generation Americans, were noted not only for their Covenanter zeal but for their dour obduracy. The Wilsons were no less pious, but an Irish buoyancy quickened their daily existence.

The Wilson home was permeated with the spirit of the Presbyterian manse. Yet Doctor Wilson was no fanatic. An eloquent and learned preacher, he enjoyed his eminence in the parish, the sallies of his ready wit, the meager perquisites of his office. To the end of his long life he combined doctrinal firmness with mundane gratifications.

From early childhood Tommy Wilson considered himself different from other boys. Of frail health, myopic, and for ten years the youngest and most cherished member of the family, he avoided rough games and give-and-take group play. Kept out of school till he was nine, he often indulged in daydreaming. He adored his father, and the Reverend Joseph R. Wilson was fondly solicitous about his ailing but alert son. Early convinced of the boy's superior mind, he devoted himself to his intellectual development. He stimulated his reading, discussed with him religious doctrine and current affairs, and trained him to express himself with explicit clarity. And Tommy exerted himself to please his beloved father. Many years later he attributed his felicitous literary style to the intensive exercises in writing prescribed by his parent.

Politics and religion dominated his adolescence. At sixteen he became a stanch admirer of Gladstone, then prime minister of England, and dreamt of becoming an equally famous American statesman. The following year he joined the church, prayed regularly, and read a portion of the Bible daily—a habit he practiced to the end of his life. Years later, in a letter to Mrs. Toy, he stated: "My life would not be worth living if it were not for the driving power of religion, for *faith*, pure and simple. I have seen all my life the arguments against it without ever having been moved by them."

In 1873 he entered the small and parochial Davidson College and remained there till the following June. Ill health kept him home the next year, but in September 1875 he enrolled as a freshman at Princeton. He was a withdrawn, reflective, yet ambitious youth. In his sophomore year he gained enough self-confidence to take part in intramural debates and to make friends with some of his classmates. The play of the mind inherent in intellectual discussion greatly appealed to him. He enjoyed the speeches of Edmund Burke and John Bright and the essays of Walter Bagehot. Soon the study of politics became his chief pursuit. In moments of make-believe he envisaged himself elected to high office and at one time he actually inscribed a number of visiting cards with the words "Senator from Virginia" after his name. In his senior year he published his first professional essay, "Cabinet Government in the United States," later to become the basis for *Congressional Government*, his first and most important book.

In the fall of 1879 young Wilson, having graduated from Princeton, began the study of law at the University of Virginia. He was seriously planning to enter politics and considered a legal training the best introduction to it. Law books bored him, however, and he gave much of his time to debating and public speaking. Soon he began to gain a reputation as an orator. It was at this time that he lopped off his first name.

In December 1880 a digestive disturbance forced him to leave for home. There he remained for more than a year, nursing his health and reading law books. In 1882 he was admitted to the bar and opened a law office in Atlanta with one of his Virginia classmates. He was not long in discovering his unfitness for the hurly-burly of legal practice. For months on end not a client came his way; nor did he make an effort to seek any. Instead he read assiduously in the field of government. After more than a year of legal inactivity he concluded that the "scheming and haggling practice" of the law was not for him. To his friend Heath Dabney he wrote: "The practice of the law, when conducted for purposes of gain, is antagonistic to the best interests of the intellectual life."

In his twenty-seventh year and still dependent upon his father for support, he wistfully decided to give up his ambition for a political career and to prepare himself for college teaching. In September 1883 he enrolled in the graduate school of The Johns

Hopkins University. Some months earlier he had met Ellen Louise Axson and became engaged to her after a brief but ardent courtship. She at once exerted a strong influence over him. Affected by her firm intellect and sensitive sympathy, he opened his heart and mind to her in a series of letters that were charged with warm affection and read like an intimate diary—in tone but not in ardor very similar to the letters he was later to send to several women friends. Shortly after he had resumed the formal study of politics he wrote to her:

I want to contribute to our literature what no American has ever contributed, studies in the philosophy of our institutions, not the abstract and occult, but the practical and suggestive, philosophy which is at the core of our governmental methods; their use, their meaning, the spirit that makes them workable.

Wilson was strongly stimulated by his teachers, who were among the most original thinkers in the country. His mind seethed with fresh ideas and new perceptions. Determined to produce a book on American government at once original and well written, he read with unflagging concentration and labored painstakingly over each sentence. When he finished a chapter he read it in one of his seminars for critical discussion and was highly pleased with the praise of his peers.

Early in October 1884 he completed the manuscript of *Congressional Government* and submitted it to a publisher with a quaking heart. He believed he had produced a work of original merit, but he was not at all certain of its reception. When the book was accepted and published several months later, it was enthusiastically reviewed by men of eminence. The older Gamaliel Bradford, who had no doubt recognized some of his own ideas in the volume, generously wrote of it in *The Nation:* "We have no hesitation in saying that this is one of the most important books dealing with political subjects which have ever issued from the American press."

Congressional Government was indeed the first book to view

American government both pragmatically and critically. Patterned after Bagehot's *The English Constitution*, it combined a keen understanding of the democratic process with an admirable analytical incisiveness. Wilson found that our government was not functioning according to the intention of its founders; that the division of power tended to develop a sense of irresponsibility; that Congress has become "predominant over its so-called coordinate branches"; that the power of the Presidency has waned as that of Congress has waxed; and that the political complexion of the Supreme Court was inevitably "taken from the color of the times during which its majority was chosen." "Power," he maintained, "is nowhere concentrated; it is rather deliberately and of set policy scattered amongst many small chiefs . . . the chairmen of the principal Standing Committees." He urged that the defects and inadequacies of our governmental processes be examined with "fearless criticism" and that the remedies be applied without equivocation. Strongly influenced by the writings of Walter Bagehot, Wilson did not hesitate to recommend the English form of government as a worthy model. "Cabinet government is a device for bringing the executive and legislative branches into harmony and cooperation without uniting or confusing their functions."

The success of the book rekindled Wilson's political ambition. Early in 1885 he confided to Ellen: "I do feel a real regret that I have been shut out from my heart's *first*—primary—ambition and purpose, which was, to take an active, if possible a leading, part in public life, and strike out for myself; if I had the ability, a *statesman's* career." Circumstances did not, however, favor the plunge into politics. He recoiled from the very idea of having to curry favor with party bosses. After serious reflection he followed Ellen's highly practical advice to complete his studies and obtain a teaching post in a college. He was eager to get married and knew that this would be feasible only after he began to earn a salary. Having made a brilliant record at Johns Hopkins and having published a highly praised book, he had no difficulty in finding a position. He accepted an offer from the newly established Bryn Mawr

College because he wanted to remain in the East. When the contract was signed he and Ellen were married.

Wilson left Johns Hopkins without completing the requirements for a doctorate. At Ellen's urging, however, he submitted his book in lieu of a thesis and was awarded the coveted degree in 1886. That year he began to write a textbook in comparative government, a work published in 1889 and widely used. Meantime he had become dissatisfied with his position at Bryn Mawr. His salary was too low to provide adequately for his growing family; even worse was the thought of having to teach girls indefinitely. To his friend Dabney he wrote in 1888, "I have for a long time been hungry for a class of *men*." He was therefore happy to accept a more lucrative offer from Wesleyan University in Middletown, Connecticut. There he enjoyed, in addition to his teaching, such extracurricular activities as coaching the football team and organizing the House of Commons for debating purposes. He also managed to lecture in different cities and thus widen his reputation as a scholar and speaker.

In 1890 Wilson accepted a professorship in jurisprudence and political economy at Princeton—refusing several other good offers in order to return to his beloved alma mater. He was a highly successful teacher, and in the course of the years he was four times chosen by the students as their most popular lecturer. Not that he catered to their tastes. Endowed with a very fastidious mind, he recoiled from slovenly thinking or loose speech. His lectures were noted for their logical preciseness, but their clarity of expression and uncommon eloquence often inspired spontaneous applause. The fact that he continued to be a football enthusiast of course added to his popularity. He also quickly established himself as a leader among his fellow teachers. According to Bliss Perry, Wilson was "the most brilliant man among the younger faculty" and one of their effective spokesman. He led the fight for the honor system and sharply criticized the stodgy conservatives on the faculty. All the while he found time to write articles and books and deliver numerous lectures outside of Princeton.

In the late 1890's Wilson was one of the best-known and highest-paid members of the faculty. His writing and lecturing brought him an additional income of around $1500 annually. Yet he felt restless and impatient. His ambition drove him hard. Fastidious and indefatigable, he worked so hard on his monograph on George Washington that he began to suffer from an acute attack of neuritis and decided to go to England for an extended rest.

On his return home at the end of the summer he became intensely interested in the turbulent 1896 campaign. The "latent politician" in him chafed at his cloistered existence. An advocate of *laissez faire* in economics and of the doctrine of social stability in politics, he disdained the dissenters of the time. He scorned the "crude and ignorant minds" of the Farmers' Alliance spokesmen; he frowned upon trade unions and condemned strikes; and he criticized both socialists and monopolists. As a Democrat he rejected McKinley; yet he considered Bryan a demagogue and charlatan. He ached to enter the contest and lead the people to the path of what he considered sound democracy. To his brother-in-law Stockton Axson he exclaimed: "I am so tired of a merely talking profession! I want to do something!"

That same fall he was to feel proud of his ability to talk well. Princeton, celebrating its sesquicentennial on a national scale, chose him to deliver the main address—an honor that went far to salve his political frustration. He prepared himself with painstaking care on the theme that a university functioned best when it served the nation. He developed his argument with impeccable logic and in a style at once dulcet and dignified. The speech made a profound impression upon the distinguished audience gathered to hear it.

The next six years were for Wilson a period of intensive work. His ambition kept him restive, dissatisfied with the crumbs of fame that came his way. He wrote a five-volume history of the United States; he broadened his active interest in public affairs; he strengthened his leadership of the younger faculty group. In his writing he scorned being either the pedant or the researcher—

preferring to be known as "a man of letters." His essays indeed sparkle with literary brilliance, although the overuse of quotations gives them an academic flavor. They do give point, however, to his avowal that he was "an idealist, with the heart of a poet."

During these years Wilson manifested the virtues and defects that characterized his later behavior. Adored by his wife and three daughters, he seemed always in need of additional sympathy and appreciation, especially from witty and cultivated women. He was feminine in his possessive claims upon his friends. As one of them remarked:

He did not explicitly demand but implicitly assumed absolute and exclusive loyalty, and always tested devotion to his cause in terms of personal loyalty to himself as its chosen delegate and inspired mouthpiece. . . . His self-confidence was fortified by the assurance that his was the voice of the people made articulate.

One was either his friend or his foe. His "inflexibility of mind and character"—markedly noticeable even in his early Princeton days—made his soul live in isolation, surrounded by an emotional hoarfrost, yet palpitatingly eager for the sympathy and warmth of human friendship. Because he tended to dominate in his leadership, he could not but react extremely in his intimacies or animosities. To quote another of his Princeton colleagues, "When he was not personally concerned he could be most generous, helpful, and nonpartisan. But if something did affect him, he could be utterly selfish and even ruthless." Once he had made up his mind on anything, it had for him the certainty of objective truth and not to be denied. It was this self-confidence, hardened by his Covenanter's spirit, that caused him to underestimate his adversaries and ultimately to suffer defeat.

After twelve years of personal preparation and faculty leadership Woodrow Wilson was neither surprised nor unready when he was suddenly called to the presidency of Princeton on June 9, 1902. The trustees voted for him unanimously and faculty approval was equally affirmative. Although less than six months previously he had written to Frederick J. Turner, "I was born a politician, and must be at the task for which, by means of my historical writing, I have all these years been in training," he turned to his new duties as if they marked the realization of a long-cherished ambition. For he was at last holding high office, in some respects superior to political preferment. Best of all, he could now act, spread his wings, give flesh to the bones of his educational ideals. "My election to the presidency," he wrote that summer, "has done a very helpful thing for me. It has settled the future for me and given me a sense of *position* and of definite tangible tasks which take the *flutter* and restlessness from my spirits."

In 1902 Princeton was still a small parochial college, strongly Presbyterian, a haven for the sons of wealth whose idea of higher education was a four-year period of social ease and casual study. It remained unaffected by the experimentation and soul-searching that was agitating Harvard, Chicago, and other universities. Under Wilson's administration, however, it quickly leaped into the forefront of modern institutions of higher learning. One of his first acts was to raise academic standards. "I'll not be president of a country club," he insisted. Nor was he in the slightest disturbed by the outcries of wealthy alumni whose sons were forced to leave the college because they were poor students. Instead he launched a new plan for Princeton that created a national sensation. First he asked for funds amounting to more than twelve million dollars —at that time by far the largest request ever made by a university president. Even more dramatic was his revolutionary preceptorial program which aimed at introducing undergraduates to a more mature and independent method of study. "The governing idea is to be that they are getting up *subjects*—getting them up with the assistance of lecturers, libraries, and a body of preceptors who are their guides, philosophers, and friends." The plan called for fifty preceptors—"proven scholars," young, alert, intelligent—who were to "transform thoughtless boys performing tasks into thinking men."

In his effort to raise the money and to obtain acceptance of his audacious program, Wilson sought to take the alumni into his confidence and to implant in their minds his own vision of Princeton's great opportunity. In a speech in New York he declared:

What this country needs now more than it ever did before, what it shall need in the years following, is knowledge and enlightenment. Civilization grows infinitely complex about us; the tasks of this country are no longer simple; men are not doing their duty who have a chance to know and do not equip themselves with knowledge in the midst of the tasks that surround us. Princeton has ever since her birthday stood for the service of the nation.

He also wrote inspiring personal letters to every man of wealth who struck him as a likely donor. For all his pleading, however, he never ceased to stress his high ideals. "I am covetous for Princeton," he insisted, "of all the glory that there is, and the chief glory of a university is always intellectual glory."

Contributions did not come in fast enough or large enough to please him. Eager to put his preceptorial program into action, he persuaded several of his rich classmates to provide enough money for the current employment of the preceptors—whom he selected with exceeding care. Meantime the new course of study was, after months of serious discussion, unanimously adopted by the faculty on April 25, 1904, and successfully initiated that fall.

Wilson reached the peak of his popularity in 1906. Most Princetonians appreciated the great improvements which he was achieving for their alma mater. He was not, however, the man to rest on his laurels. He went about the country advocating the urgency of his ideals not only in the field of education but in that of national affairs. It was after his speech at the Lotos Club on February 3, 1906, that George Harvey began to write of him as a presidential candidate. As ten years earlier, his intensive concentration began to affect him physically. One May morning he woke to find himself practically blind in one eye. A summer in Europe again helped him to regain his health, and he returned ready to launch his new plan of the quadrangle system.

The radical proposal to abolish the socially cherished eating clubs—which years before had taken the place of fraternities— quickly depleted the reservoir of good will which Wilson had built up during the first years of his administration. Although the trustees at first adopted his plan without question, the mere announcement caused an explosion of wide protest. In his impatience to act he had not troubled to take the faculty into his confidence or to consult with the leading alumni. His procedure therefore struck them as both arbitrary and arrogant. Dean Andrew F. West, fearful that the building of quadrangles at a cost of many millions would greatly handicap his own designs for the graduate school, became the leader of the opposition. Wilson, however, refused to consider a compromise. In his mind the abolition of the eating clubs had become essential to the democratic health of the university. "The colleges of the country," he asserted, "are looking to us for leadership in this matter, and if we disappoint them it will be an opportunity irretrievably lost."

The alumni, sentimental and conservative, balked. Many resented the idea of their sons being forced to "eat with muckers" or losing the social advantages of the eating clubs. Encouraged by Dean West's cutting remark to Wilson— "If the spirit of Princeton is to be killed, I have little interest in the details of the funeral" —they insisted on preserving the traditions of their alma mater. And although the faculty favored the plan by a vote of 80 to 23, the exertions of powerful alumni caused the trustees to rescind their original approval of the plan.

Wilson took defeat very hard. When Professor John G. Hibben, for years his most intimate friend, sided with the opposition, Wilson turned from him as from a Judas and never spoke to him again. Hurt to the depths of his being, he thought seriously of resigning—and refrained only out of loyalty to Princeton. The experience, however, helped to strengthen his growing awareness of the gap between the democratic ideal and the aristocracy of wealth. Meantime his precarious health made it necessary for him to seek rest in Bermuda during the winter and in Great Britain during the summer vacation.

The issue of the graduate school became acute about this time, causing Wilson to incur Dean West's active and implacable hostility. At first the two men were in complete agreement on the idea of the projected graduate school. When Wilson assumed the presidency he readily approved West's plans and helped him solicit separate funds toward their realization. It was his assumption all the while that the graduate school was to be a part of the general reconstruction and expansion of the university and was to be situated "at the heart of Princeton." With the receipt of the Swann bequest of $300,000 he considered the location a settled matter.

Dean West, however, was not one to submit to another's will. A bull of a man, solid of flesh, stolid of mien, positive and aggressive, he wanted a graduate school independent of the college, luxuriously outfitted, adapted to leisurely study, and completely under his control. When he received an offer of the presidency of the Massachusetts Institute of Technology in 1906, he placed the matter before the trustees. Wilson joined the latter in urging West to remain and develop the graduate school. He hated personal dissension and thought he could get along with the dean despite their temperamental differences. West, having received new assurances, proceeded to solicit funds on the basis of his own plan. Soon he was able to announce that William C. Procter offered a half million dollars for a graduate school building with the provision that it be erected on land away from the campus. West made no mention of the contrary provision in the Swann bequest—assuming that Wilson would not dare risk the withdrawal of the large Procter gift.

Wilson was hurt by Procter's slight in not consulting him before making public his generous offer. Yet he tried to be reasonable. He even sought to persuade Procter to alter his conditions in order to make the donation consonant with his own plans for the university. When Procter, prompted by West, refused to yield, Wilson decided to fight. Loath to deepen the quarrel between West and himself, he forfeited his advantage by making the issue not the administration of the graduate school—which was at the bottom of the dispute—but the location of the Procter building. Even those trustees who sided with him in other matters failed to agree with him that the university should refuse the gift of a half million dollars for that reason. When Procter's offer was accepted, Wilson was again ready to resign. Stating his objection to the gift, he gave his real reasons:

It has reversed the policy of the Faculty, the leading conception of my whole administration, in an educational matter of the most fundamental importance. . . . I cannot accede to the acceptance of gifts upon terms which take the educational policy of the University out of the hands of the Trustees and Faculty and permit it to be determined by those who give money.

Thus challenged the trustees, agreeing that Wilson was "the greatest asset of Princeton," could not but reconsider their acceptance of Procter's offer. News of this decision brought violent protests from the alumni. Few of them had decided opinions on either the location of the graduate school or the nature of its administration, but the rejection of a half million dollars struck them as sheer madness. Wilson, determined to have his way, sought to win alumni support by a series of speeches before Princeton Clubs in key cities. Motivated by the importance of the problem and influenced by the current political insurgency, he argued that the controversy was indeed a fight between democracy and special privilege. To the hostile New York alumni he declared on April 7, 1910:

Divorce the universities of this country from their teaching enthusiasm, divorce them from their undergraduate energies, and you will have a thing which is not only un-American but utterly unserviceable to the country. There is nothing private in America. Everything is public; everything belongs to the united energy of the nation.

Nine days later, speaking extemporaneously before the Pittsburgh alumni and smarting from attack on every side, he exclaimed:

What we cry out against is that a handful of conspicuous men have thrust cruel hands among the heartstrings of the masses of men upon whose blood and energy they are subsisting. . . . I have dedicated every power that there is in me to bring the colleges that I have anything to do with to an absolutely democratic regeneration of spirit.

The speeches—his first "appeal to the country"—did not lessen the acuteness of the crisis. Both sides had powerful support, yet neither wished to do anything that would hurt the university. A compromise seemed the only workable settlement and was in the process of consummation. Then came the news that I. C. Wyman, a New England alumnus, had died and left an estate of over two million dollars to the graduate school, with Dean West as one of the trustees. Wilson realized immediately that his fight was lost. Accepting the inevitable he said to West: "I wish to say that I desire to cooperate with you generally and in every possible way in working toward the success of the Graduate School under this bequest. The size of the gift entirely changes the perspective." Shortly afterwards Procter renewed his offer, and this time it was promptly accepted.

Outwardly acquiescent and philosophical, Wilson seethed inwardly with frustration and defeat. He considered his usefulness to Princeton at an end. The only question was what should be his next move.

In 1910 there was much political restiveness over the country. Muckraking journalists had stirred many people to a realization of graft and incompetence in government and greed and monopoly in business. The Taft Administration disappointed the liberals who had expected it to carry on Roosevelt's Square Deal. Voters everywhere were in the mood to "throw the rascals out" and elect men who promised to break up the trusts. Democratic politicians were only too eager to take advantage of this situation.

James Smith, genial Democratic boss of New Jersey, was in search of a candidate for governor who could get himself elected. George Harvey, editor, politician, friend of Wall Street men, and a neighbor of Smith, had long been advocating Woodrow Wilson's eligibility for the Presidency. Knowing that candidacy for the greater office would be enormously strengthened by successful election to the governorship, he talked to Smith about his plans for Wilson and urged his nomination. The idea appealed to the seasoned politician. He was impressed by Wilson's fight at Princeton and considered it an asset with the independent voters. Smith also assumed that Wilson's political inexperience would make it necessary for him to accept guidance and support. It did not take him and Harvey long to agree on a course of action. Wilson was offered the nomination on his own terms—an event he had been vainly hoping for ever since he had inscribed the words "Senator from Virginia" after his name.

For some years he had been pleasantly aware that his admirers considered him a potential political figure. And although his duties at Princeton kept him from taking an active interest in politics, his opinions on national affairs were too definite to be kept to himself. Essentially a nineteenth-century liberal and a strong party man, he frequently expressed his views on current events. When the 1904 political nominations came up for discussion, he favored Bryan politically but considered him a man of "no brains" and unfit for the Presidency. Later that year he disapproved of the insurgents and declared that the United States "needs and will tolerate no party of discontent or radical experiment." This opposition to reformers with a "passion for regulative legislation" he maintained until the end of his Princeton presidency. He also made no secret of his critical attitude toward organized labor. As late as January 12, 1909, he stated, "I am a fierce partizan of the Open Shop and of everything that makes for individual liberty." For the same reason he frowned upon trusts and bankers. On January 12, 1910, addressing a powerful group of financiers, including J. P. Morgan, he said admonishingly:

There is a higher law than the law of profit. You bankers sitting in this provincial community of New York see nothing beyond your own interests and are content to sit at the receipt of customs and take tolls

79

of all passers-by. You should be broadminded and see what is best for the country in the long run.

Wilson did not take seriously Harvey's campaign to make him President, but he felt genuinely flattered by the compliment and took no steps to stop it. Early in 1908, to test his availability for the Democratic nomination, he made a number of speeches on topics of general interest. When he sensed that Bryan was in control of the party and would be renominated, he left for Europe before the convention and refused to allow the use of his name for possible nomination as Vice-President. That he preferred high political office to his academic position he admitted in a letter that gives an accurate measure of the man:

I have a strong instinct of leadership, an unmistakable oratorical temperament and the keenest possible delight in affairs. . . . I have no patience for the tedious toil of what is known as research. I have a passion for interpreting great thoughts to the world; I should be complete if I could inspire a great movement of opinion, if I could read the experiences of the past into the political life of the men of today and so communicate the thought to the minds of the great mass of the people as to impel them to great political achievements.

Wilson was definitely interested in the Democratic gubernatorial nomination, provided it came to him without effort on his part and left him a free agent. He agreed not to attack the existing Democratic machine "so long as I was left absolutely free in the matter of measures and men." These conditions were agreeable to Smith, and on July 15 Wilson made public his availability for the office. The insurgent Democrats, considering Wilson the candidate of Big Business, were highly critical; labor leaders, apprized of his antiunion views, likewise opposed him; but Smith's machine functioned smoothly and Wilson was nominated on the first ballot. Harvey had arranged to have Wilson await the result at a nearby hotel in order to address the delegates immediately after they had voted for him. His acceptance speech, simply and sincerely spoken, pledging adherence to the progressive platform and asserting his

independence of bosses, served to reconcile the insurgent Democrats who had fought him. Soon after, Wilson resigned from the
presidency of Princeton.

Once he began to campaign, he manifested a surprising political
astuteness. His effective eloquence and lack of common bombast
enabled him to convince audiences of his complete sincerity. A
shrewd journalist noted that Wilson was the rare type of speaker
"who could be confidential with a crowd." His lofty tone and
dignified language, his progressive views and frank manner—these
attributes marked him as a man worthy of high office. Equally to
his advantage was his ability to appeal to progressives without immediately alienating the bosses. Smith and his lieutenants considered it good political doubletalk when Wilson condemned the
boss system and promised never to "submit to the dictation of
any person or persons, 'special interests,' or organization." Nor did
they take seriously his question-and-answer correspondence with
George L. Record, progressive Republican, in which he avowed
his liberal views on all matters of current political importance. But
the New Jersey insurgents of both parties were delighted with his
liberal position and devoted themselves to his election. When the
ballots were counted Wilson won by a landslide; reversing Taft's
New Jersey majority of 80,000 in 1908 to a Democratic majority of
49,056, the most conspicuous of Democratic victories in the 1910
election.

As governor-elect, Wilson quickly came face to face with
bossism. With a Democratic majority in the assembly, the choice
of a Democratic Senator was assured. James Smith, having held
that office some years back, decided he wanted it again. Wilson
balked. The matter had come up during the campaign and Smith
had promised Harvey he would not be a candidate. Wilson therefore wrote to his mentor to make Smith keep his word. "His election would be intolerable to the very people who elected me. . . .
They count on me to prevent it. I shall forfeit their confidence if
I do not. All their ugliest suspicions, dispelled by my campaign
assurances, will be confirmed." Smith, however, insisted on re-

81

turning to the Senate. Wilson's opposition, striking him as sheer ingratitude, if not gross perfidy, only made him the more determined. With most of the assemblymen under political or financial obligation to him, he felt assured of success. But Wilson fought him with surprising skill and effectiveness. He went personally to the elected assemblymen to familiarize them with the issues involved. He also made a number of vigorous speeches in every part of the state, arousing the people on the question of whether the state was to be governed by its elected officers or by an autocratic boss. The battle was fierce and was fought to the last hour; when the vote was counted Smith was the loser. Victory gave Wilson nationwide prominence among progressives—he having dealt with Smith more courageously than Theodore Roosevelt had dared treat Boss Platt.

Wilson began his career as governor by carrying out his campaign promises. He prepared himself thoroughly on the nature and purpose of each of his reform bills and promoted them forcefully. His intellectual acuity and intense earnestness affected favorably even the hack politician; and the aggressive insurgents, led by his secretary Joseph P. Tumulty, worked for him incessantly. With an aroused public backing him and exerting pressure on their representatives, Wilson was able to force his bills through despite the desperate opposition of the political bosses and their henchmen. His curt dismissal of James Nugent, Smith's nephew and first lieutenant, from his office gained him wide approval. By the time the legislature adjourned on April 21, 1911, Wilson had carried through every reform he had promised in the campaign—laws affecting public utilities, corruption, employers' liability, the primaries—making New Jersey, long known as the "mother of trusts," one of the most progressive states in the nation.

Conditions were forging Wilson into an admitted "radical." His ambition to become President began to dominate his thoughts and motivate his behavior. Though no professional politician and ever the intellectual, he readily sensed the drift of political thought over the nation and embraced it as his own. In the spring of 1911 and again subsequently he toured a number of western states in order to show himself to active progressives. His forthright speeches were impressive. His talk on the Bible in Denver, delivered with deep feeling and later distributed in pamphlet form, won favor with many church groups. Knowing that he needed Bryan's support, he praised his "extraordinary force of personality," his "sincerity and conviction." When they happened to speak from the same platform, he went out of his way to express his high regard for the Commoner. He did this with a full knowledge that approval of Bryan would alienate the bankers and the eastern bosses of the party. Indeed, as Harvey told Colonel House, "Everybody south of Canal Street was in a frenzy against Wilson." But like the calculating gambler he placed his faith in the rising tide of progressivism—breaking with Harvey, his original sponsor, to strengthen his position with western insurgents. When his crucial test came in January 1912 at the Jackson Day Dinner in Washington, he gave an excellent account of himself. Without disavowing his earlier criticism of Bryan in a letter written in 1907 and made public by his enemies shortly before the dinner—"would that we could do something . . . to knock Mr. Bryan once and for all into a cocked hat"—he was so gracious in his evaluation of the Commoner that he won his warm approval. The next day 32 out of 52 members of the Democratic National Committee expressed a preference for Wilson.

The battle for delegates was fought hard during the months preceding the Baltimore convention. Aided by William F. McCombs, the energetic but temperamental manager of his campaign, by E. M. House, the shrewd and suave Texas politician who quickly became his intimate friend, and by an increasing number of active and enthusiastic liberals the country over, Wilson fought for delegates with his accustomed dignity and earnestness. In a number of important states, however, Speaker Champ Clark was favored by both the voters and the politicians, so that at the opening of the convention he had the largest number of pledged delegates.

The contest on the convention floor and in the rooms of influential delegates was long and tumultuous. At first it appeared that Clark would be nominated, and he indeed obtained a majority when the New York delegation began to vote for him, but the two-thirds rule kept him from victory. His final defeat and Wilson's triumph were due largely to Bryan's exertions. Although he came to the convention an apparent neutral, he insisted that the party retain his progressive principles. One of his first acts was to offer a resolution declaring the convention "opposed to the nomination of any candidate for President who is the representative of or under obligation to J. P. Morgan, Thomas F. Ryan, August Belmont, or any other member of the privilege-hunting and favor-seeking class." Although many seasoned politicians jeered at his naive insolence, he succeeded in making the issue paramount with a large number of western delegates. As one of them remarked, "The fight is on and Bryan is on one side and Wall Street is on the other." While Wilson had the sagacity and courage to approve Bryan's fight for progressivism, Clark straddled—and lost. On the fourteenth ballot Bryan, who had been voting with the Nebraska delegation for Clark, publicly cast his ballot for Wilson with the explanation that he could not favor a candidate sponsored by Tammany. Thereafter, at first slowly but later more rapidly, Wilson began to gain at Clark's expense—winning the nomination on the forty-sixth ballot.

Wilson was less known to the voters than either President Taft or Theodore Roosevelt. To Mrs. Mary Hulbert he wrote candidly that by comparison with Roosevelt he was "a vague, conjectural personality, more made up of opinions and academic prepossessions than of human traits and red corpuscles." Eager as he was to win favor with the mass of voters, he insisted on conducting his campaign with his wonted probity and seriousness. He selected a committee without either bosses or conservatives to manage the practical matters of publicity and political contacts; he himself, aided by Louis D. Brandeis and other advisers, concentrated on the speeches that were to expound the principles of his "New Freedom."

Because the trust problem was then the dominant issue, Wilson gave it special emphasis. He took the position that American business enterprise was no longer free and that "the man with only a little capital" was finding it "more and more impossible to compete with the big fellow." Although a corporation, grown big naturally, "has survived competition by conquering in the field of intelligence and economy," trusts "have been artificially created . . . to get rid of competition" and are therefore "indefensible and intolerable" private monopolies.

If I did not believe monopoly could be restrained and destroyed I would come to doubt that liberty could be preserved in the United States. It is a choice of life and death—whether we shall allow the country to be controlled by small groups of men or whether we shall return to the form of government contemplated by the fathers. . . . What I am interested in is having the government of the United States more concerned about human rights than about property rights. Property is an instrument of humanity; humanity isn't an instrument of property.

Wilson's adherence to the ideals of Jefferson while urging government control of big business revealed his "inner contradiction." He was antagonistic to trusts because he feared their size and power; he extolled the small businessman because he sympathized with "those on the make." It never occurred to him that the successful large-scale industrialist was the small-scale manufacturer grown big at the expense of his competitors; that some of the little businessmen "on the make" in the early nineteenth century were as callous and unscrupulous as any of the rapacious trust builders of his own day. Trained in the Manchester school of economics, he had little insight into the conflict between the ethics of modern industry and the morality of the Jeffersonian agricultural society. He spoke glibly of the people taking possession of the government and determining every turn of its policy, but he failed to square that democratic ideal with the pressing reality of industrial concentration affecting every phase of modern society. His New Freedom was, in the words of Walter Lippmann, "a freedom for the little profiteer, but no freedom for the nation from narrowness, the poor incentives, the limited vision of small competitors" —indeed, no freedom "from the chaos, the welter, the strategy of industrial war."

If Wilson was fundamentally a *laissez-faire* liberal, he was in 1912 speaking for the insurgent and aggressive middle-class Americans. Neither Roosevelt nor anyone else expressed their grievances and their hopes with such earnest idealism and effective eloquence. His rhetoric was ennobling and reassuring.

We are going to climb the slow road until it reaches some upland where the air is fresher, where the whole talk of mere politicians is stilled, where men can look in each other's faces and see that there is nothing to conceal, that all they have to talk about they are willing to talk about in the open and talk about with each other; and whence, looking back over the road, we shall see at last that we have fulfilled our promise to mankind.

Most of those who heard his message gladly embraced his leadership. When the ballots were counted in November he was victorious by a wide margin—although the combined vote of Roosevelt and Taft was considerably larger than his.

The perplexities of the Presidency began to prey upon Wilson's mind the day he was elected. The need to ward off the crowds of job hunters, to choose the right men for the Cabinet and other high posts, to prepare a legislative program for Congress—these and other troubling problems confronted him daily. And he was not a man to take such matters lightly or to leave them in the hands of his associates. His conscience frowned upon the easy way. Nor did he have the benefit of advice from many friends; indeed, he had little capacity for intimacy with others. To Edith G. Reid, one of his few devoted correspondents, he confided:

Plenty of people offer me their friendship; but, partly because I am reserved and shy, and partly because I am fastidious and have a narrow, uncatholic taste in friends, I reject the offer in almost every case; and then I am dismayed to look about and see how few persons in the world stand near me and know me as I am.

The loyalty he expected ignored personal conviction or principle. He was therefore very fortunate in his friendship with Colonel House. After their second meeting Wilson felt as if he had always known him, finding in him the qualities that appealed to him so much in women: sympathy, genuine appreciation, receptivity. House in truth offered him much more. With a genius for friendship and diplomacy, he knew how to obtain the help and information Wilson needed. He was able to read his friend's mind and to ease it almost imperceptibly. Rarely contradicting him and seldom even stating an unwelcome truth, he nevertheless influenced him profoundly. Wilson early admitted this when he declared, "Mr. House is my second personality. He is my independent self. His thoughts and mine are one. If I were in his place I would do just as he suggested."

Immediately after the election House began to carry on a large correspondence with all kinds of men on matters pertaining to the incoming Wilson Administration. He obtained and sifted information on various candidates for office and prepared memoranda for Wilson's attention. He also took up various complex problems of policy and legislation and dealt with them with exceptional disinterest, skill, and good will. Refusing to hold office, he made himself indispensable and in fact served as Wilson's alter ego. It was he who suggested most of the men who were finally chosen as members of the Cabinet, and it was he who saw and pacified many of the disappointed office-seekers. All his time was dedicated to easing his friend's terrific load and in helping him with advice and information.

Wilson gratefully accepted House's invaluable assistance, but the responsibility remained his. Now that he had realized his great ambition, he became a man with a mission. He felt morally bound to fulfill his campaign promises. The pomp of office seemed to him a wasteful distraction, and he displeased many by foregoing the inaugural ball and by limiting his official obligations to the minimum. Although he wanted "the best men in the nation" for the important posts, unavoidable political debts and the pressure of circumstances forced him, much to his distress, to engage men of lesser quality. When he thought a man unfit for a coveted office, however, he could be as firm and unrequiting as he was to his campaign manager McCombs.

The functions of the President are complex and arduous even in a time of tranquillity. And Wilson assumed office at the outset of a period of strain and stress. The revolution in Mexico demanded his immediate attention. Our difficulties with England over the Panama Tolls Act required settlement. Other Latin-American incidents clamored for adjustment. And conditions in Europe seemed ominous despite the apparent quiet. All these and other foreign problems needed his careful and constant consideration. Yet he was at first most interested in obtaining domestic legislation that would help free our economy from the grasp of monopoly. In his inaugural address he stressed the urgency of social and economic reforms:

We have made up our minds to square every process of our national life again with the standards we so proudly set up at the beginning and have always carried at our hearts. . . . The Nation has been deeply stirred, stirred by a solemn passion, stirred by the knowledge of wrong, of ideals lost, of government too often debauched and made an instrument of evil.

Dedicating himself to this task, and having as he frankly admitted "a one-track mind," he could not but do first things first: he concentrated his efforts on carrying out his domestic campaign promises and looked after foreign affairs as best he could in the meantime.

He called Congress into special session on April 7. For months previously, with the help of special advisers and the leaders of the

Democratic party, he had worked hard on his reform program. An apostle of "responsible government" and a believer in the doctrine that the President was "the political leader of the nation," he insisted on taking an active part in the enactment of his proposed legislation. He knew that his projected reforms, affecting property and limiting privilege, would be fought by vested interests. To press the advantage of his office upon the members of Congress, he addressed them in person on the imperative need of a lower tariff. In his broad analysis of the nation's economy he stressed the principles on which he wanted them to act:

We must abolish everything that bears even the semblance of privilege or of any kind of artificial advantage, and put our business men and producers under the stimulation of a constant necessity to be efficient, economical, and enterprising, masters of competitive supremacy, better workers and merchants than any in the world.

In the House the tariff bill was fathered by Oscar Underwood and was passed fairly promptly. A powerful lobby blocked the measure in the Senate. For weeks no action was taken. To break the deadlock and to expose the forces fighting the bill, Wilson publicly blasted the insidious lobby.

I think the public ought to know the extraordinary exertions being made by the lobby in Washington. . . . There is every evidence that money without limit is being spent to sustain this lobby and to create an appearance of a pressure of opinion antagonistic to some of the chief items of the Tariff bill . . . only public opinion can check and destroy it.

The response on the part of the people was immediate and effective. In addition Wilson cajoled and catered to the doubtful Democratic Senators. He also invoked the caucus, long inactive, in order to compel party unity of action. All summer, with the heat at times becoming nearly intolerable, Wilson remained in Washington and would not permit Congress to recess. When the Senate finally yielded—reducing the tariff about a third on hundreds of items and putting on the free list a number of articles of common need—Wilson was highly gratified. "A fight for the people and for free business, which has lasted a long generation through, has at last been won, handsomely and completely." In 1916 this law was strengthened by the creation of a Tariff Commission. Unfortunately the entry of the United States into the war the following year hindered the full operation of the law. And by the time the world was at peace again the Republicans were once more in power and raised tariff rates to new high levels.

While the tariff bill was meeting stubborn opposition in the Senate, Wilson again addressed Congress, this time on the urgency of new currency legislation. With the lowered tariff rates about to set our economy free, he argued,

It is imperative that we should give the business men of this country a banking and currency system by means of which they can make use of the freedom of enterprise and of individual initiative which we are about to bestow upon them. . . . We must have a currency, not rigid as now, but readily, elastically responsive to sound credit. . . . And the control of the system of banking and of issue which our new laws are about to set up must be public, not private, must be vested in the Government itself, so that the banks may be the instruments, not the masters, of business and of individual enterprise and initiative.

The proposed banking bill was the product of the best minds Wilson was able to engage in and out of Congress. Himself long a student of our monetary system, he was determined to give the nation a banking law that favored the small businessman. As early as 1911 he had stated that "the great monopoly in this country is the money monopoly." In his discussions with Representative Carter Glass and Senator R. L. Owen, the sponsors of the bill, he reiterated the urgency of an elastic and responsive credit system. Throughout the summer and fall he fought the opponents of the measure—among them the most powerful bankers and businessmen in the country—with an adroit skill that assured ultimate success. Influenced by Brandeis, whom he was later to appoint to the Supreme Court despite the bitter clamor of many conservatives, he accepted Bryan's recommendation that control of the proposed Federal Reserve System be lodged with the government and not with bankers; he also agreed with Bryan that Federal Reserve notes be issued as "obligations of the United States" and not of the constituent banks. These changes assured the bill the warm support of the Bryanites in Congress.

The agitation of the leading bankers—who decried the currency measure as not adapted to their particular requirements—strengthened the opposition of the conservative Senators. When Wilson refused to permit a summer recess, they called him a "dictator." But he remained adamant. To Mrs. Hulbert he wrote on September 28:

The struggle goes on down here without intermission. Why it should be a struggle it is hard (cynicism put on one side) to say. Why *should* public men, Senators of the United States, have to be led and stimulated to what all the country knows to be their duty. . . . A man of my temperament and my limitations will certainly wear himself out in it; but that is a small matter; the danger is that he may lose his patience and suffer the weakness of exasperation.

Yet he lost neither his patience nor his persistence. He believed he had the ear of the people and would win out. When the Senate opposition refused to yield, he announced that he would not permit Congress to adjourn for the Christmas holiday before the bill was passed. Meantime public sentiment in favor of the measure became widespread and strong enough to bring about the enactment of the bill on December 19. Five days later Wilson had the pleasure of signing it, making the Federal Reserve Act the law of the land. The twelve Federal Reserve banks, spread regionally across the country, were designed to prevent concentration of the money power in New York. The establishment of the Federal Reserve Board assured supervision of the banking and credit structure in the public interest and under government control. Viewed as a whole, the Act went far to modernize the currency system and to remedy the glaring faults of the banking operations. Indeed, its enactment made possible the intricate and extensive financing of the world war in which the nation was shortly to engage.

The Federal Reserve Act became the high point of Wilson's domestic reforms. Eager to pursue his program while his hold on Congress remained strong, he lost no time in urging the passage of new measures. On January 20, 1914, he addressed a joint session of Congress on trusts and monopolies. Determined to assure freedom of enterprise for the small businessman, he proposed the following five objectives: prohibition of interlocking directorates, government supervision of railway financing, greater clarification of the Sherman Act, an interstate trade commission to eliminate business abuses and unfair competition, and individual responsibility for corporate wrongdoing. By arrangement with Representative Henry D. Clayton, who had refused elevation to the Senate in order to sponsor this legislation, bills were introduced to amend and clarify the Sherman Act and to establish the Federal Trade Commission. In the anti-trust measure farmer and labor organizations were specifically exempted from its restrictions. Indeed, the clause "That the labor of a human being is not a commodity or an article of commerce" so pleased Samuel Gompers that he prematurely hailed it as "the most far-reaching declaration ever made by any government in the history of the world." In his excitement he overlooked certain other phrases which later permitted federal judges to widen the use of the labor injunction.

Industrialists and bankers and railway executives attacked these bills as discriminatory and inimical to the nation's prosperity. The younger J. P. Morgan spoke scathingly of the Wilson Administration: "A greater set of perfectly incompetent and apparently crooked people has never, so far as I know, run, or attempted to run, any first-class country." In an effort to ward off the new legislation he and George F. Baker dramatically announced their resignation as directors from about half of the corporations in which they were financially interested. But this act of ostensible abnegation and the powerful influence exerted by businessmen upon certain members of Congress failed to stop the public clamor

against the trusts. After months of debate and stubborn opposition, the bill creating the Federal Trade Commission was passed
in September and the Clayton Anti-Trust Act was enacted a month
later.

Wilson initiated or approved other acts of Congress aiming to
democratize the nation's economy and remove certain inequities.
At his urging the Alaska Coal Lands Leasing Act was adopted in
1914, providing for private exploitation but for government control. The following year he signed the Seamen's Act sponsored by
Senator La Follette, a long-needed law to improve labor conditions
in the merchant marine. The Adamson Act of 1916, providing for
a standard eight-hour day for railroad employees, was passed at
Wilson's insistence when the refusal of the railroad executives to
grant the shorter day had made a nationwide strike imminent. In
the same year Congress also enacted the Federal Farm Loan Act,
establishing twelve federal land banks to facilitate loans to farmers
at reasonable interest rates. Other legislation to make "argiculture
more profitable and country life more comfortable and attractive"
provided for road building in rural areas, for farm-demonstration
work, and for various rural educational facilities.

By the time Wilson came up for re-election in 1916 he was able
rightly to claim that his legislative record was the most liberal
in recent history and went far to democratize the government and
to free the economy from monopoly domination. He succeeded in
demonstrating, in the words of Lincoln Steffens, "that good and
beautiful ideas and ideals work." This record was the more significant because it was achieved in the face of powerful opposition
and largely by virtue of his great capacity for leadership.

Wilson entered the Presidency as a progressive intent on adapt-
ing Jeffersonian principles to modern industrialism, on putting his
long-cherished ideals to the acid test of the national marketplace.
Yet he no sooner entered the White House than he was confronted with pressing foreign affairs. Before going to Washington,
troubled by the disturbances in Mexico, he remarked to a friend,

"It would be the irony of fate if my administration had to deal chiefly with foreign affairs." Time did turn this irony into tragedy —mockingly distorting his lofty idealism. He assumed the Presidency eager to repudiate the "dollar diplomacy" of his predecessors, yet circumstances compelled him to acquiesce in this practice as the easier way out of a troublesome situation. Long a pacifist, a member of the American Peace Society since 1908, he slowly and reluctantly became an exponent of force in his effort to make the world safe for democracy.

Two weeks before he was inaugurated President the revolution in Mexico boomeranged in the assassination of Francisco Madero and the usurpation of power by General Victoriano Huerta. President Taft left the problem of recognition for his successor's decision. Wilson immediately let it be known that he would never recognize an assassin and that he had the friendliest feelings for the Mexican people. Nor would he listen to the clamor for intervention on the part of Americans anxious to safeguard their Mexican investments, stating, "I am more interested in the fortunes of oppressed men, pitiful women and children, than in any property rights whatever." He wanted a democratic Mexico and insisted on a government elected fairly and formally by all the people. To him Huerta was "unspeakable" because he "traitorously overthrew the government of which he was a trusted part." This moral attitude was not shared by the leading European governments, but they could not act effectively without American cooperation.

Conditions in Mexico continued to deteriorate. Several armies were fighting one another for control. Life was precarious and property insecure. Foreign and American interventionists, eager to exploit the country's natural resources, insisted on the pacification of the land regardless of the means or of who headed the government. But Wilson persisted in his policy of peace and political morality. In an address before Congress on August 27, 1913, he spoke fervently of his wish to cultivate Mexico's friendship and to prove to her "that our friendship is genuine and disinterested, capable of sacrifice and every generous manifestation." He pointed out that to this end our behavior "must be rooted in patience" and that "we shall triumph as Mexico's friends sooner than we could triumph as her enemies."

Two months later, in a policy-making speech in Mobile, he gave further expression to this lofty morality in international relations. He maintained that the United States had no imperialistic ambitions and "will never again seek one additional foot of territory by conquest." On the contrary, he continued, the United States regards it as one of the duties of friendship never to make material interests superior to human liberty. Indeed, we will never sacrifice morality to expedience or "condone iniquity because it is most convenient to do so."

When Mexican officers fired upon American sailors and Huerta refused to salute the American flag in addition to his grudging apology, Wilson could not well avoid backing our naval officers. Again, when news reached him that a German shipload of munitions was about to reach Vera Cruz, he did not hesitate to order the port seized, at a cost of several lives, as a means of keeping the guns from strengthening Huerta against his enemies. But he readily accepted mediation when it was offered by the leading South American republics, and stoically disregarded the rising agitation for further intervention. To Samuel Blythe, noted journalist, he explained:

I hold this to be a wonderful opportunity to prove to the world that the United States of America is not only human but humane; that we are actuated by no other motives than the betterment of the conditions of our unfortunate neighbor, and by the sincere desire to advance the cause of human liberty.

When Huerta, at the end of his resources, finally resigned and was replaced by Venustiano Carranza, Wilson exercised long-suffering patience in his eagerness to help this well-intentioned but temperamental leader—finally recognizing him despite his inability to control the factional strife within his own ranks. When Pancho

Villa, dashing head of a bandit army, raided Columbus, New Mexico, in 1916 and killed a number of Americans, the cry for war against Mexico became general. Wilson nevertheless resisted the clamor. To Tumulty he said:

The thing that daunts me and holds me back is the aftermath of war, with all its tears and tragedies. . . . I will not resort to war against Mexico until I have exhausted every means to keep out of the mess. I know they will call me a coward and a quitter, but that will not disturb me. Time, the great solvent, will, I am sure, vindicate this policy of humanity and forbearance.

He did, however, order American troops, led by General John J. Pershing, to pursue Villa into Mexico and capture him dead or alive. After several months of futile effort the expedition was abandoned. By that time Wilson had become too involved in European affairs and left it up to Carranza to put down the opposing factions as best he could.

Wilson's idealism, again and again unable to square with stubborn reality, nevertheless achieved a modicum of success in his dealings with Mexico. His idealism failed to serve him, however, in connection with Nicaragua, Haiti, and Santo Domingo. The paternalistic New Freedom of his diplomacy, so loftily espoused in his Mobile speech, seemingly did not apply universally. The difficulties then common to most Latin American nations—domestic turbulence, financial incompetence, undemocratic and unstable government—appeared greatly aggravated in these small states because of their subjection to foreign capital. Here, however, Wilson failed to apply his expressed standard of political morality. It was with his permission that American Marines enforced tranquillity by shooting hundreds of "bandits" who sought to oppose American intervention. For several years our marines and sailors occupied these countries in the most egregious manner of "dollar diplomacy." This lapse from his professed idealism Wilson never troubled to explain.

His combining of political morality and pragmatic reality was clearly evident in his fight to repeal the Panama Tolls Act. This law, exempting American vessels engaged in coastwise traffic from payment of tolls through the Panama Canal, was enacted by Congress in 1912 in obvious disregard to the 1901 Hay-Pauncefote Treaty assuring equality of treatment to ships of all nations. Shortly after our Ambassador Walter H. Page reached England he learned that the British Government strongly resented this treaty breach. Eager to strengthen amiable relations between the two nations, Page urged Wilson to seek the repeal of the Act. The President, at the time anxious to win England to his Mexican policy, decided to act. On March 5, 1914, he addressed a joint session of Congress to demand repeal of the controversial measure.

I have come to state to you a fact and a situation. . . . We consented to the treaty, its language we accepted, if we did not originate it; and we are too big, too powerful, too self-respecting a nation to interpret with a too strained or refined reading the words of our own promises just because we have power enough to give us leave to read them as we please. The large thing to do is the only thing we can afford to do, a voluntary withdrawal from a position everywhere questioned and misunderstood.

This request of Congress met with a mixed response. A good many Senators and Representatives resented the idea of "bowing to the knee of England." Wilson, however, insisted on repeal. The struggle was heated and hard, but he fought the opposition with fine tact and resourcefulness. At one juncture he even thought of threatening to resign if defeated. Finally he pleaded that the repeal would expedite his handling of delicate foreign affairs and Congress yielded.

Another similar request, satisfaction and remuneration to Colombia for the Panama incident of a dozen years before, was rejected by the Senate after Theodore Roosevelt had denounced the proposed treaty as "sheer blackmail." Several years later, when the discovery of oil made that country attractive to American investors, the treaty was approved without the "apology" by a Republican Senate.

In August 1914 Wilson's career took a sudden sharp turn. Simultaneously with the outbreak of war in Europe, which was to tax him to the uttermost and to lift him to political apotheosis before he was broken on the wheel of his Covenanter inflexibility, his wife died after a long illness. Bereavement afflicted him more acutely than is commonly assumed. Irresponsible gossip to the contrary, the Wilsons were joined by a bond of strong intimacy. Many years of adaptation and mutual respect gave each of them clear insight into the working of the other's mind and made it possible for Mrs. Wilson to influence her husband to a degree greater than either realized. As high-minded as Wilson, but endowed with somewhat broader sympathies and much less self-centered, Ellen often served him as a balance wheel. Much as she admired his intellectual qualities and appreciative as she was of his idealistic fervor, she was not blind to his defects of character or to his overweening ambition. And with the tactful frankness of a loving and lifelong companion she again and again stopped him from making hasty decisions or helped him to resolve disconcerting doubt.

Without fully realizing how much he needed her, he missed her terribly. For months he felt acute loneliness. Colonel House came closest to his mind, but he could not give him Ellen's wifely sympathy and frank advice. When Wilson met the handsome Edith Bolling Galt, his life suddenly brightened. His heart began to surge with youthful passion and his longing to marry her became irresistible. So filled were his heart and mind with his new love that he tended to neglect the duties of his office.

Wilson and Mrs. Galt were married in December 1915 and remained passionately attached to each other to the end. But the second Mrs. Wilson, for all her remarkable devotion and good sense, did not serve her husband as a balance wheel when he needed it most. Knowing him only as the President and awed by his world-wide eminence, she was inclined to act more as the adoring wife than as the intimate and incisive helpmeet. Unlike Ellen, she had neither the mind nor the will to urge caution or compromise, or to keep him from yielding to his increasing obstinacy when tact was imperative—thereby breaking himself body and soul.

The outbreak of war in Europe forced Wilson reluctantly to turn his mind from his national program and attend to increasingly urgent international problems. Earlier in the year he had sent House to England and Germany on a mission of peace, but after weeks of futile effort his emissary returned with the conviction that British indifference and German belligerence needed "only a spark to set the whole thing off." When news came that the Kaiser's armies were on the march and that the war was engulfing most of Europe, Wilson was acutely depressed. A firm believer in the efficacy of reason and the power of righteousness, he had long felt that war was not only cruel and calamitous but that it never really settled anything. He was also aware of the industrial rivalry between England and Germany and knew that Great Britain entered the conflict not so much because Belgium was invaded as because she was anxious to protect her foreign markets from German enterprise. Hating war as he did, he determined to keep it from the United States. He therefore advised Americans not to take sides and not to embarrass him in his efforts to keep the country at peace. "The United States," he pleaded, "must be neutral in fact as well as in name during these days that are to try men's souls."

Almost at once it became evident that strict neutrality was at best a pious wish. Although the vast majority of Americans wanted to keep out of the war, many of them openly sympathized with one side or the other. Allied control of the open seas, the economic recession late in 1914, and the subsequent eagerness to fill Allied orders for food and manufactures—these and other factors tended to weaken our position of neutrality. This situation was clearly manifest in connection with loans to the countries at war. At first Secretary of State Bryan, fearful of embroilment, persuaded Wilson to discourage such transactions. When J. P. Morgan inquired of the State Department how he should proceed in the matter of foreign loans, Bryan replied, "In the judgment of this Government loans by American bankers to any foreign nation which is at war is inconsistent with the true spirit of neutrality." For nearly a year the Allies drew upon their own resources to pay for purchases from the United States. Then, as the sympathies of the majority of Americans crystallized in favor of the Allies, and particularly after Robert Lansing replaced Bryan as Secretary of State, our position on foreign loans changed from that of true neutrality to that of "strict legality." With Wilson's passive permission J. P. Morgan and Company assumed the profitable task of floating loans for the Allies, and by April 1917 it disposed of bonds amounting to more than two and a half billion dollars.

There is no doubt that Wilson wanted to keep the United States out of the war. For a long time he favored neither side. His sense of morality was affronted by Germany's ruthlessness; his sense of right was irritated by England's arbitrariness. He was not long, moreover, in conceiving the idea of becoming the world's peacemaker. It was this ambitious claim upon destiny that kept him for more than two years, despite personal impulses and public clamor, clinging heroically to the weakening pillars of peace. In 1915 and again the following year he sent Colonel House to Europe to offer mediation to both sides, only to be met with disappointment. Each time, however, astute British diplomats used these visits to strengthen the bonds of sentiment between the two English-speaking countries.

Wilson's eagerness for neutrality was strengthened by the belief that he could best succeed as mediator if the United States remained at peace. That this was not to prove easy became apparent very early in the war when both belligerents began to disregard the rights of neutrals. British violations were irritating and persistent; but since they concerned primarily property seizures they called forth nothing more drastic than sharp verbal protests. German transgressions, however, entailed the loss of many American lives and finally brought us into the war against her. Yet not before Wilson's patience was tried to the uttermost.

On April 20, 1915, Wilson stated to the Associated Press: "I am interested in neutrality because there is something so much greater to do than fight; there is a distinction waiting for this Nation that no nation has ever yet got. That is the distinction of absolute self-control and self-mastery." Seventeen days later this self-control was put to the acid test when news came that a German submarine had torpedoed the *Lusitania* with a loss of 1195 lives including 124 Americans. The nation was horrified by this shocking catastrophe, and the cry for retaliation rose over the land. Many leaders of public opinion demanded an immediate declaration of war against Germany. Wilson secluded himself to write a speech he had promised to deliver on May 10 to a group of new citizens in Philadelphia. His own shock was soon cushioned by the awareness that the majority of the people still recoiled from war. Later he gave House a second reason for his pacifistic position: "It would be a calamity to the world at large if we should be drawn actively into the conflict and so deprived of all disinterested influence over the settlement." Risking misunderstanding and condemnation he made his address in Philadelphia a plea for peace and righteousness.

The example of America must be the example not merely of peace because it will not fight, but because peace is the healing and elevating influence of the world and strife is not. There is such a thing as a man being too proud to fight. There is such a thing as a nation being so right that it does not need to convince others by force that it is right.

The phrase "too proud to fight" was immediately torn out of context and blazoned over the front pages of newspapers the world over as evidence of Wilson's pusillanimity. The abuse and indignation heaped on him would have broken a weaker man. But he stood his ground unflinchingly. Three days later he sent a note of sharp protest to Germany, demanding the disavowal of the act and a promise "to take immediate steps to prevent the recurrence of anything so obviously subversive to the principles of warfare." When Germany's reply proved unsatisfactory, Wilson wrote a second note in a much sterner tone in which he insisted on "the safeguarding of American lives and American ships" regardless of circumstances. Secretary of State Bryan, having dedicated his office to the perpetuation of peace, protested against sending so contentious a note. He argued that "Germany has a right to prevent contraband going to the Allies and a ship carrying contraband should not rely upon passengers to protect her from attack." Rather than sign a document that would make naught of his years of effort in behalf of peace he resigned his office. Wilson immediately replaced him with Robert Lansing, Counsellor of the Department, who sent the note. Germany, still short of enough submarines for an unrestricted attack, sought to be conciliatory without being submissive. Two additional protests were necessary, the last one threatening "to sever diplomatic relations" and solemnized by an address before Congress, before Germany promised not to sink ships "without warning and without saving human lives unless those ships attempt to escape or offer resistance."

Wilson had no illusions about the origins of the war or about the character of the men perpetrating it. Early in 1916 his friend House corroborated his worst suspicions. In each of the countries he visited, House wrote, he found among the government leaders "stubbornness, determination, selfishness, and cant. . . . History will bring an awful indictment against those who were shortsighted and selfish enough to let such a tragedy happen." It was this knowledge that nursed Wilson's ambition to save the world from future wars and moved him to retain American neutrality in order better to serve the peace of mankind.

German truculence gradually persuaded Wilson that neutrality was becoming untenable and that war must be the painful means to a glorious end. To gird the country in her armed might for any eventuality—even more, to blunt the propaganda of the war advocates—he went on a speaking tour in January 1916 in behalf of military preparedness. He made eloquently clear that with the world on fire there was no way of fully safeguarding the United States from the sparks; that America could not accept peace without honor—a striking change from the position he had advocated seven months before.

I should feel that I was guilty of an unpardonable omission if I did not go out and tell my fellow countrymen that new circumstances have arisen which make it absolutely necessary that this country should prepare itself, not for war, not for anything that smacks in the least of aggression, but for adequate national defense.

Although he would not "consent to any abridgment of the rights of American citizens in any respect" and successfully fought off the Gore-McLemore resolution urging Americans not to sail on armed ships, he continued to covet peace. Annoyed by the increasingly hysterical agitation of "irresponsible voices" who demanded war with Germany, he remarked to Tumulty in January 1916, "If my re-election as President depends upon my getting into war, I don't want to be President." Yet with new insight he perceived the hopelessness of neutrality in an extended conflict. "War now has such a scale," he stated, "that the position of neutrals sooner or later becomes intolerable." The sinking of the *Sussex* on March 24 indeed strained our neutrality to the breaking point, and Germany's reluctant promise not to sink passenger ships without warning was merely a precarious truce.

The increasing awareness that he might not succeed in his efforts to keep American neutrality made Wilson all the more anxious to devise a means of making future wars impossible. For years the idea of an association of nations to maintain peace had been appealing to the idealism of many leading Americans. Andrew Carnegie gave millions of dollars to further the abolition of war. In 1910 Theodore Roosevelt broached the idea in his Nobel Peace Prize speech. Senator Lodge, former President Taft, Elihu Root, Charles W. Eliot, and other eminent public men favored an association for peace. Wilson was one of its early advocates. When the war broke out in Europe he deplored the absence of such an instrument of peace. By 1916 the idea of a League of Nations became in his mind a concrete and urgent issue. He therefore readily accepted an invitation to address the League to Enforce Peace on May 27 in order to use this influential organization as a sounding board. His proposal was in essence a rephrasing of the democratic postulates of his Mobile speech and a statement of the thought that was later to become the heart of the controversial Article Ten.

We believe these fundamental things: First, that every people has a right to choose the sovereignty under which they shall live. . . . Second, the small states of the world have a right to enjoy the same respect for their sovereignty and for their territorial integrity that great and powerful nations expect and insist upon. And, third, that the world has a right to be free from every disturbance of its peace that has its origin in aggression and disregard of the rights of peoples and nations.

The speech was applauded by the entire nation and praised by the Republican leaders who were later to condemn the League of Nations to calamitous defeat.

Meantime the political parties were preparing for their national conventions. The Progressives met first, but their efforts to put a ticket in the field were frustrated when Roosevelt not only refused the nomination but urged a reunion with the Republicans, whose candidate was Justice Charles Evans Hughes. The Democrats nominated Wilson by acclamation.

With a formally united party, the Republicans could again claim a majority of the voters. But Hughes and his advisers campaigned with a conspicuous lack of boldness and imagination. They acted with neither unity nor enthusiasm. Hughes behaved like an overcautious lawyer, finding fault with his opponent and manifesting little of the breadth and passion and sympathy of the intelligent statesman. In his eagerness to avoid antagonizing any group or faction, he alienated a large number of the progressives by his negative attitude.

Wilson, on the contrary, stood fast on his record and on his democratic idealism. In his speech of acceptance he proudly declared: "We have in four years come very near to carrying out the platform of the Progressive Party as well as our own, for we are also progressives." While Hughes evaded the issue of hyphenated Americanism in his effort to retain the support of the pro-German voters, Wilson courageously, yet with calculated indignation, stated his views unequivocally in a letter to Jeremiah O'Leary, a leader of the anti-British Irish-Americans: "I would feel deeply mortified to have you or anybody like you vote for me. Since you have access to many disloyal Americans and I have not, I will ask you to convey this message to them." Perhaps his most effective maneuver was to permit Democratic speakers to stress the slogan that he had kept the country out of war—a rallying cry as potent as it was soon to prove premature.

When the votes were counted—the result was in doubt for four days—Wilson won by nearly six hundred thousand and became not merely the first Democratic President since Jackson to succeed himself but the first definitely progressive candidate to receive a majority vote.

Wilson's conscience was acutely troubled by the awareness that he probably owed his re-election to the Democratic boast that he had kept the nation at peace. None knew better the fortuitous nature of this claim; and none was more painfully conscious of the powerful forces propelling the United States into the European maelstrom. Much as he cherished neutrality, he perceived only too clearly that our heavy material and moral investment in the Allies made our truce with Germany more and more untenable.

Early in 1916 and again shortly after the election, Wilson, with House acting as his adviser and personal representative, sought to ascertain the terms of peace acceptable to both belligerents. Neither side, however, showed any real interest in peace; each thought only in terms of victory. The Allies, strengthened by the enormous flow of goods from American shores and expecting full participation fairly soon, became morally indignant at Wilson's statement that "the causes and objects of the war are obscure" and that the aims of both sides were "virtually the same." In England and in this country he was severely criticized as pro-German.

Getting no satisfaction from the heads of the nations at war, Wilson decided to appeal to the people of Europe in a final effort to bring an end to the bloodshed on their battlefields. On January 22, 1917, he addressed the Senate on what he considered fair peace terms and what part the United States should play in the peacemaking. He stated emphatically that only a peace giving victory to neither side would "keep the future safe against war."

Victory would mean peace forced upon the loser, a victor's terms forced upon the vanquished. It would be accepted in humiliation, under duress, at an intolerable sacrifice, and would leave a sting, a resentment, a bitter memory upon which the terms of peace would rest, not permanently, but only as upon quicksand. Only a peace between equals can last. . . . The right state of mind, the right feeling between nations, is as necessary for a lasting peace as is the just settlement of vexed questions of territory or of racial and national allegiance.

After outlining the democratic basis for lasting peace he expressed the hope that the United States would join other nations in an association that would guarantee the permanence of peace. Aware of the traditional American sentiment against entangling alliances, he made clear that this proposal was in effect an extension of the Monroe Doctrine to the entire world: "that no nation should seek to extend its polity over any other nation or people, but that every people should be left free to determine its own polity, its own way of development, unhindered, unthreatened, unafraid, the little along with the great and powerful."

Although extremists in this country and abroad decried the entire speech because it proposed "peace without victory," the majority of Americans applauded its lofty and liberal sentiments. Wilson, ignoring the attacks which he knew would come when he deliberately used the provocative phrase, was highly pleased with the effect of his proposal upon the people who had elected him. To a friend he wrote, "I have an invincible confidence in the prevalence of right if it is fearlessly set forth."

At the very time Wilson was preparing his address, the German war lords had already decided to resume unrestricted submarine warfare on February 1. Apprised of this late in January, he became very agitated and angry. "This means war," he exclaimed. "The break that we have tried so hard to prevent now seems inevitable." On February 3 the German ambassador was given his papers.

To the very end Wilson continued to hope that war would somehow be averted. As late as February 20 Secretary of the Interior Franklin K. Lane, impatient for war with Germany, complained: "We are all, with the exception of one or two pro-Germans, feeling humiliated by the situation, but nothing can be done." A few days later the British played a trump card when they supplied the American government with an intercepted cable from Zimmermann, German Under-Secretary for Foreign Affairs, to the German ambassador in Mexico, urging him to offer the Mexican government the southeastern part of the United States as an inducement to become Germany's ally. Wilson was outraged by this gross act of hostility but still refrained from asking Congress for an immediate declaration of war.

He did, however, ask for permission to arm merchant ships. The bill was quickly passed in the House, but in the Senate a filibuster prevented its enactment. Although he later learned that he did not need the permission of Congress and ordered the arming of American ships on his own authority, Wilson could not refrain from venting his spleen on the Senators who had opposed him. "A little group of willful men representing no opinion but their own, have rendered the great Government of the United States helpless and contemptible." This angry statement, made in a moment of nervous vexation, foreshadowed a sharpening Covenanter spirit that was in the immediate years ahead to undo the great work upon which he had set his heart. Equally ominous was the passionate antagonism of his Republican opponents. Commenting on Wilson's criticism of the filibuster, Theodore Roosevelt wrote to Lodge:

I regard Wilson as far more blameworthy than the "willful" Senators. I am as yet holding in; but if he does not go to war with Germany I shall skin him alive. To think of the folly of having cursed this country with the really hideous misfortune of four years more of Wilson in this great and terrible world crisis.

The overt act which Wilson dreaded came with the sinking of the *Laconia* and the *Algonquin*. On receiving the news he saw no alternative but to ask Congress for a declaration of war. On March 21 he called both Houses to meet on April 2 in order "to receive a communication by the executive on grave questions of national policy." The next ten days he suffered the ordeal of harrowing responsibility. Except for the bright news from Russia, which enabled him to speak of the Allied democracies without flushing at the awareness of the Czar, he could think only of the horrors of war and the grievous effects of militarism.

On the last night of March he hardly slept and spent the tense hours composing his speech to Congress. The following day he sent for his friend Frank Cobb, the astute editor of the New York *World*. When the latter arrived at one o'clock in the morning he found the President worn and weary, wretched and desperately anxious to think aloud, to give vent to his fearful perplexities. "I think I know what war means," he said nervously, then asked: "Is there anything else I can do?" When assured that the fault was obviously Germany's, he still voiced his anguish at having to place the whole world on a war basis. Then he spoke prophetically of the effect upon the nation:

It would mean that we should lose our heads along with the rest and stop weighing right and wrong. It would mean that a majority of people in this hemisphere would go war-mad, quit thinking, and devote their energies to destruction. . . . Once lead this people into war and they'll forget there ever was such a thing as tolerance. To fight you must be brutal and ruthless, and the spirit of ruthless brutality will enter into every fiber of our national life, infecting Congress, the courts, the policeman on the beat, the man in the street.

Alas, it was to infect him as much as anyone. As if subconsciously fearful of this, he exclaimed in anguish, "If there is an alternative, for God's sake let's take it!" But Cobb couldn't think of one.

The next day, emerging as the stern Covenanter, Wilson delivered his heart-quickening address before Congress. There was no shadow of doubt in his message, only foreboding and an acute sense of responsibility. He outlined the German acts forcing him to take this step, the dangers to peace from autocratic rule, the need to make the world "safe for democracy," and the obligations we must assume to assure this safeguard.

We have no selfish ends to serve. We desire no conquest, no dominion. . . . We are but one of the champions of the rights of mankind. We shall be satisfied when those rights have been made as secure as the faith and the freedom of nations can make them. . . . It is a fearful thing to lead this great peaceful people into war, into the most terrible and disastrous of all wars, civilization itself seeming in the balance. But the right is more precious than peace, and we shall fight for the things which we have always carried nearest our hearts. . . . To such a task we can dedicate our lives and our fortunes, everything that we are and everything that we have, with the pride of those who know that the day has come that America is privileged to spend her blood and her might for the principles that gave her birth and happiness and the peace which she has treasured. God helping her, she can do no other.

On his return from the Capitol, Wilson wept with grief and relief. It seemed strange to him that people should applaud his call to war. "My message today was a message of death for our young men," he commented. His speech indeed deeply stirred those who heard it. Chief Justice Edward D. White burst into applause, with tears streaming down his cheeks. Even Senator Lodge praised Wilson in person. *The Literary Digest* summarized the general reaction with the statement that the address had worked "a miracle of crystallization in American sentiment."

When Wilson determined on war with Germany, he dedicated himself to the tremendous task with concentrated zeal. Once too proud to fight and but recently pleading persuasively for a peace without victory, his "one-track mind" now concerned itself only with the defeat of the enemy. He saw less and less of people and discouraged advice; Ambassador J. J. Jusserand tartly remarked, "He doesn't want to see any of us." He behaved with remarkable singleness of purpose; he stripped his mind of everything that did not suit this purpose. Thus he now preached "force, force to the utmost." From the military leaders he demanded dashing and daring attacks. "In my view," he wrote to Admiral Sims, "this is not a time for prudence but for boldness even at the cost of great losses." Even more spirited was his address to a group of naval officers, an exhortation to be ever audacious in fighting the enemy.

Before delivering his war message he had complained to Secretary of the Navy Josephus Daniels that war would kill the reforms he had fought so hard to achieve. "War means autocracy. The people we have unhorsed will inevitably come into the control of the country, for we shall be dependent upon the steel, oil and financial magnates. They will run the nation." Yet he made no attempt to check this tendency. Directing his own efforts to military and diplomatic matters, he invited the leading industrialists to take charge of building up the arsenal of war. Soon the vastly expanded economy of the nation was operated and controlled by such bankers and businessmen as J. P. Morgan, Charles M. Schwab, James A. Farrell, Bernard Baruch, Edward R. Stettinius, Henry P. Davison, and Thomas W. Lamont.

Although Wilson had deplored the intolerance bred by war, he soon became an egregious practitioner of this warped zeal. So convinced was he of the righteousness of his cause and so possessed had he become of the spirit of the Covenanter that he became the implacable enemy of all pacifists, radicals, and other dissidents. He simply did not perceive the tragic discrepancy between his passionate profession of democracy and his practical abuse of it where his leadership was not followed. In June 1917 he cautioned the dissenters: "For us there is but one choice. We have made it, and woe be to that man, or that group of men, that seeks to stand in our way in this day of high resolution, when every principle we hold dearest is to be vindicated and made secure for the salvation of the nation." To this end he approved the Espionage Act in 1917 and the Sedition Act the following year—laws at once repressive and vindictive, imposing imprisonment up to twenty years upon resolute nonconformers. These same laws gave the Postmaster-General power to censor periodicals, and a number of newspapers and magazines were excluded from the mails. When some of the harsh sentences and bureaucratic abuses were brought to Wilson's attention, he coldly refused to intercede on the ground that war resisters were "men who do not deserve consideration."

Despite false starts and unavoidable ineptitude and inefficiency, the United States soon managed not only to provide some of the sinews of war needed by the Allies but also to build up an army and an arsenal that in a remarkably short time brought on the collapse of the mighty German army. With Congress and the people enthusiastically behind him, Wilson led the effort with surprising energy and enterprise. He early persuaded Congress to enact the Selective Draft Act, which provided the military chiefs with a pool of ten million young men. He appointed General John J. Pershing head of the American Expeditionary Force, and within three months after the declaration of war thousands of soldiers began to reach Europe—totalling over two million before the end of the summer of 1918. Equally spectacular achievements were attained in the fields of munitions, shipping, food, and finance. When it became necessary to take over and coordinate the railroads, Wilson did not hesitate to do so and gave control to Secretary of the Treasury William G. McAdoo. Indeed, the United States was demonstrating not only its enormous capacities as the world's most powerful nation but also its eagerness to defeat Germany quickly and decisively. After eighteen months of gigantic effort the American people felt the satisfaction of a job well done. By October 1918 the German generals were desperately anxious to arrange an armistice, and in accepting Marshal Foch's terms they made a resumption of war practically impossible.

From the very first, of course, the enormous war effort was for Wilson merely an unavoidable means to a glorious end. Deprived of the role of a neutral mediator, he was prepared to risk the life-blood of the nation to settle the peace of the world on a permanent basis. He wanted to do away with "alliances and competing armaments and land grabbing"—the old diplomacy with its secret treaties and selfish agreements. Early in the war, when discussing with House the need of bringing the Allied leaders to their own conception of a durable peace, he said: "When the war is over we can force them to our own way of thinking because by that time they will, among other things, be financially in our hands."

To prepare himself for the task of peacemaking with his accustomed thoroughness, he asked House to enlist a group of the best scholars in the country for the research required to give him a clear and complete picture of the complex problems likely to come up for settlement at the peace conference. For more than a year this assemblage of experts, known as The Inquiry, studied the historical claims and accrued emotional yearnings of dozens of nations and groups and factions over the complex map of the world. So effective was this research that at Versailles the American delegation, for the first time concerned with the rights and ambitions of small Continental nations, was best equipped to deal with each claim on its real merits.

One of the problems confronting Wilson insistently after October 1917 was how to deal with Bolshevik Russia. Soon after the March revolution Wilson, having "the greatest sympathy" for the provisional government, sent to Russia a commission headed by Elihu Root. The Russian radicals did not trust the conservative Americans, and the latter failed in the mission to strengthen the Russian will to fight the Germans. Yet Wilson did not lose faith in the new republic. Even after the Bolsheviki had seized power he remarked that Russia would "go through deep waters but she will come out upon firm land." When Lenin and Trotsky began to negotiate with the Germans, Wilson sought to prevent the Allies from sending an army to northern Russia ostensibly to keep the war material from falling into German hands. Personally, however, he abhorred Lenin's radical doctrines and was violently repelled by the Bolshevik repression and bloodshed.

It was largely to offset the Russian publication of the Allied secret treaties and Lenin's demand for a peace without reparations and annexations that Wilson addressed Congress on January 8, 1918, for the purpose of discussing the war aims and peace terms of the United States. The speech was based on material provided him by The Inquiry and contained in effect the fundamentals of a new and higher international morality. This program of peace, consisting of the famous Fourteen Points, was Wilson's highest expression of the ideals upon which he wanted peace to be based. His comments on Russia were deliberately sympathetic. Point Six promised her complete independence and "a sincere welcome into the society of free nations under institutions of her own choosing." He added significantly: "The treatment accorded Russia by her sister nations in the months to come will be the acid test of their good will." The underlying purpose of the address was to proclaim the validity of "the principle of justice to all peoples and nationalities, and their right to live on equal terms of liberty and safety with one another, whether they be strong or weak." To safeguard this principle and this right Wilson formally embraced the idea of a League of Nations. His Fourteenth Point read: "A general association of nations must be formed under specific covenants for the purpose of affording mutual guarantees of political independence and territorial integrity to great and small states alike."

The speech was received with great enthusiasm by liberals the world over. Even the Allied leaders whose aims were on a lower and less altruistic plane praised its idealism—hoping privately that the Americans would be more practical at the peace table. The

Republicans likewise lauded the peace program and approved the idea of an association of nations—although ten months later Roosevelt and Lodge denounced the Fourteen Points as if they were a betrayal of American principles.

Wilson's fair words toward Russia did not lessen his difficulties with that country. In February 1918 he wrote to Senator John Sharp Williams, "I do not know that I have ever had a more tiresome struggle with quicksand than I am having in trying to do the right thing in respect of our dealings with Russia." Not long afterwards, continuing to adhere to "the principle of Russian territorial integrity and political independence," he advised General Tasker Bliss that Allied military action in Murmansk or elsewhere "should proceed, if at all, upon the sure sympathy of the Russian people." In his own mind still resisting such invasion as late as July, he wrote to House: "I've been sweating blood over the question what is right and feasible to do in Russia." The next month, however, he was won over to an Allied invasion of Russia for the purpose of succoring the Czechoslovak prisoners of war. In view of his previous position on this perplexing problem, a number of his admirers considered his change of mind as evidence that he was beginning to be broken by the terrific strain of his office. Justice Brandeis regarded this acquiescence as the first of the grievous mistakes Wilson made during the ensuing eighteen months. It should be noted also that Soviet Russia has never forgiven this hostile act.

Soon afterward he made other false moves. The war was nearing its end and his thoughts were concentrating on the oncoming peace conference. He sent House to Europe to make certain that the armistice discussions were based on the Fourteen Points. His mind seethed with hopes and plans for an enduring peace. Yearning to be the architect of a new and better world, he hardened his Covenanter spirit against the crass and cynical Allied leaders and his bitter and bigoted Republican enemies. Brooding over their opposition he determined to discomfit the first by attending the peace conference in person and to confound the Republicans

114

by appealing to the voters to return a Democratic Congress in the oncoming elections. On October 26 he issued a statement that accused the Republicans of hindering his work and urged the people to give him a vote of confidence.

If you have approved of my leadership and wish me to continue to be your unembarrassed spokeman in affairs at home and abroad, I earnestly beg that you will express yourself unmistakably to that effect by returning a Democratic majority. . . . This is no time either for divided counsel or for divided leadership.

Apart from the advisability of issuing the appeal at all—as a politician he should have known that at the end of a war people are bound not only to suffer a spiritual let-down but also to level their accumulated grievances upon the men in power—Wilson's request for a Democratic Congress rather than for one that would accept his leadership was an invitation to Roosevelt, Lodge, and others to play up the partisanship of the statement and confuse the voters on the actual merits of his appeal. His good friend Charles W. Eliot was quick to point this out: "Your appeal to the voters was an unnecessary and inexpedient departure from the position you previously had, that you are President of the United States claiming and having the support of the entire people."

Although the Republican victory in November 1918 was of an equivocal nature—in the Senate the Democrats would have retained their majority with the aid of Vice-President T. R. Marshall if not for the corruption-ridden victory of Truman Newberry of Michigan—it was due as much to local conditions and antagonized progressives as to the failure of the partisan appeal. Republicans, however, insisted that the election was a direct repudiation of Wilson's leadership. Even Secretary of the Interior Lane wrote privately that the defeat was "a slap in the face."

Wilson was deeply disappointed. He knew how difficult it would be for him to deal with a Republican Senate, especially since Lodge would be the chairman of the Foreign Relations Com-

mittee. Always proud and obstinate but now a dogmatic Covenanter with an urgent mission, Wilson recoiled from the idea of
having to placate his enemies. Instead of accepting the realities of
his situation and exerting himself to dissipate the antagonism toward him, he proceeded to aggravate the opposition by completely
disregarding it. Ignoring the advice of his dearest friends and
closest associates, he announced his intention of attending the
peace conference. He also courted disaster by appointing no dominant Republican leaders as members of the American peace delegation. In addition, he further antagonized Lodge by refusing to
attend a meeting at which the Senator was to speak because he
would not associate with his opponent "in any way."

His "one-track mind" now functioned with fanatic inflexibility.
Inwardly glowing with the radiance of his lofty concept of peace,
he became irritated by whatever appeared to hinder his great purpose. Ten years earlier, in a series of lectures on American government, he had pointed out that the President had complete control
of the nation's foreign relations. "The initiative in foreign affairs,
which the President possesses without any restriction whatever, is
virtually the power to control them absolutely." He had also stated,
however, that there was no reason why a President could not
make the Senate a working partner instead of a jealous rival. Conveniently forgetting the latter precept, he remembered only his
great powers as President. He considered most Senators "pigmy-
minded," with no vision and little principle. Despite the failure of
his appeal to the voters, he continued to believe that the people
would approve of his incorporating the Golden Rule into world
politics and would force the Senate to do likewise.

Completely dedicated to his messianic mission, Wilson ignored
the sniping and carping criticism of his political antagonists. Although both Roosevelt and Lodge had preceded him in the public
advocacy of an association of nations, they now repudiated the
idea of a league as unrealistic and un-American. In like manner
they also condemned the Fourteen Points, and Roosevelt urged the
Senate to "repudiate the so-called fourteen points and the various

similar utterances of the President." When Wilson began to consider the basis for an armistice, these and other of his adversaries
raised the cry that his negotiations came "dangerously near to being treacherous diplomacy," and Senator Miles Poindexter even
talked of impeachment. Shortly before Wilson prepared to sail
for Paris on his momentous mission, Roosevelt stated jeeringly and
irresponsibly: "Our Allies and our enemies and Mr. Wilson himself should all understand that Mr. Wilson has no authority whatever to speak for the American people at this time. His leadership
has just been emphatically repudiated by them."

On December 2, 1918, Wilson addressed Congress on the State
of the Union. He advised the legislators on the domestic problems
requiring their attention and informed them that he was going
to the peace conference because he considered it his "paramount
duty" personally to elucidate the Fourteen Points which were to
form the basis for the peace negotiations. The next day he sailed
on the *George Washington* with his large staff of advisers and
associates. To Tumulty, who remained behind to keep him informed on developments in the United States, he admitted: "This
trip will either be the greatest success or the supremest tragedy in
all history; but I believe in Divine Providence. If I did not have
faith, I should go crazy." The task before him was indeed stupendous; and his inability to share responsibility made the work all
the more strenuous.

By this time he was fully convinced that a League of Nations
was the panacea that would rid the world of war and its attending evils. He conceived of it as covenant of greater importance
than the peace treaty itself—since it would serve as a continuous
means of righting wrongs the world over. When he reached Paris
he at once consulted with House and told him that he intended
"making the League of Nations the center of the whole programme
and letting everything revolve around that. Once that is a *fait
accompli*, nearly all the very serious difficulties will disappear."
This idea he reiterated a fortnight later in an address to English

sympathizers: "A League of Nations seems to me to be a necessity of the whole settlement."

Eager as he was for the peace conference to begin, he had to wait until David Lloyd George finished his "khaki" election campaign having the slogan of "Hang the Kaiser" and until Georges Clemenceau exhorted the National Assembly to give him a free hand in his demand for French security—both auguring ill for a liberal peace. Meantime he had no alternative but to accept invitations to visit England and Italy. In these countries as well as in France he was received with extraordinary homage and enthusiasm. The war-weary people hailed him as a deliverer. And wherever he spoke he gave eloquent expression to the ideals he was fighting for.

To his advisers of The Inquiry who came with him on the *George Washington* he emphasized that this would be "the first conference in which decisions depended upon the opinion of mankind, not upon the previous determinations and diplomatic schemes of the assembled representatives." This assumption was not shared by the chief of the Allied leaders. They were realists with the cynicism of seasoned diplomats. Their aims were chauvinistic and concrete: they wanted extended boundaries, economic spoils, national safeguards, and other similar advantages. They were willing enough to pay lip service to the Fourteen Points— having been forced to agree to do so during the armistice discussions—but were ready to fight any obstacle to their nationalistic objectives. When they came face to face with Wilson and found that he really believed in the ideals he advocated, they combined against him with a calculated shrewdness that again and again forced him to sacrifice the substance for the form and thereby open himself to charges of "appalling hypocrisy."

With his unbending mind concentrating on the League of Nations project and with his Covenanter's confidence in the rightness of his ideals, Wilson fought for his plans and proposals with stubborn persistence. The conference began on January 18, 1919, and at first moved at a leisurely pace. Day after day was consumed in general talk. Wilson's patience began to get shorter by the hour. Finally he insisted on action. After much discussion and striving he obtained approval for his proposal that the League of Nations become an integral part of the peace treaty. As chairman of the committee on the League he wasted no time in preparing the document. Sparing neither himself nor his associates, he worked day and night until the Covenant was drafted and accepted at a plenary session on February 14. His solemn speech and his reading of the document marked his triumphant hour. For the nonce he lifted the hardened diplomats to his own high moral plane.

The next day Wilson sailed for the United States in order to attend to the pressing duties of his office. Most of all he wanted to discuss the Covenant with the Senate Committee on Foreign Relations; it was his hope to instill a majority with his own enthusiasm for his epochal achievement. On February 24 he reached Boston, the home of Senator Lodge and of a sizable group of anti-British Irish-Americans, and spoke there on the problems of peacemaking. He discussed the grievous conditions in Europe, and mankind's dependence on the United States to make and maintain peace. "Arrangements of the present peace cannot stand a generation," he declared prophetically, "unless they are guaranteed by the united forces of the civilized world." His concluding note expressed his deep faith in the people:

Probing deep in my heart and trying to see things that are right without regard to the things that may be debated as expedient, I feel that I am interpreting the purpose and the thought of America; and in loving America I find I have joined the great majority of my fellow men throughout the world.

Before leaving Paris he had cabled a dinner invitation to the members of the Senate Committee on Foreign Relations. The affair went off poorly. Two Senators did not show up at all. Some of those who came were offish and belligerent. They spoke of the League of Nations as an entangling alliance likely to involve the

United States in activities inimical to her best interests. Wilson's elucidation of the ideal underlying the League and his appeal for sympathetic consideration fell on deaf ears. Lodge was ominously silent in Wilson's presence.

Two days later Lodge severely criticized the Covenant in a Senate speech and announced his opposition to it as it was. He and other Republican Senators, about to assume majority control in the Senate, prepared a round robin signed by 37 Senators— more than enough to defeat the treaty—asserting their definite objection to American participation in the League. To compel Wilson to call the new Congress into session at an early date they arranged a filibuster to block essential bills until the expiration of the old Congress on March 4. On that day Wilson, highly indignant at the Lodge Resolution and aware of the difficulties it would make for him in Paris, vented his anger in a speech at the Metropolitan Opera House in New York:

I cannot imagine how these gentlemen can live and not live in the atmosphere of the world. . . . I particularly cannot imagine how they can be Americans and set up a doctrine of careful selfishness thought out to the last detail. I have heard no constructive suggestion. I have heard nothing except, "Will it not be dangerous to us to help the world?" It would be fatal to us not to help it.

Then, certain from the loud applause that the people were with him, he shouted his defiance: "I do not mean to come back until it's over over there, and it must not be over until the nations of the world are assured of the permanency of peace." He also added that the Covenant would not only be a part of the Treaty but so tied to it that dissection would destroy "the whole vital structure."

That very evening he boarded the *George Washington* for the return trip to Paris. Reconciled to requesting the amendments demanded by the hostile Senators, he was determined to fight to the last for the acceptance of the League.

On reaching Brest, Wilson was met by House and given a detailed report of what had taken place during his absence. When they parted more than two hours later, Wilson looked old and haggard. Worried over the truculent opposition in the Senate, he considered the compromises made by his friend not as the unavoidable result of negotiation, of which he himself was soon to be even guiltier, but as a kind of betrayal. He grew angry at the thought that House had failed him by acquiescing in the separation of the Covenant from the Treaty. To Mrs. Wilson he complained peevishly: "House has given away everything I had won before we left Paris. . . . Well, thank God I can still fight, and I'll win them back or never look these boys I sent over here in the face again." The very next day, on reaching Paris, he announced that the agreement on January 25, making the League of Nations an integral part of the Treaty, "is of final force and there is no basis whatsoever for the reports that a change in this decision is contemplated." The news acted with the explosiveness of a bombshell and served immediately to re-establish his leadership of the conference.

The ensuing three months were for Wilson a period of extreme strain and repeated frustration. Working behind closed doors, chiefly with Lloyd George and Clemenceau, was mostly an exasperating ordeal. He had come to Paris to make a lasting peace, openly arrived at, with justice and freedom for all mankind. What he had to deal with was greed, bigotry, and chicane; in the words of General Jan Smuts, "an inferno of human passions." England wanted control of the high seas, dominion over valuable enemy territory, and the economic advantages of a victorious world power; France, with a "shell-shock" intensity, demanded national security —which to Clemenceau meant German territory and full reparations; Italy, Japan, Belgium, the new-fledged small countries—all sought to gain at the expense of the defeated enemy and even of one another without regard to justice and right. None cared to pay the price of a just and lasting peace; all scorned, in fact if not openly, the principles of the Fourteen Points.

Almost alone of the chief delegates Wilson fought for his ideals with a moral fervor that again and again, if only momentarily, lifted the members of the conference out of their mundane cyni-

121

cism. But the daily exertion sapped his strength and seared his soul. By evening, to quote R. S. Baker, he "looked utterly beaten, worn out, his face quite haggard and one side of it and one eye twitching painfully." Yet he often had to drive himself till late in the night, arguing, bickering, pacifying, pleading. Unable and unwilling to delegate work to others—he mostly ignored the other American commissioners with the exception of House—he lacked the time to see some of the men who demanded his attention and thereby encouraged antagonism and misunderstanding. All the while, of course, he labored under the severe handicap of a sniping and snarling Senate opposition—a fact taken full advantage of by Clemenceau and Lloyd George.

The chief obstacle Wilson had to contend with was the French demand for security, which was to be obtained by annexing the Rhineland and the Saar. For weeks Clemenceau sought to wear Wilson down by repeated and obstinate wrangling. In the end the two men compromised, Wilson agreeing to a security treaty in place of the Rhineland, control of the Saar for only fifteen years, and reparations that violated the principle of "no punitive damages." In like manner, fighting hard but forced to yield more and more in order to save the conference from breaking up, Wilson acquiesced in the abuse of the principle of self-determination and of other of his principles—actions resulting in egregious injustices which his enemies later stressed to his discomfiture.

One of the telling charges against him was the agreement giving Japan the "rights as an economic concessionaire" in Shantung. When the question first came up he proposed "that all governments should renounce the special rights they had acquired in China." Since neither England nor France would do so, Japan was able to press her claim to advantage. Choosing a most opportune moment—when her demand for racial equality was defeated and the Italian delegates had left on account of Fiume—she too threatened to bolt the conference if not granted economic rights in Shantung. Wilson dared not risk the collapse of the negotiations. "They are not bluffers," he said of the Japanese, "and they will go home unless we give them what they should not have." Then he added, "If the Italians remain away and the Japanese go home, what becomes of the League of Nations?" Nor was he unmindful of his need to gain approval for the amendments to the Covenant from the delegates he was fighting so desperately. Again he had to compromise, making "the best that could be gotten out of a dirty past." Always, of course, he fell back on his belief that the League of Nations, once established, would soon enough deal justice to China as well as to other weak and exploited countries.

Another objectionable act on the part of the Allied leaders of the conference—and one for which Wilson received disproportionate blame—was what many considered the obdurate and obtuse behavior toward Russia. Devastated by war, incapacitated by revolution, forced by the might of the German army to make a catastrophic peace, and bleeding freely from the wounds of civil strife, she received in effect only scorn and stabs in the back from the Allies whom she had earlier helped to save from destruction by her own sacrifices. E. J. Dillon, an eminent correspondent and no friend of Bolshevism, wrote critically of this shabby treatment: "Russia, the whilom Ally, without whose superhuman efforts and heroic sacrifices her partners would have been pulverized, was tacitly relegated to the category of hostile and defeated peoples." Wilson disapproved of this attitude on the part of Clemenceau and Lloyd George. Horrified by the excesses of Bolshevism, he knew that it could best be eliminated by food and friendship. To House he said: "We are not at war with Russia and will under no circumstances that we can now foresee take part in military operations . . . against the Russians." Yet he proved no match in this instance for the vindictive Frenchman and self-seeking Welshman. In time he not only acquiesced in military action against the Bolsheviki but permitted himself to be overruled on the question of dealing with their representatives at Prinpiko Island—to the probable hurt of the world ever since.

The final Treaty, completed and delivered to the German delegates on May 7, was a ghastly caricature of the humane idealism of the Fourteen Points. Pathetically anxious to retain the League of Nations, handicapped by his "one-track mind" as well as by the Senate opposition, and confronted by skilled cynics in crass diplomacy, Wilson made compromise after compromise until he belied the principles he had fought so hard to establish. John M. Keynes, one of his severest critics, remarked that "his thoughts and his temperament were essentially theological," and that he was incompetent "in the agilities of the council chamber." It is also true, however, that the Treaty was in many respects greatly superior to earlier similar documents and that it did give rise to the League of Nations as a potential instrument of justice and peace and equity among the nations of the world. William Allen White in a sense expressed the extent of Wilson's achievement in Paris: "He really has done wonders here; and how he has done it is past me. . . . He has really dominated the situation—and that all alone."

The final Treaty was signed by the major principals on June 28 in an impressive ceremony. The next day Wilson sailed for the United States. When House urged him to be conciliatory to the Senate, he replied, "House, I have found one can never get anything in this life that is worth while without fighting for it."

Wilson transmitted the Treaty to the Senate on July 10. His conscience seared by the acid of failure, he was in an almost truculent mood. Aloof and unyielding when he should have been pliant and appealing, he stressed the duty of the United States to approve and effectuate the Covenant. "The League of Nations," he assured the Senate, "was not merely an instrument to adjust and remedy old wrongs under a new treaty of peace; it was the only hope for mankind. . . . Dare we reject it and break the heart of the world?" And although he admitted that the Treaty was marred by bad compromises, he insisted that "none cut to the heart of any principle." Viscount Bryce shrewdly commented that Wilson persisted "in stroking the cat the wrong way."

The grim battle was immediately joined. As chairman of the Committee on Foreign Relations, Senator Lodge was determined to defeat Wilson by every means at his disposal. Instead of formally opposing the Covenant, he emphasized the need to protect the United States from vicious foreign entanglement. Playing for delay in order to confuse the issues and gain support from a people eager to forget the war, he and his supporters prolonged the hearings as long as they could and called upon any witness who cared to criticize the Treaty. They won a great advantage when Secretary of State Lansing made no denial of having told young William C. Bullitt in Paris that "the American people did not know what the treaty and the League of Nations let them in for." Even more damaging to Wilson was his own assurance to the Committee that he had not known about the Allied secret treaties until he reached Paris—an ill-considered remark readily disproved. When Lodge finally reported the Treaty to the Senate on September 10, he offered a number of reservations to safeguard the sovereignty and security of the nation. "The Committee believe," he warned, "that the league as it stands will breed wars instead of securing peace."

A week earlier, exhausted by the prolonged strain yet exasperated by the Senate obstruction and fanatically resolved to force approval of the Treaty, Wilson started out on a speaking tour westward in a direct appeal to the people. All summer he had warded off his friends who wished him to accept several mild reservations in order to obtain the necessary two-thirds vote in the Senate. Jules Jusserand, senior diplomat in Washington, had actually succeeded in getting England and France to consent to amendments that would win support of the necessary number of Republican Senators, but when he broached the matter to Wilson, the latter replied sternly: "Mr. Ambassador, I shall consent to nothing. *The Senate must take its medicine.*" The very thought of accepting reservations sponsored by Lodge—"that impossible name"—was gall and wormwood to his Covenanter's driven spirit. Nor would he listen to the anxious warnings of his friends who feared the results of a strenuous trip on his overstrained nervous system. To

Mrs. Wilson he insisted he had no choice. "I feel it is my duty, and my own health is not to be considered when the future peace and security of the world are at stake."

So convinced was he of the cogency of his appeal and of its favorable effect upon the people that he took no cognizance of either their current disillusionment or of the normally slow response of Senators to public pressure. He addressed his audiences with a charged fervor. Initially indifferent or even hostile hearers were moved by his passionate appeals for a durable peace. Over and over he pleaded with them to help him make sure that their sons and brothers had not died in vain. He depicted a disturbed and desperate Europe depending on the United States for stability and succor. "Everywhere in Europe there is that poison of disorder and distrust, and shall we take away from this unsteady world the only thing that reassures it?" He emphasized that in helping others we were not only exercising generosity but removing the seeds of trouble to ourselves. "I can predict with absolute certainty," he said ominously, "that within another generation there will be another world war if the world do not concert the method by which to prevent it."

The trip proved extremely debilitating for him. Driven by the urgency of his mission, he refused to spare his depleted strength. All day and part of the night he was spending himself meeting people, making and preparing speeches, attending to a multitude of routine tasks. He began to suffer from severe and continuous headaches, and sleep came to him only fitfully. By the time he reached the Pacific Coast he was too ill to continue his program without medication, but he refused either to cancel the tour or to take a few days' rest. "I have caught the imagination of the people," he declared hopefully. "They are eager to hear what the League stands for; and I should fail in my duty if I disappointed them." Up to Seattle he went, down to San Diego and Los Angeles, and back to San Francisco—everywhere speaking with a moral eloquence that lifted his audiences to their feet in bursts of enthusiasm. By the time he reached Pueblo on September 25 he was seriously ill, yet he turned what he promised would be a brief talk into an impassioned speech extending over more than two hours. When he stopped, his clothes were soaked with sweat and his body was feverish and spent. He lacked the will to resist when Dr. Grayson, his devoted physician, ordered him back home. On his arrival in Washington he managed to walk to his car unaided. Several days later, however, he suffered a cerebral thrombosis which paralyzed his left arm and leg and left him in a critical condition. Significantly his serious illness made little impress upon the nation. Neither in Congress nor in any state legislature were any resolutions of sympathy even considered.

The nerve specialists found that Wilson had critically debilitated his nervous system and needed absolute quiet for an indefinite period. When the question of resigning from the Presidency was raised, the doctors advised against it on the ground that such renunciation would weaken the patient's incentive to recovery. Dr. Grayson and Mrs. Wilson thereupon completely isolated the stricken President and brought nothing to his attention except such matters as seemed to them imperative. "The decision that was mine," Mrs. Wilson later stated, "was what was important and what was not, and the *very* important decision of when to present matters to my husband." By way of explanation she added: "Woodrow Wilson was first my beloved husband whose life I was trying to save, fighting with my back to the wall—after that he was the President of the United States." This attitude probably furthered the rejection of the Treaty by the Senate. Whether or not Wilson's overrighteous obstinacy would have been lessened by the urgent pleas of House and other influential proponents of the League remains a matter for conjecture, but the fact remains that none of their messages ever reached him.

As things were, the opponents of the League in the Senate had no effective resistance. Wilson's refusal to accept the proposed modifications, which House considered "of a wholly minor character," was played up by his enemies as the arrogant attitude of a dictator. And his insistence that these reservations were in effect a

127

"nullification" of the Treaty tied the hands of his devoted supporters on the Senate floor. When he was told by Mrs. Wilson
on November 19 that the Treaty without amendment failed to
receive the required two-thirds vote, he remarked characteristically:
"All the more reason I must get well and try again to bring the
country to a sense of its great opportunity and greater responsibility." By this time somewhat improved in health, he clung to
the idea that in the oncoming election the people would uphold
him in "a great and solemn referendum." When he projected this
thought in his message to the Democratic leaders gathered at the
Jackson Day Dinner on January 8, 1920, Bryan pointed out the
folly and unreality of such expectation and pled for the compromise that would assure the ratification of the Treaty in the Senate.
Unmoved by this attitude of the leaders of his party, Wilson still
refused to accept the Senate reservations. This fanatical inflexibility
and his curt dismissal of Secretary Lansing for holding routine
Cabinet meetings without his prior approval played into the hands
of the opposition. When another vote on the Treaty was taken
on March 19, it was again defeated. Two months later the Senate
passed a resolution of peace claiming for the United States all
the advantages accruing to it under the Treaty. Wilson vetoed the
measure on the ground that it "would place an uneffaceable strain
upon the gallantry and honor of the United States."

The Wilson Administration was fast losing the support of the
people. The voters' refusal to give their President a Democratic
Congress in 1918 was perhaps the normal emotional precipitation
at the end of a war. Their subsequent loss of confidence, however,
was genuine and justifiable. The fighting had no sooner ended
than the numerous war bureaus and organizations began to break
up in complete confusion. Determined to negotiate the peace
treaty in person, Wilson tended to neglect the serious domestic
problems arising out of the necessary liquidation of the military
establishment and the equally urgent adjustment to a peacetime
economy. Social dislocation, price inflation, industrial malpractices,
strikes and lockouts, political reaction—these and other irritations

plagued the nation and generated discontent. Organized workers, heretofore stanch supporters of Wilson, were particularly antagonized by government use of court injunctions to break strikes aiming to adjust wages to inflated prices. Middle-class Americans recalled longingly "the good old days" under the Republicans and turned again to that party. And the liberals, who had been in the vanguard of Wilson's active admirers, were among his strongest postwar opponents.

Many of his early supporters had opposed our entrance into the European conflict in the belief that it was primarily of imperialistic origin. But even those who had hailed his crusade to save the world for democracy were soon alienated by the harsh treatment of conscientious objectors and the savage oppression of socialists and pacifists. When the fighting ended, Wilson's curt refusal of clemency to the imprisoned dissidents convinced most liberals that his New Freedom had indeed fallen victim to the war hysteria. His compromises at Versailles seemed in keeping with the new Wilson, and his idealistic utterances struck them as sheer hypocrisy. They therefore objected to the Treaty as violently as the conservatives, though for different reasons.

Wilson's Covenanter illiberalism blighted his Administration after the armistice. Even conservative Americans recoiled from his harshness toward Eugene V. Debs, the elderly and ill Socialist leader who was serving a ten-years' sentence for an antiwar speech. "I will never consent to the pardon of this man," Wilson told Tumulty. "I know that in certain quarters of the country there is a popular demand for the pardon of Debs, but it shall never be accomplished with my consent. . . . This man was a traitor to his country." Such complete lack of sympathy for rebels and radicals made possible Attorney-General A. Mitchell Palmer's "war on the Reds." This aggressive and arrogant Quaker, eager to gain the Democratic nomination for the Presidency, organized wholesale raids upon suspected aliens and dissidents without warrant, employed spies to stir up seditious agitation in order to arrest the participants, and resorted to the third degree as a means of obtain-

129

ing evidence. Around ten thousand suspects were arrested in a nationwide raid on January 2, 1920; of these about 6500 had to be released the next day for lack of evidence, and all but a few of the rest were dismissed subsequently. Senator Thomas Walsh, who investigated these illegal and arbitrary arrests, remarked: "I find it difficult to conceive of a course more powerfully calculated to excite widespread hatred of our Government." Protesting against these same Palmer raids and prosecutions, twelve nationally eminent and conservative lawyers in May 1920 well expressed the indignation of many of their fellow citizens:

The American people has never tolerated the use of undercover provocative agents or "agents provocateurs," such as have been familiar in old Russia or Spain. Such agents have been introduced by the Department of Justice into the radical movements, have reached positions of influence therein.

By this time the attention of the nation had become focused on the oncoming Presidential elections. The Republican convention was held first. Senator Lodge made the keynote address, and his hatred of Wilson broke through his supercilious reserve. "Mr. Wilson and his dynasty, his heirs and assigns, or anybody that is his, anybody who with bended knee has served his purpose, must be driven from control." The platform was, in the words of William Allen White, "a Pandora's box of seemingly contradictory propositions"; the Presidential nominee, Warren G. Harding, was one of the "pigmy-minded" Senators reviled by Wilson. The Democrats, as disorganized and dispirited as the Republicans were buoyant and brash, met soon after to pay lip service to Wilson and the League and to nominate James M. Cox, governor of Ohio, as the party's standard bearer.

The campaign was drab and desultory. Confident of victory, the Republicans used their money and their oratory to strengthen political weak spots over the country. The Democratic politicians, equally certain of defeat in view of Wilson's unpopularity, concentrated their efforts on the stronger local candidates. Wilson himself took no part in the campaign. His health was much better, but his left arm remained inert and he could walk a little only by shuffling with the aid of a cane. He was indeed a feeble, stooped, gray-faced, white-haired old man. But his dogmatic determination remained as fixed as ever and he clung with almost pathetic optimism to the belief that the people favored his views. He looked forward with confidence to the result of the election, firm in the thought that the right would triumph. On October 3 he issued the following statement:

This election is to be a genuine national referendum. The determination of a great policy upon which the influence and authority of the United States in the world must depend is not to be left to groups of politicians of either party, but is to be referred to the people themselves for a sovereign mandate to their representatives.

When the votes were counted, the Democratic candidate was overwhelmed by a tidal wave of national discontent—receiving a little more than half as many ballots as were cast for Harding. Wilson's reaction to this verdict of the voters was characteristic: "They have disgraced us in the eyes of the world. The people of America have repudiated a fruitful leadership for a barren independence. . . . We had a chance to gain the leadership of the world. We have lost it, and soon we will be witnessing the tragedy of it all."

Only one event of interest to Wilson occurred during his last months in office—the award to him of the Nobel Peace Prize for 1920. He bought a comfortable house on S Street, and there he moved on March 4, 1921, to lead the life of a semi-invalid. At first he even thought of practising law and had actually organized a partnership with Bainbridge Colby, Lansing's successor as Secretary of State. But he soon realized the impossibility of such activity on his part and gave it up. Nor was he able to do the writing he had planned. He read a little, saw briefly a visitor on occasion, rested and slept.

His belief in the League remained fixed. As late as 1923 he

pointed out to one of his daughters that if the Treaty had been approved at the outset it would have been a "personal" triumph. "But as it is coming now, the American people are thinking their way through and reaching their own free decision, and that is the better way for it to come." On November 11 a group of admirers celebrated Armistice Day that year by a visit to his home. To them he said:

I am not one of those that have the least anxiety about the triumph of the principles I have stood for. I have seen fools resist Providence before, and I have seen their destruction, as will come upon these again, utter destruction and contempt. That we shall prevail is as sure as God reigns.

After the turn of the year Wilson was getting gradually weaker, and on February 3, 1924, he breathed his last.

The tragedy of Woodrow Wilson was rooted in his Covenanter's zeal. Endowed with a quick and finely developed mind, imbued with the moral idealism of the true believer, capable of an eloquence that sent his message straight to the hearts of men, and placed in a position of great power at a time of world crisis, he had the rare opportunity of laying the foundations of a new and nobler Decalogue. Immediately after the Armistice he indeed appeared as mankind's modern Moses. Yet on the very brink of triumph he fumbled and failed to seize the crown of inspired achievement. For notwithstanding all his real advantages he lacked the crucial ability of getting along with men. It was this flaw of character, aggravated in his last years by his stubborn dogmatism, that caused him to compromise himself at Versailles and to forfeit the Treaty and the League by needlessly alienating the "mild reservationist" Senators who had the deciding votes.

Lincoln, Wilson wrote years before, "was the supreme American in our history. He never ceased to be a common man: that was his source of strength. But he was a common man with genius." Of Wilson himself it might be said that he possessed political genius but not the strength of the common man. A sheltered minister's son, seldom participating in the hurly-burly of boyhood, refusing to play ball when he could not have his way, he never learned the give-and-take principle of basic democracy. Till late in life he knew best the cloistered activities of the university, the quick play of the mind, and the solitary theorizing of the scholar. As Justice Frankfurter observed, "He was dogmatic, intolerant; fundamentally didn't like his kind. He believed in democracy in the abstract, but didn't care for people." Consequently when the call to political leadership came to him, he had the genius to exalt man's hopes but not the "common touch" of the practical politician. It hardly occurred to him that to lead men successfully one must know how to gain and keep followers.

At first, capitalizing on the good will toward him, he achieved notable success—at Princeton, Trenton, Washington, Paris. In each place however, it did not take him long to arouse a formidable opposition. For he insisted on having his way too fast and too forcefully. Impatient with slow minds, angered by resistance, convinced that he was right, he fought his way forward with an inflexible will. In the process he alienated his closest friends and antagonized the majority with whom he had to work. When forced to contend against shrewd and resolute men like Dean West and Senator Lodge, he lacked the necessary resourcefulness of a soft answer and became perversely obstinate. In his fight for the Treaty the petulance of the overprotected boy combined with the messianic Covenanter of his old age to brook no opposition, to disdain and defy his enemies, and to break himself on the wheel of his driven spirit rather than to bend a little for the good of the ideal to which he had dedicated himself.

If Wilson failed tragically to attain the high goal he had set for himself, he succeeded eminently in glorifying the principle of democracy. During his first two years as President he achieved greater and more enduring reforms than Theodore Roosevelt had in his seven years in office. He had remarkable insight into the progressive direction of the social and political forces of prewar

America and took full advantage of it. His ignoble antiradicalism during and after the war definitely detracted from his democratic record and is best explained as the behavior of a man overcome by messianic fanaticism. For by then he had completely dedicated himself first to victory and later to the League of Nations and could not bear any kind of opposition.

Today his name is associated mainly with the ideal of the League of Nations and not with his failure to realize it. Maximilian Harden, writing in 1925, well expressed this attitude:

Is there not even to-day a halo about the head of the man who, though he was unable to bring about the moral ennoblement of peoples, nevertheless strove for this achievement with holy earnestness and pointed the way toward its attainment to generations yet unborn? America, conscious of her debt to him, will some day bow her head in reverence before his image.

134

Robert M. La Follette

UNCOMPROMISING PROGRESSIVE

EVALUATING THE PRESIDENTIAL CANDIDATES in the 1924 campaign, William Allen White wrote of Robert M. La Follette, then the independent aspirant: "Compromise is not in his lexicon. . . . Personally he is incorruptible. Politically he is immovable in his determination to battle in his finish fight for what he deems a just and righteous cause." La Follette's long political career was indeed an uncompromising crusade for good government. For more than thirty years he distinguished himself from most other reformers not only by his persistent progressivism but by his steadfast fight for principles in the face of, at times, nearly universal condemnation. So firm was his belief in democracy that he readily resorted to radical measures to safeguard it; and so fixed was his humanitarian goal that political success whetted rather than warped his idealism.

Robert Marion La Follette came of sturdy American stock, a mixture of Huguenot and Scotch-Irish pioneers. His grandfather was a neighbor of Thomas Lincoln in Indiana, and his father settled on a farm in Dane County, Wisconsin. There Robert was born on June 14, 1855, eight months before the death of his father. His widowed mother continued to live on the farm, eking out a bare existence with the aid of her four children; nor was the situation much changed in 1862 when she married again. In 1873 the family moved to nearby Madison, and two years later Robert

135

entered the University of Wisconsin. While there he not only taught in a country school but also edited and managed the bi-monthly student periodical in order to help at home in addition to earning his own expenses.

The Granger movement in Wisconsin was very active in the 1870's. Farmers resented having to pay high freight rates and exorbitant interest and they demanded legislative relief. So loud and widespread was their clamor that the conservative Republican legislature was forced to enact laws regulating the railroads.

Young Robert La Follette, serious-minded and ambitious, was deeply influenced by the Granger talk of his neighbors. He saw no reason why farmers should be deprived of much of their income by the wealthy railroads and bankers. As a student, however, he first turned his mind not to politics but to the stage. He longed to be an actor and devoted himself to the practice of public speaking. In his senior year his efforts enabled him to win the inter-state oratorical contest with an interpretation of the character of Iago. On his return to Madison he was acclaimed as the town's hero. But his dream of becoming a Shakespearean actor was punc-tured by Lawrence Barrett. That popular thespian gave him a hearing while on a visit to the city and advised him against a career on the stage.

La Follette reluctantly accepted the actor's counsel and turned to the study of law. His Granger sympathies quickened his inter-est in current affairs; his inherent idealism was strengthened by the liberal views of John Bascom, president of the university. In this receptive mood, he took to heart the words of Edward G. Ryan, chief justice of the state supreme court, whose address to the graduating class of 1873 he happened to hear:

Money as a political influence is essentially corrupt; is one of the most dangerous to free institutions; by far the most dangerous to the free and just administration of the law. An aristocracy of money is essen-tially the coarsest, the rudest, the most ignoble and demoralizing, of all aristocracies. . . . The question will arise . . . which shall rule—wealth or man; which shall lead—money or intellect.

Young La Follette knew the answer and dedicated himself to its realization. After studying law for several months he was admitted to the bar early in 1880. With legal work scarce for the newcomer, he decided to seek the office of district attorney because it paid a salary of $800 a year plus $50 for expenses. Already favorably known to the citizens of his county as an upstanding youth and the winner of the oratorical contest, he was well received by them when he promised, if elected, to save them money by doing all the work without outside aid. Ignorant of the need to obtain permission from a political boss before seeking office, he was only angered when E. W. Keyes, local postmaster and Republican leader, informed him that he had already assigned the post to someone else. Determined to win despite this opposition, he intensified his campaigning among the farmers and surprised the politicians by winning both the nomination and the election. This experience taught him the importance of appealing directly to the voters—a lesson he never forgot.

Twenty-five years old when he assumed office, he took his campaign promises literally and attended to his various tasks without outside aid; he often worked late into the night to prepare his cases for the following day. More than once he went out of his way to see justice done despite obstacles put in his way by conniving politicians.

Now earning a regular salary, he married Belle Case, a classmate with whom he had long been in love. Mrs. La Follette became his closest counselor. In possession of a keen mind, imbued with similar ideals, equipped with a legal training—she was the first woman to receive a law degree at the University of Wisconsin—she provided him with the sympathy and encouragement that sustained him in defeat and steadied him in victory. To the end of his life she helped him plan his campaigns and often worked as hard as he did in their joint striving for social justice.

In 1882 La Follette sought re-election—and was the only Republican to win locally. Two years later his friend Samuel Harper persuaded him to run for Congress. The political machine tried hard to prevent his nomination. Philip Spooner, the district boss, told him, "Don't you know nobody can go to Congress without our approval? You're a fool." But La Follette, aided by his numerous college friends, followed the formula of going directly to the people. He proceeded to canvass farm after farm and house after house—reminding the voters of his good record as district attorney and promising to look after their interests in Congress. To nearly everyone's astonishment he was nominated and elected, becoming at the age of 29 the youngest member of the House of Representatives.

Although the new Congress was not to convene till December 1885, La Follette traveled to Washington in January at his own expense in order to observe the outgoing session in action. Soon after he took office he was befriended by Senator Philetus Sawyer, a millionaire lumberman and one of Wisconsin's leading politicians. Sawyer was a rough, uneducated, self-made man, a complacent practitioner of the ethics of the Gilded Age. He guided La Follette through the routine channels, introduced him to President Cleveland, and acted the amiable uncle.

If La Follette did not establish himself as one of the House leaders, he quickly became known for his uncompromising honesty. No amount of urging and cajoling on the part of Senator Sawyer and other Wisconsin politicians affected his insistence on safeguarding the public. When Sawyer sponsored a bill that would have given the railroads millions of acres of Indian land in the Dakotas, La Follette fought it stubbornly. For more than a week both Sawyer and Henry C. Payne, Wisconsin's leading lobbyist and political boss, argued with him day after day. Payne was furious. "La Follette is a crank," he complained; "if he thinks he can buck a railroad company with 5000 miles of line, he'll find out his mistake. We'll take care of him when the time comes." Although he was apprised of this threat La Follette remained unmoved and in the end succeeded in limiting the grant of land to the normal right of way. Years later he remarked, "Payne was as good as his word. He fought me ever afterward."

During his six years in the House La Follette was uncompromising, incorruptible, and a nonconformer, but no radical. His clashes with Republican bosses arose not from principle but from a normal repugnance to political subservience. In Congress he was an honest democrat but no insurgent. Although he refused to acquiesce in deals against the public interest, he remained on friendly terms with Senator Sawyer and the House leaders. In 1889 he worked and voted for Thomas Reed as Speaker. His appointment to membership on the powerful Ways and Means Committee was gained in part because of an effective speech on the tariff which he had made the year before.

His defeat in 1890 was to him a "bitter disappointment." He enjoyed political office, had held it for ten years, and considered himself a highly useful public servant. And although he had criticized Republican extravagance and lack of scruple in Congress, he was partisan enough to resent the idea of a Democratic victory. Once out of office, however, he resumed his legal practice and soon prospered.

Shortly after his return to Madison, La Follette underwent a traumatic experience—an event that, in his own words, "changed my whole life." For many years Wisconsin state treasurers had been banking public money to their own considerable benefit. When the Democratic victors assumed office they sought to discredit the Republican party by suing the state treasurers of the previous twenty years—all Republicans—for the interest that rightly belonged to the state. Since Senator Sawyer had been bondsman for some of the accused and was in danger of losing as much as $300,000 if the state won its suit, he approached La Follette privately in an effort to have him influence his brother-in-law Judge Robert G. Siebecker, who was to preside at the trial. The two men met in a Milwaukee hotel. Sawyer, according to La Follette, took out a thick roll of bills and offered part of it as a "retainer." La Follette was deeply shocked. Restraining his impulse to violence, he hurriedly left the room. Years later he wrote:

Nothing else ever came into my life that exerted such powerful influence upon me as that affair. It was the turning point, in a way, of my career. . . . It shocked me into a complete realization of the extremes to which this power that Sawyer represents would go to secure the results it was after.

Indignant and greatly perturbed, he considered it his duty to inform Judge Siebecker of the interview. When the latter made known his decision not to try the treasury cases, Senator Sawyer immediately denied his part in the attempted bribery; whereupon La Follette made public his side of the story, thereby incurring the wrath of the most powerful man in the state. He was at once attacked by the state's newspapers for besmirching the Senator's good name. Politicians denounced him as a notoriety seeker, and his very life was threatened by anonymous enemies.

I was shunned and avoided everywhere by men who feared or sought the favor of Senator Sawyer and his organization. At every turn the way seemed barred to me. No one can ever know what I suffered. As I recall the fearful depression of those months, I wonder where I found the strength to endure them.

The Republican machine treated La Follette as a political pariah. Yet despite this ostracism, not a few independent citizens admired his integrity and sought him out as their legal counsel. But the acid of this antagonism corroded his spirit. He knew he had done right and resented the unwarranted punishment. That winter he spent many long evenings brooding over the matter and relating it to his experiences in Congress.

I began to understand their relation. I had seen the evils singly—here and there a manifest wrong, against which I had instinctively revolted. But I had been subjected to a terrible shock that opened my eyes, and I began to see really for the first time. . . . So out of this awful ordeal came understanding; and out of understanding came resolution. I determined that the power of this corrupt influence, which was undermining and destroying every semblance of representative government in Wisconsin, should be broken.

140

From that time to the end of his life he was a man dedicated to a cause. It was he and the people against the iniquitous rich and unscrupulous politicians. Ostracism no longer bothered him; he was prepared to fight alone, if necessary, against the evildoers in power. And he had the will to win. Endowed with exceptional oratorical ability and armed with hard facts, he took every opportunity to bring his message to the people of Wisconsin. Ignoring the scorn and snubs of party politicians, he persisted in speaking publicly at frequent intervals. So popular were his addresses and so determined was he to partake in President Harrison's campaign in 1892, that the state bosses had no choice but to permit him to speak at some of their meetings.

Two years later he was ready to challenge the Republican machine at the polls. He persuaded Nils P. Haugen, a liberal Congressman, to seek the gubernatorial nomination against the party candidate. Enlisting the services of over a thousand young college graduates, he managed to reach the majority of voters on the single issue of defeating the corrupt political machine. So successful was this effort that Haugen showed great strength at the caucus meetings. At the state convention he lost the nomination only because Sawyer, Payne, and other leaders stopped at nothing to block this insurgence.

Defeat did not daunt La Follette. His course was clear, and his determination fixed. He believed time was on his side, and he worked hard to speed victory. In season and out he continued to address audiences and to circularize his speeches to the extent of his financial ability. And his talks were effective. Farmers and tradesmen sat for hours listening intently to his citation of facts and data and to his denunciation of corruption. Lincoln Steffens wrote about him in 1905:

Capable of fierce invective, his oratory is impersonal, passionate; and emotional himself, his speeches are temperate. Some of them are so loaded with facts and such closely knit arguments that they demand careful reading, and their effect is traced to his delivery, which is forceful, emphatic, and fascinating.

It was this forensic aptitude combining with the timeliness of his message that made him for many years one of the most popular speakers on the Chautauqua circuit.

In the 1896 campaign, unable to find a suitable candidate ready to oppose the choice of the machine, he announced himself as the challenger. Hard work had brought to his side not only many farmers and workers but a considerable number of public-spirited civic leaders. Organized as Independent Republicans, they appealed to voters in his behalf. "Will the people take their own work in their own hands," they asked, "or will they allow, as they have too often done, a ring of shrewd bosses to select their candidates for them?"

By fighting at the voter's door for every delegate La Follette—aided by many volunteer canvassers—succeeded in coming to the convention in Milwaukee with a majority of the delegates pledged to vote for him. On the evening before the nomination, however, Senator Sawyer and Charles F. Pfister prevailed upon enough of these delegates by means of cash payment or promised preferment to insure the choice of the party delegate.

The loss of another battle only strengthened La Follette's determination to keep fighting. He now perceived that the caucus and convention system, always subject to manipulation by unscrupulous politicians, would never truly express the will of the people. In his search for a more effective nominating procedure he came upon the idea of the direct primary, then little known in the United States. With the enthusiasm of a convert he read everything he could find on the subject and began to advocate it as a political panacea. When he was invited by the University of Chicago to address its students on February 22, 1897, he prepared a speech on the direct primary with exceeding care. He spoke frankly, factually, ferociously, enlarging upon the evils of machine politics, and proposed the method of reform with solemn enthusiasm:

This is the modern political machine. It is impersonal, irresponsible, extra-legal. The courts offer no redress for rights it violates, the wrongs it inflicts. It is without conscience and without remorse. It has come

142

to be enthroned in American politics. . . . Go back to the principle of democracy; go back to the people. Substitute for both the caucus and the convention a primary election—held under the sanctions of law which prevail at the general elections—where the citizen may cast his vote directly to nominate the candidate of the party with which he affiliates and have it canvassed and returned just as he cast it. . . . The nominations of the party will not be the result of "compromise" or impulse or evil design—the "barrel" and the machine—but the candidates of the majority, honestly and fairly nominated.

This speech he delivered over and over—at county fairs, before various organizations, and on the Chautauqua circuit. He also succeeded in having a number of country weeklies distribute a total of 400,000 copies of the speech plus a primary bill to their subscribers. In addition he and several friends bought a weekly newspaper, renamed it *The State*, and made it the vehicle of their reform program. Among the measures advocated were protection for the products of factory and farm, sound money, trade reciprocity, equal and just taxation of all property, the direct primary, punishment for bribery, and abolition of railroad passes. Discussion of these controversial reforms soon became widespread. Voters all over the state welcomed La Follette wherever he spoke. And everywhere he made clear that the paramount issue was honest government versus bossism.

In 1898 La Follette again came to the state convention as the favored gubernatorial candidate. Sawyer, still in control of the party machine, once more managed by means of bribery and intimidation to defeat the choice of the people. The progressives, however, did succeed in incorporating several major reforms into the party platform.

The fight continued. While La Follette devoted much of his time to speaking and writing on the measures of good government, the Republican legislature curtly voted down the promised reforms. It was only because of the stubborn persistence of A. R. Hall, a liberal legislator, that one reform plank, the anti-pass bill was enacted into law despite the opposition of the party bosses.

By 1900 the political situation in Wisconsin was in a state of upheaval. Senator Sawyer was dead. The scramble for control among the contenders caused considerable disaffection. And La Follette's years of agitation had finally aroused the people of the state. Early in the year he announced his candidacy on the issues of the direct primary and railroad taxation—measures included in the party platform but deliberately defeated by the administration in office. At the convention all oppositon to La Follette collapsed and he was nominated unanimously. His election by a large majority followed despite the fact that the implacable conservatives worked to win votes for the Democratic rival.

La Follette assumed office eager to destroy the Republican machine and to carry out the promises of his progressive platform. He was particularly anxious to have the legislature pass the direct primary law and the act equalizing taxes upon corporate property with those upon other similar property. To impress the urgency of these measures upon unsympathetic legislators, he delivered his first message in person before a joint session of the assembly and senate. At once conservative politicians joined with railroad lobbyists in an intensive and lavish campaign to defeat the reform bills. Charles Pfister bought the Milwaukee *Sentinel*, then the only liberal newspaper in the state, and turned it into a violently antireform vehicle bent on "skinning" La Follette. The latter fought back with all the resources of his office, but he was no match for the extravagant and ensnaring lobbyists. Years later he had this to say on the defeat of his measures:

All the efforts of the lobby, combined with the opposition of the newspapers and the federal office-holders, was not without its effect upon our forces. Every moment from the time the senate convened down to the final vote on the railroad taxation bills they were weakening us, wearing us down, getting some men one way, some another, until finally before the close of the session they had not only the senate but a majority of the Republicans in the assembly. It was a pathetic and tragic thing to see honest men falling before these insidious forces.

144

Already known to his friends as "Fighting Bob," La Follette would neither compromise nor retreat. His aim was to destroy a system that "not only favors, but, logically and inevitably, produces manipulation, scheming, trickery, fraud and corruption"— and he was determined to fight it to the end. "Selfish interests," he told a farmers' institute, "may resist every inch of ground; may threaten, malign, and corrupt; they cannot escape the final issue. That which is so plain, so simple, and so just will surely triumph." He therefore took every opportunity to attack his political opponents and to castigate the recreant legislators. One of these opportunities came when the legislature, after defeating his railroad taxation bill, passed a license tax on dogs. His veto was a stinging rebuke to the cynical sponsors.

I am unwilling to present to the people of this state, in lieu of the legislation to equalize taxation which has been promised them, and which they have a right to expect from representative government, a scheme which, in a general way, may be described as an act to relieve the farmer or city home-owner of a small measure of increased tax upon his realty by imposing a license fee upon his dog.

At the end of the 1901 session of the legislature La Follette became seriously ill with a stomach ailment. For nearly a year he had to remain under medical care and relatively inactive. Thus handicapped, and further antagonizing his enemies by opposing another term for Senator John Spooner, he had difficulty in his effort at re-election. The Republican machine might have defeated him if the liberal Democrats had not come to his aid. Equally gratifying to him was the stronger liberalism of the new legislature.

After a decade of strenuous agitation La Follette was definitely gaining over his antagonists. Serving his second term as governor and dealing with a relatively responsive legislature, he had high hope of achieving at least part of his reform program. In addressing a joint session on the desired railroad legislation he analyzed the rates in nearby states and showed that in Wisconsin "151 towns were paying on an average 39.9 percent more for their transportation charges than towns located at similar distances from markets in Illinois and Iowa." When the railroad representatives questioned the accuracy of these figures, he sent the legislature a special message, prepared with the aid of a staff of state accountants, that consisted of 178 pages of irrefutable evidence. The lobbyists then brought prominent shippers to Madison to testify against the bills. Public pressure favoring the legislation was very great, however, and the lobbyists were partly defeated. The legislature passed the equalization tax bill and provided funds for accountants to check railroad gross earnings for tax purposes; but the measure regulating railroad rates, which would prevent the passing of taxes onto the public, was defeated after a strenuous struggle.

The direct primary bill was fought savagely by all conservative politicians. When they could not prevent its enactment, they managed to postpone its effectiveness by adding an amendment that put the act to a referendum vote at the next election. Another reform passed during the 1903 session was a graduated inheritance tax ranging from $1\frac{1}{2}$ to 15 percent.

With his reform program still incomplete, La Follette decided to break with tradition and seek a third term. "I felt absolutely sure," he explained later, "that another term, with another legislature, would securely ground and bulwark self-government in Wisconsin." His political enemies, who were looking forward to his retirement, felt outraged. They organized the Republican League of Wisconsin and attacked him as a demagogue and dictator. Among the charges made against him were that he was guilty of "many unwarrantable interferences with the exclusive powers of the legislature" and that he had forced it to pass "unreasonable acts and unwise experiments" inimical to the best interests of the state. At the nominating convention they sought to obtain control by rush tactics, but a force of college athletes prevented disorder. Thwarted and infuriated, they bolted the convention and met in a previously rented hall to nominate a separate slate of candidates. In this factional strife the conservatives became known as Stalwarts and the progressives as Halfbreeds.

The Republican National Convention favored the Stalwarts as the party representatives of Wisconsin. President Theodore Roosevelt, a candidate for re-election, was loath to antagonize the conservative leaders and took a neutral position. The state supreme court, however, validated the progressive faction as the legitimate Republican party. La Follette thereupon ignored the national party leaders and turned to the people for approval. His organization sent out 1,600,000 separate pieces of mail, consisting of pamphlets presenting the story of his fight for good government. He himself traversed the state in a tour that took eight weeks of intensive campaigning. Taking his own victory for granted, he concentrated on the election of a liberal legislature. In county after county he read the voting record of the conservative candidates and pleaded with the voters to favor progressives without regard to party labels. Nor did he appeal in vain. The citizens of Wisconsin had by 1904 become indoctrinated with his progressive principles. On election day he and the primary law won handsomely and the new legislature was overwhelmingly liberal.

La Follette was now in complete control of the political machinery of the state. To him this was merely a means to an end— the adoption of his reform program. His first item of business was to enact a strong railroad regulation law, and he called on the most skilled bill framers in Wisconsin to help him. Two years earlier he had learned from the state accountants that the railroads were paying large rebates to certain influential shippers. This information he made public and thereby weakened the opposition to the regulation bill. The law finally passed "provided for a commission with power not only to fix rates but to control service and to make complete physical evaluation of all the railroad property in the state. It was more sweeping than any legislation enacted by any state up to that time." Yet it worked very well, saving the people millions of dollars and giving the railroads a fair return on their capital investment.

Late in January 1905 the legislature elected La Follette to the United States Senate. Delighted as he was to enter the field of national politics, he refused to leave his state office before the reforms he was sponsoring were passed and in practice. He therefore remained in Madison for nearly a year after his election to the Senate in order to help enact the laws that made Wisconsin politically the most progressive and best-governed state in the Union. By the time he left for Washington on January 2, 1906, he had the pleasure of signing the following bills: a strong anti-lobby law, a corrupt practices act, a state civil-service law, a forest conservation measure, workmen's compensation and various social service provisions, and insurance regulation. He also had prepared the groundwork for additional legislation of a similar character.

"The Wisconsin Idea"—government by experts for the benefit of all the people—was La Follette's legacy to the state. It was his initiative that greatly enlarged the facilities of the University of Wisconsin and established close cooperation between its scholarly experts and state officials. So strong was his influence in the state even after he had left for Washington that his loyal followers continued to govern it and to make it a progressive political laboratory, with expert commissions attending to its tax, railroad, banking, conservation, insurance, public service, and industrial problems. The legislative reference service headed by Professor Charles McCarthy served the legislators so efficiently that it became a model for similar services in other states. On reflection La Follette was highly pleased with his achievements in Wisconsin.

If it can be shown that Wisconsin is a happier and better state to live in, that its institutions are more democratic, that the opportunities of all its people are more equal, that social justice more nearly prevails, that human life is safer and sweeter—then I shall rest content in the feeling that the progressive movement has been successful. And I believe all these things can really be shown, and that there is no reason now why the movement should not expand until it covers the entire nation.

La Follette entered the Senate not as an unknown neophyte but as a prominent—to some notorious—progressive. The conservative Republican leaders sought to humiliate him by seating him in "the Cherokee strip" which separated them from the Democrats. Nor would they assign him to the committees he preferred. The role of the pariah was not unfamiliar to him; but being fifteen years older and possessed of a will that knew no compromise, he proceeded defiantly to go his solitary way.

I was again alone. When I entered the cloakroom, men turned their backs on me and conversation ceased. Members left their seats when I began to speak. My amendments to bills were treated with derision. . . . They did not know the iron that had been driven into me years before.

When only three months in the Senate he rejected the rule of silence for newcomers and made a three-day speech—extending to 148 printed pages—on the Hepburn railroad bill then under consideration. With rate regulation dear to his heart, he had made a thorough study of the measure. Although he favored its general purpose, he found it basically faulty and inadequate. He was particularly anxious to strike out the provision that enabled the Interstate Commerce Commission to act against rate discrimination only on complaint of shippers and to include an amendment that gave the Commission power to change rates on the basis of the actual value of the railroad properties. Alone of all the Senators he contended that the federal government could and should regulate railroad rates. So factual were his arguments and so forceful was his discussion that he persuaded Senator Jonathan Dolliver, chairman of the Committee on Interstate Commerce, to vote for his amendment—one of a handful to do so.

The Senate leaders were not interested. They resented La Follette's impertinence and were determined to snub him. When he began to speak they rose one after another and left the chamber. Stung by this insult he declared prophetically:

Mr. President, I pause in my remarks to say this: I cannot be wholly indifferent to the fact that Senators, by their absence at this time, indicate their want of interest in what I may have to say upon the subject. The public is interested. Unless this important question is rightly settled, seats now temporarily vacant may be permanently vacated by those who have the right to occupy them at this time.

President Theodore Roosevelt sympathized with some of La Follette's other proposed reforms, but refused to support him in the face of strong opposition. Thus the two agreed that certain coal and oil lands, then in the public domain, should be saved "from being exploited by monopoly control." Roosevelt even went so far as to include the recommendation in his annual message to Congress and told La Follette that he could introduce his conservation bill as "an administration measure." Several days later, however, the President wrote to La Follette that his bill was too drastic and that he wanted to back "something which could be passed." This pragmatic position irritated the uncompromising liberal who considered half a loaf worse than none in regard to the basic principle in questions.

A halfway measure never fairly tests the principle and may utterly discredit it. It is certain to weaken, disappoint, and dissipate public interest. Concession and compromise are almost always necessary in legislation, but they call for the most thorough and complete mastery of the principle involved, in order to fix the limit beyond which not one hair's breadth can be yielded.

This difference in attitude between Roosevelt and La Follette was evidenced in other matters of policy during the next two years. Both men favored the principle of good government, but one wanted to be practical and popular and the other was ready to stand alone and immovable for what he believed right.

If Roosevelt's liberalism was more verbal than veritable, most Senators shied away from it altogether. They were practical politicians. About half owed their office to the financial backing of powerful businessmen—and acted accordingly. The idea of keeping the public domain from private exploitation or of legislation which curbed corporate profits for the benefit of the public seemed to most Senators socialistic and therefore obnoxious. Because La Follette persisted in introducing bills for just such purposes, they considered him a radical and troublemaker. Again and again they quashed his proposals and voted down his amendments, and thus made his record of positive legislation conspicuously poor. His achievement lay rather in his role as watchdog against bills favoring corporations at the expense of the public. He scrutinized every measure introduced by the conservative Senators and fought those representing "special interests" with firm persistence. Later he wrote:

It is my settled belief that this great power over government legislation can only be overthrown by resisting at every step. . . . It matters very little whether the particular question at issue is the tariff, the railroads, or the currency. The fight is the same. It is not a question of party politics. The great issue strikes down to the very foundation of our free institutions.

When La Follette entered the Senate in 1906 he was the lone social welfare liberal. His colleagues, scrupulous or self-seeking, were still oriented to the nineteenth-century spirit of *laissez faire*. They lacked La Follette's conscious zeal for the public good. Before very long, however, his factual arguments and broad outlook began to win the allegiance of one Senator after another. By 1909 he had with him a compact little group of insurgents—all excellent speakers—fighting the Payne-Aldrich high tariff bill. And these spirited liberals made themselves heard beyond the Senate chamber.

In 1909 La Follette established his personal organ in *La Follette's Weekly Magazine*, later changed to a monthly. Its forthright advocacy of political and social reform and its critical analyses of legislation and events inimical to the public gained for it a loyal audience large enough to support its existence long after the death of its founder.

By this time insurgency was indeed a rising tide. All over the country men, influenced by the writings of muckraking journalists and the stimulating speeches of La Follette and his fellow liberals, expressed their sympathy with the insurgent groups in Congress and their disappointment in President Taft's unexpected conservatism. Political house cleaning became popular. The controversy between Secretary of the Interior Richard A. Ballinger and the conservationists led by Gifford Pinchot broke into open scandal when the latter was dismissed from office. The effect of this agitation and disaffection was evidenced in the 1910 elections, when the Democrats won a majority in the House and the progressives in both parties became a powerful coalition in the new Congress. In his re-election to the Senate despite the fierce opposition of the conservatives, La Follette established himself as the recognized leader of the liberal forces in and out of Congress.

Success in the 1910 elections confirmed the insurgents in their opposition to President Taft's renomination. They believed there was a good chance of electing a liberal in 1912 and they were eager to prepare the way. In January 1911 a number of Senators, Congressmen, governors, and other nationally known progressives met in La Follette's home and organized the National Progressive Republican League. It at once began to advocate such reforms as the direct election of Senators, the direct primary, the election of delegates to national party conventions, the initiative, referendum, and recall, and a corrupt practices act. Similar leagues were soon formed in a number of Midwestern states.

When Theodore Roosevelt, coyly perched on his political fence, declined to join the League, La Follette became the obvious choice as its presidential candidate. Louis Post, a prominent liberal, wrote in *The Public*: "The logical candidate of the Republican Progressives is Senator La Follette who led the advancing column when others feared or faltered, who has proved his constructive skill, and who does not compromise." La Follette was willing enough to lead, but was too shrewd a politician to ignore the possibility of being used as a stalking horse for Roosevelt —whom he never trusted and whose recent behavior he considered equivocal and enigmatic. Indeed, after his return from Africa, Roosevelt had both favored and criticized the conservative faction. Again, on various occasions he had stated he was not a candidate and would not run against Taft; yet he was very cautious in presenting his views, and although he spoke as a liberal he refused openly to espouse the progressive platform. La Follette naturally suspected such "rhetorical radicalism." To Gifford Pinchot, one of his financial backers and a close friend of Roosevelt, he pointed out that it would be unfair to himself and harmful to the progressive movement if he were to be used to ascertain the liberal strength and then discarded for Roosevelt in the event that conditions should appear favorable. Pinchot assured him, however, that the Colonel was not a candidate. "From many talks with him I am as certain as I live that he will be found actively and openly supporting your candidacy before the campaign ends." With this assurance and with the statement that he would not be pushed aside later, La Follette announced his candidacy.

He began his campaign in July 1911. Financial limitations kept him from making much headway in the East. West of the Alleghenies, however, the response was highly gratifying. By October it became advisable to call together the key progressives of the country in order to organize effectively the activities of the numerous local groups. Three hundred men and women met in Chicago, discussed the political situation at length, and agreed on plans for their ensuing activities. Their endorsement of La Follette's candidacy was practically unanimous.

Yet the stronger the progressive movement became the more inclined were certain of its adherents to insure success at the polls by giving it the fillip of Roosevelt's leadership. These admirers of the former President believed that La Follette was too radical and uncompromising to win a national election. They therefore persisted in urging Roosevelt to run, thereby handicapping La Follette's progress. The situation became confused when George W.

Perkins, wealthy banker, began to finance the promotion of Roosevelt's candidacy because "they looked at public questions the same way." Other representatives of big business, fearing that President Taft had no chance of election, likewise made known their preference of Roosevelt over La Follette. All this while the Colonel refused to declare himself. He did, however, intimate that he might be drafted, and that gave his ardent followers the desired incentive.

Meantime La Follette made a highly successful speaking tour in Ohio, Michigan, and Illinois. On his return to Washington in January 1912 he was dismayed to find that a number of his erstwhile adherents were transferring their allegiance to Roosevelt. At a meeting of leading progressives, called together by Gifford Pinchot later that month, La Follette protested that his withdrawal as a candidate would be a betrayal of progressivism. "If this were done the campaign would be converted into a contest to nominate Roosevelt rather than advance a cause; principles would be compromised or wholly ignored, and the progressive movement would suffer untold injury."

Three days later he was scheduled to speak in Philadelphia at the banquet of the Periodical Publishers Association. With most of the country's influential newspapermen present, the event was of manifest significance to the invited presidential candidates. La Follette was particularly eager to attend in order to speak to his fellow publishers about "the powerful influence which the business system exerts directly and indirectly over the publisher through the centralized control of great national advertising agencies." He went despite the fact that he was suffering from physical fatigue and extremely worried over the outcome of a serious operation which his younger daughter was to undergo the following day. Arriving late, feeling weak and tense—but not from the effect of a stimulant, as some claimed—he failed to speak with his usual effectiveness; angered by the obvious antipathy to his point of view, he dealt bluntly with the subject of his speech—the control of business by men who considered themselves above the law.

"This condition is intolerable," he asserted. "It is hostile to every principle of democracy. If maintained it is the end of democracy." He continued this criticism of big business long after most of the audience had left in protest, and stopped only after he had spoken twice his intended time.

Gifford Pinchot and other of his sponsors seized upon this incident to abandon him as a candidate. Acting as if La Follette's temporary debility were a physical breakdown, Pinchot wired the Minnesota progressives: "In my judgment La Follette's condition makes further serious candidacy impossible." In the ensuing confusion among the country's liberals Roosevelt emerged as their inevitable leader. Nor did he any longer hesitate. In replying to an appeal signed by several insurgent Republican governors he declared, "I will accept the nomination for President if it is tendered to me."

La Follette, recuperating from physical exhaustion, felt tricked and troubled. What he had feared had come to pass. He had indeed been used as a stalking horse to gain the candidacy for Roosevelt. It was his belief that the very men who had most urged him to run and who had contributed generously to his campaign were abandoning him for a popular opportunist. He at least would not yield to expediency. Win or lose, he would continue to fight for principles. On the front cover of the next issue of *La Follette's Weekly* appeared the following announcement:

To Progressives: I take this means of answering many inquiries and misrepresentations. The statement that my health is broken is false. A brief rest will put me back as of old on the firing line. I shall continue in the contest as a candidate for well-defined principles and for a definite program of legislation which, once enacted into law, will break the hold of privilege on the industrial life of the people and free them from the burden imposed by thousands of millions of fictitious capitalization.

Because he knew he lacked Roosevelt's glamorous personality, La Follette was all the more resentful of his rival's last-minute candidacy. Since he distrusted the former President's liberalism—

he recalled his unfriendly behavior in the Wisconsin campaigns, his record of compromise and acquiescence while in the White House, his recent acts of equivocation—he determined to remain a candidate even though it would jeopardize his rival's chances of nomination. "Upon Theodore Roosevelt and his followers," he stated, "rests the responsibility of having divided the progressives in their first national contest. Stimulated by an overwhelming desire to win, they denounced loyalty to conviction and principles as stubborn selfishness." A number of prominent liberals, agreeing with him, also refused to back Roosevelt's candidacy. Brandeis expressed their sentiments when he stated: "No man in public life today expresses the ideals of American democracy so fully as does La Follette in his thought, his acts, his living."

At the Republican convention La Follette refused to cooperate with the Roosevelt forces and thus made it easier for the conservative leaders to force through the renomination of President Taft. When the angered liberals, encouraged by Roosevelt, organized the Progressive party and made him their standard bearer, La Follette refused to bolt with them. He could not accept his rival's leadership and he did not believe in founding a new political party on the ambition of a single individual.

Roosevelt's whole record demonstrates that he has no constructive power; that he is a progressive only in words; that he is ever ready to compromise in order to win, regardless of platform promises or progressive principles. He will not last. In the end the people of this country will get his true measure.

In his speeches during the election campaign he urged the people not to vote "blindly," and the only candidate he praised as a real progressive was Woodrow Wilson. In November his own state of Wisconsin, devoted to his leadership, went Democratic.

Wilson and La Follette respected each other's liberalism. In one of his campaign speeches Wilson went out of his way to say: "I take my cap off to Bob La Follette. He has never taken his eye for a single moment from the goal he set out to reach. He has walked a straight line to it in spite of every temptation to turn aside." La Follette, on his part, wrote after the election that the voters did not favor either Taft or Roosevelt because both had been found wanting. During their incumbencies in the Presidency the people "had seen Special Privilege fastening its grip upon the country, each year with firmer hold. . . . They demanded a change. And they forged their demand into a call for Wilson." He strongly supported the New Freedom program of legislation and was the only Republican Senator to vote for the Underwood-Simmons tariff bill. He was grateful when President Wilson signed the Seamen's Act, a measure which he had long sponsored and "which blots out the last vestige of slavery under the American flag."

Ever a determined man of peace, La Follette enthusiastically supported Wilson's pacific efforts toward Mexico. He opposed the general clamor for war and insisted that no amount of American capital was worth the toll of American lives paid on the battlefield.

It is well to remember that war is always cruel; that its iron tread means destruction and devastation, whether its march is across Europe or from Atlanta to the sea; that war arouses all the fiercest human passions; that there are always cases of brutality and outrage—and that usually there is quite as much of it on one side as upon the other.

When the war in Europe began in 1914 and Wilson urged Americans to observe strict neutrality, La Follette again eagerly upheld his position. As the months passed, however, and the agitation for war against Germany grew stronger and put Wilson on the defensive, La Follette became out-spokenly pacifistic. He introduced a bill that would require a referendum on war before Congress acted on that grave question. In public speeches and in his magazine he opposed the "preparedness fever"; asserting that it was largely instigated by munition makers, he advocated the nationalization of the arms industry. He particularly resented as "interference" the President's effort to quash a resolution warning American citizens to keep off armed merchant ships.

In the 1916 campaign for the Presidency he took a neutral position between Woodrow Wilson and Charles Evans Hughes and advised voters to be guided by their conscience. Himself a candidate for re-election, he concentrated on presenting his constituents with a platform that stressed peace and social welfare. The large vote by which he won the contest confirmed him in the belief that the vast majority of the people favored his pacifistic position.

Shortly after the election war clouds began to lower over the United States. When Germany's resumption of unrestricted submarine warfare caused Wilson to break diplomatic relations with her and to ask Congress for power to arm American ships, it was obvious to everyone that this measure was but a prelude to war. Senator Lodge, who favored the bill, admitted that "to arm a vessel loaded with contraband, or to convoy a vessel loaded with contraband, would be an act of war." La Follette opposed the bill with all his resourcefulness. His editorial in his own magazine was a masterly exposition of his pacifistic views. He argued that war solved nothing, that both England and Germany were guilty of violating our neutral rights, and that peaceful solutions were the more permanent.

Shall we, to maintain the technical rights of travel and the pursuit of commercial profits, hurl this country into the bottomless pit of the European horror? Shall we bind up our future with foreign powers and hazard the peace of this nation for all time by linking the destiny of the American democracy with the ever-menacing antagonisms of foreign monarchies?

He insisted that he wasn't "an extremist," that he was fully aware of the "supreme principles for which men must fight to death as a last resort." But he argued that the United States was not then at the point of last resort and should therefore seek other ways of resolving her disagreements with Germany. He reminded his fellow Senators that the people had voted for peace the previous November and if again given the opportunity "they would with even stronger voice pray God that this country be kept out of war."

The next month the country was at war. La Follette had fought against an overwhelming majority to the last moment. With defeat came condemnation and ostracism. He and his few "willful" colleagues were shunned as pariahs. Nevertheless he continued to perform his duties as Senator with the utmost conscientiousness. He concentrated his efforts on the honest and democratic execution of our war activity. Of the sixty administration measures voted on during the first eight months of war, he favored no less than fifty-five. He did oppose the draft, espionage and other restrictive acts, and he fought hard but in vain to amend the War Revenue Act in a manner to meet war costs out of current profits and large incomes. At one point he declared sarcastically that never before in his experience had there been "so much democracy preached and so little practiced as during the last few months." And in his magazine he recounted the more egregious violations of democracy which came to his attention.

On September 20, 1917, while addressing a meeting of the Nonpartisan League in St. Paul, he remarked in reply to a question that although he had opposed the war against Germany, "I would not be understood as saying that we didn't have grievances. We had." The Associated Press garbled the report and quoted the reply to read, "We had no grievances (against Germany)." The country's leading newspapers at once headlined the misleading story and accused La Follette of vicious disloyalty. The charge was taken up in the Senate, several members denounced the speech as treasonable, and a committee was appointed to investigate the charge with a view to his expulsion.

The fury generated by the incident beat about the victim's head. All over the country he was execrated and condemned. In his home city of Madison students burned him in effigy, a club of which he was a member voted to expel him, and a round robin signed by 92 percent of the university faculty denounced him for giving

159

"aid and comfort to Germany and her allies." Alarmed by this outburst of hysterical intolerance, he obtained the floor of the Senate on October 6 and made a forthright defense of the right to free speech in wartime.

Neither the clamor of the mob nor the voice of power will ever turn me by the breadth of a hair from the course I mark out for myself, guided by such knowledge as I can obtain and controlled and directed by a solemn conviction of right and duty. . . . I maintain that Congress has the right and the duty to declare the objects of the war and the people have the right and the obligation to discuss it. American citizens may hold all shades of opinion as to the war; one citizen may glory in it, another may deplore it, each has the same right to voice his judgment. . . . If the American people are to carry on this great war, if public opinion is to be enlightened and intelligent, there must be free discussion.

Many months later the Associated Press admitted its blunder and apologized. The Senate committee delayed its report for sixteen months only to find that "the speech in question does not justify any action by the Senate." Four years after the incident the Senate voted La Follette $5000 for expenses incurred "in defense of his title to his seat."

Throughout the war La Follette again experienced the isolation and ostracism that had chilled his spirit in 1891 and in 1906. As before, however, he believed firmly in the rightness of his views. He bore patiently the opprobrium heaped upon him by both old enemies and former friends; yet eager to justify his position to an intelligent sympathizer he wrote to Zona Gale:

War is a terribly destructive force, even beyond the limits of the battle front and the war zone. Its influence involves the whole community. It warps men's judgments, distorts the true standards of patriotism, breeds distrust and suspicion among neighbors, inflames passions, encourages violence, develops abuse of power, tyrannizes over men and women even in the purely social relations of life, and terrifies all communities into the most abject surrender of every right which is the heritage of free government.

160

In January 1918 his son Robert became acutely ill with anemia aggravated by a streptococcic infection. Anxious to save his life, La Follette remained at his bedside and nursed him day and night through the critical period. Then he took the invalid to California to recuperate. For eight months he remained away from his Senatorial activities—thereby giving rise to ugly rumors—but he did succeed in the task of restoring the health of his beloved son, the youth who was later to distinguish himself as his father's successor in the Senate.

Shortly after La Follette returned to Washington, the war ended. Woodrow Wilson was on his way to Paris, and everyone talked about peace and the projected League of Nations. La Follette was skeptical. Although he approved of the Fourteen Points, upon which the armistice terms were based, he trusted neither Wilson nor the Allied leaders. As eager as anyone to destroy the seed of future wars, he knew that these peacemakers were too involved in their own schemes of power to agree upon a genuine league for peace. In his magazine he maintained that such a league must be based upon two conditions: abolition of "enforced military service," and a referendum of qualified voters before war is declared. "If this really was a war for democracy," he insisted, "let us prove it by taking the warmaking power out of the hands of the rulers in all countries and getting it into the hands of the people in all countries."

An examination of the peace treaty brought back by Wilson convinced him that no real peace was achieved and that the League was in effect an alliance of the victorious powers for the exploitation of their imperialistic designs. In criticizing the document he argued that the League should include all nations and insure peace by means of effective disarmament. Little as he relished finding himself in the company of the most conservative Senators—who opposed the treaty not so much because they loved peace and democracy as because they hated Wilson and wanted to win the next election—he would not vote for the League except with the following reservations: a guarantee of all nations to the right of self-determination; abolition of conscription; prevention of forcible annexations; prohibition against the use of mandates for the exploitation of the inhabitants and resources of weaker nations. These amendments, along with those of Lodge and others, were voted down. Under the circumstances La Follette could not but vote against the Treaty.

For some time after the armistice La Follette remained highly unpopular. Once back in the Senate, however, he resumed his forthright advocacy of political and social reform. One of his first efforts early in 1919 was to prevent valuable coal and phosphate lands from being sold to private interests, and his successful filibuster late in February ultimately saved the federal government about a billion dollars. He was also very critical of the steep rise in prices and inveighed against the large corporations that forced them upwards. "You cannot name me a single industry in the United States," he contended in a Senate debate, "that has not cut the cost of production in two again and again from 1897 down to 1914, and yet the cost to the consumer has mounted steadily every year."

He fought especially hard against the return of the railroads to private management and opposed the Esch-Cummins bill with fierce zeal. He argued that the railroads were loaded with watered stock and that the payment of dividends on that stock was depriving the public of many millions of dollars annually. Fully familiar with railway finance and administration not only in the United States but the world over, he was convinced that only government ownership and control would give the nation adequate service at reasonable cost. In one of his speeches he remarked:

I expect to stand here and make a fight alone for government ownership and control of the railroads. I am for government ownership of railroads and every other public utility—every one—and I propose to show on this floor that where it has ever been given a fair chance in any part of the world it has been successful.

At that time his protests and proposals were indeed a voice in the wilderness. The powerful leaders seldom listened to him. They were busy preparing for the presidential campaign and were taking full advantage of the general postwar disillusionment to establish the spirit of "normalcy" of the 1920's. Their intellectual lag made them unaware of the need to harmonize the principles of government with the accelerating concentration of industry. Although La Follette tended to exaggerate the evil and extent of monopoly, his colleagues in Congress were sowing the wind in their blithe encouragement of unrestrained business enterprise. La Follette's role, therefore, remained that of the people's watchdog, growling at proposed iniquities. In this activity he introduced the resolution to look into the leasing of naval oil reserves and brought about the Teapot Dome investigation.

Like so many reformers before and after him, La Follette was strongly opposed to the invalidation of Acts of Congress by the Supreme Court. He particularly resented the Court's antagonism to laws furthering social welfare and to such specific measures as the child labor law and the act providing minimum wages for women and children. To him these adverse decisions were transforming the government into a "judicial oligarchy" and thus circumventing "the immortal principle *that the will of the people shall be the law of the land.*" In an address in 1922 before the American Federation of Labor he said:

The actual ruler of the American people is the Supreme Court of the United States. The law is what they say it is and not what the people through Congress enacts. Aye, even the Constitution of the United States is not what its plain terms declare, but what these nine men construe it to be. In fact, five of these nine men are actually the supreme rulers.

In the same speech he proposed "that no inferior Federal judge shall set aside a law of Congress on the ground that it is unconstitutional"; further, should the Supreme Court declare a law unconstitutional, "the Congress may, by re-enacting the law, nullify the action of the Court." This idea was quickly criticized as subversive, since by passing a law twice Congress could modify the status and powers of the other branches of government. Such criticism notwithstanding, he incorporated the proposal in the platform which he vainly submitted to the 1924 Republican convention and which became the basis of his own independent candidacy.

In the fall of 1922 he campaigned for his fourth term in the Senate. Four years earlier he had been denounced throughout Wisconsin as a pro-German traitor; now he was once more the outstanding citizen and great progressive leader. As the patriotic fervor of his constituents subsided after the fighting had ended and they began to evaluate the causes and consequences of the war more realistically, many of them felt new faith in the principles which La Follette had championed all along. Nor did he slur over his wartime activities. He boasted of his pacifism and of his fight against the war profiteers. "I would not trade my war record with any man in the world," he asserted. By the time he had finished his speaking tour his popularity reached new heights. When the votes were counted in November, his majority was the largest in his entire career.

As the warmth of resurgent popularity began to melt the glower that darkened his mien during the war period, La Follette once again turned his thoughts to the Presidency—keenly aware that age gave him only one more chance of election. Although he was able to lose himself in a cause, he also tended to identify it with himself. With the amiable but inept Harding in the White House and the conservative Old Guard firmly in control of Congress, he saw no hope for progressive legislation. He believed, however, that the obvious incompetence of these politicians was readily disillusioning the mass of the people and that a well-organized progressive movement had a good chance of success at the next presidential election.

In 1920 he helped to establish the People's Legislative Service for the purpose of spreading an interest in more democracy in government. In February 1922 the heads of the Railroad Brotherhoods—among his most grateful followers—invited other unionists and prominent liberals to meet with them in Chicago. Their avowed aim was to promote La Follette's candidacy as President. The meeting resulted in the preliminary organization of The Conference for Progressive Political Action. After electing officers and discussing various ways to further liberal legislation, the group decided to meet again in December and to invite other organiza tions wishing to cooperate with them in this political program. Their hope was that success in the fall elections would spur liberals to unite for joint action in the campaign two years later.

On December 2 leading progressives met with La Follette in Washington to formulate plans for the conference to be held in Cleveland on December 11. The problem of a third party troubled all present. They wanted La Follette as a presidential candidate, but knew his chances of success would be infinitely greater as the Republican nominee than as the candidate of a new third party. The consensus was to do nothing until after the Republican convention. At the dinner La Follette urged unity "for the purpose of bringing about the cooperation of progressives throughout the country to aid in the advancement of liberal laws and general reconstruction." These views and decisions became the agenda of the Cleveland conference, which was well attended by representatives of every sizable progressive and radical organization with the exception of the communists. After serious deliberation the program was warmly approved.

The new Congress in 1923 remained predominantly conservative, but its liberal membership grew from a helpless handful to an aggressive faction numbering around 140, with La Follette as their intrepid leader. Although they lacked enough votes to pass their reform bills, they often succeeded in blocking legislation they deprecated. They also helped the People's Legislative Service to criticize measures considered inimical to the public welfare and to publicize bills favorable to it. Many of them worked hard, in and out of Congress, to promote La Follette's candidacy.

The third meeting of The Conference for Progressive Political Action took place in St. Louis on February 11, 1924. Delegates from liberal, labor, farmer, and socialist organizations expressed themselves in favor of political candidates "pledged to the interests of the producing classes and to the principles of genuine democracy in agriculture, industry and government." Although they took no formal action they indicated their determination to back La Follette for the Presidency even if they had to form a third party to do so. They agreed to meet again early in July, after the major political conventions had been held, and to act as circumstances dictated.

Meantime La Follette, fearing the effect of communist support on many hoped-for adherents and aware of the communist domination of the Farmer-Labor party, which appeared eager to name him as its candidate, bluntly repudiated any affiliation with this group.

To pretend that the communists can work with the progressives who believe in democracy is deliberately to deceive the public. The communists are antagonistic to the progressive cause and their only purpose in joining such a movement is to disrupt it. . . . I most emphatically protest against their being admitted into the council of any body of progressive voters.

On July 4 the convention of the united liberals was called to order. The Coolidge Republicans, ignoring La Follette and his reform planks, had forced his adherents to provide him with a new party vehicle for his candidacy. There was much enthusiasm among the delegates, but the sessions had little of the emotional fervor and crusading spirit of the Progressive party of 1912. Nor was the new party motivated primarily by devotion to a personal leader; La Follette was in a real sense merely the effective standard bearer of the discontented and class-conscious farmers and workers. So eager were these dissidents to make the fight for a candidate who sympathized with their grievances that even the

Socialists, who had always insisted on a ticket of their own, and the leaders of the American Federation of Labor, who had never before deviated from their position of political neutrality, joined the other delegates in pledging their support to "Fighting Bob" La Follette.

The National Committee had offered him the nomination even before the formal opening of the convention. In his letter of acceptance, read to the delegates by his son Robert, he reiterated the principles and beliefs which had guided his political activity for the past thirty years.

To break the combined power of the private monopoly system over the political and economic life of the American people is one of the paramount issues of the 1924 campaign. . . . The private monopoly system has grown up only through long-continued violation of the law of the land and could not have attained its present proportions had either the Democratic or Republican parties faithfully and honestly enforced the law. . . . We are unalterably opposed to any class government, whether it be the existing dictatorship of plutocracy or the dictatorship of the proletariat. Both are essentially undemocratic and un-American. . . . The supreme issue, involving all others, is the encroachment of the powerful few upon the rights of the many.

The delegates acclaimed his nomination. They gladly bent their will to his. Because he was opposed to a formal third party—wishing to avoid the stigma of a radical label in order to attract voters from both major parties—they agreed to run the campaign as independents. They also adopted his Wisconsin platform, which the Republicans had scornfully rejected the month before, and acquiesced in the choice of a vice-presidential candidate by the campaign committee.

La Follette's platform was essentially a Populist document adapted to 1924 conditions. It demanded government ownership and control of public utilities, the conservation of national resources, tariff reductions, improved banking and financing facilities, adjustment in income and inheritance taxation, a federal initiative and referendum, more democracy and efficiency in government. In addition it urged the curbing of the Supreme Court, the abolition of the labor injunction, the outlawry of war, and the reduction of armaments. In an article published in the New York *Times Magazine* La Follette summarized the nature and purpose of his candidacy:

The Progressive movement in the United States, as I see it, has for its fundamental objective the economic and political freedom of the American people and the restoration of the Government to the services of the great mass of our citizens. . . . The issues are plain and clearly defined. The specific proposals of the Progressives are constructive measures advanced to meet the supreme issue of the 1924 campaign—to break the power of private monopoly and restore government to the people.

For all its intrinsic merit, his platform did not arouse the expected enthusiasm. Economic conditions were generally prosperous. Urbanized Americans were becoming reconciled to the industrial dominance of large corporations. Employed and adequately fed, most workers were not in the mood to embrace a new party or to heed the appeal of a man with La Follette's radical reputation—he was fiercely attacked as the "Wisconsin Bolshevik." The spirit of "normalcy" readily cushioned the shock of graft and corruption in government, and relatively few were deeply disturbed by the Teapot Dome exposures. Even the farmers of the Middle West, again economically pressed and inclined to think of La Follette as their true friend, failed to support him in large numbers because of a surprisingly fine crop that fall. Moreover, the progressives had neither a strong and wide-spread organization nor adequate financial support. Unable like the Roosevelt party in 1912 to attract wealthy contributors, their expenditures of $221,977—much of it collected at public meetings —compared pitifully with the Republican outlay of $4,270,469 exclusive of contributions never formally reported or spent locally. When the ballots were counted in November, Coolidge had won by a landslide. La Follette received 4,826,471 votes, or 17 percent of the total. Wisconsin was the only state to give him its electoral votes, but in ten others he led the Democratic candidate.

La Follette was disappointed but not discouraged. "The progressives," he stated, "will close ranks for the next battle. We are enlisted for life in the struggle to bring government back to the people. We will not quit and we will not compromise." These were brave words for a man nearing his seventieth birthday and in poor health, yet he meant exactly what he said. This was not true of the men who had urged him to run and who had campaigned for him till election day. Once the result became known, they quickly backslid into their former political positions. The American Federation of Labor, having never felt at ease with the Socialists, was the first to withdraw. By the time The Conference for Progressive Political Action met again, for the last time, in February 1925, the Railroad Brotherhoods were also ready to depart—their progressive impetus having stopped with La Follette's defeat. The Socialists, eager to form an organization modeled after the British Labour party, and the farmer groups, interested in Populist reform, failed to see eye to eye.

Meantime La Follette's health continued to deteriorate. Pneumonia, bronchial asthma, and a coronary condition took their heavy toll, and he died on June 18, 1925.

"La Follette," wrote Professor Frederick A. Ogg, "was for thirty years the most spirited, resourceful and relentless fighter in the American political arena." He was also the outstanding progressive of his generation. A product of Midwestern Populism, driven by circumstances and his own dynamic ambition into political insurgency, he devoted his histrionic talents and his great energy to the advancement of democratic government. Nurtured on Jeffersonian idealism and therefore unable to acquiesce in the political exigencies of an expansive industrialism, he fought a fierce but losing fight against the aggrandizing tendencies of corporate enterprise. Yet so determined was his opposition and so keen was his devotion to democracy and public welfare, that his persistence in the face of defeat served to retard the aggression of big business and to prepare the way for the success of the New Deal in the 1930's.

He was ambitious. His extraordinary energy impelled him to leadership; to exercise and to enjoy the power drives within him. He was egotistical. His strong sense of righteousness made him impatient of opposition, domineering, and tolerant of obsequiousness in his followers. Charles McCarthy, who saw eye to eye with him politically and helped him liberalize Wisconsin, wrote to William Allen White in 1915 that although "La Follette has been a great good in the country . . . his arbitrary temperament has made it impossible for me to work personally with him all these years." Yet he was no boss in the usual sense of the term, but a crusader bent on having his way. His great ambition was to turn his state into a model of good government—that and not the personal perquisites of political power. Professor Richard T. Ely, long a leading member of the University of Wisconsin faculty, well described his achievements as politician and governor:

His chief work was to transform Wisconsin into a political laboratory for advanced measures. . . . La Follette had the zeal of a reformer. He wanted an office to fulfill his mission in life and he wished to make a name for himself. He recognized what so many reformers overlook—that to secure office he must make himself a master of political methods. He knew he must outmaneuver the old politicians—beat them at their own game. This he did—and it is an amazing story.

As United States Senator, La Follette was forced to play a largely negative role. Treated as an outcast by the conservative leaders of his party and unable to vanquish them as he had those of his own state, he could only act the part of a political goad and public guard. Yet if he failed to initiate many progressive laws in the Senate, he succeeded in influencing Congress to enact a number of reform measures by virtue of his persistent agitation.

Thus of the thirteen planks that he submitted to the Republican convention in 1908, eleven were eventually enacted into law; and of the eighteen reforms he proposed four years later, no less than fifteen were later written into statute.

As a leading anti-interventionist during World War I La Follette drew upon himself the hysterical abuse of patriots bent on assuring victory over Germany. Manifesting the parochial limitations of many Midwesterners, he nevertheless served the democratic ideal more valiantly than those who supported the war to make the world safe for democracy. Nor was it long before a sizable part of the nation acclaimed him as a farsighted statesman. Twenty years after the event this attitude was given voice by Professor Ely—one of his critics in 1918:

In looking back from 1938 to the time of the World War, I do not feel so sure as I did then that La Follette was wrong and Woodrow Wilson right. If La Follette had been nominated and elected in 1912, it is quite possible that the country might be far better off than it is now.

Eager as La Follette was to become President, he never had the slightest chance of success. He was too far ahead of his generation politically and too uncompromising temperamentally to gain the confidence of a majority of the people. And he was too shrewd a politician not to know this. His persistence as a candidate came therefore not from blind ambition but from a desire to advocate his progressive views as often and on as broad a scale as possible. To him each contest was merely a battle in a war that was bound to end in favor of the people. Defeat in effect furthered his long-range goal, inasmuch as it widely publicized his proposed reforms and eventually forced his opponents to adopt many of them as their own. For he knew from long experience that much of what his enemies at first condemned as radical and subversive they would later accept as moderate and beneficial. Justice Robert H. Jackson, speaking of La Follette in 1940, remarked:

In his policy there was enlightenment, in his hope there was a glow that caught and held young men. I did not mind then and do not mind now that he was called a "radical." That name, always hurled at those who would right wrongs, has become a certificate of character.

"Fighting Bob" La Follette has made a noted place for himself in the history of American liberalism. His uncompromising and persistent battle for honest and efficient government and his broad humane ideals have favorably influenced the political course of our own time.

Louis D. Brandeis

"COUNSEL FOR THE PEOPLE"

LOUIS DEMBITZ BRANDEIS WAS for years a highly controversial figure. A sharp critic of bigness, of the concentration of capital, and of the exploitation of labor, he had antagonized many influential Americans. His appointment to the Supreme Court in 1916 caused a sharp outcry of dismay on the part of some of the nation's most eminent citizens. Their attack was so virulent and vindictive that Senator Robert L. Owen of Oklahoma considered it "the most vicious and unjust assault ever brought against a nominee for a judgeship." Yet many equally prominent men came to Brandeis's defense—praising him as an idealist dedicated to the common good and a lawyer of great distinction and broad social vision.

Time has vindicated his friends and followers. Brandeis's judicial opinions became beacons lighting the way to the social goals of the New Deal. So firmly indeed had he established his reputation as sage and humanitarian by the time he reached his seventy-fifth birthday that Justice Holmes stated a truism when he wrote: "Whenever he left my house I was likely to say to my wife, 'There goes a really good man.' I think the world now would agree with me in adding that the years have proved 'and a great judge.'"

The Brandeis family was part of a group of highly cultivated Central European Jews that migrated to the United States after the failure of the 1848 revolutions. These newcomers prized free-

173

dom. They were romantic liberals eager for the blessings of democracy. Freed of the bonds of religious orthodoxy, they were dedicated to learning and social progress. Mrs. Frederika Brandeis, mother of the Justice, possessed "pre-eminently a sense of duty to the community"; all of them were devoted to the ideals of their adopted land; and even those who had settled in the South became ardent abolitionists.

Louis David Brandeis was born in Louisville, Kentucky, on November 13, 1856, the youngest of four children. His father had prospered as a grain and produce merchant, and the family enjoyed the comforts of moderate wealth. Louis was a precocious child and an excellent student. Strongly influenced by his uncle Lewis Dembitz, who was a brilliant lawyer and a fine Jewish scholar, he early changed his middle name to Dembitz and determined to study law.

In August 1872, after suffering financial reverses, the elder Brandeis took his family to Europe. There Louis, alert and eager, remained for three years, at first taking private lessons and traveling and then attending the Dresden Annen-Realschule for three terms. As in Louisville, he was again a prize-winner and honor student. Yet he was not happy in Germany. The Prussian spirit of rigid discipline irritated him. "I was a terrible little individualist in those days," he admitted years later, "and the German paternalism got on my nerves. . . . I wanted to go back to America and I wanted to study law."

He returned to Louisville in May 1875. The following September he entered Harvard Law School, having been admitted despite his deficiency in the required college credits. With his father still in financial straits, he borrowed the necessary money from his older brother Alfred. His intellectual acuteness was at once noticeable, and in his second year he became a popular and well-paid tutor. He earned more than enough for his modest needs— including fees to students who read to him because his eyes had become strained. On graduation he stood out as the most brilliant member of his class—his record remaining unequaled in the history of the Harvard Law School. As he was also the youngest, the college trustees temporarily suspended the rule that would have kept him from receiving a diploma until he was twenty-one. Not yet satisfied with his knowledge of law, he returned for a year of graduate study.

On leaving Harvard in 1878 he went to St. Louis to work for a successful lawyer who was a friend of the family. Eager, however, to make his way "unassisted by the fortuitous circumstances of family influence or social position" and longing for the more congenial atmosphere of Boston and Cambridge, he returned there within the year to form a partnership with his friend and classmate Samuel D. Warren, Jr. To gain experience he concurrently served as law clerk to Chief Justice Horace Gray of the Supreme Judicial Court of Massachusetts until 1881, when the latter was elevated to the Supreme Court of the United States. Justice Gray stated at the time, "I consider Brandeis the most ingenious and most original lawyer I ever met." Since Warren was likewise very able and had the advantage of high social position, the partnership quickly prospered.

Brandeis enjoyed life in Boston. His pleasant personality and intellectual superiority made him a welcome guest in the best Brahmin homes. Of a sociable disposition, he took full advantage of this opportunity. It was at this time that he became a friend of Oliver Wendell Holmes.

In March 1882, when Brandeis was only twenty-five, President Charles W. Eliot invited him to give a course on Evidence at the Harvard Law School. Although he accepted the offer with alacrity, he did not want to become a teacher and subsequently refused an assistant professorship. He was more attracted to trial work and found genuine satisfaction in extending his knowledge of the social background of the law. What greatly interested him then and later were not legal abstractions or technical problems but human motivation and the quality of justice.

He dissolved his partnership with Warren in 1889, when the latter decided to succeed his late father in the family business.

Brandeis had by that time established himself as one of Boston's leading corporation lawyers and had a highly lucrative practice. From the first, however, he differed from many others in the independence of his attitude toward his clients. He strongly disapproved of the tendency for lawyers to become in fact employees of corporations. "I would rather have clients," he stated pointedly, "than be somebody's lawyer." He therefore insisted on dealing only with the heads of firms wishing his services. Nor was he satisfied to limit himself to the legal aspects of any case. What interested him much more were the broad problems of business enterprise. He took great pain to familiarize himself with the technical and economic phases of the industrial units operated by his clients. Thus prepared, he was able to advise them not merely on questions of law but on the most efficacious business practices. To a young colleague he gave this counsel in 1893:

Knowledge of decisions and powers of logic are mere handmaidens—they are servants, not masters. The controlling force is the deep knowledge of human necessities. . . . Your law may be perfect, your ability to apply it great, and yet you cannot be a successful adviser unless your advice is followed; it will not be followed unless you can satisfy your clients, unless you impress them with your superior knowledge, and that you cannot do unless you know their affairs better than they do because you see them from a fulness of knowledge.

So well did he himself follow this precept that heads of large firms began seeking his practical business advice even more than his strictly legal guidance. His office became one of the busiest in New England and his reputation spread to New York and other industrial centers.

Early in 1890 he fell in love with his second cousin Alice Goldmark and married her on March 23, 1891. She too was quick of mind, highly cultivated, and imbued with broad social sympathies. Eager to share her husband's aims and ideals, she readily agreed with him on a modest mode of life in order that he might feel free of the need to earn a lot of money. On this point his mind was fixed. He dreaded the thought of financial insecurity, the

176

possibility of having to serve another's will—believing that "the man without some capital can only continue to slave and toil for others to the end of his days." To achieve independence he had saved his money and had indeed accumulated a considerable amount of capital by the time of his marriage. Nevertheless he adhered to the rule that a man must "keep his personal needs down to a minimum so as not to be bound by them," and this feeling of economic independence enabled him to give more and more of his attention to matters having a public interest.

Brandeis worked hard, but he also knew how to relax and when to take a vacation. He enjoyed social conversation after dinner, tramping through woods, sailing on the bay, riding horseback over country roads. His wife and he, always close companions, took great delight in bringing up their two daughters and in spending much of their time together.

Brandeis's career as a social crusader began slowly. In the 1880's as a young lawyer of exceptional promise, he took a casual interest in public affairs and joined groups furthering mild civic reforms. When his friend Mrs. Glendower Evans was suddenly widowed and needed a firm hold on life, he encouraged her interest in the economic advancement of labor. In 1890 his attention was attracted to the shady political aspects of the liquor business and he furthered remedial legislation. Four years later he was engaged as counsel by a wealthy woman who was deeply distressed by the abysmal conditions in the Boston pauper institutions. For nine months he presented evidence of mismanagement and faulty organization before the aldermanic board and in the end persuaded it to reorganize the department of public institutions. What he uncovered quickened his social conscience:

Men are not bad, men are not degraded, because they desire to be so; they are degraded largely through circumstances, and it is the duty of every man and the main duty of those who are dealing with these unfortunates to help them up and let them feel in one way or another that there is some hope for them in life, and some distinction between them and the worse.

When his client paid him a fee of $3000, he donated the money to charitable and civic organizations. Thereafter, in order to remain a free agent, he refused payment for work of a public nature.

About this time, having assumed the role of "counsel for the people," he began to oppose free franchises to traction companies. It seemed to him wrong for a city to grant to private corporations valuable monopoly rights without adequate benefit to the people. When metropolitan Boston decided in the late 1890's to build subways as a means of relieving traffic congestion in its narrow streets, the traction company requested a long franchise that would place all transportation facilities in its sole control. Edward A. Filene, a wealthy and public-spirited merchant, protested against this one-sided proposal and engaged Brandeis to help him fight it. Together they organized the Public Franchise League, and with the aid of this group of civic leaders they campaigned against the franchise so persistently that in the end they succeeded in greatly reducing the term of the lease and in obtaining proper compensation for the city. When Filene insisted on paying Brandeis for his months of service, the latter said, "I'll take half of what you got out of it."

In the fight against the traction company Brandeis learned that he had incurred the sharp hostility of the wealthy men associated with it. Some of these bankers and businessmen were prominent Brahmins with whom he had long been on friendly terms. As the campaign persisted they did not hesitate to manifest their antagonism and to impugn his motives. At first he tried to assure them that his only concern was to protect the public from the designs of selfish corporations. When he perceived, however, how intensely prejudiced these privileged rich were, he decided to be guided by his sense of right and to accept the social consequences.

Another of his discoveries was that graft and corruption were perverting the city and state legislative bodies. Aldermen and assemblymen were in the habit of exchanging favors with public service corporations, and some of them had as many as two hundred friends and henchmen on company payrolls. To clean up Boston politics Brandeis and other prominent citizens formed the Good Government Association and began a publicity campaign against corrupt officials. "The politician can stand any amount of attack," Brandeis explained, "but he cannot stand the opposition of public opinion." He therefore concentrated on arousing the citizenry to insist on the enactment of certain specific laws against corruption. By writing innumerable letters and making many speeches he persuaded men of prominence to join the agitation. In time he succeeded in having passed one bill prohibiting officeholders from soliciting employment for others from public service companies and another limiting campaign expenditures.

Early in 1904 Brandeis became interested in Boston's gas problem. The newly formed Consolidated Gas Company was following the practice of other industrial combinations in its attempt to water its stock and raise prices. A number of public-spirited citizens, critical of this procedure, called on Brandeis for help. His first step was to make a thorough study of the manufacture and sale of gas. An investigation satisfied him that it was possible for the Consolidated to provide gas at a lower rate and still make a fair profit. Unlike other reformers, he believed that public ownership was no immediate solution.

To reduce the price of gas we need not only honesty but also skill, energy and initiative. And this may best be secured by following those lines of intelligent self-interest upon which the remarkable industrial advance of America has proceeded. Those who manage our public-service corporations should be permitted, subject to proper safeguards, to conduct the enterprise under the conditions which in ordinary business have a sufficient incentive to attract men of large ability and to insure from them their utmost efforts for its advancement.

This position not only antagonized the privileged capitalists but also alienated the idealistic reformers. Nevertheless he pro-

179

ceeded with his plan of action. First he sought to prevent the Consolidated from watering its stock—a financial practice which he considered hurtful both to the small investor and to our democratic form of government—and argued that such action would violate the state's antiwatering law of 1894. On finding the head of the Consolidated an intelligent and cooperative industrialist, he soon persuaded him of the wisdom not merely of relinquishing the stockwatering plan but of accepting the lower-rate proposal based on the London sliding scale. This arrangement called for a rate of ninety cents per 1000 cubic feet of gas—instead of the current one-dollar rate—and a regular dividend of 7 percent, with an additional percent for every five-cent reduction in the price of gas.

This compromise was bitterly opposed by overrighteous reformers who suspected the slightest concession to public-service corporations. Brandeis, however, believed it to be the solution most beneficial to the people and energetically advocated its adoption. He pointed out that the plan would not only reduce the price of gas but would take the Consolidated out of politics and thus serve as an example to other similar companies. "The principal evil that has been done by our public-service corporations is not excessive charges," he stressed, "but the corruption of our municipal and state governments." His agitation proved effective, and the bill legalizing this agreement was passed in June 1906. In a short time the incentive of additional dividends caused a reduction in the price of gas to eighty cents per 1000 cubic feet, thereby saving consumers nearly a million dollars annually, until the economic disturbance of World War I made a readjustment unavoidable.

Brandeis was still involved in the fight for cheaper gas when he was drawn into the life-insurance investigation. In 1905 the struggle for control of the Equitable Life Assurance Company threatened its disruption. A group of Boston's large policy holders became alarmed, formed the New England Policy Holders Protective Committee, and engaged Brandeis as counsel. Sensing the involvement of the public good, he insisted on serving without compensation. A summer's study of the life-insurance business persuaded him of the need for "radical changes in the system." At about the same time an independent investigation by the New York state insurance commissioner caused him to reach similar conclusions. Heeding the public clamor for action, the New York state legislature created the Armstrong Committee for the purpose of investigating the conduct of the large insurance companies. Extended hearings were held under the able guidance of Charles Evans Hughes, committee counsel, and the egregious malpractices of high insurance officials became headline news. The legislature thereupon promptly enacted the committee's recommendations into law.

Much as Brandeis approved of these reforms, he considered them quite inadequate. What alarmed him particularly was the realization that the large insurance companies, collecting many millions of dollars in premiums, were able, by dominating the money market, to manipulate the nation's economy to their own selfish ends. This fear he expressed that year in a speech before the Commercial Club of Boston:

The economic menace of past ages was the Church—the dead hand, which gradually acquired a large part of all available lands. The greatest economic menace today is a very live hand—those great insurance companies which are controlling so large a part of our quick capital. Such is the power which the American people have entrusted to the managers of these large companies. How has it been exercised? Substantially as all irresponsible power since the beginning of the world: selfishly, dishonestly, and in the long run, inefficiently.

Brandeis was especially disturbed by the shocking revelations in the field of industrial insurance—about which the New York legislature did nothing. He considered it highly immoral for insurance companies to spend as overhead forty cents of every dollar paid by workers. He found, moreover, that these companies permitted two thirds of their industrial policies to lapse or become forfeited within three years of issue; that workers were paid back only one third of what they actually paid in premiums. Determined to remedy this flagrant abuse, he studied the annual reports of life-insurance companies, banking institutions, and state insurance commissions until he fully familiarized himself with the nature and procedures of the life-insurance business. He was soon persuaded that it was essentially a very simple enterprise, requiring primarily "honesty, accuracy, persistence, and economy." He also learned from a study of 188 savings banks that their overhead rates were seventeen times lower than those of the large insurance companies. Anxious to reduce the cost of insurance to workers, he soon conceived the idea of savings banks adding insurance departments and operating them as economically as their other types of financial activities. As far as he could see, the only functions the banks needed to add were those of fixing insurance rates, medical examinations, and verifying the proof of death. "The savings banks," he concluded, "could thus enter upon the insurance business under circumstances singularly conducive to extending to the workingman the blessing of safe life insurance at a low cost." His detailed explanation of the proposed remedy was soon published by *Collier's*. Written with the zest of a muckraker and promoted by many liberals, the article received wide national publicity and was discussed and reprinted in numerous newspapers.

Brandeis knew the conservatism of bankers and proceeded to break down their resistance to the plan. Carrying on his campaign with great tact and energy, he succeeded in converting key men in various communities. With their help he formed the Massachusetts Savings-Bank Insurance League. Such public-spirited men as William L. Douglas, former governor and large shoe manufacturer, helped him persuade certain bank officials to give the plan a trial as soon as it was legalized. Labor leaders also promoted the idea both within their unions and before the legislative committees considering it. This mass support, made vocal and insistent by Brandeis's prodding, gradually persuaded the legislature and the governor, and the bill enpowering savings banks to issue life insurance was passed in June 1907.

This law Brandeis considered his "greatest achievement." He retained his interest in this form of low-cost insurance to the end of his life and continued to offer advice and assistance at every opportunity. Although the Massachusetts savings banks were slow to open insurance departments and made little effort to compete with the large insurance companies, the effect of the law was to force these companies to lower their rates by 20 percent and to provide their policy holders with other advantages. Years later the state of New York enacted a similar law to lower the cost of life insurance.

Brandeis early began to be troubled by the monopolistic tendency of American business enterprise. As counsel and adviser for various corporations he knew that bigness in itself was not necessarily an advantage and might be a handicap. An ardent democrat and a strong proponent of genuine competition, he could not but deplore the frantic efforts at amalgamation and consolidation on the part of leading bankers and industrialists. He was convinced that the organizers of trusts were interested not so much in furthering efficiency as in stifling competition—a matter highly inimical to the soundness of the nation's economy. "Human nature is such," he insisted, "that monopolies, however well intentioned, and however well regulated, inevitably become, in the course of time, oppressive, arbitrary, unprogressive, and inefficient."

When the New Haven Railroad Company began, at the turn of the century, to consolidate all transportation facilities in New England under its control, Brandeis was at once alarmed and on the alert. No opportunity to fight its monopolistic activities presented itself to him until 1905, when General Samuel C. Lawrence and his son William, large stockholders in the Boston and Maine Railroad Company, asked him to serve as counsel in their effort to prevent the projected merger of that railroad with the New

Haven. Brandeis accepted the case, but refused a fee on the ground that the effort was affected with a public interest—subsequently paying over $25,000 of his own money to his partners as their share of the remuneration to which he would have been entitled. He at once began to campaign against the merger, publicizing its undesirable consequences and arguing against it at legislative hearings. "There is for a community," he wrote, "a general limit where efficiency can be reached by consolidation. To that point I am in favor of it, but I am now, and always have been, directly opposed to distinct monopoly." Nevertheless the forces backing the New Haven were powerful and privileged, and the legislature did their bidding. Brandeis was criticized as a "chronic howler" and ignored.

Defeat neither discouraged nor intimidated him. It was plain to him that the New Haven's monopolistic aims would prove disastrous not only to the people it served but also to its numerous small stockholders. As in other cases, he proceeded to familiarize himself with the company's operations. When President Charles S. Mellen refused to supply him with certain information, he dug it out of state and federal and stock-exchange reports—spending $6000 of his own money for this statistical study. The more he learned about the New Haven's intricate business manipulations the more certain he became of the unsoundness of its financial foundations. He was appalled at the thought that it continued to pay its customary 8-percent dividend in 1907 despite the fact that the earnings for that year in no way justified it.

It became perfectly clear to me that Mellen was putting out reports for the purpose of misleading the public and the stockholders as to the New Haven's condition. I worked this thing up and continued working it up and with this result: I found that the New Haven didn't earn the dividend which it paid last year.

His findings, issued in pamphlet form, quickly gained wide circulation. He was sharply attacked by both interested leading citizens and paid publicists as a vicious meddler and irresponsible muckraker. They accused him of seeking to undermine the New Haven's reputation for the benefit of its rivals and that he was thereby hurting widows and public institutions that depended on the company's dividends for their existence. But Brandeis's friends and admirers were not idle. They helped him form the Massachusetts Anti-Merger League and furthered his efforts to block New Haven bills in the legislature. E. A. Filene, answering insinuations concerning Brandeis's motives in fighting the Mellen administration without a fee, pointed out that his friend was in effect contributing $50,000 in time to the public good instead of a check for that amount to charity as other men of means were doing. Nor was Brandeis himself intimidated from keeping close tab on the financial condition of the railroad or from publicizing the fact that it continued to pay its 8-percent dividend in 1908 despite the deficit it incurred in doing so. When a state committee headed by Charles Francis Adams approved the merger with the Boston and Maine, the "counsel for the people" was quick to point out that members of this committee owned New Haven stock and were biased in its favor.

The battle against the Mellen organization continued unabated, seesawing between victory for the Brandeis group and triumph for the New Haven management. In 1909 the Republican administrations both in Massachusetts and in Washington favored the railroad. The next year Brandeis, having become a warm friend of Senator La Follette, inspired him to deliver a Senate attack on the New Haven that made it a national issue. Some time later another state committee of experts gave the road a clean bill of financial health—causing its paid publicists jeeringly to recall Brandeis's pamphlet containing his "reckless assault upon the finances of the company." His comment on that slur, made to Norman Hapgood, proved to be an epitaph:

Mellen was a masterful man, resourceful, courageous, broad of view. He fired the imagination of New England, but being oblique of vision merely distorted its judgment and silenced its conscience. For a while

he triumphed with impunity over laws human and divine, but as he was obsessed with the delusion that two and two make five he fell at last a victim of the relentless rules of humble arithmetic.
Remember, O Stranger,
Arithmetic is the first of the sciences and the mother of safety.

By this time Brandeis knew that the New Haven's obligations were three times its capital stock; that its funded indebtedness had increased more than elevenfold in fifteen years and amounted to two and a half times the market value of stock outstanding. He continued to publish interviews, make speeches, and argue at hearings on the company's mismanagement by a board of directors that insisted on attaining monopoly and bigness at any price. By 1912 Mellen was no longer able to conceal the railroad's financial distress. In paid newspaper advertisements, however, he blamed Brandeis for New Haven's ills. "The cry of monopoly is an appeal to prejudice," he declared, "not to experience or judgment."

The election of Woodrow Wilson in 1912 made possible an impartial investigation of the New Haven by the Interstate Commerce Commission. The hearings that began in April 1913 brought out that the Mellen administration had made various false bookkeeping entries and that the phony sale and repurchase of Boston and Maine stock several years back had netted one man a profit of $2,700,000 without a cent of investment. Unable to defend these actions, the company sought to confuse matters by digging into Brandeis's early career and accusing him of unethical practices as far back as 1892. In newspaper advertisements, signed by Mellen, it insinuated that he was unprincipled and venal. "The people of New England are asking who is the man higher up? Who will pay Mr. Brandeis for depressing New Haven stock at a cost of millions of dollars to New England stockholders? Who is behind Brandeis? He had done this before." The company also paid C. W. Barron $133,000 in seven months for publishing a number of articles favorable to itself and highly critical of Brandeis. But the I. C. C. report, issued on July 9, placed the blame where it belonged: "Had the stockholders of the New Haven, instead of vilifying the road's critics, given some attention to the charges made, their property would today be of greater value and the problem an easier one."

Meantime the New Haven was forced to cut its dividend to 6 percent. Its financial structure continued to deteriorate, however, and at last Mellen was forced to resign. Brandeis nevertheless maintained that the root of the evil remained untouched. At his urging Senator Norris introduced a resolution in January 1914 calling for a new investigation of the New Haven by the I. C. C. At the hearings it was made clear that the financial operations of the board of directors, controlled by the late J. P. Morgan, were both "reckless and profligate." So strong was the evidence to this effect that the Attorney-General filed a bill for the dissolution of the New Haven system. Not till 1927 was the railroad in a position to resume paying dividends. Commenting on the evil consequences of banker interference in the railroad's management, Brandeis stated:

Bankers are credited with being a conservative force in the community. The tradition lingers that they are pre-eminently "safe and sound." And yet, the most grievous fault of this banker-managed railroad has already brought heavy losses to many thousands of small investors throughout New England for whom bankers are supposed to be natural guardians.

Brandeis's crusade against monopoly and bigness further antagonized New England's wealthy conservatives when he began to fight the "tying-clause" in the sales contracts of the United Shoe Machinery Company. To these economic aristocrats his action was a crass betrayal of trust. The facts were, indeed, that when the United was formed in 1899 by an amalgamation of several firms, Brandeis became a member of the board of directors in order to represent the interests of one of his clients who had entered into the consolidation. Contrary to his custom, moreover, he also invested $10,000 in the company's preferred stock. In 1906, as one of its counsel, he argued in favor of its tie-in sales policy.

187

At that time Brandeis still believed that trusts could be good for the economy as well as bad and that the United was good because it was efficient and served the interests of shoe manufacturers. Soon after, however, he was informed by some of his clients who dealt with the United that the tying-clause restricted their operations. He immediately urged Sidney Winslow, president of the trust, to modify the objectionable clause. When the latter, after months of procrastination, finally refused, Brandeis resigned both as director and as counsel.

For the next three and a half years he deliberately refused to act professionally for or against the United. Then, in 1910, he advised a client that the tying-clause was probably illegal in the light of recent court rulings and that he might safely buy the superior machines from T. J. Plant, a new manufacturer. The United then exerted pressure upon friendly bankers not to renew a loan to Plant, thereby forcing him to sell his business. Brandeis observed this financial maneuver with increasing alarm and indignation. To Senator La Follette he wrote: "The United Company's purchase of Plant's business, practically the only competitor in shoe machinery, was the most flagrant instance of violating the antitrust law that I have known."

Now ready to fight the United, he agreed to serve as counsel to the Shoe Manufacturers' Alliance without a fee. Meantime the federal government sued the corporation for violating the Sherman Act, and the governor of Massachusetts openly condemned its monopolistic practices. Congressional committees also interested themselves in its affairs. Brandeis was consulted by these officials and he testified at their hearings. President Winslow, eager to vitiate this testimony, declared that it was "grossly inaccurate and wilfully untrue" and that it was motivated by ethical inconsistency and selfish aims. The United also published a pamphlet entitled "The Reversible Mind of Louis D. Brandeis," which sought to discredit him by means of cleverly juxtaposed statements taken out of context. The attack concluded as follows: "Inasmuch as the company's methods and policies are the same today as then, the reversed attitude of Mr. Brandeis is open to but one interpretation."

It can be argued, of course, that Brandeis should have perceived the nature of the tying-clause long before 1906; that as a critic of monopoly he should never have consented to serve as director; that by acting for the corporation when he had already become the "counsel for the people," he exposed himself to insinuations having a modicum of validity. In the totality of his behavior, however, he cannot fairly be accused of more than a change of mind on the trust issue; in this case, as in others, he acquitted himself effectively as a fighter of monopoly.

Brandeis had no real contact with labor until he was at the height of his career as a corporation lawyer. Always sympathetic toward the poor and the underprivileged, he began to concern himself with the lot of workingmen after he had become familiar with the writings of Henry George and Henry D. Lloyd. The brutal Homestead strike in 1892 awakened his interest in industrial relations:

I think it was the affair at Homestead which first set me thinking seriously about the labor problem. It took the shock of that battle, where organized capital hired a private army to shoot at organized labor for resisting an arbitrary cut in wages, to turn my mind definitely toward a searching study of the relations of labor to industry.

Once his mind seized upon a subject he never let go until he had probed it to his satisfaction. He took every opportunity to observe workers in industry, to read books on labor economics, to discuss the subject with men who have given their lives to the advancement of the poor. He was soon convinced that trade unions were essential to the welfare of their members and that recognition by employers would make them responsible. In 1902 he declared: "If unions are lawless, restrain and punish their lawlessness; if they are arbitrary, repress their arbitrariness; if their demands are unreasonable or unjust, resist them; but do not oppose unions as such." In the same year he debated with Samuel Gompers on the issue of union incorporation and antagonized numerous labor leaders by his stand that incorporation would make unions less irresponsible and therefore more acceptable to employers. At about the same time, at Lloyd's urging, he helped prepare the case of the striking coal miners for consideration by a committee chosen by President Roosevelt.

In his study of the coal strike Brandeis perceived that the root of labor unrest lay not so much in low wages as in irregular employment. It surprised him to discover that neither side had ever given serious thought to this grievous problem; that both employers and workers accepted it as unavoidable. He at once began to discuss the matter with government officials and with clients who were large-scale employers and to stress the importance of annual earnings rather than hourly wages. In more than one instance he demonstrated to employer-clients the over-all advantage of steady employment and ways and means of eliminating seasonal peaks and depressions.

He also sought to persuade employers of the logic and desirability of accepting the trade union as an integral part of labor relations. In a democracy, he maintained, "we must avoid industrial absolutism, even though it be benevolent despotism." If the worker was to be a worthy citizen, he must be economically secure and in possession of the leisure to educate himself concerning his rights and responsibilities.

Politically, the American worker is free—so far as law can make him so. But is he really free? Can any man be really free who is constantly in danger of becoming dependent for mere subsistence upon somebody or something else than his own exertion and conduct? Men are not free while financially dependent upon the will of other individuals. Financial dependence is consistent with freedom only where claim to support rests upon right, and not upon favor.

Such ideas were then—and now—considered radical and dangerous. Few employers were broadminded enough to deal democratically with their workers. The large majority subscribed to the views of George E. Baer, leading coal-mine operator, who in 1902 asserted that employers were "Christian men to whom God in his infinite wisdom has given the control of the property interests of the country." Brandeis in his dealings with industrialists again and again met with this self-righteous egotism. Personally little moved by lust for money or power, he often recoiled from such callousness. After settling a strike in 1907 he wrote to his brother: "I am experiencing a growing conviction that the labor men are the most congenial company. The intense materialism and luxuriousness of most of our other people makes their company quite irksome."

He was equally disturbed by the social insensibility of certain judges—those who clung to the dead letter of the law and ignored the new industrial society knocking on the courtroom doors. Both lawyers and judges were in the habit of considerng labor abstractly, largely in the light of established principles of property rights and the freedom of contract and hardly at all from the standpoint of everyday conditions and human welfare. When the Supreme Court in 1905 invalidated a New York ten-hour law for bakers, the majority failed to consider the effect of long hours in a hot bakery on the health of its employees and maintained that the law in question was "mere meddlesome interference with the rights of individuals."

Eager to demonstrate the fallacy of this assumption, Brandeis two years later readily accepted the opportunity to defend the Oregon ten-hour law for women workers. At that time twenty states had similar laws in effect and the issue appeared paramount. He immediately engaged his sister-in-law Josephine Goldmark of the National Consumers League to gather and digest reports and statistics on the effects of overwork on the health of women. These social and medical data, obtained from various sources the world over, he studied and sifted until he was able to present them with the force of irresistible logic. In his long brief he depended very little on law and precedent—devoting almost his entire argument to the pertinent facts, bolstered by "the world's experience," of overwork on the well-being of women. Sweeping aside the abstraction of the freedom of contract, he shocked the Justices out of their legalistic lethargy into an acquiescence in the realities of modern industrialism.

The success of Brandeis's novel brief gave a sudden sharp turn to the course of American social legislation. Although certain conservative judges persisted in clinging to the obsolescent abstractions of a past era, the facts of industrial life had established their pertinence in the nation's highest courtroom. Brandeis and others after him argued successfully a number of similar cases, both state and federal. And although he failed to validate the Oregon minimum-wage law in 1914, many competent observers felt that, in the words of Judge William Hitz, "he not only *reached* the Court, but he *dwarfed the Court,* because it was clear that here stood a man who knew infinitely more, and who cared infinitely more, for the vital daily rights of the people than the men who sat there sworn to protect them."

Brandeis's efforts in behalf of social legislation enhanced his reputation as a friend of labor. When the 1910 cloakmaker strike in New York became deadlocked and the suffering of tens of thousands of strikers and their families gained the attention of social workers and certain public-spirited citizens, Brandeis was persuaded to forego his vacation in order to serve as mediator. It did not take him long to sense the tension and distrust that separated the strikers from their employers. The sweatshop drudges, rebelling against years of exploitation and wretchedness, were desperately demanding humane treatment and the closed shop; the employers, for the most part petty manufacturers caught in the vicious circle of cut-throat competition, saw no way of granting union terms and remaining in business. Nor was there a common meeting ground. The intense antagonism dividing the hot-headed extremists on both sides gave little promise of amicable agreement.

Contact with these immigrant Jews in the garment industry proved a revelation to Brandeis. He saw them for the first time in all their poverty and aggressiveness, in all their crudeness and idealism—and he strongly sympathized with their yearning for the good life. Capitalizing on his prestige among them and employing subtle tact and soft speech, he slowly calmed their fears and quieted their prejudices. He gingerly skirted the inflammable issues and dealt first with the questions less open to disagreement. When he finally brought them to a consideration of the pivotal problem of the closed shop, he offered a compromise solution that proved a milestone in the history of organized labor. Having always opposed the closed shop as undemocratic and inimical to the public good, he proposed in its place "the preferential union shop." This he defined as a shop in which union standards and conditions prevailed and in which the employer, in hiring labor, gave preference to union members if they "are equal in efficiency to any non-union applicants." The manufacturers, anxious to resume production and relieved of the closed-shop nightmare, were soon persuaded; the radical strike leaders, sensing danger in compromise, balked. It took considerable inducement on Brandeis's part and the forceful aid of Louis Marshall, the influential Jewish leader, to bring the strikers to accept the settlement.

The "protocol" ending the strike bore the earmarks of Brandeis's humanitarian views and became a notable document in the history of labor-management relations. Among other things it rid the industry of the evil sweatshop system, increased wages, limited the workweek to fifty hours, created a joint board of sanitary control, permitted neither the strike nor the lockout, and established machinery for the settlement of future grievances. Brandeis agreed to serve as chairman of the board of arbitration, but made it clear that he would consider only matters of basic policy. In the ensuing five years he sought valiantly to keep the protocol in effect despite the critical attitude of certain turbulent officials and the increasing dissatisfaction on both sides. When it finally broke down in 1916, there was general relief. Brandeis, about to join the Supreme Court, had no choice but to acquiesce in the termination of this pioneer effort at industrial mediation. He did have the satisfaction of having kept a major part of the garment industry free from strikes for six years.

The political insurgency that preceded the revolt against the boss-ridden Republican party and the election of the liberal Woodrow Wilson also brought Brandeis onto the national scene. His reputation as a highly successful "counsel for the people" made him a logical choice as the lawyer for the conservationists in the Congressional hearings of charges made against Secretary of the Interior Richard A. Ballinger. Norman Hapgood, editor of *Collier's*, having published an anti-Ballinger article by Louis R. Glavis, the official dismissed by the Secretary, and fearing a libel suit if the latter were vindicated, engaged Brandeis as counsel for Glavis.

Brandeis immediately concentrated on a careful study of the scope and functions of the Department of the Interior. Weeks of research and reading made him so familiar with its detailed activities that at the hearings he was able to prompt witnesses concerning their duties as officials in the Department. His astute mind soon discovered damaging discrepancies in the evidence offered by the government. Examination of newspaper files and various personal inquiries yielded him information that tended to substantiate his brilliant surmises. But the Committee majority, friendly to Ballinger, refused to aid him in the procurement of telltale documents and hampered his interrogation of witnesses. Fortunately for him, Representative George Norris had succeeded in placing three of his liberal colleagues on the Committee, and they again and again blocked the majority's efforts at a "whitewash." Brandeis, on his part, patiently ignored Senatorial insults and skillfully eliminated obstacles placed in his way.

After weeks of fruitless interrogation Brandeis began to direct his questioning toward certain dates and documents pertaining to Glavis's dismissal. With the aid of simple arithmetic and a knowledge of the man involved he had early perceived that Attorney-

General George W. Wickersham could not possibly have mastered Glavis's 74-page memorandum and written his "Summary and Report" for President Taft within five days as officially stated. He therefore assumed that someone else had prepared President Taft's letter justifying Glavis's dismissal and that Wickersham's report exonerating Ballinger was predated to cover up this action. His persistent queries, however, at first brought only denials from officials on the stand. His quest appeared futile—when help came unexpectedly from a young stenographer who knew the facts and was unable to quiet his conscience. He disclosed that President Taft's letter was written by Assistant Attorney-General Oscar Lawlor in Ballinger's office. Wickersham thereupon immediately sent a copy of the revelatory letter to the Committee. The White House, unaware of this action, issued a quick denial, insisting that the stenographer's statement was "absolutely without foundation" —only to admit the truth the next day.

Conservative members of the Committee were incensed at Brandeis for having caught President Taft in an untruth. Senator Elihu Root shouted in anger: "We are not here to investigate the President of the United States! We are here to investigate the Department of the Interior. Counsel has been endeavoring assiduously and not altogether ingeniously to lead the investigation into a trial of the President." Brandeis was painfully aware of the powerful enemies he was making in his relentless pursuit of the truth, but the public good was his primary concern. His closing brief was a noteworthy document. As he later restated it in part:

This investigation has been referred to as a struggle for conservation, as a struggle against the special interests. It is that: but it is far more. In its essence, it is the struggle for democracy, the struggle of the small man against the overpowering influence of the big; politically as well as financially, the struggle to establish the right of every American to equal justice in the public service as well as in the courts, that no official is so highly stationed that he may trample ruthlessly and unjustly upon even the humblest American citizen.

The Committee delayed its report for months and then cleared Ballinger by a vote of seven to five. This was bitterly criticized by minority members on the floor of the House and by liberals the country over. So persistent was this public agitation against the whitewash that Ballinger was forced to resign, thus ending a significant chapter in the struggle for the conservation of the nation's natural resources.

If Brandeis multiplied his enemies among the privileged and the conservatives, he gained many admirers among public-spirited liberals. Senator La Follette, Representative Norris, and other progressive government officials became his close friends and began to depend upon him for advice and assistance. As the country's outstanding liberal lawyer he was asked to serve in practically every important case affecting the public interest.

One such case concerned the application of the railroads north of Ohio and east of the Mississippi for a rate increase. The I. C. C., in need of counsel to protect the interest of the public, persuaded Brandeis to serve. By the time the hearings began he had completely mastered the railroad business. Taking full advantage of the new Mann-Elkins Act, which put the burden of proof upon the railroad officials, he questioned them with a disconcerting insistence on matters that revealed their relative inefficiency and incompetence in their operation of the railroads. He had by then become an enthusiastic advocate of scientific management in industry and made the startling assertion that if these managers were as interested in reducing costs as they were in raising rates and paying higher dividends they could save a million dollars a day— more than they would receive from the requested rate increase. When railroad presidents indignantly denied the possibility of such economies, he pointed out, among other things, that they were carelessly prodigal with both labor and supplies and that they were overpaying for steel and other materials because these commodities were controlled by the same bankers who dominated the railroads. He then placed eminent efficiency experts and Western railroad officials on the stand to give detailed corroboration to his criticisms. The ruffled and roiled magnates tried to scoff at the proposed economies, but failed to weaken the effect of his argument.

In his final brief Brandeis elaborated upon his proposal that the railroads substitute efficiency methods for rules of thumb and "practices hallowed by age and tradition"; that they eliminate waste, "whether of time or of effort or of material."

The investigation has developed clearly that the railroad to meet any existing needs should look not without but within. If their net is insufficient, the proper remedy is not higher rates, resulting in higher costs and lessened business, but scientific management, resulting in lower rates, in higher wages, and increased business.

Six weeks later the I. C. C. unanimously denied the higher rates. The shippers, saved nearly two hundred million dollars annually, hailed the decision and lauded Brandeis. The liberal newspapers also applauded this victory over big business. Wall Street leaders, however, denounced the action as unwarranted and detrimental to business. And in their view Brandeis was guilty of extreme radicalism.

In May 1913 the same railroads again asked for a rate increase. Although Brandeis was then known as "the most liked and most hated man at the Bar in America," the I. C. C. once more turned to him for assistance. It wanted him to be "the general channel through whom the view of others opposing the proposed advance may be presented of record." When criticism of his appointment persisted, the chairman of the Commission explained:

Mr. Brandeis is not employed as an advocate for any special interests, but is employed to assist the Commission in analysis of the big general question which underlies this proposal by the railroads. We see no reason why anyone should assume that his employment can disadvantageously affect any interest.

To bring himself up to date, Brandeis once more delved into railroad reports, economic studies, and technical memoranda. In addition to seeking ways of increasing operational efficiency, he particularly investigated the cost of free services and unnecessary gratuities. At the hearings his searching questions proved embarrassing to both large shippers and railroad officials, but the answers apprised the public of practices and manipulations of doubtful ethics and obvious inefficiency. To offset the unanswerable facts, Ivy Lee, public relations counsel for the railroads, led a barrage of unfavorable publicity against the Commission and its counsel. Brandeis's questioning also antagonized some of the opponents of the rate increase. When he finally concluded that the net income of the petitioning railroads was "smaller than is consistent with their assured prosperity and the welfare of the community," but that there were other ways of remedying the situation than by a horizontal increase, Clifford Thorne, representing the Midwestern shippers, harshly criticized him for favoring the railroads. The majority of the Commission, however, followed Brandeis's recommendations. It was only after World War I had upset the economy that the railroads were allowed a sufficient increase to assure their financial fluidity.

More than most of his contemporaries, Brandeis was deeply troubled by the problem of bigness in business. A firm believer in genuine competition and industrial efficiency, he maintained that some of the large railroads and gigantic corporations had "far exceeded the limit of greatest efficiency." When he was asked in 1911 to testify before the Senate Committee on Interstate Commerce, he stated his views on the trust problem with discerning frankness. He dwelt on the vicious effect of the so-called money trust—the group of Wall Street financiers and their allies who were able by means of their control of the country's liquid capital to dominate the affairs and policies of most of the large corporations. These powerful men, he insisted, were interested chiefly in dividends, in raising the values of stocks and bonds, and not in the long-term welfare of either industry or the nation.

The trust problem can never be settled right for the American people by looking at it through the spectacles of bonds and stocks. You must study it through the spectacles of the people's rights and people's interests; must consider the effect upon the development of the American democracy. When you do that you will realize the extraordinary perils to our institutions which attend the trusts; you will realize the danger of letting the people learn that our sacred Constitution protects not only vested rights but vested wrongs.

He further declared that, common assumption to the contrary, monopoly was "inefficient both economically and socially." In a large, monopolistic business, with a multitude of complex problems, the man at the head usually possessed a diminishing knowledge of the underlying facts and consequently a lesser opportunity to exercise good judgment on them. Indeed, "there develops a centrifugal force greater than the centripetal forces."

An even greater evil in his eyes was the attitude of trusts toward their employees. Democracy, he explained, thrives only when men are free; and men are not free without industrial liberty. By refusing their workers the right to organize, corporations were denying them the essential rights in a living democracy. "Without the right to organize, short hours, high wages, and the best of working conditions, whether introduced by legislation or by the welfare departments of great corporations, can do no more than to make slavery luxurious." He ridiculed the claim that a nonunion policy favored efficiency. Real efficiency, he asserted, was never obtained by repression and intimidation; it came only with the development of cooperative effort in the individual worker.

Some months later Brandeis had a further opportunity to express himself on the labor policies of trusts when he was asked to assist another Congressional committee in an investigation of the United States Steel Corporation. Judge E. H. Gary, its chairman of the board, had testified boastfully that its labor policy "compares favorably with that of any line of industry in this country or any other country at the present time or any period in the history of the world." Brandeis countered this assertion with the information that the corporation employed tens of thousands of men twelve hours a day and seven days a week at bare subsistence wages—a system more onerous and more degrading than Negro slavery ever was. He further criticized the firm's brutal repression of any effort at union organization among its employees. "All the power of capital and all the ability and intelligence of the men who wield and who serve the capital have been used to make practically slaves of these operatives." Such industrial oppression, he concluded, was "alien to American conditions" and intolerable on American soil.

The 1912 election enabled Brandeis to inject his antitrust views into the political campaign. Because he considered La Follette "the best statesman we have for the accomplishment of the reforms that are needed at this time," he readily joined the National Progressive Republican League in order to promote his candidacy for President. During the spring he spoke in La Follette's behalf in a number of Midwestern cities. When the Senator was sidetracked in favor of Theodore Roosevelt, Brandeis balked. He did not consider the latter a real progressive and did not agree with his trust policy.

When Woodrow Wilson was nominated, Brandeis hailed him as a genuine progressive. At Wilson's invitation he visited him on August 28 and explained his views on trusts. When Wilson came to Boston several weeks later, the two again discussed campaign issues. Subsequently he telegraphed Brandeis: "Please set forth as explicitly as possible the actual measures by which competition can be efficiently regulated. The more explicit we are on this point, the more completely the enemy's guns will be spiked." Shortly thereafter Brandeis published in *Collier's* a series of editorials and signed articles that defined and highlighted the basic issues of the campaign. He was especially critical of Roosevelt for acquiescing in the legalization of monopoly and attacked George Perkins for his business tactics—insisting that one cannot "serve both God and Mammon."

President-elect Wilson felt very grateful to Brandeis and wished to offer him a Cabinet post. Highly placed Bostonians and a number of powerful politicians immediately expressed their shock at the very idea and accused him of unfitness for so high an office. Although an investigation by Hapgood readily disproved the charges and insinuations made against Brandeis, Wilson was persuaded on grounds of party harmony not to make the appointment. He did offer him the chairmanship of the new Commission on Industrial Relations, but Brandeis refused. He preferred instead to serve as informal adviser to Wilson and several members of the Cabinet. During the fight on the currency bill he persuaded its proponents not to yield to the bankers but to insist along with Bryan on governmental control of the currency. He was even more influential in the antitrust legislation, and his ideas prevailed in both the Clayton Act and the bill authorizing the Federal Trade Commission. "The fearless course is the wise one," he counseled Wilson, and the President acted accordingly.

In 1914 Brandeis's views on banking and business were given permanent form in two books, *Other People's Money and How the Bankers Use It* and *Business—a Profession.* The first consisted of a series of pungent and provocative articles which had previously appeared in *Harper's Weekly;* the second volume was a collection of papers and speeches reflecting his activities as business analyst and social critic. Eager to further the cause of Wilson's New Freedom, he used the Pujo Committee report on Wall Street finance to strike hard at the evils which the currency bill under debate sought to remedy. After stressing the fact that the large New York banks controlled corporations capitalized at more than twenty-two billion dollars, he wrote:

These banker-barons levy, through their excessive exactions, a heavy toll upon the whole community; upon owners of money for leave to invest it; upon railroads, public service and industrial companies, for leave to use this money of other people, and, through these corporations, upon consumers. . . . More serious, however, is the effect of the Money Trust in directly suppressing competition. That suppression enables the monopolist to extract excessive profits; but monopoly increases the burden of the consumer in other ways. Monopoly arrests development; and through arresting development prevents that lessening of the cost of production and of distribution which would otherwise take place.

His criticism of interlocking directorates was particularly stringent. The problem was currently under heated debate and its solution was to be attempted in the projected antitrust legislation. Brandeis urged the prohibition of the practice.

The practice of interlocking directorates is the root of many evils. It offends laws human and divine. Applied to rival corporations, it tends to the suppression of competition and to violation of the Sherman Law. Applied to corporations which deal with each other, it tends to disloyalty and to violation of the fundamental law that no man can serve two masters. In either event it tends to inefficiency; for it removes incentive and destroys soundness of judgment. . . . It is the most potent instrument of the money trust.

Nor did he favor the spread of stock-ownership, then coming into favor. In his view such extension, instead of helping to democratize business, was in fact "absentee ownership of the worst kind." The small stockholder, knowing that he had little or no influence upon the company, tended to assume no responsibility whatever and to be interested only in dividends. This condition permitted the management to exercise absolute control without any corresponding responsibility except to assure dividends to the stockholders.

Another of his criticisms, which he frequently reiterated, was directed against the general assumption that bigness in industry made for efficiency. He maintained that every business had a unit of greatest efficiency and grew less efficient as it exceeded that particular norm. Thus "most of the trusts which did not secure monopolistic positions have failed to show marked success or efficiency, as compared with independent competing concerns." He cited the United States Steel Corporation as a conspicuous example. The cost of steel had risen markedly since its formation a decade earlier, while that of European steel makers remained unchanged, so that American exports declined sharply during that period.

Brandeis also advocated compulsory and full publicity regarding new issues of stock, maintaining that the facts should be stated clearly and in large type in order to minimize the dangers of fraud and unsound speculation. This idea proved too novel even for the New Freedom proponents and remained ignored until the advent of the New Deal.

These and other of his criticisms and proposals, expressed in articles, books, speeches, and at public hearings, received careful attention from the men in power during the Wilson Administration. They deferred to his intimate knowledge of the trust problem and they respected his zeal in furthering the rights of the individual in the face of the absolute power of the industrial leviathans. Taking advantage of his influential position, he strongly advocated the democratization of business. He insisted that labor be given the right freely to organize and that no corporation be permitted to become "larger than is consistent with the public interest." He proposed, what in 1914 seemed a revolutionary concept, that "the State must in some way come to the aid of the workingmen if democratization [of business] is to be secured."

The social world for which we are striving is an incident of our democracy, not the main end. It is rather the result of democracy—perhaps its finest expression—but it rests upon democracy, which implies the rule of the people. And therefore the end for which we must strive is the attainment of the rule by the people, and that involves industrial democracy as well as political democracy.

Brought up in a liberal, nonreligious atmosphere, Brandeis knew little of Judaism and had scant interest in Jews as such. He had never attended a synagogue service and belonged to no Jewish organization. Although he felt a strong attachment to his family and greatly admired his uncle Lewis Dembitz, who was both a Zionist and a student of Jewish lore, he made no effort to participate in the activities of the Jewish community in Boston. He early became a part of the exclusive Brahmin circle and limited his friendships largely to its members. Not that he denied his Jewish origin or refused to contribute to worthy Jewish causes; it was merely that his interests and predilections lay elsewhere.

When his concern for social reform led him to oppose the customary franchise privileges demanded by certain corporations, and particularly after he had begun his attack upon the New Haven's efforts at monopoly, he found himself no longer welcome in homes where he had previously been courted. These privileged Bostonians resented his tampering with their vested rights and showed their displeasure by shunning him socially. More than one suddenly remembered his personal origin and referred to his "oriental" mind. The thrust cut deep. Reflection made him resentful, but it also caused him to probe the nature of the slur. The more he learned about antisemitism the more sympathetic he felt toward his fellow Jews. Always ready to fight injustice and prejudice, ever inclined to follow a problem to its source, he soon familiarized himself with the history of the long-suffering Jewish people.

In his role as mediator in the New York cloakmaker strike he came to respect the Jewish immigrant workers. He found them wretchedly poor, ignorant of the language and customs of their new environment, either steeped in their spiritual past or aglow with the ideal of the cooperative commonwealth. Thinking about them, he began to feel close to them, to admire their intellectual zestfulness, to sympathize with their just grievances. It was this bond that made him give so much of his time and thought to the problem of industrial peace in the garment industry.

Brandeis's interest in Zionism was a logical consequence of his New York experience. When the idea of a Jewish homeland came to his attention, he embraced it as a desirable solution to the problem of finding relief for the oppressed European Jews. It was not till March 1913, however, that he made his first public avowal of Zionism by serving as chairman at a reception in honor of Nahum Sokolow, a leading European Zionist.

In 1914 the plight of the Jews along the battlefronts of Eastern Europe forced Brandeis to act in their behalf. Never one to do things casually, and impelled by the emergency to plunge whole-heartedly into the breach, he went to New York late in August to attend a Zionist conference and accepted the chairmanship of the Provisional Executive Committee for Zionist Affairs, which was to replace the stranded Zionist organization in Europe. He was very frank in stating why he agreed to serve:

I feel my disqualification for this task. Throughout long years which represented my own life, I have been to a great extent separated from Jews. I am very ignorant in things Jewish. But recent experiences, public and professional, have taught me this: I find Jews possessed of those very qualities which we of the twentieth century seek to de-velop in our struggle for justice and democracy; a deep moral feeling which makes them capable of noble acts; a deep sense of the brother-hood of man; and a high intelligence, the fruit of three thousand years of civilization.

Himself exemplifying these worthy traits, he threw himself into the work with his wonted intensity. The first to donate a thousand dollars to the emergency fund, he toured the Jewish communities in a number of cities in an effort to collect money and to further the cause of Zionism. In his speeches he stressed the need of Jews to exercise the rights common to others—the right to live where they wished, the consistency of Zionism with Americanism, the duty of Jews to advance Palestinian settlement regardless of whether or not they wanted to live there themselves. "Indeed, loyalty to America demands rather that each American Jew be-come a Zionist. For only through the ennobling effect of its striv-ings can we develop the best that is in us and give to this country the full benefit of our great inheritance."

For more than two years he devoted a large part of his time to Jewish affairs—ending his concentrated activity only upon assum-ing his duties as Justice. Always the democrat, he fought energeti-cally for the establishment of a congress that would represent every faction within the Jewish community and strongly disagreed with the wealthy leaders of the American Jewish Committee who wanted only a conference of a few selected organizations. In 1916 he emerged victorious when the delegates from twenty-six groups assembled to form the Jewish Congress.

Yet his success as a leader was gained at considerable cost to his popularity among Zionist officials. For all his sympathy and insight, he found it difficult to exercise patience with those who were bent on presenting their own views rather than cooperating with others. Moreover, making scientific use of his own time and expending his great energy with remarkable efficiency, he tended to make equally severe demands upon his associates. His insistence on careful attention to details, on regular and specific reports from committees and subordinates, and on the prompt payment of pledges—matters previously carried out only laxly and haphazardly —gave his leadership the semblance of "autocratic" arrogance.

Although he resigned his active Zionist offices on becoming a Justice of the Supreme Court, he retained his deep interest in Zionism and devoted his free time to its advancement. When the question of a Jewish homeland in Palestine became a live issue among the Allied diplomats in 1917, he took the initiative in discussing the matter with President Wilson and the British Foreign Secretary Arthur Balfour. He was also in frequent communication with Chaim Weitzmann and other eminent British Jews and helped greatly in the preparation and general acceptance of the Balfour Declaration on Palestine, announced in November 1917. Two months later, when England sent a commission to Palestine headed by Weitzmann, Brandeis wrote to him to stress the socio-economic objectives:

The utmost vigilance should be exercised to prevent the acquisition by private persons of land, water rights or other natural resources, or any concessions for public utilities. These must all be secured for the whole Jewish people. In other ways, as well as this, the possibility of capitalistic exploitation must be guarded against.

These recommendations were enthusiastically adopted by the 1918 convention of the Zionist organization.

At the end of the Supreme Court term in June 1919 Brandeis

sailed for Europe. He visited England and France and consulted with leading Zionists and peace delegates. Then he went to Palestine by way of Egypt. His tour of the promised Jewish homeland greatly strengthened his enthusiasm for Zionism. The potential prospects of the eroded and arid land excited his optimism and he called it "a miniature California." To his wife he wrote: "The problems and difficulties are serious and numerous—even more so than I had anticipated; but there is none which will not be solved and overcome by the indomitable spirit of the Jews here and elsewhere." On his return to the United States he reported his findings to the Zionist convention and urged economic and agricultural rehabilitation of the ancient land of Israel. He also exerted himself to invalidate the secret Sykes-Pecot Treaty, which gave part of Palestine to Syria, and persuaded President Wilson to write from his sickbed to Lloyd George requesting rectification of the Palestinian boundary. This was done at the San Remo Conference.

In July 1920 Brandeis attended the world Zionist convention in London. One of the leading participants, he insisted on practical action to strengthen the Jewish position in Palestine and clashed with those who were primarily interested in that country's political problems. When Weitzmann reneged on his stand favoring Palestine's economic development, Brandeis withdrew from further active participation in the meetings. Subsequent developments widened the rift between the two leaders. In 1921 Weitzmann attended the American Zionist conference and succeeded in having the majority reject the program advocated by Brandeis and his followers. Thereupon they resigned from the leadership and took their places as "humble soldiers in the ranks"—certain that their policies would sooner or later "be recognized as the only ones through which our great ends may be achieved." In the years that followed Brandeis kept himself relatively aloof from formal Zionist activities, but his dream of a flourishing Jewish homeland in Palestine remained bright to the end of his life.

On January 28, 1916, President Wilson, without consulting any Senator or party leader, named Brandeis to the Supreme Court.

Outcries of shock and horror were immediate and emphatic. Eminent lawyers, prominent bankers, powerful businessmen, and leading college presidents considered the appointment an insult to the nation and opposed it vigorously. Former President Taft, whom Brandeis had caught in an untruth during the Ballinger-Glavis hearings and who had himself expected the Justiceship, was quick to join the attack. "It is one of the deepest wounds that I have had as an American and a lover of the Constitution and a believer in progressive conservatism that such a man as Brandeis could be put on the Court. . . . He is a muckraker, an emotionalist for his own purpose, a socialist." He and six other former presidents of the American Bar Association sent the following protest to the Senate Committee on the Judiciary: "The undersigned feel under the painful duty to say to you that in their opinion, taking into view the reputation, character, and professional career of Mr. Louis D. Brandeis, he is not a fit person to be a member of the Supreme Court of the United States." Fifty-five outstanding Bostonians, including President A. Lawrence Lowell of Harvard and a number of Brandeis's former friends, sent the Committee a similar joint objection to the nomination. (It is of interest to note that four former presidents of the American Bar Association and those of many state and local bar associations strongly supported Tom Clark's nomination, despite his legal mediocrity, because of his reputation as a conservative.)

At the Senate Committee hearings, witness after witness tried to besmirch Brandeis's reputation. Louis A. Coolidge, treasurer of the United Shoe Machinery Company and one of the first to testify, remarked curtly: "It is customary to consign crooks to jail and not to the bench." When asked what evidence he had to justify this characterization, he could offer only vague insinuations. Clifford Thorne, still nursing his misconceived resentment against Brandeis since their disagreement at the railroad rate hearings, hurried to Washington to vent his spleen. On the stand he asserted that the nominee was "guilty of infidelity, breach of faith and unprofessional conduct in connection with one of the greatest cases of this generation"—a view quickly contradicted by the record and by other witnesses. C. W. Barron, current publisher of *The Wall Street Journal*, was especially vicious. "Brandeis at the bar may represent individual wrongs," he wrote, "but Brandeis on the bench puts the United States before the world below even the present standards of his Teutonic ancestors." Having carefully combed the nominee's career for possible slips and imputable charges, he insisted on testifying concerning his alleged misconduct and doubledealing. On interrogation he had to admit he had no direct proof of his own, but he named a number of bankers, industrialists, and lawyers who could provide the incriminating information. When these men were summoned they were free enough with criticisms of their adversary, but their specific accusations and imputations turned out on examination to be without substance or deliberately misleading. *The Outlook* remarked editorially: "Hearsay, opinions, prejudice, gossip, and rumors unrelated to any fact have been put before the Committee as if they were evidence of value."

These critics were obviously anxious to block confirmation because they feared that Brandeis on the Supreme Court would undermine their vested position in society. They could not forget his persistent and powerful blows against their favorite business firms, and they hated him the more because they thought of him as a brilliant lawyer who was disloyal to his class. Moorfield Storey, eminent counsel for some of the men of large property who had come under Brandeis's attack, spoke for those who distrusted the latter's altruism and therefore impugned his motives: "I think his reputation is that of a man who is an able lawyer, very energetic, ruthless of the attainment of his objects, not scrupulous in the methods he adopts and not to be trusted." He and other aristocrats of the Boston bar resented the idea of having one who was not of them chosen for such honor. One of the witnesses admitted frankly: "They cannot, I think, consider with equanimity the selection of anybody for a position on the great court of the country from that community who is not a typical, hereditary Bostonian."

Brandeis's friends did not fail to rush to his support. Composed mostly of loyal liberals, they planned to expose the nature of the opposition and stress the motives and corporate associations of the hostile witnesses. Administration advisers stopped this plan of attack, insisting that victory could come only on a strict party basis and that the injection of the progressive issue would alienate conservative Democratic Senators. Brandeis agreed. Outwardly completely passive in the battle concerning him, he skillfully guided the men who supported him at the hearings. He countered every charge and insinuation with documents that often proved almost the exact opposite.

Prodded by his friends, a number of prominent men spoke up in his favor. Nine of the eleven professors at the Harvard Law School, including Roscoe Pound, wrote to the Senate Committee urging confirmation. Men active in public affairs joined well-known social workers, teachers, labor leaders, and other persons of good will in supporting the nominee. At the end of the first hearings La Follette asked Brandeis for a brief of the testimony in order to attack the unfriendly witnesses the more effectively in a Senate speech. "There will be some hot work before the vote comes," he explained, "and these hell-hounds must get what is coming to them—I mean the Bar Association presidents, University presidents—these sleek respectable crooks—whose opinions have always been for sale."

On April 1 the subcommittee of five Senators recommended Brandeis's confirmation by a strict party vote of three to two. The Republicans opposed him on the ground that he had made too many enemies and was therefore unsuited to the office. Senator John D. Works stated: "To place a man on the Supreme Court Bench who rests under a cloud would be a grievous mistake. . . . Whether suspicion rests upon him unjustly or not, his confirmation would be a mistake." It evidently did not matter to him who had cast the cloud or why. The Democrats reacted very differently to the same evidence. Senator W. E. Chilton was impressed by the fact that friend and foe spoke of Brandeis's great legal ability, that the evidence showed him "absolutely fearless in the discharge of his duties," and that the late Chief Justice Fuller had written of him as "the ablest man who has ever appeared before the Supreme Court of the United States." He therefore considered it his duty "to give him the benefit of a pure life and his upright conduct, regardless of the slander."

Senator Thomas J. Walsh, the ablest member of the subcommittee, was caustic in his criticism of the traducing witnesses and praised Brandeis's exertions in behalf of the public good. He stressed his "herculean labors" in the New Haven fight and in other engagements against monopolistic corporations.

The real crime of which this man is guilty is that he has exposed the iniquities of men in high places in our financial system. He has not stood in awe of the majesty of wealth. . . . He has been an iconoclast. He has written about and expressed views on "social justice," to which vague term are referred movements and measures to obtain greater security, greater comfort, and better health for the industrial workers—signifying safety devices, factory inspection, sanitary provisions, reasonable hours, the abolition of child labor, all of which threaten a reduction of dividends.

When weeks passed with no word from the Committee on the Judiciary, President Wilson was asked to exert political pressure by making public expression of his confidence in the nominee. His response was a letter to the chairman of the Committee declaring his highest admiration for Brandeis as a man and lawyer.

I have tested him by seeking his advice upon some of the most difficult and perplexing public questions about which it was necessary for me to form a judgment. I have dealt with him in matters where nice questions of honor and fair play, as well as large questions of justice and public benefit, were involved. In every matter in which I have made test of his judgment and point of view I have received from him counsel singularly enlightening, singularly clear-sighted and judicial, and, above all, full of moral stimulation. . . . I knew from direct personal knowledge of the man what I was doing when I named him for the highest and most responsible tribunal of the nation.

211

At the same time Wilson also went out of his way to placate the doubtful Democratic members of the Committee. He created opportunities to compliment them and express his confidence in their judgment. Brandeis himself went to Washington to meet these Senators socially, and his judicious conversation helped considerably to gain their good will.

At this juncture Charles W. Eliot, the venerable former president of Harvard and in 1916 probably the most distinguished living American, issued a statement that effectively stultified the criticism of his successor and other hostile Bostonians:

I have known Mr. Louis D. Brandeis for forty years and believe that I understand his capacities and his character. He was a distinguished student in Harvard Law School in 1875–8. He possessed by nature a keen intelligence, quick and generous sympathies, a remarkable capacity for labor, and a character in which gentleness, courage, and joy in combat were intimately blended. His professional career has exhibited all these qualities, and with them much practical altruism and public spirit. He has sometimes advocated measures or policies which did not commend themselves to me, but I have never questioned his honesty and sincerity, or his desire for justice.

On May 24, nearly four months after receiving Brandeis's nomination, the Senate Committee recommended confirmation by a strict party vote of ten to eight. A week later the recommendation was affirmed by a vote of 47 to 22. On June 5 Brandeis took the oath of office. Evaluating the fight against him, the bitterest in the history of the Supreme Court, he could not restrain a surge of anger. He pointed out that his opponents were either representatives of big business or privileged and prejudiced Bostonians, and that they had sought to besmirch his reputation by resorting to slander and innuendo. "And the community permitted them to do so almost without a protest. This seems to me the fundamental defect."

Brandeis was the first genuinely progressive Justice of the Supreme Court. He was also the first to possess deep insight into the working of modern business. As a proponent and practitioner of "the living law," he helped mightily to coordinate the judicial process with the current practices of industrial society. Always the warm-hearted liberal, he approached every case with a humane realism that at times antagonized his conservative colleagues; but before long his dissents became guideposts for subsequent decisions. In the words of Professor Paul A. Freund, "Every case that fell to him for opinion gave fresh occasion for the application of his principle that knowledge should precede understanding and understanding should precede judging." The dire predictions of his detractors were happily lost in the high praise of his major contribution to constitutional doctrine. By the time he retired after twenty-three fruitful years on the bench, he was universally acclaimed as one of the greatest Justices in our history.

It was a wrench for him to sever his legal and public connections. Yet he was not one to cloister himself in the respectable anonymity of his colleagues. He continued to participate diligently, if only informally, in the advancement of Zionism. And the exigency of war made him a focal center of counsel and direction to many of the leading members of the Administration. In addition to making himself available to them during the Court sessions he remained in Washington both summers of the war period in order to help adjust many pressing problems, particularly those concerning labor.

His Court opinions early dispelled the fears of all but the most bigoted of his enemies. Without modifying his social views, he proceeded to apply them to pertinent cases with such cogency and temperateness as to impress even his parochial colleagues. His breadth of view and his warm sympathies jarred the conservatives and strict legalists, but in time his opinions forced a fresh evaluation of the quality of justice. Neither a political doctrinaire nor a legal theorist, he insisted on relating the law to the facts at hand and on placing the rights of the weak and of the minority on a par with those of privilege and property.

Endowed with an enormous capacity for work and scrupulously

213

conscious of the ambiguity of language, he was in the habit, when preparing an opinion, first of making a very careful study of the practical aspects of the statute under consideration, then of familiarizing himself with the legal precedents cited in the briefs, and finally of writing and rewriting his opinion until he gave every word its clear meaning—in one instance revising it twenty-six times before he was satisfied. It was this kind of contribution that later caused Chief Justice Taft, his one-time emphatic opponent, to remark, "I do not see how we could get along without him." His revered colleague Justice Holmes was from the first profoundly impressed with his thorough knowledge of business practices as well as with much of his social progressivism, and the two frequently joined in dissents that made judicial history.

During his first Court term Brandeis wrote more than a score of majority opinions and five dissents. One of the latter concerned a State of Washington law prohibiting employment agencies from taking fees from workers. The majority, considering only its legal aspects, invalidated it as a violation of the due process clause of the Fourteenth Amendment. To Brandeis this action seemed unwarranted by the facts of the case. He indicated that the majority had not taken into account the abuses connected with employment agencies or the remedies sought by the state law. Citing such evils as extortionate fees, discrimination, and collusion with foremen—which plagued the hapless worker in time of little employment—and stating that half of the states were similarly seeking to remove these evils by like laws, he brought forth the positive notion motivating the statute in question—elimination of irregular employment. "The problem," he insisted, "which confronted the people of Washington was far more comprehensive and fundamental than that of protecting workers applying to the private agencies. It was the chronic problem of unemployment— perhaps the gravest and most difficult problem of modern industry." This dissenting opinion was at once recognized as a highly effective means of stating advanced social views. Having the force of factual realism and the prestige of the Court rostrum, this and other dissents impressed the legal profession as well as members of legislative bodies and thus prepared the way for eventual acceptance of these social ideas.

A number of Brandeis's opinions—whether with or against the majority—dealt forcefully and favorably with questions of labor and civil liberties. At no time either persuaded or intimidated by the eighteenth-century shibboleths of natural rights or freedom of contract, he insisted on relating these hallowed dogmas to social realities. It was easy for him to sympathize with the aims of labor not only because he always favored the underdog but also because he believed that organized labor would serve as a brake upon the current domination of business. He therefore maintained that legislators had the right to experiment in the fields of labor and industry. "The divergence of opinion in this difficult field of governmental action should admonish us not to declare a rule arbitrary and unreasonable merely because we are convinced that it is fraught with danger to the public weal, and thus close the door to experiment within the law."

Another of his dissents differed vigorously from the majority opinion which validated the "yellow dog" contract in the Hitchman Coal Company case. He argued that the judgment was based on legal technicalities rather than on the fundamental facts at issue. Although he did not specifically condemn the labor injunction or the open shop, he stressed labor's economic and social rights. "If it is coercion," he pointed out, "to threaten to strike unless plaintiff consents to a closed union shop, it is coercion also to threaten not to give one employment unless the applicant will consent to a closed non-union shop." Such frank and realistic reasoning, never before heard from the Court bench, served to hearten disgruntled workers and to give them notice of the relief to come.

The Duplex Printing Company case brought forth another of his sharp dissents against the majority's calloused conservatism. In granting the company an injunction restraining the printers union from boycotting its products, the majority disregarded the provision to the contrary in the Clayton Act on the ground that "Congress had in mind particular industrial controversies, not a general class war." It further maintained that the union's interference in the affairs of the Duplex Company was not only irrelevant but malicious. Brandeis strongly objected to this unrealistic view of an industrial controversy. He brought out the facts, completely ignored by the majority, that there were only four manufacturers of printing presses in the United States, that all but the Duplex Company were unionized, and that two of the companies had informed the union of their intention to give up union conditions in their own establishments unless the Duplex Company were organized and placed on an even footing with them on labor costs. Since the union had failed to win its strike against the Duplex, it sought to safeguard its existence by seeking to stop installation of Duplex machines. In this attempt, Brandeis continued, the defendants "injured the plaintiff, not maliciously, but in self-defense." The workers were faced with the dilemma of either unionizing the Duplex shop or accepting lower wages and other disadvantages in the factories competing with it. "May not all with a common interest join in refusing to expend their labor upon articles whose very production constitutes an attack upon their standard of living and the institutions which they are convinced supports it?" In taking a narrow view, he concluded, the Court had restored the industrial evil which the Clayton Act had sought to remedy.

Brandeis took the opportunity in another case to explain that he was opposed to labor injunctions for the simple reason that they usually favored property rights over human rights and thereby intensified industrial strife. He asserted, moreover, that in seeking labor injunctions employers were interested not so much in protecting their property as in endowing it "with active, militant power which would make it dominant over man." The Court therefore must be very careful not to interpret property law abstractly or to interfere in industrial disputes.

Many disinterested men, solicitous only for the public welfare, believed that the law of property was not appropriate for dealing with the forces beneath social unrest; that in this vast struggle it was unwise to throw the power of the State on one side or the other, according to principles deduced from that law; that the problem of the control and conduct of industry demanded a solution of its own; and that, pending the ascertainment of new principles to govern industry, it was wiser for the State not to interfere in industrial struggles by the issuance of an injunction.

Several years later, with the antilabor position of the Court strengthened by the accession of Justices Taft and George Sutherland, Brandeis found it necessary once more sharply to remind his colleagues that the Sherman and Clayton Acts were designed to curb large industrial combinations rather than union activities and that their peculiar interpretation of these laws imposed "restraints upon labor which reminds of involuntary servitude." The issue in question was whether the stone-cutters union was within its rights in seeking to organize the Bedford Cut Stone Company by calling upon local unions to refuse work on stone cut by non-union labor. Justice Sutherland, speaking for the majority, maintained that the problem was similar to the Duplex case and adjudged it accordingly. Brandeis, having found on investigation that the stone-cutters union was a small, struggling organization in danger of destruction if it failed to unionize the Bedford Company, countered that the Court was not dealing even-handed justice by applying the Sherman Act against this weak union— having held that the same Act permitted such gigantic trusts as the United States Steel Corporation and the United Shoe Machinery Company to dominate their respective industries.

It would, indeed, be strange if Congress had by the same Act willed to deny to members of a small craft of workingmen the right to cooperate in simply refraining from work when that course was the only means of self-protection against a combination of militant and powerful employers. I cannot believe that Congress did so.

217

Wholly sympathetic as he was to the efforts of labor unions to improve the condition of their members, he was as opposed as any conservative to union abuses. He had long maintained that unions must be responsible and law-abiding organizations. "Industrial liberty, like civil liberty," he held, "must rest upon the solid foundations of law." He therefore joined with the majority in ruling that a trade union was suable under the Sherman Act. He also spoke for the majority in adjudging a strike unlawful when ordered for purposes of coercion.

A strike may be illegal because of its purpose, however orderly the manner in which it is conducted. To collect a stale claim due to a fellow member of the union who was formerly employed in the business is not a permissible purpose. . . . To enforce payment by a strike is clearly coercion. . . . Neither the common law, nor the Fourteenth Amendment, confers the absolute right to strike.

Brandeis was the humanely outspoken jurist in numerous other areas of social disagreement—ever concerned for the protection of the public welfare. In no field, however, was he as incisive and eloquent as in that of civil liberty. Together with Justice Holmes, who had become his partner in dissent, he struck forcefully against bureaucratic arbitrariness and majority irresponsibility. After World War I, which had burdened the nation with laws curbing the rights of citizens in order to guard against danger both from within and without, the two men worked mind to mind in an effort to preserve civil liberties from unwarranted abuse. Their criterion for the test of the freedoms guaranteed by the Bill of Rights was clearly stated by Holmes in the famous dissent in the Schenck appeal: "The question in every case is whether the words used are used in such circumstances and are of such a nature as to create a clear and present danger that will bring about the substantive evils that Congress has a right to prevent."

This touchstone of "clear and present danger" was subsequently used by both men in a number of potent opinions. In 1920, with Holmes concurring, Brandeis spoke out sharply in several dissents.

In the Schaefer appeal he argued that no jury acting calmly, could reasonably conclude that the publication set forth in the indictment endangered the republic. "Men may differ widely," he cautioned, "as to what loyalty to our country demands; and an intolerant majority, swayed by passion or by fear, may be prone in the future, as it has often been in the past, to stamp as disloyal opinions with which it disagrees." In the case of the socialists convicted for distributing a pamphlet critical of the war, Brandeis again contended that the leaflet did not constitute a genuine danger and was in a real sense no more critical of the government than certain of President Wilson's statements in *The New Freedom*. To uphold the conviction of the leaflet's distributors "would practically deny members of small political parties freedom of criticism and of discussion in times when feelings ran high and the questions involved are deemed fundamental." He added:

The fundamental right of free men to strive for better conditions through new legislation and new institutions will not be preserved, if efforts to secure it by argument to fellow citizens may be construed as criminal incitement to disobey the existing law—merely because the argument presented seems to those exercising the judicial power to be unfair in its portrayal of existing evils, mistaken in its assumptions, unsound in reasoning, or intemperate in language.

This forthright defense of civil liberty was restated in two other cases dealt with about the same time. Dissenting from a majority opinion that validated an order by the Postmaster-General barring *The Milwaukee Leader*, a socialist newspaper, from second-class mailing privileges, he punctured the official's specious reasoning and argued that the order was deliberately a punitive rather than a preventive measure. If administrative bureaucrats were permitted to issue such orders, he insisted, "there is little of substance in our Bill of Rights, and in every extension of governmental functions lurks a new danger to civil liberty." The other case concerned the Minnesota antipacifist law, validated by the Court majority. In his dissent Brandeis explained that "the statute invades the privacy and freedom of the home" and suppresses that "frank expression of conflicting opinion" which sparks democratic government. He also took this occasion to remind his colleagues that although they had not hesitated to invoke the Constitution in order to invalidate state legislation regulating property and contract, they apparently assumed that laws restricting the "liberty to teach . . . the doctrine of pacifism" were not inimical to the public welfare. "I cannot believe," he concluded, "that the liberty guaranteed by the Fourteenth Amendment includes only liberty to acquire and enjoy property."

Because Anita Whitney, convicted under California's criminal syndicalist law as a communist, appealed to the Supreme Court to set aside the verdict on the ground of its unconstitutionality rather than on the question of a clear and present danger, Brandeis concurred in the conviction. He took the opportunity, however, to restate the fundamental philosophy motivating American democracy and to make clear his objection to the arbitrary suppression of free speech. His concluding words are truly eloquent of his democratic faith:

Those who won our independence by revolution were not cowards. They did not fear political change. They did not exalt order at the cost of liberty. To courageous, self-reliant men, with confidence in the power of free and fearless reasoning applied through the process of popular government, no danger flowing from speech can be deemed clear and present, unless the incidence of the evil apprehended is so imminent that it may befall before there is opportunity for full discussion. If there be time to expose through discussion the falsehood and fallacies, to avert the evil by the process of education, the remedy to be applied is more speech, not enforced silence. Only an emergency can justify repression. Such must be the rule if authority is to be reconciled with freedom. Such, in my opinion, is the command of the Constitution. It is therefore always open to Americans to challenge a law abridging free speech and assembly by showing that there was no emergency justifying it.

Late in 1931 the nation's most eminent citizens—and many of lesser prominence—paid homage to Justice Brandeis on his seventy-fifth birthday. Fifteen years on the Supreme Court had established him as one of the great American jurists. Learned articles in leading law reviews discussed various aspects of his work on the Court, and laudatory essays and editorials in his honor were published in influential magazines and newspapers. A number recalled, with an air of incredulity, the fear and anger aroused by his appointment in 1916; the very idea seemed to these commentators as unreal as it was absurd. For Justice Brandeis had indeed become one of America's most venerable elders.

Honor lay lightly on him. Age hardly slackened his pace. He still rose very early every morning and worked intensely through the day. Throughout the 1920's his deep interest in the world about him had remained as strong as ever. Having developed a desire to strengthen the University of Louisville, he contributed much to its library facilities and legal training. In the 1920's, also, he had been greatly perturbed by the Sacco-Vanzetti case. His Dedham home had sheltered the hapless Sacco family, and he must have long struggled with his conscience before he decided, because of his personal interest in the two men, not to grant the petition in their behalf. Another matter that had troubled him greatly was the hectic prosperity of the period. In 1926 he wrote: "I wish to record my utter inability to understand why a lot of folks don't go broke. These consolidations and security flotations, plus the building boom, beat my comprehension— unless there is a breakdown within a year."

When the crash did come, a little later, he was less concerned for the shorn lambs in the stock market than for the innocent victims of unemployment. Having long considered the problem of irregular work as fundamental to an industrial economy, he greatly sympathized with the millions suffering from the lack of jobs. He despaired of any solution under President Hoover—for whom he had had great respect a decade earlier—and hoped that the crisis would bring forth a leader of vision and courage.

He was in this state of mind in 1932 when he wrote his dissent in connection with the Oklahoma law requiring a certificate of public need of new ice companies. The majority invalidated the law on the ground that an ice manufacturer was not in a business "affected with a public interest" and its regulation by the state contravened the Fourteenth Amendment. Stress was also placed on the monopolistic direction of the statute. Brandeis the realist perceived that under certain conditions the production of ice did assume the attributes of a public utility. Moreover, foe of monopoly though he was, he insisted that in this instance the fundamental issue was not the danger of monopoly but the power of the state to experiment with "economic practices and institutions to meet changing social and economic needs." The nation, he explained, was confronted by the grievous problems of unemployment and technological overproduction. To expedite their solution, a state had the right to try various remedies.

To stay experimentation in things social and economic is a grave responsibility. Denial of the right to experiment may be fraught with serious consequences to the Nation. It is one of the happiest incidents of the federal system that a single courageous State may, if its citizens choose, serve as a laboratory; and try novel social and economic experiments without risk to the rest of the country. This Court has the power to prevent an experiment. . . . But in the exercise of this high power we must be ever on our guard, lest we erect our prejudices into legal principles. If we should be guided by the light of reason, we must let our minds be bold.

The opinion was headlined in most of the country's influential newspapers, and its audacious spirit was both praised and pounced upon. Even his critics, however, admitted the incisiveness of the argument. And they were even more strongly disturbed the following year by his dissenting opinion against a majority invalidation of the Florida law that placed a special tax on chain stores. Here was his opportunity to strike against corporate bigness, which he considered largely responsible for the extent of the depression, and he struck hard. He asserted "that size alone gives to giant corporations a social significance not attached ordinarily to smaller units of private enterprise." And he explained why:

The typical business corporation of the last century, owned by a small group of individuals, manager by their owners, and limited in size by their personal wealth, is being supplanted by huge concerns in which the lives of tens or hundreds of thousands of employees and the property of tens or hundreds of thousands of investors are subjected, through the corporate mechanism, to the control of a few men. Ownership has been separated from control, and this separation has removed many of the checks which formerly operated to curb the misuse of wealth and power. And as ownership of shares is becoming continually more dispersed, the power which formerly accompanied ownership is becoming increasingly concentrated in the hands of a few.

This change, he contended, was having a fundamental influence upon the nation and was in effect leading "to the rule of plutocracy." The large corporations, by furthering inequality in the distribution of wealth and by discouraging the individual initiative of small men, were in large part responsible for widespread unemployment and suffering. "Only through participation by the many in the responsibilities and determinations of business," he concluded, "can Americans secure the moral and intellectual development which is essential to the maintenance of liberty."

Though these dissenting opinions were hardly socialistic, as many conservatives asserted, they were bold and brilliant briefs for economic democracy. Appearing in a period of crisis, and widely publicized, they served to prepare the way for the election of Franklin D. Roosevelt and the enactment of the New Deal laws. Indeed many of the bright young men who gave the impetus and direction to the New Deal were in one way or another influenced by Brandeis's social and economic views. From Roosevelt down, the liberals in office revered him and frequently sought his advice. They sometimes referred to him as "Isaiah" with a fond respect that bordered on adulation.

Yet Brandeis was only a partial New Dealer. Bolder than most as a social experimenter, he never lost his distrust of bigness or his fear of monopoly. Giving his full blessing to laws liberating and safeguarding the system of banking and investment, and to acts of employment relief and social security, he frowned upon measures favorable to large corporations. To the disappointment of enthusiastic liberals he joined his conservative colleagues in invalidating the National Industrial Recovery Act because of its provisions encouraging monopoly. He also voted against the Lemke-Frazer Farm Bankruptcy Act because he considered it a piece of class legislation against private property. Nor did he approve of government efforts to raise prices by limiting production or of the fumbling of the unemployment problem. Yet he joined wholeheartedly in the efforts of the Roosevelt Administration to establish social justice and argued cogently for the validity of laws aiming in that direction.

Brandeis liked Roosevelt and admired his "fighting qualities." Yet he considered Roosevelt's court-packing plan both extreme and dangerous. Although he kept his reticence to the end and would not discuss the matter even with his intimate friends, his disapproval was unmistakable. It was his suggestion that brought forth the letter of explanation from Chief Justice Hughes to Senator Burton K. Wheeler which killed the bill in the Senate.

At eighty-three Justice Brandeis's work was nearly done. Though still mentally alert, he was beginning to decline physically. A mild heart attack a month earlier made him decide to retire from the Court on February 13, 1939. He continued, however, to take an active interest in Zionism and called on President Roosevelt to solicit his help in dealing with the painful and pressing refugee problem resulting from Nazi barbarism. Nor did he slacken his attention to matters of national and international concern.

Six weeks before he was to reach his eighty-fifth birthday he suffered another heart attack and died on October 5, 1941.

Louis D. Brandeis combined in himself an exceptionally quick mind with a surging impetus toward social justice. He began his legal career with a strong craving for success, but in his lexicon success meant not the acquisition of wealth nor the attainment of political power but the opportunity to function as a highly useful citizen. A true product of his early liberal environment and endowed with a strong capacity for moral indignation, he could not in the manner of many lawyers close his mind to vested wrongs or industrial malpractices. Although he became, by virtue of his remarkable ability, a leading corporation counsel and had every opportunity of rising financially to the top of his profession, he refused to barter what he conceived to be his obligations as a lawyer for the emolument flowing to the devoted counselor of big businessmen. He disapproved of those eminent men of law who were in a position to serve the community and yet preferred to act as corporate mercenaries. At the height of his career he wrote:

At the present time the lawyer does not hold that position with the people which he held fifty years ago; but the reason is in my opinion not lack of opportunity. It is because, instead of holding a position of independence between the wealthy and the people, prepared to curb the excesses of either, the able lawyers have to a good extent allowed themselves to become an adjunct of the great corporations, and have neglected their great obligation to use their powers for the protection of the people.

That is just what he did: devote his remarkable talents to the protection of the people from the greed and aggrandizement of certain large corporations. In this task he had one distinct advantage—he was not tempted by the opportunities to amass great wealth. Although he did become rich by virtue of wise investment —leaving an estate of over three million dollars—he never wanted more than enough for modest comfort and personal independence. "I have only one life," he once remarked, "and it's short enough. Why waste it on things I don't want most. And I don't want money or property most. I want to be free." And he wished to be free in order to serve the public good.

Dedicating himself to the ideal of public service, he inevitably assumed the role of the social crusader. He fought privilege and inequity wherever they clashed with the public interest and thereby earned the hatred of many men of wealth. Yet neither vilification nor defeat turned him from his course. And in the end triumph was his: he gained much for the people and he thrived on the enemies he made.

Many of his adversaries, aware of his superior ability, found it difficult to understand why he should have deliberately rejected the course that would have made him rich in order to serve as "counsel for the people." To him the question was irrelevant.

Some people buy diamonds and rare works of art, others delight in automobiles and yachts. My luxury is to invest my surplus effort, beyond that required for the proper support of my family, to the pleasure of taking up a problem and solving, or helping to solve it, for the people without receiving any compensation.

For all his breadth of view and definite social ideals, Brandeis was not of a philosophic bent of mind. "I have no general philosophy," he told Hapgood in 1912. "All my life I have thought only in connection with the facts that came before me. It is true, however, in order to work intelligently with the facts, one must see the general direction." As an economic realist and social moralist he perceived the welfare of mankind in the direction of political and economic democracy. He fought vested privilege and industrial monopoly because he believed that these manifestations in society tended to weaken, if not destroy, industrial democracy. In fighting the abuses of various corporations he sought primarily to remedy the pathologic aspects of capitalism; knowing full well that an uncontrolled industrialism prepared the way for either plutocracy or socialism—and he wanted neither. Max Lerner has well stated Brandeis's position:

He has so much respect for private property that he wishes it more equitably distributed, so much respect for capital that he wishes it to flow freely instead of being concentrated in a Money Trust, so much respect for competition that he wishes the conditions created under which it will be possible, so much respect for profits as an incentive that he wishes it to operate unobstructed by the monstrous weight and the artificial power of corporations, so much respect for business enterprise that he wishes to make of it a respectable creative force.

226

With these ends in view he exerted his great talents to improve the conditions of labor, to give workers both status and a sense of responsibility, to keep business from getting too big, to prevent bankers from using "other people's money" to control the country's economy, to provide small businessmen with the opportunity and incentive to function independently and profitably, to preserve our civil liberties and democratic principles, and to imbue Americans with his own great love of freedom and justice.

He was a relentless fighter. He asked for no quarter and gave none. Always he kept his eyes on the main goal, and he seldom faltered. All through the years as crusader and Justice he was the valiant protagonist of dynamic democracy. And it was his good fortune to have become during his lifetime an honored prophet in his own land.

PART TWO

THE
NEW DEAL AND AFTER

Franklin D. Roosevelt

PROTAGONIST OF THE NEW DEAL

A READING OF THE NUMEROUS BOOKS on Franklin D. Roosevelt reminds one of the story of the blind men and the elephant. Neither his admirers nor his detractors saw him whole. His complex character and rich personality, his unconventional attitude and his tendency to deviousness, his warm humaneness and his occasional vindictiveness—these and other facets of his being, seen singly or in blurred perspective, made men write about him either with flattering favor or with warped hatred.

Few men without bias will deny that Roosevelt has achieved pre-eminence among his contemporaries. Entering the national arena in a time of acute crisis, evidencing at first little more than a politician's will to succeed, he quickly and dramatically demonstrated his pragmatic leadership in the war upon the nation's severest depression. If his actions did not always achieve the promised results, they established the principle that the government is responsible for the welfare of the citizen. And when fascist aggressors began to make unprovoked attacks upon their neighbors, he had the acumen to perceive the danger of such rapacity to the world as a whole and the duty of the United States, as the most powerful nation, to resist such aggression. Confronted by a widespread American isolationism that sought to avoid involvement in war at any cost, he assumed the herculean task of educating the people to the realities of international relations

231

and of leading them step by step to an awareness of the oneness of the world and the pervasive menace of fascism.

When the Japanese assault on Pearl Harbor catapulted the United States into the war, Roosevelt at once assumed allied leadership. His courage and his bright vision of a peace-enforcing United Nations gave heart to millions in the throes of calamity. Taxing his strength to the uttermost, he planned and promoted war offensives and persuaded his principal associates to work with him toward an enduring peace. This effective leadership in defeating the fascist aggressors and in uniting the nations of the world crowned a career that brought him to the pinnacles of immortality.

The Hyde Park branch of the Roosevelt family maintained a high social position. James Roosevelt, its head in the latter decades of the nineteenth century, had a large enough income to enjoy the pleasures and privileges of both the country squire and the worldly gentleman. A widower in 1880, he married Sara Delano, a handsome and intelligent member of a prominent merchant-shipping family. Although she was only half his age—exactly as old as her stepson—she loved and admired her husband and greatly enjoyed her role as mistress of a large estate.

On January 30, 1882, Mrs. Roosevelt gave birth to Franklin Delano. As she had no other children subsequently, she and her husband devoted themselves to the upbringing of their son. Franklin was a bright youngster, full of fun and zestful at play. Although he was deprived of nothing he really wanted, this indulgence was accompanied by lessons in responsibility that taught him reasonableness and self-discipline. He began to be taken to Europe at the age of two and these frequent visits familiarized him with the ways of peoples other than Americans. He attended a German school for a term and never forgot the irritating restrictions upon individual freedom.

Franklin was educated privately by governesses and tutors. He enjoyed reading but was not of a scholarly bent. More than most boys, he devoted himself to collecting things. His stamp albums soon became valuable and in his later years were a rich source of recreation. In his early teens he shot and preserved more than 300 bird specimens of his neighborhood. Boating and sailing were his particular delight and his devotion to naval lore became, as with stamps, a lifetime interest.

When he entered Groton in his fifteenth year he was a tall, handsome youth, well-mannered, friendly and extrovert, but with little experience in the group life of boys of his own age. His mind was crammed with much miscellaneous information but relatively untrained in academic study. Another handicap was the fact that the other boys of his class had come to the school two years earlier and at first regarded him as an outsider. He was not long, however, in making a successful adjustment. Punctual in his habits, pleasing of manner, active in the school's sports, he gradually gained the confidence of his classmates and in his senior year he was chosen manager of the baseball team.

Franklin was no grind, and he was too active in extracurricular events to seek academic distinction, but his grades were above average. One of his early interests was debating. Strongly affected by the war with Spain, he argued against the annexation of Hawaii and the purchase of the Philippines. Although his point of view undoubtedly reflected the position of his Democratic father, the content of his speeches revealed a love of justice and a respect for the weak that remained with him throughout life. The typical boy, however, he did not let his anti-imperialist beliefs keep him from wanting to enlist, and only an attack of scarlet fever prevented his scheme to join the fighting forces.

Harvard College was the choice of his parents and he entered it in 1900 as a matter of course, although his own preference had been Annapolis and a naval career. As a freshman and later he associated with youths whose families equaled his in wealth and social prestige. He was inclined to be conventional and priggish; yet he evidenced an individual enterprise and a liberalism not common among his comrades. The death of his father on December 8, 1900, added to his sense of responsibility. He worked hard on the *Crimson* and thereby not only broadened his knowledge of current events but also achieved a modicum of prominence among his college mates, becoming in turn manager and president of the student daily.

His interest in politics, strongly stimulated by the meteoric career of his fifth cousin Theodore, was cultivated by courses in history, political science, and economics. A Democrat like his father and therefore strongly opposed to Republicanism, he nevertheless took pride in the success of his cousin's dynamic leadership. Yet he was still too much his father's son to approve Theodore's efforts to end a coal strike by exploiting the prestige of his office. Ironically enough in view of his own later actions, he wrote to his mother on October 2, 1902:

In spite of his success in settling the trouble, I think the President made a serious mistake in interfering—politically, at least. His tendency to make the executive power stronger than the Houses of Congress is bound to be a bad thing, especially when a man of weaker personality succeeds him in office.

Early in 1903 he fell in love with his distant cousin Anna Eleanor Roosevelt. He had known her since early childhood but had seen her only infrequently until he was at Harvard and began to attend parties to which she was invited. His mother opposed the affair because she believed her dear Franklin deserved a wife with a happier background. In the hope that separation would cool his ardor, she took him on a Caribbean cruise. On their return he was even more determined to marry Eleanor and Mrs. Roosevelt yielded reluctantly. The engagement was an open secret before his graduation from Harvard in June 1904 and the wedding took place the following March. The bride was given away by her uncle, President Theodore Roosevelt. Because Franklin had entered Columbia Law School the previous fall, the newlyweds postponed their honeymoon trip till June, when they went for a summer's tour of Western Europe. On their return they occupied a house rented and furnished by Sara Roosevelt.

The young couple's first child, Anna, was born in May 1906. Eager to assume his responsibilities as head of the family, Roosevelt took his bar examination the following year and left school before graduation. He was at once employed by a prominent law firm and served his apprenticeship without marked distinction, although he did well enough in admiralty cases. The management of the Hyde Park farm interested him much more and he exercised both ingenuity and enterprise in his agricultural experimentation. He was also taking an active part in the communal affairs of the village and was solidifying his position as one of its prominent citizens. Meantime Eleanor gave birth to James in 1907, to Elliott in 1910. Later she was to become the mother of Franklin D., Jr., and of John.

Roosevelt's interest in politics persisted. He followed national developments with keen attention. The liberals in and out of Congress aroused his deep sympathy. When "Uncle Ted" returned from Africa and called for a resumption of his progressive policies, Franklin was cheered by the enthusiastic response. Along with many other liberals he felt that most voters were in a mood to demand a return of democracy in government.

Stimulated by this spirit of insurgency, he readily accepted the nomination for state senator. It did not matter to him that no Democrat had won the office in 32 years. As he saw it, he had little to lose. Years later he explained that he accepted the odds against him "because at that time a group or ring of politicians was completely in control of my own and other up-state counties, and it seemed to me that any sacrifice of pride or any use of my time would be an essential service." At his formal nomination he made sure to insist on complete freedom of action. "As you know," he told the delegates, "I accept the nomination with absolute independence. I am pledged to no man; I am influenced by no specific interests; and so I shall remain."

Eager personally to reach as many of the voters as he could, he decided upon the then novel method of campaigning by car. For a month he traveled in a bright red automobile, making an average of ten speeches a day. Never before had he worked so hard; never before was he so happy with what he was doing. He concentrated his efforts on the rural districts and trudged over many a field to shake hands with farmers at work. His broad smile and sincere demeanor won him many friends. Men believed him when he promised to serve their interests. When the ballots were counted he surprised the local leaders by receiving a majority of 1140 votes.

Roosevelt rented a house in Albany for the legislative session. The election of a United States Senator was the first task of the Democratic majority. Tammany Boss Charles F. Murphy and his upstate associates had agreed to give the office to "Blue-eyed Billy" Sheehan, a prominent corporation lawyer. Most of the Democratic legislators accepted the choice as a matter of course, but about twenty upstate members, including Roosevelt, balked. They considered Sheehan unworthy of the high office and refused to acquiesce in his selection. Though a political novice, Roosevelt quickly established himself as leader of the insurgents and his home became their headquarters. For ten weeks, despite cajolery and threats on the part of the bosses, they refused to attend a binding caucus or vote on a candidate. Their insubordination became national news and Roosevelt's name made headlines. Newspaper editors hailed his rebellion against bossism. Finally Murphy yielded and Justice James A. O'Gorman, a Tammanyite lacking Sheehan's notoriety, was elected to the Senate.

Roosevelt's total achievement during his three years in the state senate was relatively minor. He worked with Alfred E. Smith and Robert Wagner in the promotion of a number of liberal measures, among them the direct primary bill, antisweatshop legislation, and a restricted work week. Years later he enjoyed reminding conservative opponents that he was called a communist for favoring the 54-hour week for women.

Governor Woodrow Wilson's progressive achievements in Trenton excited Roosevelt's admiration and late in 1911 he called on him to see for himself what manner of man he was. When he left he was persuaded that the former president of Princeton University was the hope of liberal Democrats. He immediately talked with other progressives about him and with their help formed the New York State Wilson Conference. For the next six months he promoted Wilson's candidacy with energetic enthusiasm. At the Democratic Convention in Baltimore he worked exuberantly among the delegates. When he learned that those favoring Speaker Champ Clark, Wilson's chief contestant, had bribed a doorkeeper to permit clackers wearing Clark buttons into the convention hall, he quickly rounded up over a hundred toughs, provided them with Wilson buttons, and had them outshout the rival rooters with "We Want Wilson" outcries. By the time Wilson was finally nominated, Roosevelt had met and made friends with hundreds of politicians from every part of the country and knew at first hand the intricacies and maneuverings of national party politics.

Opposed by Tammany for renomination, Roosevelt fought back and won. Soon after, however, he became sick with typhoid fever. Fortunately for him Louis Howe, one of the reporters in Albany who had come to regard him as a rising star, agreed to carry on the campaign for him. By means of large newspaper advertisements and other forms of publicity Roosevelt managed to win by a safe margin.

Early in March 1913 he went to Washington to celebrate Wilson's inaugural. He was in high spirits, elated by the fine prospects of the new Administration. On the train going to the capital he had been offered a good job in the Treasury Department, but financial matters did not interest him and he begged off. When Josephus Daniels, the new Secretary of the Navy, met him the next day and asked him if he would care to become his Assistant Secretary, he jumped at the offer. Nothing appealed to him more than an opportunity to deal with ships and help build up the Navy. For many years he had been collecting a naval library and had become intimately familiar with the history of ships and the problems and progress of modern navies. He resigned from the state senate at the earliest opportunity and moved his family to Washington.

Secretary Daniels was a shrewd politician, an ardent pacifist, and a gentlemanly Southerner. He was more at home with members of Congress than with admirals of the Navy. Roosevelt, on the other hand, saw eye to eye with the officers of our fighting ships. Given a free hand by his genial chief, he immediately set about to put the ships and yards on an efficient basis. To his wife he wrote during his first summer in Washington, "I will have to work like a new turbine to master this job—but it will be done if it takes all summer."

His examination of Navy yards and Navy personnel having convinced him that the Navy as a fighting machine was in a deplorable condition, he did not hesitate to make his findings public. He maintained that American ships must be able to protect not only "our shores and our own possessions but our merchant ships in time of war, no matter where they go." Unable to obtain appropriations for the kind of Navy he believed we needed, he proceeded to make the most of the means at his disposal. He rehabilitated every Navy yard with remarkable proficiency; he also reorganized the methods of purchasing supplies and thereby saved the nation millions of dollars. Secretary Daniels looked with favor upon his assistant's zeal, although he was sometimes troubled by Roosevelt's brashness; the admirals naturally sided with their energetic young superior and abetted his efforts. With their help Roosevelt put the Navy in fighting trim—ready for the titanic task ahead.

Roosevelt's feverish efforts to strengthen the Navy were motivated by his belief, as early as 1913, that a war in Europe seemed unavoidable. When it did break out he became impatient with his superiors for failing immediately to perceive its worldwide effects. On August 1, 1914, on learning that the German armies were on the march, he wrote to his wife, "Mr. D[aniels] totally fails to grasp the situation and I am to see the President Monday

A. M. to go over our own situation. . . . These are history-making days. It will be the greatest war in the world's history." The next day he wrote again:

These dear good people like W. J. B[ryan] and J. D[aniels] have as much conception of what a general European war means as Elliott [age four] has of higher mathematics. They really believe that because we are neutral we can go about our business as usual. . . . It is *my* duty to keep the Navy in a position where no chances, even the most remote, are taken. Today we are taking chances and I nearly boil over when I see the cheery "mañana" way of doing business.

This attitude of concern and annoyance continued till the nation became reconciled to military preparedness. In October he once more wrote to Eleanor: "The country needs the truth about the Army and Navy instead of a lot of soft mush about everlasting peace which so many statesmen are handing out to a gullible public." When Secretary of State Bryan resigned in June 1915 rather than sign Wilson's stiff note to Germany, Roosevelt was "disgusted clear through" with this kind of pacifism. All the while he kept urging the enlargement of the Navy.

Roosevelt was so completely absorbed in his job that he followed the progress of the New Freedom legislation only incidentally, though with much satisfaction. In 1914, eager to serve the President's cause in the Senate, he entered the New York primaries—and was soundly beaten by the Tammany candidate, James W. Gerard, then Ambassador to Germany. Four years later, politically in a much stronger position, he was urged to run for governor; but at that time he was concentrating on naval operations in the war and refused. And although he was too busy in 1916 to take an active part in the campaign to re-elect Wilson, he was delighted with his victory over the conservative Republicans. "I hope to God," he remarked in this connection, "I don't grow reactionary with advancing years."

When Wilson severed diplomatic relations with Germany, and our entrance into the war seemed only a matter of days or weeks,

Roosevelt immediately began to acquire materials needed by a fighting Navy—proceeding without authority and before Congress voted the money. Among other things he ordered 20,000 tons of nitrate from Chile and vital equipment from American manufacturers amounting to $40,000,000. So thoroughly did he do his job that he practically monopolized certain materials and President Wilson had to request him to share them with the Army.

Often in his role as Acting Secretary and always as Secretary Daniel's chief aide he took full charge of managing the gigantically enlarged Navy Department. He concerned himself with naval strategy and the problems of logistics and supply. Quickly learning the art of handling men, he dealt fairly and effectively with the many thousands of workers in the Navy yards and with the numerous and intricate issues arising out of a greatly enlarged Navy personnel. His capacity for hard work combined with a sympathetic intelligence belied his outward insouciance and his occasional flippancy.

In July 1918 he went to Europe to inspect naval stores and installations as well as to see the fighting at first hand. He met government leaders in both England and France and visited the front-line trenches. On his way back he had determined to resign his office and join the Navy in a combat capacity. On shipboard, however, he contracted double pneumonia and did not recover until the fighting was practically ended. Again in good health after the Armistice, he went once more to Europe in order to dispose of the tremendous naval stores and implements—a task he performed with marked proficiency. In February he returned on the *George Washington* together with President Wilson and had an opportunity to study the first draft of the Covenant of the League of Nations and knew that parts of it would antagonize the Senate majority. Later, when the struggle between the President and the Senate leaders had come to a tragic impasse, he was distressed to think of the unhappy consequences. The stubborn clash of strong personalities taught him a lesson in human relations he was seldom to forget.

FRANKLIN D. ROOSEVELT

The Democratic Convention of 1920 in San Francisco was a dismal affair. Most of the delegates felt the hopelessness of their party's chances but proceeded dutifully to approve the Covenant and to choose candidates with simulated optimism. During the demonstration in honor of the invalided President the Tammany-controlled New York delegation refused to join the marchers. Roosevelt, angered at this show of disrespect, wrenched the state standard from the delegate protecting it and shouted to those about him to follow him into the Wilson ranks. Later, when his name was proposed for the Vice-Presidential nomination, he was chosen by acclamation.

Roosevelt made an energetic campaign. He traveled many thousands of miles over most of the country, met with innumerable people, and spoke at scores of meetings. He extolled the League of Nations and argued for the liberal policies of the Democratic party. It was strenuous work and he enjoyed it tremendously, but defeat was apparent from the outset and he persisted in it out of loyalty to the stricken Wilson.

Having resigned his Navy post the previous August, he resumed his law practice shortly after the election and looked forward to happy days in Hyde Park. When a friend of his offered him a lucrative vice-presidency in the Fidelity and Deposit Company of Baltimore with the task of establishing and managing a New York office, he eagerly accepted it. On January 2, 1921, he opened the office for business and within six months he was operating the new branch of the insurance company with notable success. Then, in need of a vacation, he agreed to join his friend in a leisurely cruise to Campobello, Maine, where his family was spending the summer.

Roosevelt played as zestfully as he worked. Agile and athletic, endowed with a splendid physique, he enjoyed every active sport. Sailing and swimming were his favorite forms of relaxation. On August 10, while on a sailboat near his home, he espied a forest fire and went with his companions to help put it out. Back at the

241

beach, he went for a swim in the cold ocean surf. On his return to Campobello, still in his wet bathing suit, he sat down to look over his sizable mail. Feeling suddenly chill, he went indoors. Several hours later he was desperately ill with poliomyelitis and became in large part paralyzed. After several weeks of emergency care he was well enough to be moved on a stretcher to the train going to New York. There he was hospitalized for observation and treatment. The doctor attending him finally concluded that Roosevelt would remain permanently crippled and wrote to a colleague:

He has such courage, such ambition, and yet at the same time such an extraordinary sensitive emotional mechanism that it will take all the skill which we can muster to lead him successfully to a recognition of what he really faces without crushing him.

Soon enough Roosevelt learned that although his hands and torso were fully recovered he would never again have the full use of his legs. Only thirty-nine years old and in midpassage of a career that was without limit of achievement, he refused to live the life of an invalid. With or without the ability to walk he insisted on carrying on as normally as his altered circumstances permitted. As optimistic as he was determined, he was no sooner able to leave the hospital on crutches than he resumed his business activities. His chief preoccupation, however, became the improvement of his flabby leg muscles. He followed doctors' orders zealously, exercised regularly and diligently, and remained ever alert for new methods of treatment. When he learned that swimming was good for him, he swam at every opportunity and went to Florida in the winter in order to take advantage of its warm waters.

In 1924 a good friend of his told him of a pool in Warm Springs, Georgia, that had seemed helpful to another victim of poliomyelitis. Roosevelt went there at once. He worked out his own swimming exercises. The water's constant temperature of 88 degrees enabled him to remain in it for two hours daily, and its minerals served to stimulate the muscles not completely atrophied.

After a month of treatment he felt sufficiently improved to be able to walk with the aid of canes.

The news spread; other polio patients came to Warm Springs. To ascertain the beneficent value of the pool for these newcomers, Roosevelt persuaded the American Orthopedic Association to investigate its contents. The experts soon confirmed the helpful results on the patients exercising in its waters. In 1926 Roosevelt, eager to facilitate the use of the pool for scores of patients, bought the large tract of land that included the pool and the run-down hotel, and formed the Georgia Warm Springs Foundation on a nonprofit basis. The project required the investment of a large share of his capital, but he made it gladly and worked hard toward its successful establishment.

In his eagerness to lead a normally active life, he was encouraged by his wife and children—and especially by Louis Howe. After Roosevelt was stricken at Campobello Howe gave up his job and devoted himself completely to his friend's needs. He served him as secretary and political adviser and cajoled him into activities that would keep his name before the public. To the same end he urged Mrs. Roosevelt to assume civic tasks, make speeches, visit people and places, and thus keep her husband informed of happenings and trends in various parts of the country.

At Howe's advice Roosevelt undertook the management of Al Smith's 1924 preconvention campaign for the Presidency. When he was asked to make the nominating speech for Smith, he arrived on a wheel chair, walked up to the rostrum on crutches, and gave the "Happy Warrior" address that became the highlight of that dissident and dismal gathering. After the election he wrote to more than three thousand Democratic leaders to urge them for the sake of the party never again to permit such display of disunity. In stressing the need of harmony he inferentially invested his name with the aura of an elder statesman.

Roosevelt was also active in civic affairs. In 1923 he submitted a detailed plan to the Bok peace prize contest—in essence the League Covenant revised in a manner to overcome Senate opposition and renamed the Society of Nations. During the next five years, in addition to attending to his insurance business and developing the Warm Springs Foundation, he served as president of the American Construction Council, as chairman of the Boy Scouts of Greater New York, as national chairman of the fund-raising committee for the Cathedral of St. John the Divine, as chairman of the New York branch of the American Legion Endowment Fund, as president of the Taconic Parkway Commission, as a trustee of Vassar College, and as a member of the executive committee of the Woodrow Wilson Foundation. It was as if he were anxious to prove to himself and the world that his lifeless legs in no way handicapped his interests and activities as a good citizen.

In June 1928 Roosevelt journeyed to Houston, where he again nominated Al Smith at the Democratic Convention. This time he walked to the rostrum with a cane in one hand and the other holding his son Elliott's arm. Once more he spoke eloquently of his friend's qualifications for the office; now with success assured, since the party leaders were agreed on making Smith their standard bearer. Not that friction had disappeared—the consequences of the rift were to become evident on election day—but they were determined to avoid another disastrous deadlock. All of them, however, looked with favor upon Roosevelt's efforts at unity and went out of their way to show it.

As in other election years since 1920, Roosevelt refused to consider political office. He was still concentrating on the improvement of his legs and wanted nothing to disrupt his swimming exercises at Warm Springs; hoping that in another two years he would be able to discard the heavy steel braces and stand on his feet unaided. He therefore begged off in August when Smith asked him to run for governor of New York in order to help him carry the state. The following month he went to Georgia for his course of treatment.

The popular tide ran strongly in favor of a Republican victory.

The feverish stock-speculation boom had begun and Herbert Hoover symbolized the perpetuation of prosperity. Smith's religion, moreover, was becoming a major issue against him; and his choice of John Raskob, also a Catholic and a conservative industrialist, as chairman of the Democratic National Committee only aggravated the handicap.

When the New York Democrats met in Rochester to nominate their state ticket they failed to find a strong enough gubernatorial candidate. Roosevelt seemed to them the only one likely to carry the state for the party. Desperate, Smith and Raskob sought out Mrs. Roosevelt, who attended the convention, to consult with her about her husband's possible acceptance. At their urging she telephoned Warm Springs, spoke to her husband, and turned the receiver over to Smith who, on the basis of personal loyalty, managed to obtain the desired acquiescence.

Once Roosevelt accepted the nomination, he was "in this fight to win." Republican newspapers criticized his draft as "both pathetic and pitiless." His response was to project a campaign that would duly demonstrate his physical fitness for office. In addition to making a number of speeches for Smith he toured New York state by automobile with the zeal and flair of the ardent campaigner. On his staff were Louis Howe, James A. Farley, Samuel I. Rosenman, and Edward J. Flynn—a group of shrewd and hardheaded associates. In his speeches he announced himself "a disciple in a great cause." He pledged unequivocal continuance of Governor Smith's progressive policies and outlined a number of reforms in behalf of labor, agriculture, public power, and social welfare. In justification of these proposed measures he explained:

The phrase "the best government is the least government" is a sound phrase, but it applies only to the simplification of governmental machinery and to the prevention of improper interference with the legitimate activity of the citizens. But the nation or state which is unwilling by governmental action to tackle new problems caused by immense increase in population and the astounding strides of modern science is headed for a decline and ultimate death from inaction.

245

The voters reacted favorably to his frankness and friendliness. His majority of 25,564 was the more remarkable in view of the fact that Hoover won the state by 103,481.

Defeat disconcerted Al Smith. Nor did he take well to Roosevelt's emergence as the stronger and more popular of the two. Still he appreciated the latter's devotion and was eager to help him in the administration of the gubernatorial office. He was therefore disagreeably surprised to find his friend deferential but definitely unwilling to delegate any of his responsibilities. What hurt Smith particularly was Roosevelt's refusal to retain such proved stalwarts as Belle Moskowitz and Robert Moses. Feeling himself wronged, he retreated as nonchalantly as he could; but the hurt rankled and caused a rift between the two long-time friends that time only deepened and widened.

Roosevelt was aware of what he was doing, yet he could not act otherwise. Much as he liked Smith personally and highly as he thought of his liberal achievements as governor, he saw plainly his predecessor's mind turning conservative and being influenced by such men of wealth as John Raskob. Having in recent years deepened the roots of his own liberalism and intensified his belief in social reform, he was determined to supplement and strengthen Smith's earlier progressive measures rather than be guided by his present narrowing views. Moreover, he was too ambitious a man to remain under Smith's tutelage. He was looking ahead and wanted to achieve his own leadership of the Democratic party.

In his inaugural address he paid high homage to Smith as "a public servant of true greatness." He pledged himself to carry on the same progressive policies and recommended such reforms as state control of water power and its development for the benefit of all the people. In the course of the legislative session he proposed laws favoring the worker and farmer, the regulation of public utilities, better housing for the poor, old-age assistance, and other forms of social welfare. Later, with the depression affecting more and more people, he urged additional legislation that essentially forecast the New Deal laws enacted during his

Presidency. These welfare and reform measures were his intuitive response to new and acute conditions, clarified and concretized by means of informal interviews with experts whom he invited to his home and squeezed dry of information he wanted.

The Republican legislative majorities during his terms of office opposed his reforms with obtuse obdurateness, objecting even to measures that favored their constituents for fear that credit for these laws would redound to a Democratic governor. Roosevelt's chief form of redress was to appeal to the people of the state by means of informal radio talks. His resonant voice and frank manner proved highly effective, and each speech brought hundreds of letters to the balky legislators. This response from voters helped the passage of many of the reform bills. Later Roosevelt commented, "In New York, as later in the Nation, I was able to accomplish reform and progress only because the public was ready for them, and was willing to help me carry out the people's will."

Observation and reflection had during the 1920's nurtured in his mind the conviction that modern industrial society was too complex and made men too dependent upon one another to be able to function well under the *laissez-faire* principles of a simpler civilization. He saw that the urban worker relied wholly on his job for his livelihood, that the merchant and farmer could not exist without credit from the bank and adequate consuming ability on the part of the public, and that the tendency of the large industrialists and financiers was to control and exploit the economy with little regard for the public welfare. To bring government back to the source of its powers, to assure a living to those willing to work, and to re-establish equality of opportunity for all—to put these simple democratic principles back into practice required a new political orientation.

Roosevelt was ready for it, and so were the people. Having come to believe in the concept of the state's responsibility for the individual who was no longer able to stand alone as he did in the time of the open frontier, he discussed the problem in his Phi Beta Kappa address before the 1929 graduating class at Harvard.

247

The change in social relationships, he explained, was best described in the phrase "the age of social consciousness." At the time of the Declaration of Independence the main concern was for "the equality of rights"; in our own day we have come to seek "the realization of that wider more essential equality of opportunity." In addition "we have evolved community obligations undreamt of a hundred years ago." Regardless of how one felt about it, it was no longer possible to turn back or aside. "Rather it is our privilege to direct the course."

The following January, with the depression already under way, he again gave expression to this political principle:

The most striking and important difference between the civilization of today and the civilization of yesterday is the universal recognition that the first duty of a State, and by that I mean Government, is to promote the welfare of the citizens of that State. It is no longer sufficient to protect them from invasion, from lawless and criminal acts, from injustices and persecution, but the State must protect them, so far as lies in its power, from disease, from ignorance, from physical injury, and from old-age want.

As the depression deepened and thousands of men, without work, were unable to provide food for their families, Roosevelt added the protection of citizens from hunger to the obligations of government. On March 13, 1930, having just appointed a committee to study the problem of unemployment, he pointed out to its members that "unemployment is a problem for the entire community. It is a major social tragedy."

Meantime he had to campaign for re-election. Having established himself as an able and liberal governor, he had an excellent chance of victory. Nevertheless he fought vigorously in every part of the state. In his acceptance speech he attacked the Hoover Administration for its lack of leadership in relieving the unemployed, so that "each State must meet this situation as best it can." He also accused it of irresponsibly stimulating the conditions that brought about the financial crash and then concealing its seriousness from the people. Calling for action on the part of the federal government, he made clear what he had already done to relieve distress and promised to do much more during his second term. The Republicans, put on the defensive, offered only feeble opposition, and on election day Roosevelt's majority of 725,001 was the largest on record. Such unprecedented approval in the most populous state in the Union made him at once the leading Democratic candidate for the Presidency.

The election over, Roosevelt lost no time in dealing with the increasingly pressing problem of unemployment and human suffering. Previously, at governors' conferences, he had discussed the matter to little avail. The executives of other states either lacked the means to succor the needy or believed with President Hoover that individual relief was the concern of the local community. Roosevelt knew that no city was any longer able to cope with this acute hardship; that only the state, with the help of the federal government, was in a position to care for the destitute. "The important thing to recognize," he asserted, "is that there is a duty on the part of government to do something about this—it just can't sit back and expect private charity or even local government to take care of it entirely." Considering ordinary relief as a degrading dole, he began to develop a state program of public works and to coordinate the relief agencies of the larger cities with the private social service facilities. He soon found, however, that the needs of the unemployed far exceeded the available resources. With President Hoover refusing to act, he called the state legislature into extraordinary session and requested authorization to spend $20,000,000 on public-work relief.

The duty of the State toward the citizens is the duty of the servants to its master. The people have created it; the people, by common consent, permit its continual existence. One of these duties of the State is that of caring for those of its citizens who find themselves the victims of such adverse circumstances as make them unable to obtain

even the necessities for mere existence without the aid of others. . . .
To these unfortunate citizens aid must be extended by Government,
not as a matter of charity, but as a matter of *social duty*.

The Republican majority reacted violently against this measure.
Disregarding the urgency of the situation, they were adamant
against the radical appropriation because they knew that it would
give Roosevelt the leadership which President Hoover had refused
to assume. They therefore prepared a watered-down bill of their
own. Roosevelt at once exposed its defects and insisted that if
they passed it he would veto it and call them back into special
session. So powerful was his public support that the legislators
were forced to capitulate by incorporating the original stipulations
into the final measure. This legislation focused the nation's
attention upon the difference between Hoover's *laissez-faire* principle of letting the depression work itself out unaided regardless
of cost in human suffering and Roosevelt's doctrine that it was
the duty of government to help citizens in want.

Although Roosevelt refused to discuss his candidacy for the
Democratic nomination for the Presidency until he formally announced it on January 23, 1932, by filing his name in the North
Dakota primaries, his friends and associates had been working
for him since the 1930 election. James Farley soon demonstrated
his great capacity as political organizer by personally visiting hundreds of Democratic leaders in every part of the country and
gaining their pledges. Louis Howe, at last seeing the realization
of his life's ambition, worked indefatigably to win friends for his
hero. Numerous others, either personally devoted to Roosevelt or
in sympathy with his humane liberalism, joined the crusade in his
behalf. He himself wrote hundreds of friendly letters to politicians
in a position to influence delegates and entertained at his home
as many as cared to accept his cordial invitations.

To help with the research for campaign materials and with the
actual preparation of speeches, Roosevelt asked Samuel Rosenman,

who had been assisting him in this respect since 1928, to obtain the services of academic experts. Soon Professors Raymond Moley, Rexford Tugwell, and A. A. Berle, Jr.,—all of Columbia University—became regular members of what a reporter dubbed "the brains trust." More experts joined the little group from time to time. Moley, a good organizer of ideas, was in charge of the research and planning and Rosenman, who had come to know Roosevelt's mind intimately, supervised the drafting of the speeches. Roosevelt himself not only indicated the nature and emphases of this material but read carefully every paragraph, inserted many pungent phrases, and simplified the style throughout. Thus, although a number of persons partook in the writing of every speech, the final draft emerged characteristically Rooseveltian—especially when delivered over the radio in his exceptionally effective manner.

Opposition to his candidacy came early and from various sources. His exuberant personality and informal manner caused some persons to mistake his ready laughter for unbecoming levity, his jesting quips for insincerity. Even so astute an observer as Walter Lippmann overlooked Roosevelt's notable achievements as governor when he wrote on January 8, 1932: "F. D. R. is no crusader. He is no tribune of the people. He is no enemy of entrenched privilege. He is a pleasant man who, without any important qualifications for the office, would very much like to be President." Social and political reformers, indignant at the disclosures of Tammany graft and corruption, accused him of treating the New York crooked officeholders too warily in the hope of retaining their support at the Democratic convention.

His chief antagonist was Al Smith. He had long resented Roosevelt's independence. Learning of his formal candidacy, Smith exclaimed, "He has ignored me!" What galled him particularly was to see himself relegated to the background when the chances of Democratic victory appeared excellent. Convinced that he was entitled to another opportunity—that the nomination was his by right—he announced his candidacy in February and proceeded to marshal numerous admirers, many of them wealthy conservatives, in a campaign to take away the nomination from his former friend.

Roosevelt, shrewdly disregarding this opposition as well as his setbacks in the Massachusetts and California primaries, concentrated on the basic issues of the campaign. On April 7, in a ten-minute nation-wide radio broadcast, he dramatically questioned the aims of the newly established Reconstruction Finance Corporation. It was President Hoover's idea that by lending huge sums to big banks and large corporations the RFC would succeed in stimulating economic recovery from the top down. Roosevelt argued for the completely opposite remedy—the direct relief of "the forgotten man."

In my calm judgment, the Nation faces today a more grave emergency than in 1917. These unhappy times call for the building of plans that rest upon the forgotten, the unorganized but the indispensable units of economic power, for plans like those of 1917 that build from the bottom up and not from the top down, that put their faith once more in the forgotten man at the bottom of the economic pyramid.

He again took issue with Hoover when the latter declared on May 27, "The urgent question today is the prompt balancing of the budget. When that is accomplished I propose to support adequate measures for relief of distress and unemployment." Insisting that the hungry must be fed regardless of the condition of the budget, Roosevelt demanded "bold, persistent experimentation. . . . The millions who are in want will not stand by silently forever while the things to satisfy their needs are within easy reach."

At the end of the pre-convention campaign a majority of the delegates were pledged to Roosevelt. But to obtain the necessary two-thirds vote he had to win the delegates committed to favorite-son candidates. Farley, Howe, and other of his lieutenants went to Chicago eager to cajole and bargain. With the Smith faction implacably hostile, they began to woo the leaders of the Texas and California delegations. By promising to favor Speaker John N.

Garner for second place on the ticket they succeeded in securing the needed votes. On the fourth ballot Roosevelt received 945 votes to Smith's 190¼.

Roosevelt immediately announced that he would fly to Chicago to accept the nomination—a precedent-breaking action that was to be the first of many innovations. His address to the delegates, carefully prepared in advance, was a stirring call to arms against the depression, against reaction, against panic, against prohibition. He urged a positive program that would provide the people with what they wanted and needed: work and security.

Ours must be a party of liberal thought, of planned action, of enlightened international outlook, and of the greatest good to the greatest number of our citizens. . . . Let us be frank in acknowledgment of the truth that many amongst us have made obeisance to Mammon, that the profits of speculation, the easy road without toil, have lured us from the old barricades. To return to high standards we must abandon the old prophets and seek new leaders of our own choosing. . . . I pledge you, I pledge myself, to a new deal for the American people.

Although a number of Roosevelt's advisers assured him of the certainty of his election, he insisted on making his political philosophy and projected plans crystal clear to the voters before they went to the polls in November. He therefore arranged with Moley to plan rough drafts of speeches on every major issue. All through the summer the men enlisted in the "brain trust" worked on the spadework for these addresses—material which Roosevelt later suffused with his own clear and colorful phrasing.

The vexing problem of Tammany corruption had to be dealt with first. Having satisfied himself concerning the malfeasance of Sheriff Tom Farley, he dismissed him from office with a scorching denunciation of public officials who betrayed their trust and sought immunity on the ground of self-incrimination. The case of Mayor James J. Walker was more complex. Impatient reformers wanted him removed before the charges against him were proved in open hearing. Roosevelt insisted on treating the debonair mayor

253

fairly and legally. But after fourteen days of direct testimony, extending to September 2, Walker saw the inevitable outcome and decided on immediate resignation.

President Hoover, anxious for the preservation of the status quo, warned the voters, and Roosevelt agreed, that the 1932 contest was "between two philosophies of government"; but Hoover's insistence that a change from his doctrine would "crack the timbers of the Constitution" brought emphatic dissent. Roosevelt insisted, on the contrary, that his program was bringing the Constitution back to its original purposes. To him, as to most liberals, the New Deal idea was the culmination and triumph of a half century of social protest against the economic aggrandizement of an industrial oligarchy; a peaceful revolution seeking democratically to amend the American economy for the benefit of all the people. In nearly a score of major speeches, delivered in important centers across the country, he not only presented his criticism of the men largely responsible for the financial crash and the subsequent depression but also enlarged upon the measures he considered necessary to bring the nation back to economic health and to insure it against similar catastrophes in the future.

In his first speech on August 20 at Columbus, Ohio, he made a forceful case for the regulation of banks, stock exchanges, and holding companies. He denounced the "few powerful interests" who in the name of individual liberty sought "to make industrial cannon fodder of the lives of half of the population." Because he respected private property, he continued, "I do not believe that it should be subjected to the ruthless manipulation of professional gamblers in the stock markets and in the corporate systems."

In Portland, Oregon, he discussed public utilities and the development of hydroelectric power and lashed out against the unscrupulous enterprisers in this field:

Let me speak plainly. Through lack of vigilance in State capitols and in the national Government, we have allowed many utility companies to get around the common law, to capitalize themselves without regard to actual investment made in property, to pyramid capital through holding companies and, without restraining of law, to sell billions of dollars of securities which the public have been falsely led into believing were properly supervised by the Government itself.

Probably his most important address was delivered in San Francisco before the Commonwealth Club, an organization of conservative financiers and industrialists. Discussing the relation between business and government, he argued for "an economic declaration of right" that would assure "a more permanently safe order of things." He pointed out that since every man has a right to life, "he has also a right to make a comfortable living"; likewise, since every man has a right to his own property, he must be assured of "the safety of his savings." And he continued:

In all thoughts of property, this thought is paramount; all other property rights must yield to it. If, in accord with this principle, we must restrict the operations of the speculators, the manipulators, even the financiers, I believe we must accept the restriction as needful, not to hamper individualism but to protect it.

The talk he made in Pittsburgh on balancing the budget came back later to plague him. Eager to capitalize on Hoover's inability to keep within the national budget, he declared: "I regard reduction in Federal spending as one of the most important issues of this campaign." Yet he did point out that he would let no man starve and if that meant unbalancing the budget, "I shall not hesitate to tell the American people the full truth and ask them to authorize the expenditure of that additional amount." What he failed to clarify was the distinction he later made between the basic cost of government and emergency expenditures for the people's welfare.

The addresses taken together formed a clear and bold exposition of American progressive politics—a realistic and contemporary synthesis of the reforms and ideals preached by the Populists, William Jennings Bryan, Theodore Roosevelt, Woodrow Wilson, and Robert M. La Follette. Professor Charles A. Beard, no admirer of Roosevelt, thus commented on these speeches in *Mid-passage*:

It was well within the circle of factual description to say that in his numerous discourses Franklin D. Roosevelt discussed the basic human and economic problems of American society with a courage and range displayed by no predecessor in his office; that he thrust their challenge into spheres hitherto indifferent or hostile; that he set in swift circulation, through the use of radio, ideas once confined to groups more or less esoteric; that he both reflected and stirred the thought of the nation to the uttermost borders of the land.

President Hoover, dignified and indignant, struck back by attacking Roosevelt's radicalism. He insisted that his method was best in the long run and that if it were not followed, "grass will grow on the streets of a hundred cities, a thousand towns; the weeds will overrun the fields of a million farms." Most voters were not convinced. They wanted a change and they believed Roosevelt would give it to them. On election day 22,813,786 cast their ballot for a New Deal; only 15,759,266 favored the status quo.

The interim between election and inauguration was a period of accelerated economic deterioration. The unemployed numbered upward of fifteen million and their distress was acute. The international financial situation also worsened and cries for help and cooperation assailed the State Department. Action became imperative. Hoover was anxious to do something—but on terms Roosevelt could not accept. Thus by early March chaos darkened the financial and industrial marts of the nation. The "bank holiday" in important states was putting a brake on all forms of business. Fear and gloom gripped the people.

Roosevelt's inaugural address electrified the nation with its comforting courage and bold call to action. Writing most of it himself, he intuitively hit upon the exact note of optimism needed at that moment.

This is pre-eminently the time to speak the truth, the whole truth, frankly and boldly. Nor need we shrink from honestly facing conditions in our country today. This great Nation will endure as it has endured, will revive and prosper. So, first of all, let me assert my firm belief that the only thing we have to fear is fear itself—nameless, unreasoning, unjustified terror which paralyzes needed efforts to convert retreat into advance.

He offered the people leadership and asked for their support. He pointed the way toward economic recovery and requested them to follow him. Now that "the money changers have fled from their high seats in the temple of our civilization," he wanted it rededicated "to ancient truths." "The measure of restoration," he declared, "lies in the extent to which we apply social values more noble than mere monetary profit."

The speech went to the heart of those who heard it, evoking spontaneous hope and warm gratitude. And Roosevelt acted quickly, fearlessly, zestfully, pragmatically. First he stopped financial panic by closing all banks. Then he called Congress into extra session. When it met on March 9 both Houses passed the emergency banking measure on the same day—empowering Roosevelt to open the solvent and solvable banks and to keep the insolvent ones closed. This Act, explained in a Fireside Chat in clear, simple, and comforting language, went far to assure the people that the new Administration was working smoothly and in their behalf. The next day Congress bolstered their confidence still further by passing the Economy Act, reducing government expenses by a half billion dollars.

During the hundred days of the special session Congress, guided, goaded, and cajoled by Roosevelt and his administrators, enacted more social and experimental legislation than in any previous session. Since a number of these laws aimed more at economic recovery than at social reform, even the conservatives thought well of them. Among the more important measures were: AAA, which gave farmers protection against low prices on crops; CCC, Roosevelt's imaginative effort to save a half million idle youths from vagrancy by putting them to work on national forest lands; the Security Act, which aimed to protect innocent investors; TVA, "a corporation clothed with power of government but

possessed of the flexibility and initiative of a private enterprise";
Farm Mortgage and HOLC Act to save farms and homes from
foreclosure; the Gold Clause Resolution, aiming to stop speculators
and hoarders from draining the gold reserve and to give the dollar
a truer purchase value; FERA, providing a half billion dollars
for unemployment relief; the Railway Reorganization Act, which
kept the railroads from financial bankruptcy; NIRA, a recovery
measure to stimulate business enterprise, safeguard the rights of
organized workers, abolish child labor, and initiate public works.
When Congress adjourned on June 16, Roosevelt made public his
gracious note of appreciation:

I am certain that this Special Session of Congress will go down in the
history of our country as one which, more than any other, boldly
seized the opportunity to right great wrongs, to restore clearer thinking and more honest practices, to carry through its business with practical celerity and to set our feet on the upward path.

Practically every new law was a pragmatic attempt to adapt
policy to exigency; all aimed to combine recovery with reform.
There was no formal, inclusive master plan; there was only the
impulse to initiate economic rehabilitation in the spirit of social
welfare. Although every piece of legislation required government
planning and control, the underlying purpose was to save the existing economic system and not to weaken or destroy it. Both
Roosevelt and his top aides favored the system of private enterprise; yet some of the young men in the various departments and
bureaus, motivated by high ideals and antagonized by the harmful
aspects of large-scale industrialism, sought to remove these wrongs
without full regard to consequences.

It was relatively simple to pass laws and make plans, but to
execute them successfully was much more difficult. It became a
matter of trial and error, making mistakes and starting anew, of
stepping on toes and smoothing ruffled feelings, of fitting established policy to unforeseen exigencies. And although many hailed
the efforts at recovery, very few accepted the necessary restraints

or the abridgment of previous privileges. Criticisms and complaints crowded Roosevelt's desk, forcing him to make snap judgments, to compromise and reverse himself. His multitude of visitors, charmed by his warm smile and cheering presence, often left him in the belief that he sympathized with their plaints—when in fact he was only pleasant. Thus trouble continued to brew, now and then flowing over onto the first pages of newspapers.

One of the commitments Roosevelt inherited from his predecessor was the London Economic Conference which began late in June. This gathering was planned when there was still hope of retaining and strengthening the old order of international trade. Conditions were changing quickly, however, and the emergence of economic nationalism had made the agenda obsolete. The American delegation headed by Secretary of State Cordell Hull reflected the confused thinking of the Administration on such subjects as the tariff, inflation, and financial stabilization. Moley's arrival in London as Roosevelt's spokesman only confounded the confusion. When he, by a process of rationalization, prepared a statement favoring stabilization, Roosevelt was forced to repudiate it in his famous "bombshell" cable.

Concerned primarily with raising domestic prices and suspicious of the aims of the sound-money advocates, he rejected the "old fetishes of so-called international bankers" and favored national currencies with a "continuing purchasing power which does not greatly vary in terms of the commodities and needs of modern civilization." He therefore advised the delegation not to be "diverted by the proposal of a purely artificial and temporary experiment affecting the monetary exchange of a few nations only." In view of the impression of cooperation he had given to the European dignitaries who had visited him in the spring for that very purpose, his "bombshell" indeed exploded the Conference. It was basically a matter of self-interest on both sides, and Roosevelt insisted on the policy that favored the United States.

The most conspicuous and controversial of the early New Deal laws was undoubtedly the National Industrial Recovery Act. Emergency conditions had made the law a hasty improvisation to stimulate business enterprise and at the same time improve the conditions of labor—with the appropriation for public works tacked on as a means of priming the industrial pump. It was a composite measure, based on the one hand on the policies and procedures of the numerous trade associations developed during the 1920's and on the other on the increasingly vocal demands of organized labor. In order to stop "the kind of unfair competition that results in long hours, starvation wages, and overproduction," Roosevelt was willing, at least temporarily, to overlook the several antitrust laws then in effect. The Act was indeed a bold, if unrealistic, stroke toward reconciling the contending forces in a sick and changing economy, predicated on the vain hope that capital and labor would cooperate in the interest of the national welfare. In a Fireside Chat on July 24 Roosevelt explained the purpose of the law and stressed its labor provisions.

The essence of the plan is a universal limitation of hours of work per week for any individual by common consent, and a universal payment of wages above a minimum, also by common consent. I cannot guarantee the success of this nation-wide plan, but the people of this country can guarantee its success.

Under the dynamic and dazzling leadership of General Hugh S. Johnson industry after industry was prodded into preparing an acceptable code and received the blessing of the Blue Eagle. In time nearly 750 codes were drafted and approved. Each code authority, consisting of representatives of industry, labor, and government, established its own rules of operation regarding hours, wages, and working conditions; no fixed production quotas or prices were required.

Trouble began almost at once. Leading liberals, remembering the long struggle for the enactment of antitrust laws, criticized their virtual annulment under the new law; independent industrialists complained that the codes favored the gigantic corporations; organized labor denounced the company unions formed by large employers everywhere for the purpose of circumventing the recognition of independent unions. The expected cooperation failed to materialize; the hoped-for acceleration of industrial enterprise proceeded at a snail's pace. Johnson's frenetic efforts to adjust differences and crack down on code violators only increased the confusion and disharmony. Nor did Roosevelt's attempts to keep the codes in operation result in more than temporary extensions. It became a matter of carrying water in a leaky pail, and by the time the Supreme Court declared the law unconstitutional it was already in general disfavor. Roosevelt was indignant at the Court's illiberal attitude, but he told Frances Perkins, "I think perhaps NRA has done all it can do. I don't want to impose a system on this country that will set aside the antitrust laws on any permanent basis." For by 1935 the panicky atmosphere of two years earlier had been largely replaced by the exuberance of economic recovery.

Throughout this period Roosevelt was pulled by his advisers to the right as well as to the left. The more conservative wanted him to concentrate on economic recovery; the confirmed liberals besieged him with plans for social reform. His own position was at first "a little left of center." He was essentially a humane democrat eager to see the mass of people earning a comfortable living. Consequently he was opposed to the efforts of the rich again to arrogate to themselves the rights and privileges of the pre-depression era. In addressing the code authorities on March 5, 1934, he said:

The real truth of the matter is that for a number of years in our country the machinery of democracy had failed to function. Through inertia on the part of leaders and on the part of the people themselves the operations of government had fallen into the hands of special groups, some of them vociferously led by people who undertook to obtain special advantages for special classes.

On June 8, in a farewell message to the retiring Congress, he outlined his plan for the elimination of gross economic inequity:

These three great objectives—the security of the home, the security of a livelihood, and the security of social insurance—are, it seems to me, a minimum of the promise that we can offer to the American people. They constitute a right which belongs to every individual and every family willing to work. They are the essential fulfillment of measures already taken toward relief, recovery, and reconstruction.

Congress had indeed enacted additional legislation, some of it passed over strenuous opposition, enabling him to establish SEC, FCC, additional relief facilities, trade agreements with other nations, and machinery to expedite housing improvements. Roosevelt also issued a number of Executive Orders tending in the same direction, such as the formation of the Committee on Economic Security and the National Resources Board. In a letter to Colonel E. M. House on New Deal progress he wrote, "We must keep the sheer momentum from slackening up too much and I have no intention of relinquishing the offensive in favor of defensive tactics." And in a Fireside Chat on June 28 he asked his listeners, "Are you better off now than you were last year?" The thundering answer came in the November elections, when the large Democratic majorities in Congress were further increased.

Roosevelt regarded this victory as a mandate from the voters to complete his New Deal program. In his message to the incoming Congress on January 4, 1935, he stated that the people continued to suffer from "old inequities" and that "sporadic remedies" have had little effect. "In spite of our efforts and in spite of our talk, we have not weeded out the overprivileged and we have not effectively lifted up the underprivileged."

During the course of the session he recommended additional legislation pertaining to social security for 30,000,000 Americans, the regulation of public utility holding companies, further relief, and new taxes. He also issued Executive Orders establishing the Resettlement Administration, the Rural Electrification Administration, and the National Youth Administration. When the Supreme Court invalidated the NRA, he approved Senator Wagner's National Labor Relations bill. These measures were enacted despite strong opposition and greatly augmented the New Deal form of government.

The more business improved the more obstreperous certain of its spokesmen became. They fought strenuously every reform bill and lobbied with a lavish hand. In an effort to defeat the New Deal in the 1936 elections they formed the Liberty League and made Al Smith its mouthpiece. These attacks only intensified Roosevelt's determination to carry through his avowed program. To Farley he said, "I am going to do all in my power to prevent a continuance of conditions which would permit Wall Street to dominate not only the policies but the politics of the nation."

With 1936 a campaign year, both New Dealers and their opponents let loose a barrage of invective and denunciation. No holds were barred, no hyperbole was withheld. For the Liberty League spokesmen it was a crucial combat—and Roosevelt engaged them with the zeal and zest of the aggressive champion. In his Jackson Day speech on January 8 he asserted: "Our frontiers of today are economic, not geographic. Our enemies of today are the forces of privilege and greed within our own borders." The same idea, and the call to action, he reiterated three months later in a talk to the Young Democratic Club of Baltimore. In his speech accepting the renomination he lashed out against his critics, asserting that the "new economic dynasties, thirsting for power, reached out for control over Government itself." These monopolists, he claimed, limited opportunity and crushed individual initiative; they made private enterprise privileged enterprise—for themselves. In words reminiscent of Brandeis he declared, "A small group had concentrated into their own hands an almost complete control over other people's property, other people's money, other people's labor—other people's lives." It was therefore the "inescapable obligation" of the government to re-establish "a democracy of opportunity."

Throughout the campaign Roosevelt's opponents accused him of fostering communism and lusting after dictatorship. His response was to attack. With organized labor, grown greatly in number and power under his benign legislation, backing him wholeheartedly, he contrasted again and again the superiority of "workers with hand and brain" over the owners of property. Yet he maintained that as a realistic liberal he was a true conservative in that he sought "to protect the system of private property and free enterprise by correcting such injustices and inequalities as arise from it." And he quoted Macaulay to give the keynote of his philosophy: "Reform if you would preserve."

In speech after speech he compared current economic advancement with the dark despair at the time of his inauguration. He pointed out that businessmen who in 1933 had pleaded with him for "a quick hypodermic to end the pain" now insisted on throwing "their crutches at the doctor." He also stressed that the underlying political issue throughout our history had been between those who favored the many and those who fought for the few. "We are now coming to learn that the interests of the few are best served when the interests of the many are best safeguarded."

At the end of the campaign, in his speech at Madison Square Garden, Roosevelt again struck back at his detractors. Certain of re-election, he permitted himself the satisfaction of gloating.

Never before in all our history have these forces been so united against one candidate as they stand today. They are unanimous in their hate for me—and I welcome their hatred. I should like to have it said of my first Administration that in it the forces of selfishness and of lust for power have met their match. I should like to have it said of my second Administration that in it these forces have met their master.

The Republican publicists at once pounced upon this statement as sinister evidence of his dictatorial intentions. But the mass of voters knew better. On election day he won by the overwhelming majority of 27,476,673 to 16,679,583 for Alfred Landon—gaining the electoral votes of all states but Maine and Vermont.

Roosevelt began his second term in a truculent mood. He was angered to think that his great popular victory was being nullified by the Supreme Court's invalidation of important New Deal laws. Nor did he forget the ingratitude of big businessmen who made no effort to conceal their hatred of him. In his inaugural speech of January 20, 1937, he deplored the fact that one third of the nation was still "ill-housed, ill-clad, ill-nourished" and declared that this condition was shameful in a country as rich as ours, where "natural wealth can be translated into a spreading volume of human comforts hitherto unknown." He believed that the democratic control of our national resources would help bring about a happier state of affairs—and he was determined to fight for greater democracy in matters pertaining to the general welfare.

In fact, in these last years, we have made the exercise of all power more democratic; for we have begun to bring private autocratic powers into their proper subordination to the public's government. The legend that they were invincible—above and beyond the processes of democracy—has been shattered.

The inauguration over, he was ready to deal with the Supreme Court. The majority of that august body was deeply antipathetic to the philosophy of the New Deal. In interpreting the Constitution in line with their prejudices they ignored Chief Justice Taft's warning back in 1923: "It is not the function of the Court to hold Congressional acts invalid simply because they are passed to carry out economic views which the Court believes to be unwise or unsound." Nor did they heed their own Chief Justice Hughes's dissenting comment on their invalidation of the Railroad Retirement Act: "The power committed to Congress to govern interstate commerce does not require that its government should be wise, much less perfect." In the past two sessions of the Court they had annulled such important measures and prerogatives as the "hot oil" law, NIRA, the Frazier-Lemke Act, the President's right to remove a Federal Trade Commissioner, AAA, the Guffey Coal Act, the New York Minimum Wage Law, and the Washington State Utility Law.

These decisions, Roosevelt declared, "cast a deep shadow of

doubt upon the ability of the Congress ever at any time to protect the Nation against catastrophe by squarely meeting modern social and economic maladjustments." To him they seemed a complete reversal of the established theory that an Act of Congress must not be questioned by the judiciary "unless the act was beyond all reasonable doubt unconstitutional." The Justices showed their displeasure at his critical remarks by making no effort in the fall of 1936 to pay their customary visit to the White House.

Roosevelt was in a good position to take successful issue with the Court. The voters had given overwhelming approval of the New Deal and would have certainly supported his challenge to the "Nine Old Men"—six of them over seventy and all appointed before 1933. Congress, too, would have joined him in a straight fight to stop the tortured interpretation of the Constitution. Instead of making the fight frontal and open, he proceeded deviously and indirectly—and made the crudest blunder of his political career. Working secretly with Attorney-General Homer Cummings and two of his aides, he devised a plan of attack based not on the Court's usurpation of power but on a congested calendar and overage. His request to Congress on February 5 for power to appoint a new Justice whenever one of the incumbents refused to retire on reaching his seventieth birthday—which would also have struck at Justice Brandeis, arch-prophet of the New Deal—was immediately condemned by both enemies and adherents as a dictatorial act of "packing." All the hatred and resentment that his adversaries had stored up against him in recent years burst forth in a storm of censure and abuse.

Roosevelt now realized his mistake—one he would not have made if Louis Howe were still alive—and tried to make amends by turning to the frontal attack. At the Democratic Victory Dinner on March 4 he claimed that the Court's attitude toward New Deal reforms had incited a "widespread refusal to obey the law" and hindered his Administration from carrying out his campaign promises. "If we would keep the faith with those who have faith in us, if we would make democracy succeed, I say we must act

NOW!" Five days later, in a Fireside Chat, he appealed directly to the nation:

We must find a way to take an appeal from the Supreme Court to the Constitution itself. . . . I want—as all Americans want—an independent judiciary as proposed by the framers of the Constitution. That means a Supreme Court that will enforce the Constitution as written— that will refuse to amend the Constitution by the arbitrary exercise of judicial power—amendment by judicial say-so.

This tactical change came too late. The damage was done. Passions were at white heat and unreasoning anger prevailed. The acrimonious fight in Congress was prolonged for several months, but time merely made defeat more certain. For in the interim the Supreme Court had deliberately altered its attitude toward New Deal laws. On March 29 Justice Roberts joined the liberals in validating by a vote of 5 to 4 the Washington State Minimum Wage Act, a measure very similar to the New York law which the Court had nullified the year previous. On the same day it also unanimously approved the new Frazier-Lemke Farm Mortgage Act. Two weeks later it dealt a body blow to Roosevelt's Court Reorganization bill by giving a constitutional bill of health to the crucial National Labor Relations Act. The next month it also validated the important Social Security Act. Meantime, in reply to inquiry, suggested privately by Justice Brandeis, Chief Justice Hughes wrote to Senator Burton K. Wheeler, chief opponent of the Court bill, that the federal judiciary had no crowded calendar. Then Justice Willis Van Devanter, one of the stubborn conservatives, submitted his resignation. Thereafter the fate of the hapless bill was sealed. In defeat, however, Roosevelt achieved his essential aim of liberalizing the Court. The Justices were again following the election returns.

Not so the members of Congress. The opposition to Roosevelt's leadership, during his first term sporadic and futile, now became strong and ominous. Never again was he able to have Congress enact a reform measure without persistent personal prodding—

sometimes only after the greatest political pressure. In 1937 he failed to obtain approval for certain important bills and had to introduce them again—and still again—before they were adopted; the only reforms enacted that year were the Bankhead-Jones Farm Tenant Act and the Wagner-Steagal Housing Act.

Another setback to the New Deal program was the "recession" that began about the middle of 1937. Up to that time the economic index had been climbing upward steadily, if irregularly. Then, goaded by critics of the New Deal to retrench public spending on relief and recovery, Roosevelt initiated reductions in government spending. At the same time a number of industrialists and financiers, antagonized by the judicial validation of the Wagner Act and other reforms, slackened their investment of new capital. A series of severe strikes also served to unsettle economic recovery. The result was a considerable drop in national income and a grim rise in unemployment. Anxious to avert further industrial decline and to alleviate renewed suffering, Roosevelt quickly enlarged his program of relief and public works. Soon, however, a number of European orders for airplanes and munitions and our own extensive rearmament program started the national economy on its subsequently spectacular upward climb.

The recalcitrance of Congress to the Court bill and to important reform legislation such as the Wages and Hours measure so irritated Roosevelt that he embarked on another ill-considered and futile enterprise. Angered by the persistent opposition of certain conservative Democratic members of Congress, he decided actively to resist their nomination. He spoke against them in their own states and criticized them for favoring "the kind of dictatorship which has enslaved many of our fellow citizens for more than half a century." In his appeal to the voters he maintained that "the Democratic Party will live and continue to receive the support of the majority of Americans just so long as it remains a liberal party. . . . As the leader of that party, I propose to try to keep it liberal." The people gave him ovations everywhere, but in the polling booths most of them voted for the men he had attacked.

268

Much as they admired him personally, they subconsciously resented his interference in local politics. This snub, reminding him of Woodrow Wilson's experience in the 1918 elections, taught him a lesson in politics he never again forgot.

From the beginning of his first term as President the troubled international situation grew progressively more ominous. Japan's aggressions in Asia, the truculent march of Nazism in Germany, Mussolini's attack on Ethiopia, and the civil war in Spain—these events kept the world in an increasing state of anxiety. Throughout the 1930's, however, the prevailing sentiment in the United States was pacifistic and isolationist. Memories of World War I, disillusionment with the bickering of European nations, and the sensational exposures by the Nye Committee tended to alienate many Americans from the rest of the world.

In his first inaugural speech Roosevelt had little to say on world affairs except to comment briefly on his Good Neighbor policy. Indeed he and the State Department made a positive and on the whole successful effort to win the friendship of the Latin American nations. Hitler's assumption of power, however, immediately became a threat to the peace of the world. Roosevelt was quickly aware of the danger and one of his early acts as President was to make an eloquent and fervent appeal to all nations for disarmament. It was met with hostile suspicion by isolationists at home and by cold silence or polite mumbling from foreign diplomats. That fall he arranged for a resumption of diplomatic relations with the Soviet Union, broken since the Bolshevik Revolution in 1917, as a means of furthering world amity. On December 28, speaking before the Woodrow Wilson Foundation, he praised the League of Nations as "a prop in the world peace structure," denounced the few nations "with a leadership that seeks territorial expansion at the expense of neighbors," and "wondered with Woodrow Wilson whether people themselves could not some day prevent governments from making war."

In 1934 the Nye Committee investigation of the munitions industry exposed the graft and greed that went far to fan the flames of war. The Committee further revealed that these "merchants of death" were even then helping to arm Nazi Germany, Bolivia, and Paraguay. The Hearst and other newspapers cynically headlined the investigation and used it to strengthen isolationism. Such demagogues as Father Charles Coughlin, some members of Congress, and their sympathizers brazenly insisted not on controlling the munitions industry, as liberal pacifists did, but on an American foreign policy of political isolation. Their harangues found favor with millions of Americans who sincerely hated war and believed that the United States could remain aloof and at peace regardless of what happened elsewhere.

Roosevelt saw further and more clearly what lay ahead. He knew only too well that the world could not remain at peace when a powerful aggressor was on the march; that no country could any longer build a wall of isolation along its borders. With the war cloud then no bigger than a man's hand, however, he hopefully signed the Neutrality Act of 1935, which completely contravened our traditional insistence on the freedom of the seas. The avowed aim of this law was to prevent activities that brought the country into World War I: the shipment of munitions, the lending of money to belligerents, and the traveling of Americans on ships belonging to a nation at war. This Act was later strengthened by amendment.

Fascist Italy's attack on Ethiopia seemed to make the Neutrality Act a weapon against aggressors; but Roosevelt was fully aware of the double-edged nature of the law, which soon enough became evident in connection with the Franco revolt and Japan's aggression against China. What concerned him deeply was the inevitable spread of hostilities. In an Armistice Day speech in 1935 he stated warily:

America must and will protect itself. Under no circumstances will this policy of self-protection go to lengths beyond self-protection. Aggression on the part of the United States is an impossibility so far as the present administration of your government is concerned. Defense against aggression by others—adequate defense on land, on sea and in air—is our accepted policy.

Time merely aggravated the international situation. The war in Spain showed the way the ill wind blew. Roosevelt proclaimed our neutrality as required by law—more reluctantly than he would have otherwise only because Franco's forces had the greater shipping facilities. At a Chautauqua meeting he expressed his great concern and reminded his audience "that so long as war exists on earth there will be some danger that even the nation which most ardently desires peace may be drawn into war." Hitler's unopposed remilitarization of the Rhineland earlier that year, the formation of the Axis among Germany, Italy, and Japan, and the latter's renewed aggression in China in 1937 were additional omens of the threat of fascism.

Roosevelt felt it his duty as President to apprise his fellow Americans of these dangers of war. At the same time he sought to warn the peaceful nations of Europe against the menace confronting them. On October 5, 1937, he delivered in Chicago—the center of isolationist sentiment—his famous "Quarantine" speech. After discussing clearly and concretely the illegal and brutal outrages perpetrated by the fascist governments upon innocent peoples, he appealed to the world for "positive endeavors to preserve peace." To this end he called upon all peaceable nations to "make a concerted effort in opposition to those violations of treaties and those ignorings of humane instincts which today are creating a state of international anarchy and instability from which there is no escape through mere isolation or neutrality." With "the epidemic of world lawlessness" spreading in Europe and in Asia, he proposed a quarantine of aggressors for the protection of their victims. Meantime, he asserted, the United States was alerted to the danger and was taking all precautions.

We are determined to keep out of war, yet we cannot insure ourselves against the disastrous effects of war and the dangers of involvement. We are adopting such measures as will minimize our risk of involve-

271

ment, but we cannot have complete protection in a world of disorder in which confidence and security have broken down.

The articulate reaction to the speech was violently hostile. Public men, popular commentators, and newspaper editors denounced Roosevelt as a meddler and warmonger. Only a small minority praised him for putting an end to what they considered our weak and ignoble foreign policy. The speech was indeed a beacon of bright light piercing international confusion. To a friend he wrote, "As you know, I'm fighting against a public psychology of long standing—a psychology which comes very close to saying 'Peace at any price.'" But he soon realized that he had taken too long a step ahead of the people he was trying to lead and made sure not to be guilty of the same mistake again—much to the irritation of the ardent anti-fascists. What did hurt him was the knowledge that he was not being supported by his own party.

As if to prove the grave dangers of which he spoke, Japanese fliers boldly and brazenly bombed and sank the American gunboat *Panay* in the Yangtze River. A sharp note of protest brought the required apology and compensation from a Japanese government not yet ready to challenge us openly. The incident was closed and Roosevelt said no more about it in public, but his requests of Congress for additional rearmament appropriations spoke firmly of his concern for American safety.

The greatest threat to the peace of the world came from Germany. Hitler and his henchmen were feverishly rearming the nation and concentrating on the mass production of tanks and airplanes. American officials in Berlin kept the State Department informed of the plans of aggression. Aware of the explosiveness of the situation, Roosevelt was distressed at the demoralized condition of the European democracies. The French government, lulled by its dependence on the Maginot Line and torn by inner political dissension, was able only to fumble and grumble. The English nation, led by the pacifistic and pathetic Neville Chamberlain, preferred to appease rather than oppose aggression. In January 1938, anxious to stop the Germans before it was too late, Roosevelt intimated to Chamberlain that he should initiate a European conference that would strive to achieve understanding and amity, but was politely ignored. With isolationists at home still cresting the tide, he dared not interfere more directly. He did, however, ask for enough ships to develop a two-ocean navy.

About this time German plans of conquest were reaching maturity. Early in 1938 Hitler unilaterally annexed Austria to the German Reich and then began a violent propaganda campaign against Czechoslovakia. By the end of the summer war appeared imminent. With a chain of treaties making certain the spread of the conflict over the whole of Europe, in view of the ineptitude and dissension thwarting the diplomatic efforts to avert the threatened aggression, Roosevelt again risked domestic criticism by making a strong appeal to the heads of the five affected nations to keep the peace of Europe. "On behalf of the 130 millions of people of the United States of America and for the sake of humanity everywhere I most earnestly appeal to you not to break off negotiations looking to a peaceful, fair, and constructive settlement of the questions at issue." Chamberlain saved the "peace in our time" by appeasing Hitler at the expense of Czechoslovakia. Roosevelt knew better. When Hitler shortly thereafter intensified his efforts at rearmament, the President publicly announced further increases in American arms. He also stiffened his opposition toward Japanese aggression. Anxious both to warn warmongers abroad and to educate Americans to the realities of world conditions, he said in a speech on October 26, 1938:

It is becoming increasingly clear that peace by fear has no higher or more enduring quality than peace by the sword. There can be no peace if the reign of law is to be replaced by a recurrent sanctification of sheer force. There can be no peace if national policy adopts as a deliberate instrument the threat of war.

Six weeks later, continuing his efforts at education and leadership, he stated in another speech:

What America does or fails to do in the next few years has a far greater bearing and influence on the history of the whole human race for centuries to come than most of us who are here today can ever conceive. We are not only the largest and most powerful democracy in the whole world, but many other democracies look to us for leadership in order that world democracy may survive.

Hitler, bent on conquest and aware of the position of Congress on foreign affairs, paid little attention to Roosevelt's warnings. He brazenly marched into Prague and destroyed Czechoslovakian independence. Sumner Welles, with Roosevelt's approval, denounced the action and reiterated our "condemnation of a policy of military aggression." On April 14, 1939, Roosevelt again appealed to Hitler—and also to Mussolini—to keep the peace in the name of humanity and promised that if they agreed not to attack their independent neighbors he would urge the democracies to reduce their armaments and to foster international trade. To this plea neither gave any answer.

It now became evident to a good many responsible Americans that appeasement had failed and they heartily supported Roosevelt's efforts to repeal the Neutrality Act. Secretary of State Hull assured a group of influential Senators that the arms embargo clause was "an incitement to Hitler to go to war." But the majorities in both Houses of Congress balked. In July their leaders came to the White House at the President's invitation. He informed them that war in Europe was imminent and pleaded with them to help repeal the law on the ground that it hindered his efforts to save the peace. This was disputed by some of the Senators, and Senator William Borah claimed that he had more trustworthy sources of information than the State Department and that he saw no prospect of war.

Six weeks later Hitler ordered the invasion of Poland and World War II was on. With Nazi planes bombing the civilian population of Warsaw, Roosevelt declared in a Fireside Chat:

You must master at the outset a simple but unalterable fact in modern foreign relations between nations. When peace has been broken anywhere, the peace of all countries everywhere is in danger. . . . This nation will remain a neutral nation, but I cannot ask that every American remain neutral as well. Even a neutral has a right to take account of the facts. Even a neutral cannot be asked to close his mind or his conscience.

Then he called Congress into extraordinary session and again requested repeal of the Neutrality Act. This time, after weeks of heated debate, the legislators nullified the arms embargo clause.

It was natural for Roosevelt to think of mediating between Hitler and the democracies, but he was loath to consider a peace "that would consolidate or make possible a survival of a regime of force and aggression." To William Allen White he wrote on December 14, "I do not want this country to take part in a patched-up temporizing peace which would blow up in our faces in a year or two." In his annual message to Congress on January 3, 1940, he again said that the United States must keep out of the war but should "strive with other nations to encourage the kind of peace that will lighten the troubles of the world." And he added with hopeful determination: "We must as a united people keep ablaze on this continent the flames of human liberty, of reason, of democracy and of fair play as living things to be preserved for the better world that is to come."

As the Nazi armies steamrollered over the Low Countries and into France, driving the British divisions into the ocean at Dunkirk and destroying the ill-equipped and poorly led French troops, millions of Americans were shocked into a realization of the terrible menace of fascism. They began to insist on strengthening our defenses still more and on helping England in her fearful efforts at survival. This change in public opinion encouraged Roosevelt to increase the sale of war supplies to Great Britain to the legal limits. Army and Navy chiefs were instructed to declare old material obsolete in order that it might be turned over to English purchasing agencies. When Winston Churchill, who had replaced Chamberlain as prime minister, wrote to Roosevelt of his desperate need of American overage destroyers as a means of keeping up the fight against German submarines, the President was eager to comply but considered the legal and political obstacles insurmountable.

Until the outbreak of war in Europe Roosevelt had assumed as a matter of course that he would retire at the end of his second term. The Presidency during the eight years of economic depression and world crises had been a very severe strain and would have affected harshly one without his remarkable resilience. Moreover, he had long looked forward to living in Hyde Park and to the vocation of a gentleman farmer. Having a very keen historical sense, he was also eager to arrange his papers at the library he had established in Hyde Park to house them. In addition he planned to record the events of his life in book form. So certain was he of political retirement that he had conditionally agreed to serve as special editor on a popular national weekly at a handsome salary.

Not that he longed to yield the powers and prestige of his office. A man of extraordinary ambition, fully aware of his great achievements as President, deeply perturbed by the gross immorality of fascist aggression, he found it very difficult to persuade himself that his successor would be able both to retain liberalism at home and to lead the fight against fascism abroad. The more he considered the available candidates the less acceptable they appeared to him. They were either not internationally minded, or no genuine New Dealers, or personally not strong enough, or unable to command the required popularity.

Hitler's invasion of Poland came as a pounding on his sense of duty. To his thinking the brutal attack had endangered the very foundation of Christian civilization. Unless such political rapacity were successfully stopped and its perpetrators driven from power and destroyed, mankind was doomed to dark barbarism. And who but the United States was strong enough to challenge this cruel enemy of society? And who of the likely candidates had the vision and the will to lead this crusade? Had he the moral right at this crucial juncture to respect the third-term taboo and leave the colossal task to an inexperienced and probably less able successor?

Torn between personal inclination and a prodding sense of duty combined with a sublimated ambition, he continued for months in a state of vacillation—now bent on retirement, now remaining equivocally silent. All the while his ardent admirers kept urging him to run again. Democratic politicians, anxious to remain in power, overcame their scruples concerning a third term and jumped on the bandwagon. Conservatives like Al Smith, Farley, and Garner were definitely opposed to Roosevelt's renomination, but their protests were little heard in the general clamor.

The German invasion first of Denmark and Norway and then of Belgium and Holland forced Roosevelt's decision. He determined that Hitlerism must be purged from Christian society and that it was his duty to help defeat it. This attitude was strengthened by France's collapse. To Farley, who urged him to reply to popular demand for his renomination with General Sherman's famous dictum, he said: "Jim, if nominated and elected, I would not in these times refuse to take the inaugural oath, even if I knew I would be dead within thirty days."

The selection of a candidate for Vice-President nearly disrupted the Democratic Convention. The delegates were overwhelmingly in favor of Roosevelt because of his extraordinary hold on the voters, but they balked at his choice of Henry Wallace as his running mate. The leaders wanted one of their own men in that office—fully aware of the possibility that the President might not last through the full term. This was also in Roosevelt's mind, and he insisted on Wallace because of his genuine New Deal liberalism. At one point the bickering so annoyed him that he was ready to refuse the nomination—and it was this warning that forced the delegates to yield. The isolationists insisted on a plank against involvement in war and Roosevelt agreed to the following phrasing: "We will not participate in foreign wars, and we will not send our armies, navies or air forces to fight in foreign lands outside the Americas, *except in case of attack.*"

Roosevelt's speech of acceptance, radioed to the convention floor, explained how he had reluctantly concluded that he had no right to retire from office in this period of acute world crisis if the people wanted him to remain at his post. He made clear that he would continue to resist aggression in every way he could despite criticism and slander.

I have pursued these efforts in the face of appeaser fifth columnists who charged me with hysteria and war-mongering. But I felt it my duty, my simple, plain, inescapable duty to arouse my countrymen to the dangers of new forces let loose in the world. So long as I am President, I will do all I can to insure that that foreign policy remain our foreign policy.

His immediate task was to help England hold off the Nazis. Assured of his popularity by public opinion polls, yet aware of Congressional opposition to any move which might involve us in the war, he tried to find a way that would enable him to give Britain the badly needed overage destroyers without legislative action. Soon he evolved the plan of exchanging destroyers for bases—air and naval stations which Churchill had offered gratis but which Roosevelt insisted on accepting as part of a deal in order to make the exchange more palatable to his opponents. Upon inquiry he learned from Attorney-General Robert Jackson that as Commander-in-Chief he could arrange the transaction without approval of Congress since it concerned the country's defense. To avoid making the matter a campaign issue, prior acquiescence was obtained from Wendell Willkie, the Republican candidate. On September 3 Roosevelt made public announcement of the exchange and it was favorably received by most Americans.

Meantime Roosevelt greatly accelerated the enlargement of our defense apparatus by the formation of the National Defense Advisory Commission, requests for military preparedness totaling around seven billion dollars and for the enactment of the Selective Service Act, the appointment of Henry L. Stimson as Secretary of War and Frank Knox as Secretary of the Navy—both leading Republicans and active internationalists—and other measures that bespoke the President serving his country well in a time of great danger. In speeches to Congress and to the people he kept reminding them of the critical situation abroad and of our own needs at home. His was a voice of watchful warning, but also of moral courage and confidence in the eventual triumph of right and justice. Although he resisted being pushed into the war by some of his advisers as well as by many eminent Americans who wanted to erase fascism from the world—so much so that they deplored his presumed timidity—he did not hesitate to condemn Hitler's barbarism and Mussolini's "stab-in-the-back" jackalism or to criticize Americans who were ready to "do business with Hitler."

His prodigious activity aimed to prepare the United States not only militarily but also psychologically. He wanted the people to realize that "the only peace possible with Hitler is the peace that comes from complete surrender"; to stand resolutely against oppression and to maintain our American liberties at all cost. In a Fireside Chat on May 26, after the debacle in the Low Countries and the approach of Dunkirk, he urged them to rid themselves of their "fears and illusions" and to concentrate on defense with "the spirit and morale of a free people." He informed them of the plans to multiply military production and cautioned them against those who would try to use preparedness as a means of vitiating social and economic progress.

We must make sure in all that we do that there will be no breakdown or cancellation of any of the great social gains that we have made in these past years. . . . There is nothing in our present emergency to justify a retreat from any of our social objectives—conservation of resources, assistance to agriculture, better housing, and help to the underprivileged.

At the time of his renomination he announced that he would be too preoccupied to make a full-scale campaign but that he would not hesitate to refute lies and falsifications of fact. On August 31, acting as President in a time of danger rather than as a candidate seeking votes, he called out the National Guard. A fortnight later he proclaimed the Draft Registration Day—the first in time of peace—and called upon the youth of the land to consider this call to duty as an enrichment of responsible citizenship.

It was not easy for him, however, to remain passive in a campaign against a strong candidate and he soon yielded to the urging of party leaders to answer some of Willkie's broad assertions and accusations. Taking advantage of his office, he made several "non-political" addresses in addition to a few campaign speeches. The first of the latter talks, given before the Teamsters Union, was a direct appeal for the labor vote. He reminded American workers of the advanced standard of living under the New Deal and stressed the progress of organized labor:

Much of this progress has been due, I like to think, to the one thing that this Administration from the very beginning has insisted upon: the assurance to labor of the untrammeled right, not privilege, but right to organize and bargain collectively with its employers. That principle has now become firmly imbedded in the law of the land; it must remain as the foundation of industrial relations for all time.

In a speech to the nation on Columbus Day he called attention to the evil designs of fascist aggressors and declared our decision to make our defense impregnable. "I speak bluntly," he asserted. "I speak of the love the American people have for freedom and liberty and decency and humanity. That is why we arm. Because, I repeat, this nation wants to keep war away from these two continents." This insistence on his peaceable intentions became the thesis of his final campaign speeches. He stressed his record as a defender of democracy and lashed out against the "record of timidity, of weakness, of short-sightedness" of Republicans in both domestic and foreign affairs—especially their opposition to his rearmament program. He reiterated over and over his sincere efforts to preserve peace. In Boston, piqued at Republican accusations of warmongering, he asserted irascibly:

While I'm talking to you mothers and fathers, I give you one more assurance. I have said this before, but I shall say it again and again and again: Your boys are not going to be sent into any foreign wars. They are going into training to form a force so strong that, by its very existence, it will keep the threat of war far away from our shores. The purpose of our defense is defense.

If in these speeches he occasionally resorted to the pragmatic tricks of the politician, he usually spoke with the fervor of the patriotic statesman. He was quick to condemn the Republicans for taking a page advertisement in the *Daily Worker*—in 1940 opposing Roosevelt as a warmonger—and for accepting assistance from "organizations that make no secret of their admiration for the dictatorship form of government." He prided himself on his liberalism at home—never having called out the army while governor or President "except in the cause of humanity"—and on opposing aggression and injustice everywhere. In his final address in Cleveland he lifted his vast radio audience to the heights of his own vision of the future America:

The true measure of our strength lies deeply imbedded in the social and economic justice of the system in which we live. . . . I see an America where factory workers are not discarded after they reach their prime, where there is no endless chain of poverty from generation to generation, where impoverished farmers and farm hands do not become homeless wanderers, where monopoly does not make youth a beggar for a job. . . . I see an America devoted to our freedom—unified by tolerance and by religious faith—a people consecrated to peace, a people confident in strength because their body and their spirit are secure and unafraid.

The majority of Americans, listening to his remarkably effective radio voice, shared with him his noble vision of American democracy. Impressed by his strong sense of international morality and by his hatred of injustice at home and abroad, they thrust aside hallowed tradition and elected him to a third term by a vote of 27,243,466 to 22,304,755.

With the campaign ended and with the economic depression at last driven out by military preparedness, Roosevelt focused his attention upon the very grave international situation. Together with Secretary Hull he continued his diplomatic attempts to stop Japan from carrying out her ambitious plans of conquest—now invoking the principles of international morality, now intimating economic sanctions, and always making clear American disapproval of aggression. His chief concern, however, was to stop Hitler from crushing England and becoming master of a continent. For the Nazi "Blitz" was making a shambles of British cities and the German submarines were sinking many British ships—and he knew that if England went down the United States would have to face the Axis powers alone.

On December 8, 1940, Churchill wrote a long personal letter to Roosevelt, giving him a detailed and impressive account of England's economic plight and of her determination to fight the Nazis to the end. He explained frankly that the British had reached the bottom of their financial resources and were no longer able to pay for American arms and supplies already ordered and needed desperately. Roosevelt was deeply affected. It was obvious to him that "the best immediate defense of the United States is the success of Great Britain in defending itself"; that the loss of the British Navy would greatly imperil the American continent. After days of reflection he hit upon the brilliant idea of supplying England and other active enemies of fascism with the implements of war by means of "Lend-Lease." This bold act of generosity would not only strengthen the hands of the opponents of aggression, and thus contribute to American defense, but also eliminate the system of loans which in the 1920's caused the United States to be called "Uncle Shylock." To make this idea acceptable to Congress and the people, he explained its essence with the following homely analogy:

Suppose my neighbor's home catches fire, and I have a length of garden hose four or five hundred feet away. If he can take my garden hose and connect it with his hydrant, I may help him to put out his fire. Now, what do I do? I don't say to him before the operation, "Neighbor, my garden hose costs me $15; you have to pay me $15 for it." What is the transaction that goes on? I don't want $15. I want my garden hose back after the fire is over.

On December 29 he gave a Fireside Chat to elaborate the idea —which in essence was his long-known effort to make the United States the arsenal of democracy. With the Axis powers bent on dominating the world, it was of most vital concern to us that these European and Asian warmakers should not gain control of the oceans leading to this hemisphere. The downfall of England would have forced us "to convert ourselves permanently into a militaristic power"—ever faced with the "threats of brute force." This disaster had to be prevented by every means at our command.

The experience of the past two years has proven beyond doubt that no nation can appease the Nazis. No man can tame a tiger into a kitten by stroking it. There can be no appeasement with ruthlessness. . . . The people of Europe who are defending themselves do not ask us to do their fighting. They ask us for the implements of war. . . . Emphatically we must get these weapons to them, get them to them in sufficient volume and quickly enough so that we and our children will be saved the agony and suffering of war which others have had to endure.

A week later, in his annual message to Congress, he developed the twin ideal of an unlimited arsenal of war matériel and demo- cratic morale. Making clear that circumstances not of our own choosing had committed us to a course not only of unrestricted national defense but also of full support of those resisting fascist aggression, he requested the necessary authority and appropria- tions. Then, eager to inspirit Congress and the people with his great goal of making the United States the wellspring of social and economic justice, he outlined the "basic things" inherent in it:

Equality of opportunity for youth and others.
Jobs for those who can work.
Security for those who need it.
The ending of special privileges for the few.
The preservation of civil liberties for all.

The enjoyment of the fruits of scientific progress in a wider and constantly rising standard of living.

On the foundation of these New Deal objectives he placed the "four essential freedoms" that would rid the world of tyranny:

The first is freedom of speech and expression—everywhere in the world.

The second is freedom of every person to worship God in his own way —everywhere in the world.

The third is freedom from want, which, translated into world terms, means economic understanding which will secure to every nation a healthy peacetime life for its inhabitants—everywhere in the world.

The fourth is freedom from fear—which, translated into world terms, means a world-wide reduction of armaments to such a point and in such a thorough fashion that no nation will be in a position to commit an act of physical aggression against any neighbor—anywhere in the world.

This New Deal for the world, he assured Congress, was "no vision of a distant millennium" but "a definite basis for a kind of world attainable in our own time and generation." And he rightly gauged the sentiment of the nation. Men in every walk of life felt imbued with the loftiness of his idealism.

The next day he sent Harry Hopkins to England for the purpose of having him see how the people were faring under the German air raids and to discuss with Churchill the country's needs under the projected Lend-Lease arrangement. This was to be the first of a series of foreign missions in which Hopkins distinguished himself as Roosevelt's *alter ego*. The two men had been developing a strong intimacy throughout the late 1930's. Louis Howe's death in 1936 had deprived the President of an adviser who was completely devoted to his interests and had the courage and the political shrewdness to keep him from making mistakes. Hopkins never became as familiar with Roosevelt as Howe had been, nor did he dare be as critical; but he was equally loyal and in command of a superior intellect; and with his mind lying closer alongside Roose velt's he was able the better to approximate his thoughts and aspirations. Unlike Howe he seldom asserted his own views when there was a difference of opinion, but he always sought to explore an idea to its limits and to indicate its good and bad aspects. Once Roosevelt decided on a course of action, Hopkins proceeded to carry out his wishes with selfless devotion. His six weeks in England early in 1941 served to bring Churchill and Roosevelt much closer together and to give the latter a clear understanding of British needs in the fight for survival. To make sure that the matériel to supply these needs was dispatched expeditiously, Roosevelt appointed Hopkins administrator of Lend-Lease when the measure became law.

All the while Hopkins was abroad, Roosevelt exerted his great gifts of expostulation and persuasion in behalf of the Lend-Lease bill. His opponents in and out of Congress fought desperately to defeat the generous measure, but the nation as a whole shared his anxiety for England's fate and made its feeling known without equivocation. On March 11 Congress sent the enacted bill to Roosevelt for his signature and soon after voted appropriations amounting to $7,000,000,000. Ironically enough, one of the first items shipped to England as part of Lend-Lease consisted of 900,-000 feet of fire hose.

Nazi bombers and submarines continued to weaken English resistance. British ships were being sunk three times as fast as the shipyards were able to build them. It became obvious that the United States would not only have to supply airplanes and essential goods but also the ships needed to bring this material across the Atlantic. When the powerful *Bismarck* emerged into the open seas for its brief career of uncontrolled prowling, the great danger to British ships stimulated the extension of American patrols. Later the United States occupied bases in Iceland and Greenland, thereby risking a shooting war with Germany. Anxious as Roosevelt was to avoid this contingency, he nevertheless felt impelled to disregard diplomatic caution. In a worldwide radio address on May 27 he proclaimed an unlimited national emergency. He pointed out that Hitler was determined to obtain control of the seas in order to further his drive for world power. With modern warfare capable of lightning speed, it was imprudent to wait until the enemy appeared in the front yard. The United States could not permit Germans to occupy strategic outposts in the Atlantic and was therefore ready to resist with all its resources "every attempt by Hitler to extend his Nazi domination to the Western Hemisphere, or to threaten it." Moreover, to strengthen its own defense it must continue to "give every possible assistance to Britain. . . . I say that the delivery of needed supplies to Britain is imperative. I say this can be done; it must be done; it will be done."

Hitler made no move to involve the United States in the conflict as he was then eagerly preparing to attack the Soviet Union. When this crucial event occurred on June 21, Churchill and Roosevelt immediately realized that the involvement of the Red Army radically altered the problems and prospects of the war. Roosevelt again sent Hopkins to England to discuss the new situation with the war leaders there and to facilitate a personal meeting between Churchill and Roosevelt. The latter, anxious to winnow hard fact from wild rumor, also asked Hopkins to fly to Moscow and learn directly from Stalin what his strength was and what aid he required most. This mission the frail but fearless Iowan accomplished with a sympathetic directness that greatly expedited the ensuing interchanges between Stalin and Roosevelt.

With world conditions at an acute stage, Roosevelt requested Congress to extend the draft beyond the year limit. The isolationists fought the amendment with all their resources, and on July 21 the House passed it by the barest majority of 203 to 202.

Early in August Roosevelt set out, with the secrecy he enjoyed, to meet Churchill at a rendezvous on the Atlantic. Together with their military and diplomatic staffs they explored conditions the world over and the ways to meet them most proficiently. Hopkins having returned from Moscow in time to join Churchill at his invitation, was able to report to the conferees that the Red

Army was much stronger than was generally assumed. Roosevelt and Churchill readily agreed that since the Russians were being forced to face the full might of the powerful Nazi army, it was incumbent upon both the United States and England to give them all the help they needed.

We realize fully how vitally important to the defeat of Hitlerism is the brave and steadfast resistance of the Soviet Union and we feel therefore that we must not in any circumstances fail to act quickly and immediately in this matter of planning the program for the future allocation of our joint resources.

The two leaders easily established an intimacy that in time ripened into close friendship. They admired each other's qualities and respected one another's differences. Both were dominated by the wish to destroy the Nazi tyranny, and neither permitted extraneous factors to turn his mind from the main goal. In their first joint statement, embodying the principles of the Atlantic Charter, it was Roosevelt's views that prevailed. Despite Churchill's insistence that nothing in the pronouncement should affect the British Empire, the thesis of the Charter was definitely anti-imperialistic. In effect it proclaimed the application of democratic ideals to every part of the world—no aggrandizement, no exploitation of weak or backward peoples, economic equality to all nations, freedom from fear and want for everyone, and "the abandonment of the use of force." In a real sense Roosevelt succeeded in extending his New Deal philosophy as a goal for the entire world.

Hitler's response was to order his submarines to attack American vessels entering within their range of operations. On September 4 the destroyer *Greer* was fired upon while on its way to Iceland to deliver mail. A week later Roosevelt gave a Fireside Chat to announce the attack and to state that he was ordering the Navy to protect itself as well as the ships carrying supplies to England. He pointed out that Hitler was seeking "to control the seas by ruthless force and by wiping out every vestige of international law and humanity." Although the United States sought "no shooting war," it did not want peace so much as to refrain from fighting back. "When you see a rattlesnake poised to strike," he commented, "you do not wait until he has struck before you crush him." Hereafter Nazi vessels of war would enter the waters under American protection "at their own risk. . . . I have no illusions about the gravity of the step. I have not taken it hurriedly or lightly. It is the result of months and months of constant thought and anxiety and prayer. In the protection of your nation and mine it cannot be avoided."

The next month, as more American ships were attacked, Roosevelt asked for authority to arm merchant vessels and ordered the Navy "to shoot on sight." These provocations on both sides were not followed by a formal declaration of war for the simple reason that the United States acted defensively and Hitler wanted to avoid full-scale combat with the American leviathan before he had crushed the Red Army.

Although the danger seemed greatest in the Atlantic, the enemy in the Pacific was the more determined. From the beginning of Japan's march of conquest in Asia in 1931 the United States refused to acquiesce in its acts of aggression. After 1937, when China proper was invaded, Roosevelt and Hull made no secret of their sympathy with the Chinese government, but they were careful to use their economic sanctions in a manner to lessen Japan's temptation to further acts of conquest. Throughout 1941 they tried vainly to persuade the Japanese government to cease its imperialistic activities. The Nipponese warlords, however, refused to relinquish their plans to dominate Asia.

From April 9 to September 6 five different Japanese drafts for an agreement were presented to Hull, but each one demanded American acceptance of greater Japanese aggression than the previous proposal. Roosevelt and Hull remained firm but friendly—their replies urging respect for international morality and offering greater economic trade as the advantage of an agreement. But the Nipponese militarists insisted on appeasement, and this the United

States refused. In a stiff note to Ambassador Nomura on August 17 it stated that if Japan continued to attack her neighbors it would be "compelled to take immediately any and all steps it may deem necessary" to safeguard its legitimate rights and interests. When the meeting between Roosevelt and Churchill was made public, the Japanese proposed a similar conference between the President and Premier Konoye. Roosevelt was agreeable, but stipulated a prior understanding between the two governments in order to assure the success of the talks between the principals. To this the Japanese would not agree, and soon after the premiership was taken over by General Tojo.

Negotiations between the two countries continued, but no progress was made and neither side hoped for more than to gain time for its own advantage. The American Navy had broken the Japanese code and knew that Tojo was planning further aggression but not how or against what country. As late as November 7 Roosevelt and Hull assumed that the attack would be made in South Asia. Two weeks later Nomura and Kurusu, Japan's special representative, delivered their government's final terms—an ultimatum which we could not accept without sacrificing China's independence. In our reply on November 26 we sought to be conciliatory while insisting on that country's territorial integrity. Roosevelt knew such an argeement would be unacceptable to the Japanese war party and said in a cable to Churchill, "This seems to me a fair proposition for the Japanese but its acceptance or rejection is really a matter of internal Japanese politics. I am not very hopeful and we must all be prepared for real trouble, possibly soon." Although he learned from intercepted cables that the Japanese had placed a deadline for the acceptance of their demands, he did not know that a mighty task force had left its home base on November 10 and was to end its mission at Hawaii.

Much has been written to the effect that Roosevelt had deliberately provoked a Japanese attack in order to plunge the United States into the war. The known facts do not substantiate this serious charge. They indicate that Roosevelt and Hull did not expect the Nipponese leaders to be reckless enough to strike directly at the United States. They assumed that the next aggression would be southward. Since such an attack would very likely force us into the conflict, they sought to prolong the negotiations as long as possible in the hope of postponing it—or perhaps even averting it altogether. At a cabinet meeting on November 25 Roosevelt and his advisers agreed that the United States must act peacefully even at the risk of letting Japan strike first in order to leave no doubt in anyone's mind as to who was the aggressor. And as a last-minute effort to avoid hostilities the President on December 6 appealed to Emperor Hirohito to stop the war moves of his government.

A day later the reply came from Pearl Harbor, where Japanese dive bombers sank American ships, destroyed airplanes on the field, and killed Americans in large numbers. That afternoon Nomura and Kurusu kept their appointment with Hull to hand him their government's latest communication. The Secretary, informed of the attack, felt free to tell them that although he had not "uttered one word of untruth" during their nine months of conversations, he had never in all his fifty years of public service seen a document so crowded with "infamous falsehoods and distortions on a scale so huge that I never imagined until today that any government was capable of uttering them."

The next day Roosevelt appeared before Congress to ask for a declaration of war. "Yesterday December 7, 1941—a date which will live in infamy—the United States of America was suddenly and deliberately attacked by naval and air forces of the Empire of Japan." Congress was as shocked and outraged by the assault as the rest of the nation and eagerly complied. The British Commonwealth of Nations similarly declared war on the aggressor. Three days later practically the entire world became engaged in the conflict when Germany and Italy joined Japan against the democracies. In a Fireside Chat Roosevelt emphasized that the war was the "climax of a decade of international immorality," and now that we were in it we must make sure not to fight in vain:

The true goal we seek is far above and beyond the ugly field of battle. When we resort to force, as now we must, we are determined that this force shall be directed toward ultimate good as well as against immediate evil. We Americans are not destroyers—we are builders. . . . Together with other free peoples, we are now fighting to maintain our right to live among our world neighbors in freedom and in common decency, without fear of assault.

This confidence in victory and this hope for the future he maintained to the end—to the great encouragement of many millions the world over.

Americans did not need to be told that they were facing the most dangerous enemies in their entire history. Japan was punishing our crippled Navy with ferocious effectiveness and driving our army in the Philippines to unavoidable surrender. But Roosevelt's embattled stand united the nation in its determination to fight back—and win. Political differences were for the time being forgotten; men and women accepted hardship without flinching; and the country's mighty industrial machine was geared into high speed to perform miracles of production.

Roosevelt immediately took full charge of the national war effort. As President and Commander-in-Chief he issued Executive Orders and laid plans for the prodigious work ahead. He assembled a first-rate group of generals and admirals to devise military strategy and forge the weapons of victory. While he acted on their advice in matters of warfare, they sympathized with his war aims and admired his extraordinary qualities of leadership. For he had at once established his stellar position among the heads of the democracies and guided their councils by the boldness and breadth of his political idealism.

The day after Pearl Harbor he invited Churchill and his staff to Washington for a conference. He was firmly convinced that the Axis powers would be defeated in the end and he was from the first anxious to evolve a peace that would eliminate all bloody conflict among nations. The British came on December 22 and immediately proceeded to discuss matters of war strategy. Although the serious defeats in the Pacific cast a pall of gloom over these fighting men, Roosevelt, ably abetted by Churchill, strengthened their wills by demands for aggressive preparations and offensive action. Agreement was soon reached that Hitler's armies were the prime target and that they must be engaged in battle on the Continent as quickly as possible. With 280 Nazi divisions driving deep into Russia and endangering the ability of the Red Army to hold them back, victory for the allies depended on an early second front that would draw a good many Nazi divisions from Russian territory. The fight in the Pacific must wait until Germany was defeated.

Simultaneously with military plans Roosevelt argued for the initiation of a peace program. Keenly aware of the psychological value of concrete hope, he wanted to provide the nations fighting fascism with an encouraging symbol of unity and justice. He therefore proposed the high principles of the Atlantic Charter as the rallying point for the antifascist peoples. Quick negotiation brought representatives from every country at war with the Axis powers to the White House on January 1, 1942, and a total of twenty-five nations joined the United States in signing a pledge not to make a separate peace, to cooperate toward victory, and to abide by the principles of the Atlantic Charter. Roosevelt himself provided the name of the organization that was to bind these peoples together: United Nations.

Five days later, in his annual message, he rallied the people with an inspiring confidence that did not gloss over defeats but stressed ultimate victory. "The militarists of Berlin and Tokyo started this war. But the massed, angered forces of common humanity will finish it." After recounting our war aims and peace objectives, he called for an industrial productivity that staggered the imagination but soon enough became the realistic result of American ingenuity and enterprise. On February 23, when conditions in the Pacific were desperate and mourning pervaded thousands of American homes, he gave a Fireside Chat in which he discussed the war situation frankly and factually in all its immense global aspects but with infectious courage and a persuasive boldness of spirit.

Throughout 1942 he devoted his extraordinary energies to establish the colossal war machine and to make sure that the people at home got butter while the armed forces abroad received the guns. He formed numerous war boards to help accelerate production and enforce economic controls—and drafted the ablest men he could find to serve on them. To help him expedite matters he asked Justice James F. Byrnes to resign from the Supreme Court and take charge of the Office of Economic Stabilization, and later of the Office of War Mobilization, thereby relieving him of much of the detailed attention to domestic affairs. This replacement of "Dr. New Deal" by "Dr. Win-the-War," while signifying his concentration on beating the enemy, entailed no slackening of interest in domestic democracy on his part.

Accelerating war production having made necessary the rationing of civilian goods, a national economic policy was devised to keep down inflation and profiteering. On April 28 Roosevelt made another Fireside Chat to explain his seven-point program requiring sacrifices on the part of every citizen. "The price for civilization," he insisted, "must be paid in hard work and sorrow and blood. The price is not too high. If you doubt it, ask those millions who live today under the tyranny of Hitlerism." All through the war he continued to fight inflation and to urge the principle of equality of sacrifice—with the result that the price spiral rose only a fraction of what it did both in World War I and shortly after the fighting ended in 1945.

The conduct of the war effort absorbed most of Roosevelt's time and thought until victory was plainly in view. After Churchill and he had agreed early in 1942 on a general program, their Joint Chiefs of Staffs were asked to prepare specific plans of action. The task seemed at first impossible to square with reality. Although their plans called for the seizure of the initiative and the opening of a second front without delay, an inadequacy of supplies and men combined with major disasters in Africa and on the high seas tended to frustrate the carefully developed strategy and required frequent revision.

A series of conferences in Washington and London dealt with the ever-pressing problem of a second front. The Russians were being severely pommeled during most of 1942 and the danger of their complete collapse greatly worried the allied leaders. Stalin urged an invasion of France as the most effective means of releasing the crushing grip on his armies and sent Molotov to London and Washington to plead his cause. Roosevelt and his advisers were heartily in favor of such a front. They knew that the Russians were killing and crippling hundreds of thousands of Nazis; they also knew that the collapse of the Red Army would make the destruction of Hitlerism terribly costly in American lives. Although Churchill pretended to be agreeable to the opening of a second front, he argued that an attempted invasion of France in 1942 would result in a "river of blood." The Americans at first insisted, pointing out that it would be to allied advantage to relieve the Russians—and thus keep them fighting—even at the risk of sacrificing part of the invasion forces. "Russia had successfully fought off the German army for six months," Secretary Stimson maintained, "and it was now up to us to do our share." While this debate was in progress in June, news reached the conferees that Tobruk had fallen and that the entire Middle East was in danger —forcing Churchill's immediate return to England.

When Hopkins, General Marshall, and Admiral King flew to London the next month to complete the interrupted conference, they found Churchill adamant against an early attack on Normandy. Instead he stressed the advantages of an invasion of North Africa. Roosevelt reluctantly agreed, persuaded that a second front in France was still premature and that a clearance of the Mediterranean route would expedite the shipment of supplies to Russia.

Feverish preparations were begun at once and a mighty armada reached the African shore early in November. It was the hope of American leaders that the Vichy government would not seriously oppose the landings, but instead it fought back hard for several days until overwhelmed by vastly superior forces. If the military invasion was successful, the subsequent political deals with Vichy officials were inept and caused considerable bad feeling both at home and abroad.

By late 1942 the war situation had improved markedly. The Japanese advance was stopped in the Coral Sea and at Midway; the Russians were holding the Germans in the streets of Stalingrad; Rommel's army was being fought back in Libya; and the invasion of North Africa gave evidence of the allied offensive in full swing. Roosevelt said on Armistice Day that the Nazis "know they have conquered nothing. Today, they face inevitable, final defeat. Yes, the forces of liberation are advancing."

At the end of 1942 he took the time to give WPA an "honorable discharge." He praised its notable achievements in the construction of public roads, bridges, buildings, utility plants, outdoor recreation facilities, flood-control projects, and in the advancement of education, the arts, and public health. In a retrospective mood he once said to William D. Hassett:

I shall be remembered by historians as the great spender, the greatest spender we have ever had. What the historians won't know, what the public doesn't know, is the enormous sums I have been able to save by careful scrutiny of bills, paring down extravagant and unwarranted and unnecessary expenditures.

Early the next January he submitted to Congress a war budget of over one hundred billion dollars. In his annual message he surveyed the progress in production at home and in the fighting abroad and explained the kind of peace he was striving for. He maintained that only by furthering the four freedoms in every part of the world could we safeguard the future welfare of the United States. "We cannot make America an island in either a military or an economic sense. Hitlerism, like any other form of crime or disease, can grow from the evil seeds of economic as well as military feudalism."

Two days later he left for Casablanca for another meeting with Churchill. He had tried hard to persuade Stalin to join them, but the crusty Russian, annoyed by the delay in the promised invasion of France, insisted he was too preoccupied with the conduct of the war to leave his country. In the sessions of the Joint Chiefs of Staff as well as in those including Roosevelt and Churchill the Americans continued to favor the prompt opening of a second front in Normandy. The British now argued for a Sicilian invasion as a first requisite in eliminating the Axis threat to allied shipping and in obtaining air bases in Italy. The final decision was to attack Sicily next but at the same time to accelerate preparations in England for the Channel invasion of France. An incidental product of the conference was Roosevelt's policy of unconditional surrender—a principle that was later severely criticized by certain military experts. In reporting on the achievements of the meeting shortly after his return, he again stressed that the peace to come must recognize that "the whole world is one neighborhood" and must therefore do justice to the whole human race—or "the germs of another world war will remain as a constant threat to mankind."

The fighting in 1943 was definitely in favor of the Allies. The Nazis suffered a crippling defeat at Stalingrad and were driven out of North Africa; in the Pacific, Americans were winning battles and driving the Japanese back toward their home bases. In May British leaders came to Washington again to confer on the next steps to be taken. For various strategic reasons Roosevelt had to agree to postpone the invasion of France to May 1, 1944, and in the meantime to invade Italy. Agreement was also reached on the forthcoming campaign against Japan.

The immediate objective of knocking Italy out of the war began to be realized in July with Mussolini's abdication and with his successor Bagdolio's secret negotiations for an armistice. Late that month Roosevelt announced over the radio: "The first crack in the Axis has come. The criminal, corrupt Fascist regime in Italy is going to pieces." He stated that he would "have no truck with Fascism in any way" and that the terms were "unconditional surrender," but he assured the people of Italy that they would be helped to reconstitute themselves and to choose a "government in accordance with the basic democratic principles of liberty and equality."

Rapidly developing war conditions made necessary a new top-level conference. In May Roosevelt had sent Joseph E. Davies to Moscow to seek Stalin's agreement to a meeting in Alaska, but the Russian leader refused. Roosevelt and Churchill thereupon met in Quebec on August 17. They readily agreed to attack in the Toulon-Marseilles area to complement the Normandy invasion; to give supreme command to an American general; to form a Southeast Asia Command headed by Lord Louis Mountbatten; and to work out a four-power declaration providing for the postwar establishment of an effective international organization. Stalin was informed of these decisions and he indicated his approval by agreeing to a meeting of foreign ministers in Moscow that fall.

Secretary Hull was in his seventies and not in good health. Yet so strong was his antagonism to Sumner Welles, whom Roosevelt had expected to attend the Moscow Conference, that he insisted on making the long and arduous trip himself—thus forcing Welles to resign as Under-Secretary. Roosevelt accepted the situation despite his good opinion of Welles because he valued Hull's influence in the Senate and needed him to help gain approval for the projected international organization. Nor did Hull disappoint him in Moscow. He represented the United States with a friendly firmness that won Stalin's respect—so much so that he voluntarily offered to join the war against Japan immediately after Hitler's defeat. "The Marshal's statement of his decision was forthright," Hull wrote later. "He made it emphatically, it was entirely unsolicited, and he asked nothing in return." And even while the Secretary was on his way home the Senate, impressed with his work in Moscow, approved by a vote of 85 to 5 the Connally Resolution favoring American participation in the United Nations.

The more territory the allied armies occupied the more anxious Roosevelt became to alleviate suffering among the victims of war. He knew that such relief, apparently altruistic, was in fact a practical means of avoiding the danger of chaos and revolt among the starving populace. To expedite this work and to give it an international character, he called the representatives of forty-four nations to the White House for the purpose of forming the United Nations Relief and Rehabilitation Administration. On November 9 the delegates signed the agreement to set up this organization. Roosevelt assured them that UNRRA would "help put into practical effect some of the high purposes" of the United Nations. He also pointed out that "Nations will learn to work together only by actually working together." As an act of poetic justice he appointed Governor Herbert Lehman director of UNRRA.

At Moscow Hull had obtained Stalin's concurrence for a meeting with Roosevelt and Churchill at Teheran late in November. Roosevelt looked forward to this personal conference with the powerful Russian. He was well aware that the Red Army, having borne the full brunt of the Nazi fury, was growing in power and would in the end emerge as the strongest force in Europe. The peace of the world therefore depended upon the amicable relations between the Soviet Union and the United States. To achieve this goal he had to meet and become friends with Stalin.

Roosevelt went first to Cairo, where he conferred with Churchill and Chiang Kai-shek about the Asian war program. The promises of assistance given to the Generalissimo had to be postponed temporarily as a result of agreements reached in Teheran, but the political decisions assured a Japan stripped of her empire and military prowess, a united and strong China, and an independent Korea.

At Teheran the Russians dealt respectfully with Roosevelt and persuaded him to occupy a villa in their compound in order to avoid the inconvenience and danger of daily travel through the city. Stalin was blunt and tough in debate, but he was quick to grasp essentials and to compromise on secondary issues. More than once he spoke harshly to Churchill when the latter insisted on directing the second front to "the soft under-belly of Europe," but always he treated Roosevelt courteously and considerately. Once he obtained assurance on the invasion of Normandy, he readily agreed to attack simultaneously from the east, to enter the Japanese war within six months after the defeat of Hitler, and to participate fully in the organization of the United Nations.

Roosevelt was extremely pleased with the outcome. To his son Elliott he explained, with acute foresight, that he was most gratified with his success in convincing Stalin "that the United States and Great Britain were not allied in one common bloc against the Soviet Union. . . . The one thing that would upset the applecart, after the war, is if the world is divided again, Russia against England and us. That's our big job now, and that'll be our big job tomorrow, too." The Declaration of Teheran, issued by the three principals after the meeting, expressed their determination to "work together in war and in the peace that will follow."

Emerging from these cordial conferences we look with confidence to the day when all peoples of the world may live free lives, untouched by tyranny, and according to their various desires, and their own consciences. We came here with hope and determination. We leave here, friends in fact, in spirit, in purpose."

Although the exertions of these meetings proved extremely fatiguing, Roosevelt found it necessary on the way back to confer with President Ismet Inonu of Turkey in order to keep his allegiance to the allies. He also stopped at Tunis to tell General Eisenhower that he was to be the commander of the allied invasion of France—for various reasons giving him the high post that was originally reserved for General Marshall.

On Christmas Eve, a week after his return to Washington,

Roosevelt reported on these conferences in a Fireside Chat. With the actual fighting progressing very well, he stressed peace and international good will. His references to Stalin were laudatory. It was his firm belief that the Russian subscribed to the intent and spirit of the Teheran Declaration.

To use an American and somewhat ungrammatical colloquialism, I may say that I "got along fine" with Marshal Stalin. He is a man who combines a tremendous, relentless determination with a stalwart good humor. I believe he is truly representative of the heart and soul of Russia; and I believe that we are going to get along very well with him and the Russian people—very well indeed.

On his recent trips to the fronts Roosevelt had obtained the impression that the people at home were not doing enough to win the war. He also thought of the millions of young men who would soon be returning home and would need jobs and security. His report to Congress on January 11, 1944, combined a request for a national service law and other associated measures with a declaration of an economic bill of rights. The war legislation aimed to "mobilize our total resources" and to "give our enemies demoralizing assurance that we mean business—that we, 130,000,000 Americans, are on the march to Rome, Berlin, and Tokyo."

The second part of his message dealt with "the fact that true individual freedom cannot exist without economic security and independence." The keynote was security "for all—regardless of station, race, or creed." Among the elements constituting the economic bill of rights were the rights to work, to adequate wages, to a decent living for farmers, to freedom to do business, to a comfortable home, to medical care, social security, and a good education. He urged Congress "to explore the means for implementing this economic bill of rights." A majority of both Houses of Congress, however, consisting of a combination of conservative Republicans and Democrats, balked at these as well as at other of his proposed postwar reforms.

Roosevelt followed the daily developments in the several fighting areas with unflagging concern and dealt with emergency problems as they arose. The building of the peace, however, began to occupy his closest attention, and he worked hard to lay a democratic foundation. He believed that the day of colonial exploitation was gone forever, and he was critical of Churchill's insistence on keeping the British Empire intact. To his son Elliott he said, "I've tried to make it clear to Winston—and the others— that while we're allies, and in it to victory by their side, they must never get the idea that we're in it just to help them hang on to the archaic, medieval Empire ideas." When the problem of Indo-China came to the fore in 1944, he opposed its return to France and suggested to Hull that it be administered by an international trusteeship. "France," he explained, "has milked it for one hundred years. The people of Indo-China are entitled to something better than that." He also was alert to developments in Eastern Europe and was determined on democratic solutions everywhere.

Preparations for the invasion of Normandy were meanwhile coming to a head and it was only bad weather that delayed the attack to June 6. The day before Roosevelt spoke on the radio concerning the fall of Rome—"one down and two to go!"—and again assured the Italians that they would be fed and helped to regain their independent national existence. Twenty-four hours later he was once more speaking over the radio to announce the successful landings on the Normandy beaches. In characteristic fashion he considered the long-awaited invasion not a time for boasting but for humble supplication; his speech consisted of a deeply felt prayer for guidance and strength to the armed forces and for "a peace that will let all men live in freedom, reaping the just rewards of their honest toil."

Despite his absorption in matters of war and peace, Roosevelt was not permitted to forget that 1944 was an election year. It was obvious that he could not well refuse to remain in office in the midst of war and he was reconciled to his fate. To a friendly Congressman he wrote, "I would give a great deal personally to return to Hyde Park and Georgia just as soon as the Lord will let me."

301

He was by then a very tired man, greatly bothered by a chronic sinus condition and by a persistent cough; no longer in possession of his quality of quick resilience, he longed for the relaxation of retirement. But he knew his duty to his country and to the world. To Robert E. Hannegan, chairman of the Democratic National Committee, he wrote, "If the people command me to continue in this office and in this war, I have as little right to withdraw as the soldier has to leave his post in the line." Not for a moment, of course, was he unaware of his position as chief architect of the oncoming peace and of his eagerness to guide its structure to successful completion.

As in 1940, one of the vexing problems was the choice of a nominee for the Vice-Presidency. Much as he liked Henry Wallace personally, he no longer considered him a politically desirable running mate. He knew that the party politicians disliked him; nor did he forget Wallace's tactlessness in permitting his quarrel with Jesse Jones to deteriorate into a public scandal. Wishing to avoid a fight within his own party and anxious to retain the good will of Congress toward the projected United Nations organization, he finally acquiesced in the choice of Senator Harry S. Truman. Yet loath to hurt Wallace's feelings, he did not tell him of his decision and even stated publicly to the convention that if he were a delegate he would vote for his renomination; after the election he dismissed Jones, whom he had come to consider disloyal, from the office of Secretary of Commerce and gave the post to Wallace. Meantime Truman, unaware of Roosevelt's assent, continued to promote James Byrnes's candidacy for the Vice-Presidency till near the end. It was this deviousness that led to the "clear it with Sidney" charge—made much of by Republicans as evidence that the CIO and Sidney Hillman were in control of Roosevelt Democrats.

While the convention was in session, Roosevelt went to Hawaii to confer with the Pacific leaders of our armed forces. From there he proceeded to Alaska to inspect installations and returned by way of Bremerton, Washington, where he made a radio address.

302

Read on shipboard, far from the assembled crowd and in the face of a fresh wind, the result was poor and caused much speculation about his health. Thomas Dewey, the Republican candidate, and his associates made much of this incident and campaigned on the slogans of the government being run by "tired old men" and that it was therefore "time for a change"—much to the President's annoyance.

He was not long in demonstrating that he had lost nothing of his mastery as a campaigner. On September 23 he delivered his first political speech before the Teamsters Union. With a fine mixture of irony and satire, as well as an array of facts overlaid with incisive indignation, he ridiculed the charges against his Administration and pointed out the political bankruptcy of his opponents. He capitalized on Republican claims that they approved of many of the basic New Deal laws but promised to administer them more efficiently. "Can the Old Guard pass itself off as the New Deal"? he asked derisively, and the thunderous roar of the audience gave the answer he wanted. The highlight of the speech was his mock anger at the canard that his dog Fala had been left behind in Alaska and had to be brought back by a destroyer sent there specially for that purpose. He asserted that although he and his family did not resent personal calumny, Fala's "Scotch soul was furious" at the very thought of so extravagant a gesture on his account. "I am accustomed to hearing malicious falsehoods about myself . . . but I think I have a right to resent, to object to libelous statements about my dog." His delivery suited the occasion to perfection. The appreciative guffaws of the hilarious labor and political leaders encouraged him to give the best oratorical performance of his career. Thereafter any talk about his being a "tired old man" seemed silly.

In the heat of the campaign the charges against him became vicious. He fought back with unwonted fervor. No previous political rival had angered him as much as did Dewey. In a radio address on October 5 he repelled the persistent accusation that he favored communism:

303

Labor-baiters, bigots, and some politicians use the term "communism" loosely, and apply it to every progressive. ·. . . I have never sought and do not now welcome the support of any person or group committed to Communism, or Fascism, or any other foreign ideology which would undermine the American system of government or the American system of free enterprise and private property.

He insisted, however, that this attitude toward communism did not conflict with American friendship toward the Soviet Union. "The kind of economy that suits the Russian people, I take it is their own affair."

He next went to New York City to tour its streets and to deliver an important address before the Foreign Policy Association. Although a cold, driving rain swept the metropolis, he insisted on riding for hours in an open car to prove that he was strong enough to endure it. This extreme exposure, oddly enough, left him without bad aftereffects. His speech that evening made clear his policy "not to bargain with tyrants" and to provide future generations with "a heritage of peace" by means of an international organization that would use force, if necessary, to keep war from breaking out. "Peace, like war," he maintained, "can succeed only where there is a will to enforce it, and where there is available power to enforce it." He brought this novel policy home to the American people by the following apt simile: "A policeman would not be a very effective policeman if, when he saw a felon break into a house, he had to go to Town Hall and call a town meeting to issue a warrant before the felon could be arrested."

In later speeches at Philadelphia, Chicago, Boston, and intermediate points, he took issue with Republican criticism of his domestic and foreign policies. His ridicule, understatement, and direct retort exposed the spuriousness of the charges. In Boston he responded with indignation against the snide insinuations concerning Hillman and other foreign-born Americans: "Never before in my lifetime has a campaign been filled with such misrepresentation, distortion, and falsehood. Never since 1928 have there been so many attempts to stimulate in America racial and religious intolerance."

When the election was over he had won for the fourth time— by a vote of 25,602,505 to 22,006,278 for Dewey.

Eager to prepare the machinery for peace while the war was still in progress, Roosevelt was instrumental in initiating the Dumbarton Oaks Conference. It assembled in August 1944 and remained in session till October, when it finished preparing the preliminary organization of the United Nations. At this gathering the American representatives, mindful of the probable will of Congress, favored the veto in all matters involving the use of economic sanctions and armed forces.

Early that fall Churchill, fearful of the postwar fate of the Balkans with the Red Army fighting its way through it, insisted on an immediate meeting with Stalin. Unable either to dissuade the apprehensive prime minister or to leave the country in the middle of an election campaign, Roosevelt stated pointedly that he would "retain complete freedom of action after this conference is over." At this meeting in Moscow Churchill and Stalin agreed to give Great Britain full responsibility in Greece, to grant Russia predominance in Bulgaria, Hungary, and Rumania, and for both countries to have equal influence in Yugoslavia—an arrangement in violation of the Atlantic Charter and a later source of trouble.

The election out of the way, Roosevelt was ready for another conference with his co-principals. In the occupied territory behind the battlefront many problems were emerging that required intelligent settlement. Even more important to him was the organization of the United Nations. With victory in sight, spokesmen for national interests were beginning to press their selfish ends at the expense of international amity. This he was anxious to forestall. Again Stalin pleaded his inability to leave Russia and suggested Yalta as a meeting place. Although Churchill objected strenuously to the idea of going to the war-devastated town, Roosevelt was too eager to strengthen the sympathetic understanding among the principal nations to bother about possible inconveniences.

President Roosevelt's mind remained keenly alert, but he was no longer able to throw off the ill effects of the long and concentrated strain of his office. He had lost considerable weight and looked emaciated and frail. His body shook visibly and his hands trembled. Nor was he able to relax before making the long trip. In the midst of his preparations he had to accept the resignation of the ailing Cordell Hull—the post going to Under-Secretary Edward R. Stettinius. He also had to take the time to prepare and deliver his annual message to Congress and his inaugural address. Both documents dealt with the pressing problems of war and the requirements of a democratic peace. He once more reminded the nation that our own peace depended on other nations, near and far. "We have learned that we must live as men and not as ostriches, not as dogs in a manger. We have learned to be citizens of the world, members of the human community."

The day after the inauguration he left for Yalta, with a stopover at Malta to meet with Churchill and the Joint Chiefs of Staff for preliminary discussions. Now that the war was nearing its triumphant end, he thought chiefly of the coming peace. He knew that success or failure depended on Russia's attitude and he was determined to win Stalin's cooperation by practicing his own quoted precept from Emerson: "The only way to have a friend is to be a friend."

The sessions at Yalta were brisk, at times contentious, with Roosevelt acting the moderator with his wonted skill. Both Churchill and Stalin insisted on concessions favoring their countries; Roosevelt, taking the larger view, again and again turned the debate to the major problems of peace. He prevailed upon them to reaffirm the principles of the Atlantic Charter in connection with the liberated areas—although Stalin proved stubborn regarding Poland, and its political establishment had to be left for later agreement. He also obtained approval for the organizational meeting of the United Nations to begin on April 25 at San Francisco—although he had to acquiesce in Stalin's demand for two additional votes for the Ukraine and White Russia. At the urging of his military advisers Roosevelt made final arrangements for the Red Army's early entrance into the war against Japan—although he had to grant the Soviet Union the return of Asian concessions that once were hers. It was a give and take all around, but not for a moment did Roosevelt compromise with his grand aim of a people's peace. As Stettinius stated years later, "The record of the Conference shows clearly that the Soviet Union made greater concessions at Yalta to the United States and Great Britain than were made to the Soviets." It was only after Roosevelt's death, when the Russians became apprehensive of Churchill's antagonism and when their fears of the Truman Administration were confirmed by the sudden stoppage of Lend-Lease supplies and the unexpected reversal of a projected loan that they began to act arbitrarily in their own national interests.

On his way back Roosevelt stopped in Egypt for sessions with its King Farouk, Ibn Saud of Arabia, and Haile Selassie of Ethiopia. He was by then sapped of energy and strength—"all burned out." The sight of him shocked people who knew him well. Nor did he respond, as always before, to the sea voyage home. The sudden death of one of his close aides grieved him deeply. It was only by conscious effort that he managed to complete his report to Congress, which he delivered shortly after his return to Washington. He no longer made any attempt to wear his steel braces and sat in his wheel chair while making the address—for the first time referring publicly to his infirmity. And if his speech reflected his fatigued condition and lacked the buoyant spirit of his earlier discourses, it was an earnest appeal to his countrymen to assume their destined part in the world and work patiently with other nations for a durable peace.

The Crimea Conference was a successful effort by the three leading Nations to find a common ground for peace. It ought to spell the end of the system of unilateral action, the exclusive alliances, the spheres of influence, the balances of power, and all the other expedients that have been tried for centuries—and have always failed. We propose to substitute for all these a universal organization which all peace-loving Nations will finally have a chance to join.

The fighting was nearing its end in Europe and reaching a climax in the Pacific. The latest reports from secret scientific laboratories—on which Roosevelt had gambled two billion dollars in the attempt to develop a nuclear fission bomb before German scientists succeeded in a similar effort—were very encouraging. All was going well, but there was still a great deal to be done. Tired as he was, Roosevelt persisted in attending to his manifold tasks. At the urging of his doctors he rested at regular intervals, yet his body failed to respond properly. He lacked his former ability to laugh away sniping criticism, of which there was an ever-increasing chorus after his return from Yalta; he also worried about the outcome of the United Nations conference in San Francisco. Emergency cracks in the friendly relations between the Soviet Union and the West perturbed him even more. On March 27 he cabled Churchill that he had been "watching with anxiety and concern the development of the Soviet attitude" since Yalta and that he was "acutely aware of the dangers inherent in the present course of events, not only for the immediate issue involved but also for the San Francisco Conference and future world cooperation." On April 1 he sent Stalin a firm reminder on the thorny Polish situation and urged him to send Molotov to San Francisco as evidence of full Russian cooperation. Five days later, referring to Russian complaints regarding the German surrender in Italy, he cabled Stalin: "Frankly, I cannot avoid a feeling of bitter resentment toward your informers, whoever they are, for such vile representations of my actions or those of my trusted subordinates." Yet he yearned to maintain our friendly relations with Russia and on the day he died he urged Churchill to "minimize the general Soviet problem as much as possible because these problems, in one form or another, seem to arise every day, and most of them straighten out, as in the case of the Berne meeting. We must be firm, however, and our course thus far is correct."

Two days later he went to Warm Springs for an extended rest. Although he could not escape the essential duties of his office, and he insisted on keeping up with daily events, he was able to stay in bed longer and to relax more frequently. After several days in the warm Georgia sun he began to feel better and worked on a speech he was to deliver on April 13 in honor of Thomas Jefferson. He wanted it to be not on war or politics but on peace. While working on various paragraphs or on state papers, he sat for his portrait. On the afternoon of April 12 he was to attend a barbecue picnic. In fine spirits and at ease, he chatted with the artist while revising a draft of his speech. Suddenly he felt a sharp pain, complained of "a terrific headache," and collapsed. Two hours later, despite immediate medical care, he died from a massive cerebral hemorrhage. On his desk was his undelivered speech—the final paragraphs being his true testament to mankind:

Today we are faced with the pre-eminent fact that, if civilization is to survive, we must cultivate the science of human relations—the ability of all peoples, of all kinds, to live together and work together, in the same world, at peace. . . . Today as we move against the terrible scourge of war—as we go forward toward the greatest contribution that any generation of human beings can make in this world— the contribution of lasting peace, I ask you to keep up your faith. I measure the sound, solid achievement that can be made at this time by the straight edge of your own confidence and your resolve. And to you, and to all Americans who dedicate themselves with us to the making of an abiding peace, I say: "The only limit to our realization of tomorrow will be our doubts of today. Let us move forward with strong and active faith."

Cordell Hull, who knew Roosevelt long and intimately and who had reason to resent his own forced acquiescence in crucial dealings with foreign governments, wrote of him as follows:

President Roosevelt, in my opinion, was one of the greatest social reformers in our modern history, even though many persons might disagree with certain of his reforms. As Commander-in-Chief, his achievements were outstanding among those of other commander-in-chiefs. In my opinion he had no contemporary rival in political skill. As long as I knew him he was always an earnest follower of individual liberty, freedom, and other basic rights and privileges necessary for the welfare of the private citizen.

Roosevelt became a social reformer out of his profound belief in democracy. From early manhood, despite his aristocratic environment and sheltered upbringing, he manifested a desire for fairness to others and a concern for those in adverse circumstances. Endowed with personal charm, the object of his mother's adoration, his every reasonable wish granted as soon as it was made, he grew into an easy-going, urbane, and upright citizen. He was neither interested in making a lot of money nor driven by selfish motives. His inclination was to live, like his father, the full, simple life of a country squire. Yet deep within his being stirred a potentially strong social conscience. His entrance into politics in 1910 was induced as much by an impulse toward reform as by the wish to emulate his eminent fifth cousin.

The fight against Tammany, into which he drifted rather casually, wakened his latent political talents and, though a newcomer and young, he at once assumed leadership of the small band of insurgents. Much as it pleased his vanity, then and later, to act the iconoclast, he was at no time impelled by the urgency of the radical or the severity of the fanatic. In 1911 he wanted fairness and honesty in government; assured of this within the orbit of the New Freedom, he enjoyed the next decade on the crest of an active and amiable existence.

His physical tragedy, leaving him permanently crippled, only roused his fighting qualities. He refused to acquiesce in his misfortune, as his mother strongly urged, and spend the rest of his life among his beloved trees in Hyde Park. Instead he undertook courses of treatment which would have frustrated most men but which he endured without complaint. Day after day and month after month he persisted in the varied exercise of his feeble leg muscles. For a time he even crawled on the floor and up stairs, dragging his legs, in the hope that these movements might be helpful. Undoubtedly the mettle of his character was tested and tempered in the fire of agony—preparing him for goals beyond the mere personal gratification of being able to walk unaided.

Still the life-loving, light-hearted gentleman despite his adversity, he found the tragic years had activated his social conscience. Although his gay demeanor and loud laugh fooled even astute observers, his interest in the welfare of the underprivileged was genuine and soundly based. Once in office, he readily applied his liberal views to emerging events and new needs. And political activity having whetted his strong ambition, he fixed his eyes on the Presidency.

It is very likely that Roosevelt might have been elected President even in normal times that under these circumstances he would have retired into oblivion reserved for good but not great men. But the time was not normal—and he met the critical need to his everlasting remembrance. Assuming office in a day of extreme economic crisis, he electrified the nation with the magic of his reassuring voice, his sanguine air of confidence, and his unprecedented activity. He fumbled and made mistakes, but he was daring and imaginative in his successful efforts to find the right formula. His bold and buoyant spirit gave comfort and courage to a people on the verge of despair. And they were grateful and trusted his leadership.

Recovery was to him a means; the end was reform. He had come to believe that the rapid rise of large-scale industrialism had on the one hand brought into existence a small but aggressive group of enterprisers who tugged at the reins of the American economy and on the other placed millions of workers at the mercy of their jobs. This gargantuan manifestation of capitalism greatly aggravated the normal conflict, inequality, and exploitation— social ills endangering the foundation of democracy. To remove this threat to the principles he cherished, he improvised laws that sought to nullify class privileges and provide each American with the security and basic comforts to which he had a right in a functioning democracy. These laws, like all legislation, were imperfect and had to be revised and improved; nor was their administration more efficient or more faithful than the men charged to execute them. Yet despite balky Congresses, the fierce opposition from "economic royalists," the self-seeking and shortcomings of his advisers, and the inadequacy implicit in human effort, Roosevelt's New Deal unquestionably altered the relation of government to the people. Notwithstanding continued lip service to freedom of enterprise and rugged individualism, Americans have in practice accepted the doctrine that in a modern industrial economy, where most workers are wholly dependent on their jobs with gigantic corporations, it is the government's solemn responsibility to see that no man starves and that the basic rights of all men are adequately protected. Thus the right of workers to organize, flouted by employers for over a century, was made the law of the land; the benefits of social security became the essential right of nearly all who needed them; and the goal of economic democracy was stated and sanctioned as a worthy ideal. And the sum of it all was the spirit of good will that had come to symbolize the greatness of Franklin D. Roosevelt.

In the 1960's, when Hitler and Mussolini and Tojo are only evil memories and the western democracies are in dread of an aggressive communism, it requires an effort of the imagination to recall the ominous specter of fascism two decades earlier. But in the late 1930's its menace was very real—all the more so because the democracies were in the grip of an enervating pacifism and refused to see the threat of Hitlerism until it nearly overwhelmed them. Unlike most of the European statesmen, however, Roosevelt was quick to perceive the true nature of fascism and dedicated himself to its destruction. Well aware of world conditions and of the prevailing will to appeasement, he began a course of public education that was slow to take effect because of strong opposition by isolationists but that eventually prepared the American people for the oncoming ordeal. He was excoriated as a militarist and warmonger, but he persisted in his warnings against the menace of fascist aggression—not with the zeal of the prophet crying in the wilderness but with the pragmatism of the politician who knew he could not lead unless he kept within sight of his followers.

When appeasement failed to satisfy Hitler's lust for power and he ordered his armies and planes to devastate Poland, Roosevelt did his utmost to strengthen the wills and arms of the nations fighting German aggression. He believed that a victorious Hitler would be a dread danger not only to the United States but to the civilization of which it was a dominant part. But a good many Americans—isolationists who accepted "the wave of the future" and pacifists who wanted peace at any price—resisted him shrilly and bitterly. Against this opposition he and other antifascists fought skillfully and persistently. His speeches made the issue of democracy versus dictatorship crystal clear and persuaded more and more people of the urgency to keep England from collapse. Thus, by the time he was ready to launch his magnificent Lend-Lease program, most Americans were heartily with him and impelled Congress to do his will.

As an associate of Churchill and Stalin in the deadly struggle against fascist forces, his greatness of spirit made him first among his equals. For although the British and Russian titans fought heroically and indomitably, their motives were essentially limited by their national interests. From the first, however, Roosevelt, never doubting final victory, was passionately eager to make such future blood orgies impossible. From the outset, therefore, he dedicated himself to making the peace democratic and beneficial to the people of the entire world. Beginning with the signing of the Atlantic Charter on January 1, 1942, by the United Nations formed that day at his insistence, he promoted the idea of a world organization for peace to the day of his death. Over and over he forced Churchill to curb his quest for imperial gain in the interest of international good will. Aware of the crucial position of the Soviet Union in the postwar world, he twice journeyed halfway across the globe in order to deal with Stalin face to face and to induce him to cooperate with the democracies.

Roosevelt worked heroically to assure the realization of his magnificent ideals—ideals encompassing not only the United States but the entire world. And countless millions everywhere felt his love for them and blessed him as their great leader and benefactor. And he gave his life to bring them to the peak overlooking a world of peace and justice; and like Moses on Mount Pisgah he urged them in his last hour of consciousness to "move forward with strong and active faith."

George W. Norris

EMINENT PROGRESSIVE

THE CAREER OF GEORGE W. NORRIS well exemplifies the fine flowering of American democracy. Of pioneer stock, bred in bleak poverty, uplifted by Jeffersonian ideals, Norris worked his way through college, established a fair legal practice, and gradually drifted into politics. He did not, however, become a mere politician. A homespun idealist with an implicit faith in the hallowed principles of the Declaration of Independence, he in time denied party conformity, defied political bosses, suffered rebuff and obloquy—fighting for his beliefs with a firmness and fervor that finally gained him the respect of his opponents and the plaudits of the nation. Without guile, avoiding histrionics, abiding by simple truths, exuding good will, yet combatting greed and double-dealing with unslackening zeal, he truly personified the dynamic democracy of his generation.

George W. Norris was born on a farm near Sandusky, Ohio, on July 11, 1861. Before he was four years old his only brother died from a battle wound in the Civil War and his father succumbed to exposure resulting from an attempt to stop a runaway horse— leaving him the only male in a large family. He worked hard from early childhood to help his mother on the farm. In his eleventh year he also began earning extra money as a laborer on nearby farms. "Long before I became a man," he wrote later, "I was able to do a man's work."

During the winter months he went to school. In his early teens he joined a debating club and frequently sharpened his adolescent mind on current topics. He was already a confirmed Republican— as were most people he knew—and grew eloquent in praise of his party's principles. "I have often thought and I firmly believe that the experience I received in that old country schoolhouse, where we met once a week to debate various questions, was one of the main things which started me on my political career." Success on the platform turned his mind to the study of law. In 1877, after teaching school for a term at a salary of $150, he and two of his sisters entered Baldwin College in the nearby town of Berea, where they worked at odd jobs to earn their few cash expenses. A year later he transferred to Valparaiso University, then known as the "poor boy's school," to enroll in the law school. Although he had to alternate studying with teaching, he became a leader in his class and received his law degree in 1882.

Lacking the capital to open a law office of his own and loath to begin as a clerk for one of the established lawyers, he decided to migrate to Washington Territory, where a land boom was reported in progress. After a tedious and tiring journey to Walla Walla he was greatly disappointed to find the town "dusty, and dirty, and desolate, and uninviting." Worse still, the boom had collapsed and he could find no employment of any kind. Nor had he the fare for the return trip. After frantic efforts he found a teaching post in a wretched hamlet along the railroad and taught there long enough to earn the money for a ticket east.

He traveled as far as Nebraska, where one of his sisters had made her home. The open prairie and the wholesome atmosphere of the place appealed to him and he decided to remain. Eager to practice law, he borrowed several hundred dollars and opened an office. When no clients sought his services for months on end, he moved to Beaver City, the center of a fertile farm section. There he soon prospered. People liked his honesty and amiability. Gradually he began to take an active part in local politics and found favor with those in control. "My loyalty and zeal as a

Republican never faltered in those years. I became acquainted with nearly every man in Furnas County, and without any definite plan or effort I became in a slight way a party leader." The rising tide of Populism irritated him; in his high esteem of the Grand Old Party he tended to be critical of the discontent and disdain of its detractors.

In 1890 he married Pluma Lashley and in the course of time became the father of three girls. In March 1901, while giving birth to the third child, Mrs. Norris died. His distress was deep, and for many months he was emotionally depressed. In 1903 he married Ellie Leonard, a schoolteacher in McCook, where he was then living, and she remained his devoted helpmeet to the end of his life.

By now a well-established lawyer and popular Republican, he was in line for political preferment. When the office of district attorney became available, the party leaders readily offered it to him. Hard work and a fine record earned him the nomination for the district judgeship. Although the Populist tide was running high in 1895, placing the Republican party on the defensive, Norris's personal popularity enabled him to win over his active Populist rival—but only by two votes.

Judge Norris quickly established a good reputation for fairness and honesty. It was a period of poor crops and unpaid mortgages, and he had to deal with a large number of suits against farmers for the nonpayment of interest. "Only those who lived in the heart of the nation's food-producing regions," he explained, "know fully the agony of these cycles of crop failure, heavy indebtedness upon the land, and ruinous farm commodity prices." Anxious to keep his sympathy under control, he studied each case with scrupulous care. He usually knew the defendant and his capacity as a farmer, the worth of his land, and his ability to repay his debts.

If the evidence clearly showed that the indebtedness was much in excess of the value of the land, and it would not in the end benefit the owner to postpone confirmation, I confirmed the sale at once. If

317

it appeared to me that under normal conditions the farmer would be able to pay out, I postponed confirmation until the next term. . . . In the end, hundreds of farmers paid off their mortgages, and hundreds of farms that otherwise would have become vacant or operated under absentee ownership, remained in the hands of those who settled upon the soil.

Norris found his work congenial. He felt a sense of accomplishment and enjoyed his relations with the people about him. His social prestige rose with his reputation as a humanitarian and he was chosen for high office in the Order of Odd Fellows. He was also re-elected to a second term despite continued stiff opposition from the Populists. It was this success against the radicals that caused Republican leaders in 1902 to offer him the nomination for a seat in Congress. At first he was very reluctant to make the change. He saw no advantage in leaving either the bench or his home in McCook. At that time still "a bitter Republican partisan," however, he acquiesced as a matter of duty. His prestige as a humane and intelligent jurist stood him in good stead, and the local newspaper headlined him as "Norris, the Poor Man's Friend." Despite the fusion of the Democrats and Populists, he campaigned hard and won by the slim majority of 14,927 to 14,746.

Norris reached Washington in 1903 with a copybook notion of government. He assumed that elected officeholders were dedicated to the advancement of the public welfare, especially if they were Republicans.

I believed that all the virtues of government were wrapt up in the party of which I was a member, and that the only chance for pure and enlightened government was through the election of only Republicans to office. I was conservative, and proud of it—sure of my position, unreasonable in my convictions, and unbending in my opposition to any other political party, or political thought except my own.

Disillusionment came quickly. One of his first disappointments was the discovery that the House leader who had sent him money and literature during the campaign had done so as a matter of party routine and not out of personal interest. His first speech in the House favored civil-service reform. It was obvious to him that an efficient civil-service system would eliminate the evils of partisanship and would exclude the incompetent and the unqualified. Much to his surprise he found both parties opposed to such legislation. Another shock came on February 20, 1904, when he found himself the only Republican voting in favor of declaring a holiday on Washington's Birthday—the others of his party opposing the resolution simply because its proponent was a Democrat. To his consternation he learned that in the Senate the Republicans voted for the holiday because it was sponsored by a member of their party.

His political education proceeded from jolt to jolt. Anxious as he was to cling to his illusions, he simply could not make party compliance square with a prodding conscience. Again and again he found his party supporting the evils he had ascribed to the Democrats. His attacks on spoils and patronage practices met with curt rebuffs.

The same cold antagonism greeted his resolution to lengthen the term of Representatives to four years—a proposal which seemed to him both logical and meritorious. He saw no reason for a situation that normally kept an elected Representative from assuming his office for thirteen months—from the November elections to the first regular session of the new Congress in December of the following year. "Their term of office," he pointed out, "has practically half expired before they take the oath. Before they are fairly started in the work for which they are elected they are plunged into a campaign for renomination." Defeat of his resolution did not lessen its merit in his estimation and years later he achieved his main goal in his successful fight for the "Lame Duck" or 20th Amendment.

In 1904, aided by President Roosevelt's popularity, Norris was re-elected by a large majority. Shortly thereafter, finding the Nebraskan intractable, Republican leaders deprived him of the customary patronage and later made no effort to help him during election campaigns. To them he was a renegade and the sooner rid of the better. But opposition only made him fight all the harder. Notwithstanding increasing opposition from both parties, he won elections time and again because the people of Nebraska had come to believe in him and wanted him as their representative in Congress.

In the 1900's Norris's conception of society was still that of the insular idealist. Honest government and the public welfare were the two pillars of his political credo. His interest in liberalism derived from these beliefs. He applauded President Roosevelt's criticism of monopoly and advocacy of the conservation of natural resources because his aim was the general good. Not constructive policies, however, but the evils of machine politics long claimed his closest attention. The dictatorial rule of Speaker Joseph Cannon especially irritated him. Having more than once felt the sting of Cannon's whip, he was determined to liberalize the House rules, to limit the absolute and arbitrary power exercised by one man.

Norris did not underestimate Cannon. "He was, perhaps, the most efficient and the most articulate representative of that blighting philosophy in America which places loyalty to party at the top of the list of duties and responsibilities of citizenship." Because Cannon ruled the House with an inflexible will, Norris realized that the only way to defeat him was to resort to a stratagem. The first occasion came in January 1910, when House members were about to be chosen to participate in a Congressional investigation of Secretary Ballinger's dismissal of Gifford Pinchot and Louis Glavis. Normally Cannon named the House members as a matter of course. Norris knew that the Speaker wanted to clear Ballinger and would appoint men to do his will. Aware of Cannon's custom of leaving the chair at a certain hour, Norris obtained recognition from the unsuspecting acting Speaker and moved that the members be named by the House as a whole.

Aided by his fellow insurgents and abetted by the Democrats, Norris won by 149 to 146—a shocking rebuke to Cannon.

Victory stimulated his efforts to democratize the procedure of appointing committee members. He maintained that the Speaker's arrogation of the right to name all majority members inevitably led to dictatorial evils, since it forced Representatives to do his bidding in order to gain places on preferred committees. In the quiet of his office, and with the approval of his liberal colleagues, he prepared a resolution calling for a new Rules Committee of 15—nine from the majority party and six from the minority—to be chosen on the basis of equally divided population areas. This Committee, of which the Speaker was not to be a member, was to appoint the members of all other committees. He kept this resolution in his coat pocket, ready to propose it at an opportune moment—knowing only too well that Cannon would never permit its introduction under ordinary circumstances.

An erroneous ruling by the Speaker gave Norris the occasion he sought. In March 1910 a census bill was in danger of not being acted upon before the oncoming adjournment of Congress. When the chairman of the committee in charge requested special consideration, Cannon ruled favorably on the ground that the census provision in the Constitution gave it preference over general House rules. An appeal from the decision was made and won. The next day, however, Cannon gathered his forces and had his ruling sustained. Thereupon Norris immediately offered his resolution. "Mr. Speaker, I present a resolution made privileged by the Constitution," the alert Nebraskan insisted.

The long-repressed struggle for control suddenly burst into the open, and everyone present was aware of it. The crisis caught the Cannon forces depleted by absences, so that a vote would have favored Norris. Cannon therefore played for time by asking discussion of the resolution. He and his stalwarts tried every trick and stratagem to avoid a ruling, but the insurgents were equally skillful. All through the night both sides sparred for advantage.

321

Knowing that his resolution would be defeated without the full support of the Democrats, Norris regretfully modified the wording so as to give the House the power to choose the members of the Rules Committee. With this compromise arranged, he was able the following afternoon to vote down Cannon's ruling against him by 182 to 160. Thereupon the amended resolution was passed by a vote of 191 to 156—and Cannon was shorn of his dictatorial powers.

Victory gave Norris national prominence. A writer in *World's Work* commented, "One man without position against 200 welded into the most powerful political machine that Washington has ever known, has twice beaten them at their own game. Mr. George Norris is a man worth knowing and watching." Yet success did not make him vindictive. Unlike other insurgents he refused to press his advantage against Cannon; insisting that he was opposed to the system and not to the man, he voted against the motion to accept the Speaker's resignation.

Heretofore Norris had been primarily concerned with reforming the machinery of government rather than with its broader national aspects. After 1910, however, having won his fifth term by a large majority despite Republican opposition and a national Democratic victory, he turned his attention to the prevailing spirit of progressive insurgency. His growing friendship with Senator La Follette stimulated him to grapple with the problems of unbridled monopoly and economic inequality.

About that time he became interested in the case of an independent coal mine owner who was being forced into bankruptcy by the unfair competition of the Delaware, Lackawanna and Western Railroad, which charged higher freight rates on coal shipped by independents than on coal from its own mines. On investigation he found that one important factor against the independents was that Judge Robert W. Archbold always ruled in favor of the railroad. Norris immediately moved for impeachment, and the Senate upheld him. Another of his campaigns aimed at the dissolution of the coffee trust, which had obtained firm control of the product. On the House floor he expounded his opposition to monopoly with forceful, if naive, candor:

When any combination has succeeded in monopolizing and controlling the production or distribution of any given article, the price to the ultimate consumer is increased and the unfair or unreasonable profits are pocketed by the men or corporations in control. . . . The favored few have unduly profited at the expense of the unorganized thousands.

For more than a decade a warm admirer of Theodore Roosevelt, he joined other of the Colonel's followers in advocating his candidacy for President. To promote this idea he became a founder and vice-president of the National Republican Progressive League. When in 1911 Roosevelt definitely refused to become a candidate and permitted La Follette to be the choice of the progressives, Norris became active in the latter's behalf. Early in 1912, when the Colonel changed his mind, Norris joined his bandwagon despite his feeling "that in this matter Roosevelt was far from treating Senator La Follette fairly." When the progressives were beaten at the convention, Norris described the Taft victory as "one of the worst political highway robberies that has ever been committed in this country." He joined the dissidents in forming the Progressive party and worked for Roosevelt during the campaign.

In 1912 Norris was seriously considering the idea of leaving politics. He did not really relish the role of the rebel. The constant strain and struggle of the past few years had had a depressing effect upon him; yet he knew that so long as he held office he would be duty-bound to fight the greed and venality that spurred much of the proposed legislation. He was in this frame of mind when a lobbyist called on him with an offer of generous backing if he ran for governor of Nebraska. The more the man talked the more convinced Norris became that the companies represented by the lobbyist believed he would be less harmful to them in Lincoln than he was in Washington. Irritated by this blatant overture, he decided to act on the suggestion of his friends and announced his candidacy for the Senate. His friends worked hard in his behalf. Louis D. Brandeis, in Nebraska as a speaker for La Follette, urged the voters to favor Norris because he had made the Ballinger inquiry a thorough investigation instead of a whitewash. And Nebraskans thought well of their representative. Notwithstanding strong opposition from the Republican machine and a Democratic sweep of other offices, Norris won in the primaries by a vote of 126,022 to 111,946. With Nebraska following the Oregon plan of having state legislators vote for the successful candidate for the Senate, the will of the majority prevailed.

In the United States Senate, Norris met with cold hostility on the part of the conservatives. He was refused membership in the Judiciary Committee, for which he felt himself qualified, and placed instead on the Agricultural and Public Lands Committees. The liberal Senators, however, welcomed him warmly and his friendship with La Follette grew even closer. The two men saw eye to eye on whatever favored the underprivileged and benefited the country as a whole. Both were equally sincere, similarly devoted to democratic ideals, and alike in their zealous tenacity. Yet while La Follette was militant and grim, driving himself with drama and doggedness and ever insistent on dominance, Norris was quiet and genial, employing shafts of gentle satire against opponents and accepting defeat philosophically—only to fight on persistently till final victory. For all their temperamental differences, they stood shoulder to shoulder against angry and contemptuous majorities and expressed their strong beliefs clearly and fearlessly.

Though nominally a Republican, Norris was very favorably impressed with Woodrow Wilson's exposition of his New Freedom platform and was eager to further the proposed Democratic legislation. As before, however, he refused to vote for measures that failed to meet his test of the general welfare. Thus he opposed the tariff bill because it put northern wheat on the free list but kept a duty on southern rice. He also went much further than President Wilson on such matters as inheritance taxes, the development of water power, and the public ownership of basic utilities. Wilson's tolerance of political machine methods, particularly in connection with civil service jobs, likewise met with his sharp criticism.

As a member of the Public Lands Committee Norris interested himself in the bill proposing a dam on the Hetch-Hetchy in California and providing that the power generated there was to be used by the people in the San Francisco area. The Pacific Gas and Electric Company opposed the measure with all its resources. Its energetic lobbying stimulated Norris's opposition. A firm believer in the public ownership of water power, he fought for the bill on the Senate floor—maintaining that the dam would provide the people of California with a hundred thousand horses that needed no food and could be put to work for the common good forever.

The passage of this bill means to lighten the burden of every man who toils in any of the Pacific cities. It means that the woman who breaks her back over the washtub will be able to do her washing with electric power. It means that the citizen who has to buy electric light by means of which to educate himself and his children will have the price cut in two. It means that the street railways of San Francisco and other cities will be operated by this power. It means a three-cent fare to the poor.

The law was finally passed in December 1913. Because it prohibited the sale of power generated by the dam to private companies, the latter immediately challenged its legality in the courts, thereby holding up the completion of the dam for many years. Not till 1925 was enough electricity developed for use in San Francisco and not till 1937 was the dam fully completed. And local politicians violated the provisions of the law from the beginning by disposing of the electricity to private companies. The legal struggle ended only in 1940 when the Supreme Court upheld the law.

The outbreak of the war in Europe gave Norris a sharp jolt. He had never thought much about the world outside of the United States. A true product of the Middle West, he had little interest in foreign affairs and was definitely opposed to imperialistic enterprise. Proud as he was of the greatness of the American nation, he had no notion of its dynamic impetus as a world power. Nor did he know that the force of industrial gravity had made the United States the economic capital of modern society—for good or ill a dominant factor in international diplomacy. He therefore opposed any action that tended to disturb American insularity or undermine its pacific polity.

President Wilson's advocacy of complete neutrality in 1914 met with Norris's hearty approval. He also favored Secretary of State Bryan's peace treaties with other nations and applauded the required cooling-off period as a notable advance in diplomatic relations. Late in 1915, however, perturbed by Bryan's forced resignation and resenting Wilson's conversion to military preparedness, Norris joined his pacifistic colleagues in a desperate struggle against the increasing propaganda for war. Believing that this agitation was largely stimulated by munition-makers, he urged that the manufacture of armor plate and guns be made a government monopoly.

The private ownership of munitions factories is responsible for the enormous effort which is nationwide to artificially create a sentiment for increased army and navy expenditures by those who would make a financial profit out of such increases. . . . I think we ought to have a navy and army well equipped and of reasonable size but I cannot agree with the widespread contention that we ought to enter a military race.

He took every opportunity to condemn war as barbaric and to stress its grave dangers to modern society. "The greatest disgrace of the present century," he insisted, "is that war between civilized nations is still a possibility." As a means of avoiding future wars, he called upon President Wilson to seek the establishment

326

of an international court of arbitration and to arrange for an international navy to patrol the high seas.

Meantime he actively participated in the debates on proposed social legislation. Advocating a bill to utilize neglected water power sites, he pointed out that the electricity developed by damming various streams would serve industry and agriculture nearly as much as the railroads. When the Adamson Act came up for discussion, and the question of government ownership was raised in criticism of the bill, Norris expressed his readiness to let logic lead where it would:

I do not care whether or not it leads toward government ownership or whether it leads in the other direction. The question is, Is it logical, is it right, and is it fair? When we pass a law that is fair and that is just, we ought to be willing to follow the results wherever they may lead.

At the end of 1916, following Wilson's re-election on a peace platform, relations between the United States and Germany were rapidly reaching the breaking point. Early in February, having been informed by the German ambassador of his country's intention to resume submarine sinkings, President Wilson severed diplomatic relations with Germany and asked Congress for authority to arm merchant ships and to employ other means necessary to defend American shipping. The publication of the notorious Zimmermann cable to Mexico helped to put the bill through the House by an overwhelming majority. Administration leaders in the Senate also expected approval by a wide margin. A number of Senators, however, fearing that the legislation would hasten American entry into the war, joined the debate with troubled minds. Though most of them agreed to vote for the bill—a total of 76 pledges were obtained by its proponents—not a few privately confessed acting against their conscience. No less than twelve, led by Senators La Follette and Norris, refused to yield either to political pressure or popular clamor. With the session of Congress nearing its end, they decided to prevent passage of the bill by a filibuster and began talking around the clock. When it became obvious that this would go on till noon on March 4, the proponents of the measure took over in order to deprive La Follette of the opportunity to partake in the oratorical marathon.

Two days later President Wilson announced that despite the opposition of "a little group of willful men" he had learned that he did not need Congress approval and had already ordered the arming of merchant ships. Meantime the newspapers performed an "intellectual lynching" on the dozen dissidents. Prominent men excoriated them; editors denounced them; state legislatures censured them. They were everywhere scorned as pacifists and renegades. Only a scattered few dared praise them. Dr. David Starr Jordan, eminent scientist, wired Norris wishfully: "We believe you represent vast, though unknown, numbers of Americans whose earnest desire is that this country should not be drawn into war directly or indirectly."

Norris was grievously perturbed by this hysterical denunciation. He believed the filibuster was justified and his conscience was clear. Yet he did not wish to remain in the Senate if the people of Nebraska thought he was not representing them to their satisfaction. On March 17 he informed the governor that he wished to resign his office in order to give the voters an opportunity to express their opinion on his conduct in the Senate.

I have no desire to hold public office if I am expected blindly to follow in my official actions the dictation of a newspaper combination, controlled and influenced by stock-jobbers of Wall Street, who desire to coin the lifeblood of my fellow citizens into dollars for their own private benefit.

The governor thought it best to ignore this extraordinary request. But Norris persisted in his wish to tell the people his side of the story and let them decide. He hired the city auditorium in Lincoln for the Monday evening of March 26. On his arrival in the city on Sunday morning no reporters sought him out— except a neophyte late at night—and only the bravest of his friends visited him furtively in his hotel room to warn him that he would be mobbed on making his public appearance. Years afterwards Norris wrote in the *Nation:* "I cannot remember a day in my life when I have suffered more from a lonely feeling of despondency than upon that particular Sunday."

The following evening he found the auditorium filled to over-flowing, some farmers having come from far distances. When he stood up to speak he was greeted with complete silence. Determined to speak his mind, he began by saying that he had come from Washington to tell them what they could not learn from the newspapers. Thereupon "the people stood up and yelled." Cheered by this unexpectedly quick and warm response—definitely silencing the few opponents who had come to jeer—he told them frankly and freely how he felt about war and peace, about the munitions-makers and their lobbyists and lackeys, about President Wilson's change of heart, and about his own insistence on acting in accord with his conscience. The audience cheered him lustily and encouragingly. Later he declared:

It seemed to me a demonstration that the American mind demands fair play; that it insists that the underdog shall have his hearing and his day in court; and it demonstrated to me that underneath the deception and the misrepresentation, the political power and the influence, there was, in the hearts of the common people, a belief that there was something artificial about this propaganda, and that the so-called leaders of public sentiment, both in and out of public life, were being carried off their feet by misrepresentation and even by falsehood. In that hour I felt repaid for all the turmoil, the agony, and the suffering that I had endured.

He returned to Washington with confirmed faith and renewed fervor. The martial madness in the Capitol repelled him. President Wilson had called Congress into extraordinary session, and on April 2 his forceful address requested a declaration of war against Germany. Only the few members of Congress who opposed war to the end remained silent and sorrowful. Norris was of this "willful" group, but he was not an extreme pacifist. When the war

resolution came up for debate in the Senate, he opposed it vehemently and resolutely, yet not blindly or irreconcilably. He said:

Mr. President, while I am most emphatically and sincerely opposed to
taking any step that will force our country into the useless and sense-
less war now being waged in Europe, yet if this resolution passes I
shall not permit my feeling of opposition to its passage interfere in
any way with my duty either as a Senator or as a citizen in bringing
success and victory to American arms.

Nevertheless he considered it his solemn duty to make clear his
reasons for opposing the resolution. He in particular condemned
the bankers and munitions-makers, whom he accused of responsibility for the war hysteria.

I know that this war madness has taken possession of the financial
and political powers of our country. I know that nothing I can say
will stay the blow that is soon to fall. . . . I feel that we are about
to put the dollar sign upon the American flag. . . . Upon the passage
of this resolution we will have joined Europe in the great catastrophe
and taken America into entanglements that will not end with this war
but will live and bring their evil influence upon many generations yet
unborn.

Several Senators immediately denounced the speech as border-
ing on treason and were particularly incensed against the remark
associating the flag with the dollar sign. But Norris stood his ground
without flinching. "I am not apologizing for what I said. I believe
myself that we would not be on the verge of war now if it were
not for the influence of money, and that is the idea I expressed."
When the savage attack continued, he declared that he would
not be silenced because the majority was against him and that
it was his right and his duty to state his view as emphatically
as he could. The next day's headline in the New York *Times* read:
"Nebraska Senator Denounced for Hinting that Commercialism
Prompted Nation's Course." When the resolution finally came
to a vote on April 6, 82 Senators favored it and only six—half of
the original "willful" group—opposed it.

Although Norris loyally supported war measures, as he had said he would, he fought certain bills with his usual zest. He opposed the draft law, and resisted the espionage and similar measures as needless and coercive. "While we are engaged in making the world safe for democracy we ought to remember that America is a part of the world, and it will be of little consequence if we establish democracy in Europe and at the same time establish autocracy here." He further objected to the conscription of men and not of money. "If we demand by law that there should be equality of service where human lives are at stake, then why should we not demand by law equality of contribution when funds for the prosecution of the war are necessary."

Throughout the war he was spied upon. His files were ransacked and his family was harassed in his absence. Like La Follette he was a marked man, scorned and vilified by officious patriots. Depressed by this situation, he was inclined not to seek re-election in 1918. His friends, however, persuaded him not to yield while under fire and, despite false accusations and fierce opposition, he won by a vote of 120,086 to 99,960.

The wave of reaction following the armistice—the inevitable consequence of great emotional strain and intensified frustration—grieved him deeply. He watched the violation of democratic ideals with a heavy heart, himself a victim of the abuse and execration heaped upon liberals and radicals alike. "Right now," he wrote, "our government is in the hands of reactionaries and every executive official is afraid of his life if he undertakes to be friendly to such men as myself."

With the war ended, thoughts of a peace that would perpetuate itself dominated Norris's mind. Having long reflected upon the subject, he welcomed President Wilson's idea of a League of Nations. He envisioned it as an agency that would abolish the tools of war, enable all nations to achieve real independence, and thus remove what seemed to him the basic causes of war. On March 18, 1918, he had written to a friend:

We ought to destroy every fort along every international boundary line in Europe. This would be an easy thing to do if we and our allies would announce that it must be done. And when it is done, we ought to follow the example by disarming ourselves. No nation ought to keep a navy larger than is necessary to do police duty. If the world is disarmed, and remains disarmed, there will be no more world wars. If these leading nations would agree, in addition to this, that an international court of arbitration should be set up, that no nation should engage in conquest, and that no secret treaty would be entered into or recognized, the danger of war would be as completely averted as it is possible for human beings to avert it.

Having this simple and idealistic solution in mind, he could not help questioning Wilson's procedures and decisions. The choice of peace delegates seemed to him unfortunate. The President's insistence on regal luxury while away from Washington also struck the frugal Nebraskan as unseemly and inconsistent with the solemnity of the mission. And the more Norris heard about the activities at Versailles the less hope he had for the League. The final treaty confirmed his worst suspicions. He was particularly indignant about the secret treaties and the award of Shantung to Japan. When Wilson invited the recalcitrant Senators to the White House for a private discussion, Norris declined—not wishing to be bound to secrecy on international affairs.

Although he disliked only certain parts of the Treaty, he referred to it in the heat of the debate as "the most unholy thing that man ever tried to put over on an innocent world." He also declared, "If my people insist that I shall officially give my approval to such a dastardly thing I will give them my resignation instead. I would rather go out and starve." In the final voting he, unhappily, found himself on the side of Senator Lodge and other of his long-standing conservative opponents.

Norris never regretted his opposition to the war and the Treaty. On the tenth anniversary of our entrance into the conflict he emphasized its failure to accomplish any of the purposes of which it was fought.

We went to war to make an end to militarism, and there is more militarism today than ever before.

We went to war to make the world safe for democracy, and there is less democracy today than ever before.

We went to war to awaken the American people to the idealistic concepts of liberty, justice, and fraternity, and instead we awakened them to the mad pursuit of money.

The inauguration of President Warren G. Harding in March 1921 initiated a twelve-year period noted for its lack of democratic idealism, its excesses of venality and corruption, its shoddy prosperity, and its catastrophic depression. "The early twenties," Norris wrote, "brought the American people to their knees in worship at the shrine of private business and industry. . . . Great wealth took possession of the Government." Although he was nominally a member of the party in power, he was at even greater odds with it than in the early years of his Congressional career. In 1921 he said, "I cannot rest while there are so many inhuman things going on." And all that decade he found himself intensely engaged in one fight after another—often in several at once—in the pursuit of the public good.

As chairman of the Committee on Agriculture he sought to provide help to the farmers then suffering from a postwar market collapse, but his conservative colleagues thwarted every effort in that direction. Equally futile was his resistance to the Harding doctrine of "less government in business." Goaded into outbursts of sarcasm, which during this period became his ready weapon of attack, he said on one occasion:

The government is all right in business when it will take a risk for financial men that they are not willing to take themselves. The government is all right in business if the middleman, the banker and the trust company can get their rake-off. Then it's all right. Then it's a virtue. If they're eliminated it's a crime, it's foolish, it's reactionary, it's populistic, it's dishonorable, it's unpatriotic.

Anxious to stop the practice of rich men buying their election to the Senate, Norris fought the seating of Truman H. Newberry, who had defeated his opponent in Michigan, Henry Ford, by spending several hundred thousand dollars during the campaign. Unable to budge the Senators in control, he resorted to satire, mockingly favoring the seating of Newberry as a means of establishing a precedent that would bring more rich men to the Senate. "Seats will be put up in the market place, just as seats in the stock exchange. This will insure a high-class membership." Soon thereafter Newberry resigned. In the next few years Norris had to make the same fight against Frank Smith of Illinois and William S. Vare of Pennsylvania, thus preventing the contenders from reaping the reward of their moneyed efforts.

Although Norris was glad to cooperate with the few liberals in Congress, he had become disillusioned with the efficacy of party organization. An admirer of La Follette, joining him readily in various legislative efforts, he reluctantly declined to help him form a third party. It had become his firm belief that partisanship of any kind was destructive of the democratic form of government.

I have small faith in a new party. There is too much belief in parties in this country. Unless its leaders were Christlike men—in which case they would not be political leaders—its candidates would be dictated by a few bosses conferring in private, just as in the old parties.

Although he voted for La Follette in 1924, he refused the following summer to replace him as the leader of the progressives.

He was generally discouraged during this period, having accomplished relatively little of the good he had sought to achieve by means of legislation. When it became necessary for him to seek another term in 1924, he again spoke of leaving politics.

Under the present conditions in Washington and conditions which have existed since I came to Congress, it is almost impossible to obtain effective legislation in the interest of the people. I have been bucking this game for twenty years and there is no way of beating it. Now I'm through.

He actually dictated a telegram requesting that his name he omitted from the ballot. By chance a well-known liberal journalist happened to be in the outer office at that time and managed to prevent the delivery of the message. Unwittingly Norris found himself a candidate in the primaries and was nominated without any effort on his part. He had planned to make no campaign, but the attempt of the Republican state bosses to put him off the ticket as a renegade caused him to fight back vigorously. Ironically both he and President Coolidge won the state by landslide proportions.

Upon the death of La Follette, Norris became the most prominent liberal in the Senate. Aware of his inability to initiate legislation with any hope of success, he was ever vigilant against any bill or amendment that favored a privileged group over the good of the nation. He was particularly incensed against the increasing power of large corporations and their monopolistic control of essential goods. In one of his speeches he exclaimed:

How long are we to stand for that? How much longer will we stand for it before we realize that we are just hired men of corporations; that we are just slaves; that we have nothing to say about anything that shall be done unless we get the consent of some great big corporation which through its interlocking directorate controls practically every avenue of human activity?

Defeat, however discouraging, never stopped him from pursuing the public good. Basing his decisions on principle rather than on a political label, he never voted for a Republican candidate for the Presidency after 1920. In 1926 he campaigned throughout Pennsylvania in opposition to Vare's candidacy as Senator. Two years later he spoke in favor of Al Smith. In each instance he knew he was on the losing side, but he also knew that he must fight for what he considered the right regardless of the outcome. Nor was he too impatient for the millennium. "I realize," he remarked, "I cannot revolutionize the world. I cannot expect to improve very much the conditions that exist, if I do so at all. I only know that I have done my best and while I am here I am still going to continue."

When President Hoover in 1930 nominated Judge John J.

Parker of North Carolina to a seat of the Supreme Court, organized labor, Negro groups, and many liberals objected on the ground that the nominee had ruled in favor of the "yellow dog" labor contract and against equal rights for Negroes. Norris took up the opposition and persisted skillfully till a majority of his colleagues voted with him against confirmation. Commenting on this liberal victory, he said: "It will serve to strip away the absurd notion that judges are invested with a sanctity that puts them above just and proper criticism. I believe it will hasten legislation to put an end to the abuse of the injunction."

In that year he again thought of retiring at the end of his term. The Republican leaders, anxious to remove him from the Senate and afraid to chance his voluntary retirement, planned his sure defeat by using as a rival candidate an obscure grocery clerk bearing the same name. Their reasoning was that since under Nebraska law no identification of candidates on the ballot was permissible and no voter was allowed to indicate his preference, all votes for either George W. Norris would automatically become void. To confuse the citizens still more, the Republicans charged that this political chicane was Norris's own doing—a way of arousing sympathy for himself in reverse.

Senator Norris was outraged by this piece of criminal trickery. He now insisted on running and was determined to forego the Republican primary and become an independent candidate. It happened, however, that the grocer's affidavit of candidacy reached the secretary of state a day late and the supreme court ruled him off the ballot. An easy victor in the Republican primary, Norris was forced to make the hardest campaign of his career in order to win over a popular Democratic opponent backed by the machines of both parties. Among other things, the Republicans sent to all district leaders a forged letter from Tammany Hall in praise of Norris. The liberals were not idle, of course, and a number of national leaders came to the state to speak in Norris's behalf. William Allen White wrote a forceful editorial in his Emporia

Gazette and sent the issue to all parts of Nebraska. Norris himself stood fast on his record:

I would rather be right than regular. I offer no apology for the course I have pursued and the only promise I make is that if I'm re-elected to the Senate I will continue to pursue it. I submit the issue to the constituency which has stood so loyally behind me all these years.

At the end of a mean and dirty campaign, in which conservatives stopped at nothing in their attempt to defeat the liberal Senator, Norris won the election by a vote of 247,118 to 172,795.

The Senate Campaign Funds Committee, headed by Gerald Nye, investigated the charges made by Norris and found that the Republican politicians had resorted to "corruption, perjury, fraud, and forgery" in their efforts to balk his candidacy in the primary. It took numerous hearings and persistent questioning to discover that the conspiracy was furthered by top national leaders of the party and that it involved some of the most prominent citizens of the state. Grocer Norris and his immediate sponsor were cited for perjury and found guilty. At the close of this ugly episode Norris commented: "I had met up with the force great wealth and Big Business could bring against the political life of a rebel fighting its rule."

The high-water mark of Senator Norris's career was of course his long and heroic struggle for legislation that initiated the majestic achievement of TVA. The potential magic of electricity generated by water power had long fascinated him. He envisioned a time when it would lighten man's work and brighten his home. On the farm in particular he saw it revolutionizing the old way of life and bringing ease and comfort to every member of the family.

All that is needed to give humanity the full enjoyment of this modern giant is to cheapen its production. If stock manipulation can be eliminated and if financial legerdemain and unconscionable profits can be removed, it is the cheapest source of power and light known to man.

He did not underestimate the strength and resourcefulness of the so-called power trust. He studied its Hydra-headed ramifications, its tortuous tactics, and its great influence in high places. Toward the end of his life, despite resounding victories, he still feared it and continued to warn the people against it.

The power trust is the greatest monopolistic corporation that has been organized for private greed. The investigations instigated by the Federal Trade Commission, covering a period of years, have revealed some of the most disgraceful, distasteful, and disreputable means by which it attempted to perpetuate its control of the natural resources of the nation. . . . The fight has never ended. It is still in progress, sometimes secret, sometimes bold, but consistently against the construction of all great national undertakings.

At the end of World War I he knew little about the Muscle Shoals project and was too busy with other matters to take an active interest in it. In 1920, however, he became chairman of the Committee of Agriculture and had to take charge of the Muscle Shoals bills under consideration. Never doing anything half-heartedly, he studied them with care and soon learned that Muscle Shoals had been intermittently occupying the attention of the federal government since 1824, at first militarily for better navigation and in 1916 as a war site for the production of much-needed nitrate. A dam and a nitrate plant were authorized at the outbreak of the war, but the armistice in November 1918 came before the project was completed. When no private offers to take it over materialized, Secretary of War Baker urged authorization of a government corporation to finish the job. In January 1921 the Democrats in the Senate, aided by Norris, passed the bill, but the measure died in the House.

A month after Harding became President he initiated his policy of taking the government out of business by stopping all work on the dam at Muscle Shoals. Secretary of War John W. Weeks placed the project on sale and asked for bids. In July one came from Henry Ford. He offered $5,000,000 for the nitrate plant which had cost over $100,000,000 to build; he also asked for a hundred-year lease on the dam, which the government was to complete at a cost of $50,000,000, and for which he was to pay a relatively low rental. Under the terms of this offer his profits from the production of nitrogen fertilizer was not to exceed 8 percent.

Ford was at that time one of the nation's popular heroes. His friends and publicists promoted him as a public benefactor. They enlarged upon the presumed advantages of his offer, and described the prospect of low-cost fertilizer for the farmer in glowing terms. Although Secretary Weeks acknowledged the bid without enthusiasm and even made Ford amend certain specifications before submitting it to Congress, everyone else seemed greatly in its favor. The American Farm Bureau Federation lobbied actively for it, Secretary of Commerce Hoover praised it as a generous proposal, and businessmen around Muscle Shoals swamped Congress with letters of approval. The mere prospect of Ford's participation in the project started a real estate boom of fantastic proportions.

Norris saw the matter differently. To him Muscle Shoals became more than a means of cheap fertilizer. He was even more interested in developing "the entire Tennessee River to its maximum for power, for navigation, and for flood control." He studied power reports and engineers' plans, the intricate details of hydroelectric generation and transmission, and the regional prospects of an improved waterways system. At his own expense he went a number of times to the Tennessee Valley to examine its resources at first hand; each time he noted that while millions of gallons of water roared over the dam's spillways unattached to generators, thousands of farmers below were without the benefit of electric power. He also learned the chemistry of nitrogen and the processes for making it—thereby ascertaining that the cyanamid method employed in the Muscle Shoals plant had been made obsolete by the simpler and cheaper Haber process. Later he wrote:

For two years I have been absolutely absorbed in the Muscle Shoals problem. It is so difficult, so far-reaching in its ramifications, that in order to master it I have had to concentrate upon it and to exclude from my mind all other matters that were not absolutely essential.

339

An examination of the Ford bid persuaded him that it assured neither cheap power nor low-cost fertilizer. What perturbed him in addition was the possibility that Ford might transfer the enterprise to Wall Street manipulators, thus surely bartering away the people's heritage. He therefore opposed the offer and introduced a bill that would assure government operation of Muscle Shoals. Months of debate and tactical maneuvering failed to bring agreement.

Late in 1923 Ford came to Washington to consult with President Coolidge. The nature of their talk was not made public, but rumor insinuated that the two men agreed for Ford to forego his ambition to seek the Presidency and for Coolidge to exert the power of his office in favor of the industrialist's bid. At any rate Ford did express approval of another term for President Coolidge and the latter urged Congress to sell Muscle Shoals for private exploitation. Norris was very critical of this alleged complicity. When Ford accused him of impugning the President's motives, the provoked Nebraskan replied:

I am sincerely endeavoring to save for the people of the United States the valuable inheritance of our national resources and I will continue to do this regardless of results, and regardless of who may be involved. I do not want a controversy with the President or anyone else, but I will not deviate from what I believe to be my duty in bringing out the proper evidence before the Committee, regardless of what the effect may be upon me or anyone else.

In January 1924 the House Military Affairs Committee, acting on President Coolidge's recommendation, offered a bill favoring Ford's bid. With most Representatives opposed to government ownership, the legislation was readily approved by a vote of 227 to 142. The Senate Committee on Agriculture, however, ended a prolonged debate in May by voting against the House bill and in favor of Norris's resolution. Other legislation, however, prevented the Senate from acting promptly on these recommendations, and in June Congress adjourned for the political conventions—thereby leaving the Muscle Shoals proposals in abeyance.

By this time the deficiencies of Ford's offer had become generally known and public opinion began to turn against it. Aware of this situation, Ford suddenly announced his withdrawal. "More than two years ago," he declared, "we made the best bid we knew how to make. No definite action has been taken on it. A simple affair of business which should have been decided by anyone within a week has become a complicated political affair." And he added pointedly that he was not in politics.

With Ford eliminated, Norris promoted his bill with renewed vigor. In the discussion Senator Oscar Underwood, an able and experienced politician from Alabama, emerged as his most forceful opponent. Though a leading Democrat, he joined the Coolidge forces and proposed legislation for the private operation of Muscle Shoals as a fertilizer plant. He accused Norris of "dreaming dreams" and extolled the virtues of individual industrial enterprise. Norris was quick to send his satiric shafts in the Southerner's direction. He was equally vehement in his criticism of President Coolidge and the electric power companies. Not till January 13, 1925, was a final vote taken, and the Underwood substitute bill was approved by a vote of 46 to 33. Fortunately for Norris, however, the House leaders, pressed for time, made the mistake of sending to conference its earlier proposal, which was quite unlike the Senate bill. When the compromise measure was reported out of conference, Norris moved a point of order against it on the ground that new matter had been introduced into it. The Senate thereupon voted to recommit the legislation. Since the session was nearing its end, Norris managed to arrange a filibuster. "We gave the machine a taste of its own medicine," the Nebraskan remarked drily. Yet he knew that the struggle would be resumed in the new Congress, and he was not sanguine about the outcome.

President Coolidge moved next by appointing a commission to make a study of Muscle Shoals and report its recommendations. With the members known to be opposed to government ownership, Norris countered with the offer to write their conclusions in a few hours. And he was right. After months of research and investigation the commission found in favor of private operation and Coolidge again urged Congress to act accordingly. Although the response was a joint resolution of approval, no definite action was taken for the next two years. Meantime Norris resigned his chairmanship of the Committee on Agriculture, yielding it to his friend Charles L. McNary, in order to give more of his time to the study of water power and its application to the Tennessee River region. He also enlisted the aid of other sympathetic Senators as well as a number of eminent citizens in a nationwide campaign for the public ownership of water power.

In January 1928 he introduced a bill providing for partial government operation of Muscle Shoals. Another bill favoring private exploitation was also presented, but this time Norris had relatively little difficulty in obtaining a majority vote. Meantime the House Military Affairs Committee, considering several bills, listened to four hours of Norris's testimony on the matter and recommended the one coinciding with the Senate measure. Late in May, with Representative Fiorello H. La Guardia's help, the bill was passed and sent to conference. An attempt in the Senate to filibuster the report failed and both Houses accepted it shortly before adjournment. President Coolidge, however, nullified the legislation by a pocket veto—causing Norris to comment caustically that the action "was not only unfair but lacked the courage that a public official ought to show."

Disappointed but not disheartened, he persisted in his study of water power. In Toronto he learned that in one of the homes he visited the family used 334 kilowatt hours of electricity at a cost of $3.35. The same amount of power, he pointed out, cost $32 in Birmingham and $40 in Nashville—cities within the Muscle Shoals area. "Some day," he added, "we are going to have a system such as Canada has, . . . some day there will not be a home, either in the country or in the city, but will be supplied by electricity. . . . We cannot escape that; it is as sure as the law of gravitation."

In May 1929 he once more presented his bill to the Senate. Although it was reported out of committee by unanimous vote, no action was taken that year in view of President Hoover's known opposition. During this period a Senate investigation of lobbying, activated by Senator Hugo Black, provided Norris with fresh support by making public that in 1925 Hoover, then Secretary of Commerce, had sought diligently to bring the power and fertilizer interests together against the Norris bill. The Committee further disclosed that the Farm Bureau Federation had worked closely with the American Cyanamid Company and had helped write the Muscle Shoals section in President Coolidge's message to Congress.

Senate discussion of the pending bill was finally begun in April 1930. For nearly two days Norris discussed its history and purpose. Little opposition developed and the vote in its favor was 45 to 23. In the House, however, the Republican landslide in 1928 enabled opponents of public ownership to pass a bill of their own by a vote of 196 to 114. As was generally expected, the two conflicting measures remained in conference when Congress adjourned. The 1930 elections, affected by the economic depression, sent to the House a sizable number of liberals who favored public power. The "lame duck" session continued its opposition, but early in March 1931 the new Congress voted favorably on the bill. President Hoover, however, immediately vetoed it in a sharply critical statement. He maintained that government operation would tend "to break down the initiative and enterprise of the American people; that it would destroy equality of opportunity and our civilization."

This bill would launch the Federal Government upon a policy of ownership and operation of power utilities upon a basis of competition instead of by the proper Government function of regulation for the protection of all the people. I hesitate to contemplate the future of our institutions, of our Government, and of our country if the preoccupation of its officials is to be no longer the promotion of justice and equal opportunity but is to be devoted to barter in the markets. This is not liberalism, it is degeneration.

Norris considered the veto unfair and unjust. But he was not discouraged. He was already looking ahead, reconciled to wait till the end of Hoover's term in office—convinced that the future was on his side.

The struggle for government operation of Muscle Shoals absorbed most of Norris's attention and energy, but it did not keep him from working for other important reforms. His eagerness for functional democracy had early made him critical of the lag in government procedure which enabled defeated Congressmen to function as legislators for months after the election of their successors. He maintained that with acceleration in travel it was no longer necessary to retain provisions requisite in the stagecoach era. He also pointed out that this anachronistic situation tempted outgoing Congressmen to barter their votes for federal jobs.

The matter became focused in his mind in 1922 when a group of Congressmen favoring ship subsidies met with emphatic defeat at the polls. President Harding, approving these subsidies, nevertheless called upon the "lame duck" Congress to pass the controversial legislation. A Senator opposed to subsidies introduced a resolution stating that no defeated member of Congress "has the moral right to support or vote for any measure which the people by their votes have repudiated." The matter was referred to Norris's committee and he reported that only an amendment to the Constitution would remedy the situation.

On December 5, 1922, he offered such an amendment for consideration. Its purport was to advance the terms of the Presidency and Congress from March to January in the interest of administrative and legislative efficiency. The original draft also provided for the abolition of the Electoral College, which Norris considered undemocratic, but he deleted that portion because of strong opposition. On the Senate floor he argued that since campaign issues were debated at length, it was fair to assume that the victors at the polls best represented the wishes of the people and should therefore be given an early opportunity to formulate these wishes into legislation. The Senate on February 13, 1923, passed the resolution by the overwhelming vote of 63 to 6. In the House, however, no action was taken.

Norris became determined to work for the passage of his resolution, soon known as the "Lame Duck" Amendment. On March 18, 1924, the Senate again passed it by a large majority. In the House it was reported favorably, placed on the calendar—and ignored. Norris charged that "entrenched behind the breastworks of the old constitutional provisions were the organized political machines of special privilege." Yet he persisted, and in the next Congress the Senate passed the resolution for the third time on February 24, 1926. And for the third time the House leaders refused to bring it to a vote. Two years later the Senate once more voted favorably on the amendment. This time it came up for a vote in the House but failed to obtain the required two-thirds majority. A year and a half later the Senate passed the measure for the fifth time, but for the next ten months Speaker Nicholas Longworth did nothing about it. He referred it to a committee only after Norris called this situation to the attention of the Senate. Meantime the House leaders introduced and passed a similar resolution but with provisions quite contrary to those in the Senate bill. In conference the House members refused any compromise and thus again killed the proposed amendment.

A turn for the better came with the Democratic victory in the 1930 elections. On January 6, 1932, the Senate passed Norris's resolution for the sixth time. Speaker John N. Garner immediately gave it the right of way in the House, and on February 16 it was adopted by a vote of 335 to 56. The conference report was prepared amicably and was quickly approved by both Houses. The required number of state legislatures readily ratified the 20th or "Lame Duck" Amendment—Missouri being the 36th state to do so on January 23, 1933.

Another important reform measure began to germinate in Norris's mind in 1926, when he was in Pennsylvania campaigning against Vare. There he saw the hovels of the coal miners, the drab towns they lived in, and the oppressive conditions around the coal mines. For the first time he discovered the onerous effects of the "yellow dog" contract system. It became clear to him that the combination of venal sheriffs, unfriendly courts, and arrogant managers served to develop "a type of bondage that enslaved the miner to a life of toil without any opportunity to make a decent effort to improve or to better his position." He particularly deplored the free use of injunctions in an effort to force the miner into a kind of "involuntary servitude." Three years later, dedicating a statue of Abraham Lincoln in Freeport, Illinois, he had these miners in mind when he said:

Economic slavery is as great an injustice, as cruel, as any political slavery ever established by man; and if, by the combination of vast amounts of wealth, the economic and political and social functions of our race are controlled and dominated by those who own the combination, then those who are controlled are, in reality, slaves.

About that time Senator Henrik Shipstead was persuaded by the doughty labor leader Andrew Furuseth to introduce a bill outlawing the "yellow-dog" contract. In committee discussion Norris and other members thought the wording inadequate and probably unconstitutional. After prolonged open hearings the committee appointed five eminent lawyers and economists to draw up a substitute bill that would be juridicially foolproof. To this end they perused all important Supreme Court decisions bearing on labor before they prepared the new legislation. Norris commented:

After all of the study and research and energies devoted to hearings, and the deep desire among members of the subcommittee to remedy frightful conditions in the coal-mining industry, we were concerned chiefly with framing legislation that would pass the test of the courts.

The new bill was presented to the Senate by Norris. In explanation he remarked:

It limits the injunction to such causes as common, ordinary justice demands it should be limited. It admits laboring men to organize for the purpose of improving their conditions. It recognizes their right to organize in defense of their rights and their labors. It prevents great aggregations of capital from continuing against the weak and poor in any way which would deprive them of the ordinary rights of free American citizens.

A companion bill was introduced in the House by La Guardia. In 1930, however, antiunion sentiment in the Senate was still dominant, and the proposed legislation met with strong and stubborn resistance. President Hoover also made known his opposition to the bill. Both Norris and La Guardia worked in vain for the passage of anti-injunction legislation during the life of that session.

With the 1930 elections markedly liberalizing the membership of Congress, the Norris-La Guardia bills were received much more sympathetically. Workers' organizations, representing many thousands who were either unemployed or suffering from oppressive employers, besieged the open hearings to urge enactment of this legislative relief. Liberals everywhere also spoke up for the bills. The result was that a number of Congressmen who had opposed this legislation in the previous session decided to vote in the affirmative. In the Senate there were only five nays against 75 yeas, while in the House the vote was 363 to 13. Although President Hoover was still opposed, he reluctantly signed the law which in effect outlawed the "yellow-dog" contract, greatly limited the issuance of labor injunctions, made mandatory a jury trial of most contempt cases, and permitted defendants to request that their trial proceed before a judge other than the one who had issued the injunction. The Norris–La Guardia Act thus became the first of the favorable labor laws in the 1930's which in combination helped organized workers to achieve their present strength and influence.

Early in 1929 Franklin D. Roosevelt's favorable position on public power brought him to Norris's attention. By the time the New York governor announced his candidacy for President, the Nebraskan had come to know him well enough to hail him as the best of the men seeking the high office. "We disagree only on prohibition," he remarked. "He is the nearest right on the power issue of any man in public life." To a fellow liberal he wrote:

I have said and I believe that Governor Roosevelt comes much closer to representing the idea of standing for the people as against monopoly than any other man who apparently has any show for the Democratic nomination. I may be, of course, as you have intimated in your letter, entirely wrong about this, but from what I know and what I have been able to gather I am convinced I am right about it.

Shortly after Roosevelt was nominated, Norris made public his opposition to President Hoover's re-election and campaigned actively for the national Democratic candidates. This party switch was inevitable. Hoover's conservative dogmatism had completely alienated Norris from the Republican party and Roosevelt's New Deal coincided with his own idea of dynamic democracy. Indeed the 1932 Democratic platform to a great degree spelled out the liberal reforms for which he had been working for twenty years. This philosophy of economic justice he expressed simply and truly in his acknowledgment of the 1933 Cardinal Newman Award at the University of Illinois:

The right to acquire property and make unlimited profits is not a sacred right. The laws which gave this permission were framed in accordance with the conditions then existing, and when changes in economic conditions occur regardless of the wish or the demand of man, and especially when these rights, if continued, will bring about the destruction of government and civilization, then new laws and new rules must be enforced to protect the rights of humanity and save our civilization from annihilation. That personal liberties of individuals will be modified and somewhat changed by such laws and rules cannot be denied, but personal liberty of man is always a relative one, and he cannot exercise this liberty in a way which is destructive of the rights of his fellowmen.

Roosevelt genuinely admired Norris as "the very perfect gentle knight of American progressive ideals." To do him honor he, on September 28, 1932, made a special stop at McCook. About 16,000

348

people gathered to hear him, some farmers traveling long distances to be on hand. In introducing Roosevelt to his townsmen, Norris asserted that "patriotism demands that we put our country's interests above our party's interest." Roosevelt's response was high tribute to his hosts's greatness as a public servant:

History asks "Did the man have integrity?" "Did the man have unselfishness?" "Did the man have courage?" "Did the man have consistency?" . . . There are few statesmen in America today who so definitely and clearly measure up to an affirmative answer to the four questions as does the senior Senator from Nebraska, George W. Norris. In his rare case, history has already written the verdict.

A month after his election Roosevelt invited Norris to join him in January on an inspection of Muscle Shoals. Norris was delighted to find the President-elect so wholeheartedly in favor of the widest possible development of the region. He was particularly pleased to hear him say:

We have an opportunity of setting an example of planning, not just for ourselves but for the generations to come, tying in industry and agriculture and forestry and flood prevention, tying them all into a unified whole over a distance of a thousand miles so that we can afford better opportunities and better places for living for millions of yet unborn in the days to come.

"I can see my dreams coming true," Norris told Roosevelt that day. And in the evening he was given a copy of a bill embodying the broad provisions of what was to become the Tennessee Valley Authority.

During his first weeks in office, in the midst of an avalanche of demands upon his time, Roosevelt managed to see Norris several times concerning the Tennessee project. On April 10 he sent to Congress a brief but forceful message advocating the desired legislation.

It is clear that the Muscle Shoals development is but a small part of the potential public usefulness of the entire Tennessee River. Such use, if envisioned in its entirety, transcends mere power development:

it enters the wide fields of flood control, soil erosion, afforestation, elimination from agricultural use of marginal lands, and distribution and diversification of industry. In short, this power development of war days leads logically to national planning for a complete watershed involving many States and the future lives and welfare of millions. It touches and gives life to all forms of human concerns. I, therefore, suggest to the Congress legislation to create a Tennessee Valley Authority—a corporation clothed with the power of government but possessed of the flexibility and initiative of a private enterprise.

The following day Norris, in the happy frame of mind of a man who was about to realize his fondest hopes, introduced the TVA legislation in the Senate. Its objectives were those outlined by President Roosevelt. A similar bill was presented in the House. Hearings began at once, and both Houses passed separate bills by large majorities. When conflict developed in the conference committee, a pro-Norris member appealed to Roosevelt for help—which he gave promptly and effectively. On May 18 he signed the law—at long last making TVA a fact. Norris, jubilant, declared:

The Muscle Shoals legislation . . . is a monument to the victorious ending of a twelve years' struggle waged on behalf of the common people against the combined forces of monopoly and human greed. It is emblematic of the dawning of that day when every rippling stream that flows down the mountain side and winds its way through the meadows to the sea shall be harnessed and made to work for the welfare and comfort of man.

TVA was indeed the largest and most comprehensive engineering project ever undertaken in the United States. No single government agency was ever assigned so gigantic a task or the responsibility for the inclusive development of so vast a region. When the job was finished a dozen years later, there was nothing in the world to compare with it. To mention only one main aspect, it comprised the coordinated functioning of 28 dams along a watershed of over 40,000 square miles—all operated with the sole aim of controlling a vast river system for the maximum good of the people inhabiting the region. The use of electricity was made general and cheap in the home and factory and on the farm, and the economy and culture of hundreds of thousands of families were radically improved and broadened. TVA became in truth the symbol of dynamic democracy intelligently applied.

Norris rightly considered TVA his special responsibility. He helped Roosevelt choose the three directors and kept in close contact with them throughout the 1930's. He also combatted the private companies that sought to belittle the objectives of the gigantic project and to handicap its successful development. Great was his relief and satisfaction in 1937 when the Supreme Court routed the enemies of TVA by validating the law which had created it. And painful as the choice was to him, he favored Arthur E. Morgan's dismissal when a persecution complex had begun to vitiate the engineer's earlier notable accomplishments. In Congress he made sure that the needed moneys were duly appropriated. He was also ever alert for a bill or rider tending to affect the project adversely. And the TVA personnel and the people of the region honored him as their beloved patron. The first new dam was named after him, and so was the model city built to house the influx of population.

Having achieved the major reforms he had long fought for in Congress, Norris devoted the summer of 1934 to the campaign for the unicameral amendment in Nebraska. He had for many years been critical of the two-house legislative system of government. Of a practical bent despite his idealistic outlook, he knew that it was hopeless to expect a change on the federal level, since the small states would never yield their advantage in the Senate; moreover, he saw a certain logic in having both a small and relatively continuous Senate and a larger but short-lived House. He could perceive no reason but that of political lag for the similarly organized two-house state legislature.

As early as 1923 he published in the New York *Times Magazine* an article entitled "A Model State Legislature," in which he compared the state organization to a corporation, with the governor as president, the legislators as directors, and the people as stock-holders. As his ideas on the subject became crystallized, he maintained that it was illogical and inefficient to elect members to two separate bodies having similar qualifications, the same tenure of office, salary, duties, responsibilities, and jurisdiction. Such a system, he pointed out, was the relic of monarchical conditions that required checks and balances. Deprived of its original purpose, it merely repeated each action taken by either house and perpetuated the politically weighted conference procedure. In a democracy predicated on a one-class society, he concluded, the politicians were the only beneficiaries of the two-house legislature.

Until 1934 he was too preoccupied with his work in Congress to take definite action toward the proposed unicameral legislation. Moreover, he knew that the political apathy of the people in the 1920's did not favor the success of such a reform. With the advent of the New Deal there was everywhere a decided turn to liberalism and experimentation. Judging the time to be ripe, Norris went to Nebraska immediately after the close of Congress. He had the initiative petitions printed at his own expense and organized a corps of volunteers, many of them college students, to obtain the required signatures. Originally his amendment provided for a single legislature of 21 members, elected on a nonpartisan basis for four-year terms. Sensing the rising, widespread opposition, he enlarged the membership and reduced the term to two years. He insisted, however, on the nonpartisan ballot as an essential part of the basic reform.

Even with these revisions the proposed amendment aroused greater antagonism than he had anticipated. The politicians of both parties were furious. Nearly every newspaper opposed the change and fought it without let. Bankers, lawyers, and corporation heads spoke up against the proposed reform as the death of the American system of government. Despite this resistance, the volunteers succeeded in obtaining around 85,000 signatures— nearly 30,000 more than the required number. Norris himself canvassed every part of the state, traveling day after day and from

town to town, explaining the nature of the amendment and pleading with his listeners to believe that he had their interests at heart.

I know that those who live by politics are opposed to this amendment.
I have served you more than thirty years with no other interest than
that of the people of Nebraska and the people of our country. I have
always been called the worst demagogue who ever walked down the
pike until the things I wanted began to work. Do you think that in
my declining years I would desert the cause of the people, to which I
have given my life? If you ever believed me, believe me now when I
say that I have no other interest in this amendment than to make
Nebraska a better place in which to live.

As before, the people of Nebraska believed him and voted in
favor of the amendment by 286,086 to 193,152. His comment on
the unicameral victory was that an honest study of the subject
could not but convince everyone of the reform's validity. When
the single-chambered legislature met for the first time on January
5, 1937, Norris was on hand as an honored guest to witness the
first session—preferring to be there rather than in Washington,
where the new Congress began its accelerated opening on the same
day in accord with the 20th Amendment.

In Congress Norris welcomed the economic and social legislation of the Roosevelt Administration, but he was strongly opposed
to its big-navy program, its patronage policies, and especially its
machine politics. He was critical of Roosevelt for permitting James
Farley, chairman of the Democratic National Committee, to hold
the office of Postmaster-General. "I am sorry that the President
has permitted machine politics to operate. It is a very serious defect
in his armor." When Roosevelt did nothing in 1934 to stop Farley
from seeking the defeat of the liberal Republican Senator Bronson
Cutting for re-election, Norris was incensed. Since Cutting had
endangered his position with the New Mexico Republican party
machine by working for Roosevelt's election, Norris termed the
President's passivity "a case of awful ingratitude." Later, when
Cutting died in an airplane crash while on his way to Washington
to refute the claims of his Democratic rival, Norris walked out of

the Senate chamber in protest against the seating of the latter as Cutting's successor. "It is a blot upon the record of the Roosevelt Administration," he insisted.

Despite these shortcomings, Norris thought that Roosevelt had done much to better social conditions and early expressed himself in favor of a second term. He himself was strongly inclined to leave politics. He considered himself too old to undertake another six years of legislative exertion. Moreover, he felt "completely discouraged" by the sordid practices of both parties. He wrote subsequently:

I had no desire to be the candidate of a party whose state and national leaders had undertaken to steal an election by imposing a dummy candidate bearing my name unknown to the people of Nebraska. That decision was genuine, whatever others may think. Under no circumstances could I have been induced to have become a Republican candidate for the United States Senate in 1936. Under no circumstances would I have accepted a Democratic nomination.

When his decision became known he was inundated with urgent requests to reconsider. His friends and admirers made every possible effort to change his mind. At one of his press conferences President Roosevelt took the unprecedented step of telling correspondents "on the record" of his hope that Norris would remain in the Senate.

If I were a citizen of the State of Nebraska, regardless of what party I belonged, I would not allow George Norris to retire from the United States Senate, whether he wanted to or not, for the very good reason that I feel he is necessary not only to Nebraska but to the United States as long as he lives.

Thereupon Norris again yielded to the dictates of duty. His admirers in Nebraska assured the legality of his independent status by collecting 40,504 signatures instead of the required 1000. Leading liberals, including such men as Senators Hugo Black and La Follette, came to Nebraska to speak in his behalf. President Roosevelt, on his campaign tour, took time out in Omaha to plead eloquently for Norris's return to the Senate:

On this platform sits a man whose reputation has been known in every community—a man old in years but young in heart—a man who through all these years has had no boss but his own conscience. . . . George Norris's candidacy transcends State and party lines. In our national history we have had few elder statesmen who like him have preserved the aspirations of youth as they accumulated the wisdom of years. He is one of our major prophets of America. . . . Nebraska will be doing a great service not only to itself, but to every other State in the Union and the Nation as a whole, if it places this great American above partisanship, and keeps George Norris in the Senate of the United States.

Ironically, one of the men who came to Nebraska to attack Norris was Al Smith. In his talk he not only berated the man who had broken with his party in order to campaign for him in 1928 but also denounced Roosevelt for "betraying" the Democratic party by his espousal of Norris's candidacy. But with liberal leaders that year reaching their peak of popularity, the aged Norris won a hard three-cornered fight by a plurality of 25,424 votes—thereby becoming the first successful independent candidate for the Senate.

Early in 1937 the more active progressives in Congress united in an effort to curb the conservatism of the Supreme Court. Norris, as their informal leader, held that the Court was not "responsive to the pulsations of humanity." He declared that it was "a sad commentary on democracy that when a law is passed by the House and Senate and signed by the President, it can be nullified by a majority of one in the Court." Earlier, angered by the invalidation of AAA, he had pointed out sarcastically that "the people can change the Congress, but only God can change the Supreme Court." Knowing that the remedy, if effective, had to be of a fundamental nature, he proposed the slow but sure method of constitutional amendment as a means of stopping this "legislation by judiciary." His resolution gave the Court original and exclusive

355

jurisdiction to declare an Act of Congress invalid by a vote of 7 to 2. Its provisions would not only make invalidation more difficult but would stop district and circuit judges from enjoining government agencies—thereby saving millions of dollars in legal expenditures and in the loss of business till the Supreme Court decided the constitutional issue.

Although President Roosevelt appeared to favor the resolution, he made no move to help. His own proposal, sprung upon Congress without warning, greatly displeased Norris and other liberals. Although they did not oppose it publicly, they knew that the allegation of an overcrowded docket was at best questionable and that the plan to enlarge the Court was only a temporary expedient. "It might easily happen," Norris pointed out, "that a majority out of fifteen members would see through glasses fitted to meet the needs of another generation, just as it is true with only nine members." He admitted that it might take considerable time to pass a constitutional amendment, but he saw no alternative if the reform of the Court was to be "fundamental."

If he did not regret the failure of Roosevelt's Court plan, he hailed the appointment of Senator Black as Justice. When the latter was attacked for his one-time membership in the Klan, Norris defended him loyally. "Actually, Justice Black is being subjected to all this criticism because he is a liberal, because he wants to bring the Supreme Court closer to the people, not because he may have been a Klansman."

Throughout the 1930's Norris was largely concerned with domestic social reform. After 1935, however, international problems forced themselves on his attention. In the hope of keeping the United States out of the next war in Europe, portents of which were becoming more and more apparent, he furthered the passage of the Neutrality Act and its amendments. The disclosures of the Nye Committee served to justify his pacifistic position. In 1937, marking the twentieth anniversary of the American declaration of war on Germany, he asserted gloomily that the event had been an evil influence:

We have political corruption, such as we have never dreamt of before. We have a new crop of millionaires such as the world has never before witnessed. We have a crime wave that staggers the imagination of the world. We have gigantic, war-grown combinations of trade and money that are squeezing billions out of the people who gave till it hurt. We have a national avariciousness, a sense of grab, grab, grab, that cannot be eradicated from the national consciousness for generations to come.

It was this melancholy reflection that led him to remark in 1939, "After the work of a lifetime I can't see much progress."

Even more than war he abhorred the rising fascist menace. The threat of Hitlerism grew more and more real to him—not only in Europe but in the United States. He recognized that the advent of the airplane had nullified the protection afforded by the expanse of the oceans. When the Nazi invasion of Poland plunged Europe into another desperate continental struggle, Norris admitted that "there was no similarity in the challenge which confronted the American people" in the two wars. Although he continued to insist he was right in opposing the carnage in 1917, when the German menace to the United States was in his opinion more a freak phantom than a stark reality, he now had no doubt of the German-Japanese threats to American democracy. Unlike the stand-pat isolationists who resisted the steps taken by President Roosevelt against the fascist aggressors, Norris joined the liberal internationalists in the struggle to save the democratic countries of the world. He favored Lend-Lease, campaigned hard for Roosevelt's re-election to a third term, and voted for war after the Pearl Harbor attack.

Once in the war, Norris was as anxious as Roosevelt to achieve a lasting peace. Acutely conscious of the blunders at Versailles, he favored the unconditional surrender and complete disarmament of the enemy nations; but he also insisted on a peace without hate and "the absolute equality of nations." In addition to a number of speeches and articles he published a pamphlet in which he made clear his conception of a lasting peace. He maintained, as he had after World War I, that permanent disarmament was "the real cornerstone of the peace"; that it could be achieved by first de-

357

stroying the weapons of the defeated enemies and then by gradually reducing the arms of the victorious allies. To this end he urged restraint of the normal passions and natural hatreds so strongly aroused in a time of war.

We must remember that if we are to have a perpetual peace we must not establish, under any circumstances, a rule of government that practices the same things and is guilty of exactly the same wrongs that we charge against our enemies. A permanent peace will not come out of any peace that is framed in hate and dedicated to posterity with the spirit of vengeance. . . . Only by comtemplation of the future—only by thinking in terms of endless time—will we find the strength, the inspiration, and the vision to restrain the natural impulses of our nature and to give us strength to forego revenge upon enemies who do not deserve mercy.

In 1942 he was rounding out his fortieth year in Congress. An octogenarian and yearning for the quiet of retirement, he nevertheless considered it his duty to serve his country at war as he had in time of peace. In the campaign for re-election he once again met with the bitter opposition of the conservative politicians. They spread false rumors about him and hammered constantly at the disadvantage of his old age—although he was at that very time fighting as actively as any of the younger Senators for the repeal of the poll tax. With the war effort absorbing the energies of President Roosevelt and other of his influential friends, and with his own efforts limited to a few speeches, the citizens of Nebraska failed to give him a majority for the first time in nearly a half century.

Norris left Washington without regret. Although he did not relish defeat, especially in an unequal fight and to an opponent unworthy of him, he looked forward to days of quiet and ease at McCook. But the repose of retirement was not for him. Before long he grumbled that he could not "stay quiet and live." Besides, there was still much to be done—and his friends and followers implored his help. A month after the election a dinner was given in his honor with the aim of initiating a "popular front" among the liberals. Loath as he was to assume the role of leader, especially at his age, he could not remain passive in the face of the anti-democratic upsurge. As before in Congress, so now as a venerated free lance he spoke out against the evils of the day—lending his name, or his presence, or his voice, as the occasion demanded. In addition he worked on his autobiography, published posthumously under the title of *Fighting Liberal.*

In 1944 he again entered the campaign on President Roosevelt's behalf and accepted the honorary chairmanship of the National Citizens Political Action Committee. Late in August, however, he was stricken fatally with a cerebral hemorrhage.

George W. Norris never achieved the prestige of a popular hero because he lacked the quality of self-dramatization, the drive and impetus of the demagogic leader. Yet he was unquestionably a very great American. No other Senator ever attained his record of constructive work. For thirty years he was the goad and the conscience of the United States Senate. As William Allen White has well stated:

How piffling seem the pigmies who held power in Congress while Norris worked there—men like Cannon and Aldrich and Bois Penrose, the Congressional bosses whose loyalty to their party was their god. What a false and mocking god they served compared to the purpose and vision that held George Norris in his course!

Norris's mind and aspirations were shaped during the quarter century following the Civil War, when life on the midwestern prairies was hard but hopeful, where democracy prevailed as a pristine yet potent force. A typical, yet rare and refined, product of this environment, he proudly adhered to the principles expounded by the Founding Fathers and boastfully echoed by political orators every Fourth of July. Throughout his youth he believed that the nation established in 1776 was God's final answer to man's democratic striving.

When, on entering Congress, he found that the politicians he admired disregarded in practice the ideals they espoused in theory, he could not acquiesce in the equivocation. In addition to being a man of principle and an idealist, he was a stubborn fighter. In time he dissociated himself from these politicians and the party they controlled and followed his true bent. The years of conflict and cogitation sharpened his ardor and heightened his aspirations. The welfare of the people became to him the basic criterion; whatever clashed with it he opposed on principle. It was this dynamism that caused Senator Arthur Capper of Kansas to refer to Norris as "a living, perambulating Declaration of Independence in human form."

Experience and reflection convinced him of the social irresponsibility of unbridled industrialists and financiers. Their drive and greed seemed to him the antithesis of the public good. A corollary of this assumption was that private monopoly of a public utility was inherently evil. "A free people," he argued, "cannot permanently submit to a private monopoly of a necessity of life." He therefore advocated the public ownership and operation of those utilities and natural resources that are essential to the general welfare.

Because the struggle for the control of water power was most vigorous in his time, he devoted many years to combating what he termed the power trust. Throughout the 1920's he remained adamant in his fight for the public operation of Muscle Shoals and scoffed at the Republican dogma of "less government in business." No wonder that Herbert Hoover called him ominously "a most consistent Socialist." But labels never bothered Norris. Undeterred by defeat, certain of the rightness of his position, he persisted in preaching the doctrine of public water power—broadening and brightening his vision of millions of horses harnessed and working for the entire nation. As R. L. Duffus aptly explained:

Muscle Shoals has come to symbolize for him a philosophy of the proper relation between government and people. Behind his long fight for government ownership and control of the great Tennessee River plant is a belief that the power industry must necessarily be a monopoly—that it cannot effectively be anything else—and that the public welfare demands that it be publicly controlled.

Norris was for years characteristically the Middle Westerner in the insularity of his world outlook. An ardent advocate of peace, he hated war and those responsible for it. For years he failed to perceive the American position as a leading power because he did not want the United States to assume the duties and involvements incumbent upon a mighty and enterprising nation. He believed it could—for all its accelerating power, and perhaps because of it —well take advantage of its fortunate geographical position and remain aloof from the rivalries and jealousies and petty squabbles of the European governments. It was this naively idealistic attitude that caused him to oppose American participation in World War I. Twenty years later, however, he viewed world affairs with greater sophistication. Still a confirmed pacifist, he acquiesced in the urgency to destroy fascism as a matter of self-defense. He never quite gave up his preference for an aloof America, but he hoped that the defeat of Germany and Japan would not only assure our own safety but bring permanent peace to the rest of the world.

As an outstanding dynamic democrat he became the most persistent advocate of progressive reforms in Congress. Liberals claimed him as their own and, especially after the death of the elder La Follette, pleaded with him to become their active leader. This he refused. He had neither the drive for power nor the personal vanity of the successful head of a party. His interest lay in specific reforms and not in the generalship of a reform movement. He dreaded, and also despised, the rivalries and bickering within any political group. And he knew better than to succumb to the glamor and glory of a presidential candidacy. By this preference to act alone, or at most as the protagonist of a specific cause, he forfeited the opportunity to organize the liberal factions into a permanently active force in contemporary American politics. During the last twenty years of his life he was time and again forced into the position of temporary leadership, but each time he relinquished it at the first opportunity.

Notwithstanding this limitation—if such it be—Norris is rightly honored as one of the most forthright and effective liberals in American history. His honesty of purpose, his warm humanity, his selfless dedication to the public welfare, and his remarkable persistence as a fighter combine to make him "the perfect gentle knight" of democratic liberalism.

Hugo L. Black

NEW DEAL JUSTICE

Although President Roosevelt's maladroit move against the Supreme Court in February 1937 resulted in a political battle lost from the outset, his defeat soon became the springboard leading to decisive victory. By "a switch in time that saved the nine," the Court sharply reversed its previous position and validated a number of New Deal laws. At about the same time Justice Van Devanter announced his retirement. With Senator Joseph Robinson, who was to have been appointed to the first vacancy, suddenly dead of a heart attack, Roosevelt found the choosing of a new Justice a highly intricate political problem. He knew the Senate was in a recalcitrant mood and would resist the confirmation of a known progressive. Yet he was resolved to name a genuine and aggressive liberal. After considering scores of likely candidates he surprised the nation and nonplused the Senate by nominating Senator Black of Alabama. Thus Roosevelt once again revealed himself the shrewd politician: defiantly selecting an ardent New Dealer and yet assured of his confirmation by the wonted rule of Senatorial courtesy.

The outcry against the nominee was vociferous and vituperative. He was denounced as a demagogue devoid of the judicial temper and accused of intolerance, inquisitorial arrogance, and juristic ignorance. Ominous reference was also made to his one-time connection with the Ku Klux Klan. Despite this harsh criticism he was confirmed within two days.

363

Hugo LaFayette Black, the eighth and youngest child of an Alabama merchant, was born on February 17, 1886. After spending his first three years on a farm in Clay County he was taken to live in a nearby village, where he attended school. The community was extremely poor, the whites little better off than their black neighbors. When Hugo first became aware of his environment in the early 1890's, the men around him were strongly affected by the Populist movement. His eager ears absorbed the arguments and political harangues, and his keen mind retained the distilled doctrines, although his relatively prosperous father condemned them vigorously. Also influential were the stories he heard from his maternal grandfather, who was proud of the family's Irish ancestors because their sympathy for the French Jacobins had forced them to flee to this country.

At seventeen Hugo enrolled in Birmingham Medical College because his father wanted him to follow in his older brother's footsteps. The next year, however, he transferred to the University of Alabama Law School, his original preference. Though poorly prepared academically, he studied hard and made the honors list. On graduation in 1906 he opened a law office in his home town of Ashland. For a year he did little more than investigate policy applicants for an insurance company—at fifty cents per applicant. When a fire destroyed his office, he decided to settle in Birmingham. His first client was a Negro convict who had been kept at work by a private concern 22 days after his prison term had expired. So ably did he handle the case that he made a favorable impression on both the judge and his older opponent.

Ambitious and gregarious, Black in time joined the Masons, the Knights of Pythias, and the Odd Fellows; he also became an active member of the Baptist church and taught Sunday school. Conventionally religious, he attended service fairly regularly and continued teaching till he moved to Washington twenty years later.

In 1911, at twenty-five, Black was appointed police judge. For two years he dealt with the dregs of the Birmingham population —mostly Negroes whose ignorance and poverty led them to violate the law and become the victims of a vicious prison system. Black insisted on treating them with sympathetic fairness.

His private practice, in conjunction with various partners, was growing rapidly. He became skillful at research and in examining witnesses and soon gained a reputation as a very shrewd trial lawyer. Most of his cases were personal damage suits; practically none came from corporations. By 1914 his net annual income ranged around $7500. Not satisfied with mere money-making, however, he decided to seek election as county solicitor.

Successful at the polls, he lost no time in initiating promised reforms. At once he ran afoul of men who profited from vested crime and slum conditions. They fought him relentlessly throughout his three years in office. Nevertheless he persisted in instituting certain improvements. Ruthless in the prosecution of major criminals, murderers in particular, he relaxed the former harsh and corrupt treatment of petty culprits. Among other reforms he stopped the practice of keeping Negroes in jail longer than was necessary.

He was shocked by the third-degree methods employed by Bessemer police when dealing with Negro defendants. "Such practices," he stated, "are dishonorable, tyrannical, and despotic, and such rights must not be surrendered to any officers or set of officers, so long as human life is held sacred and human liberty and human safety of paramount importance." So strongly did he antagonize politicians and local officials by his zealous conduct that his chances of re-election appeared doubtful.

The declaration of war against Germany in April 1917 gave Black's career a sharp jolt. A Bryan pacifist during the "preparedness" period, he nevertheless considered it his patriotic duty to enlist without delay. He remained in the United States throughout the fighting and was discharged from the Army as a captain in the artillery.

Resuming his law practice in 1919, he soon represented the United Mine Workers and other unions in important suits. He was also handling some of the most prominent trial cases in the state and receiving large fees. When Mobile citizens conspired against the Prohibition Act, he was engaged by the federal government as special counsel.

In 1921 he married Josephine Foster and in time became the father of two sons and a daughter. Mrs. Black's sense of reality and her high ethical standards helped him later to stand his ground under attack and to persist in the fight for his ideals. Essentially modest and self-effacing, she encouraged him to do as he thought best without regard to consequences. When she died in December 1951 she left him deeply bereaved. Five years later he remarried.

On September 11, 1923, Black joined the Klan. It was an act of neither impulse nor conviction. The Klan was then at the height of its political influence and had more than two million members in the South. It was promoted aggressively as a fraternal organization, allegedly serving Protestants as the Knights of Columbus served Catholics and the Bnai Brith served Jews. The crimes and violence committed in its name were attributed by its sponsors to members unrepresentative of the order. In Birmingham all the Protestant ministers and most of the prominent citizens, among whom were Black's best friends, were members of the Klan. It was at the insistent urging of these intimates, and with their assurance that the Klan really favored law and order as stated in its by-laws, that he finally enrolled.

At no time, then or since, did he have the disdain for the Klan that many Northerners have. He deplored its intolerance and denounced its acts of violence, but he knew that the membership was for the most part as peaceable and humane as he was. Though suspecting skulduggery among its chief promoters, he remained enrolled for nearly two years because he thought it was good for his career to belong to social organizations and because he wanted to please his friends. In 1925, when he decided again to enter politics, he resigned his membership but remained friendly with the local leaders and welcomed their support in the oncoming campaign.

Black's decision to seek election to the United States Senate was the result of serious soul-searching and frank discussion with his wife and close friends. Inspired by Jeffersonian ideals and by such ethical philosophers as Spinoza, he was moved by the ambition to distinguish himself in the service of his fellow men. Fully aware of his abilities as a speaker and lawyer, he had neither the southern demagogue's drive for power nor the aggressive lawyer's desire for financial gain. His years in office as police judge and county solicitor had convinced him of the futility of superficial reform. His six years of private legal practice after his discharge from the Army had brought him to the top of his profession in Alabama, with an annual income of nearly $50,000, but not the personal gratification he yearned. While thus contemplating the future direction of his career he learned that the aged Senator Underwood was not to run for re-election in 1926. With his wife's strong encouragement he decided to seek the office.

On June 10, 1925, he announced his candidacy. With no political machine to work for him, little known outside of Birmingham, and opposed by four aspirants with official backing, he knew he had to work hard to win. Proclaiming himself the poor man's candidate and relying on the sympathy of many Klansmen, Prohibitionists, and labor unionists, he stressed in his platform such planks as veterans' aid, farm relief, Prohibition enforcement, immigration restriction, and the public operation of Muscle Shoals. For more than a year he toured the highways and byways of the state in his Model T Ford, shook hands with as many voters as he could reach, spoke to groups in every town and hamlet, and systematically solicited the support of active citizens everywhere. Although the national Klan officially supported one of the other candidates, he was able to retain the friendship of the state organization. So energetic and effective was his long campaign—carried on at considerable financial cost to himself—that in the August 1926 primaries he received 40 percent of first-place votes and enough second-place votes to win the nomination and thus the election.

Three weeks later the Birmingham Klan met to honor Governor Bibb Graves. Black, as the successful nominee for the Senate, was also invited, and both men were presented with Grand Passports or honorary Klan life memberships. In a speech made that evening Black, in an expansive mood, declared that he had been chosen to serve in the Senate "by men who believe in the principles that I have sought to advocate, and which are the principles of this organization." He added, however, that he would rather resign that coveted office than pander "to the things that are wrong and contrary to American tradition and instincts." He also expressed his devotion to the Fathers of the "principles of liberty which were written in the Constitution of this country and in the great historical documents."

Black took his public career very seriously. Knowing that as Senator he would have to deal with grave national and international affairs, matters with which he had only superficial acquaintance, he began a course of intensive study in the fields of economics and government that before long made him one of the best-informed men in the Senate. For months after assuming office he said little because he first wanted to familiarize himself with legislative procedure and the issues under debate.

When the Muscle Shoals bill came up for discussion he spoke in favor of the bid made by the American Cyanamid Company in the belief that the firm would provide farmers with cheap fertilizer. Senator Norris soon convinced him, however, of the collusive agreement between that company and the power corporation and thus made him a loyal supporter in the crusade for the public development of Muscle Shoals.

Having learned the ways and means of Senate politics and having taken his stand as a Norris liberal (the Nebraskan's photograph is still in the most prominent position on the wall of his study), he became in 1929 an active opponent of the Hoover Administration. Again and again he stanchly supported the progressive faction in their fight against conservative legislation. In 1930 he favored John Bankhead, whom he had defeated four years earlier, over the incumbent Senator Heflin and thus helped to defeat the notorious demagogue.

Two years later, seeking re-election, Black was again opposed by four rivals. This time the Klan was working actively for his defeat, having broken with him in 1928 because of his open support of Al Smith's candidacy. Among other things it made public its award to him of the Grand Passport in 1926. Despite this strong opposition and his own relatively passive campaign he polled 49 percent of the votes in the May primary. Returning to Alabama immediately thereafter, he worked intensively and at his own expense during the few weeks prior to the run-off nomination, and this time he obtained 60 percent of the votes. A notable factor in this campaign was the strong support of organized labor.

Like all conscientious Americans, he was deeply perturbed by the distress resulting from the economic depression in the early 1930's. He studied numerous reports, consulted with businessmen and labor leaders, and concluded that the most likely immediate remedy was the spread of work among the unemployed. On the opening of the Senate session in 1933 he introduced a bill limiting the work-week to thirty hours. Offering a vast amount of statistics on economic and industrial conditions, he argued that such legal limitation of the hours of work would not only lessen unemployment but help stabilize industry and thus improve the general economy. He condemned employers who forced their workers to labor excessive hours at low wages, and insisted that the shorter work-week was a natural corollary of labor-saving machinery. The New Deal Congress, however, preferred to heed Administration advisers; although the bill passed the Senate by a vote of 53 to 30, it was sidetracked in the House for the more comprehensive NIRA experiment.

For all his liberal sympathies, Black would not accept the validity of the NIRA bill. Mostly he feared the powers the measure gave to business. Speaking against it in the Senate, he asserted:

This bill, if it shall pass and become a law, will transfer the law-making power of this nation, in so far as the control of industry is concerned, from the Congress to the trade association. There is no escape from that conclusion. That is exactly what has happened in Italy and as a result the legislation passed by the parliamentary body in Italy, as expressed by one economist, has reached the vanishing point.

In his own mind the thirty-hour plan seemed a safer and sounder means of industrial recovery. Writing on the subject in 1936, when NIRA was already a failure, he maintained that national production would have been greater during the years 1930–1935 with a thirty-hour week. This spread of work, he contended, would have created an effective demand for labor and thus "speed up production, require more efficient operation, and make useful invention profitable."

Black's objection to NIRA, the bonus veto, and certain aspects of the Economy Act did not affect his generally cordial agreement with the aims and activities of the New Deal. His chief usefulness to it derived from his great ability as an investigator. As far back as 1928 he had suspected corruption and inefficiency in the United States Shipping Board, but he was prevented from looking into its operation by the Republican majority. Five years later, with the Senate largely Democratic and himself one of its prominent members, he introduced a resolution to investigate mail-carrying contracts and became chairman of the committee. In his scrutiny of ocean mail-carrying contracts he was chagrined to discover that many of the telltale records had been destroyed by previous administrators. Questioning only strengthened the suspicion of fraud and favoritism.

He next investigated the airmail contracts. By piecing diverse facts together, by persistent interrogation of witnesses, and by close examination of the available records he succeeded in uncovering bribery, collusion, and general extravagance in connection with airmail subsidies. He disclosed that between 1928 and 1934 $28,-000,000 of the total have been excessive and illegal, that 90 percent of all subsidies were awarded to only four companies, and that small firms not in the "airmail trust" were ignored despite their low bids. Scrutiny of the books of the favored corporations revealed that certain influential individuals had turned investments of a few dollars into millions of paper profits. These men were also paid lavish salaries and bonuses while their firms received millions in subsidies from the government. Of these businessmen he asked: "Do you think it is right for the United States Government to subsidize any companies when the officers draw salaries and bonuses of several hundred thousands dollars?"

The information brought forth at the public hearings angered a large part of the nation and protests against the subsidies were general and vigorous. In January 1934 President Roosevelt canceled all airmail contracts and directed the Army to fly the mails. Exceptionally bad weather forced the inexperienced pilots into a series of tragic accidents. By the time twelve of the men were killed the people forgot the scandalous aspects of the subsidies and began to clamor for the return of the airmail to the private fliers. In less than a month this was done. The new agreements, however, called for awards of contracts to lowest bidders and for limitation to no more than three contracts for any one company. These modifications soon reduced airmail costs by half. Senator Black regretted the unanticipated casualties. Yet wishing to keep the record straight and to remind his critics of the inescapable facts, he said in a nationwide radio speech:

Since 1925 taxpayers of this nation have paid $1,143,255,705 for the developments of aviation. The tragic part of this picture is that investigations have revealed recently that these huge government expenditures have, in great part, found their way into the pockets of profiteers, stock manipulators, political and powerful financial groups who never flew a plane, who never invented an engine, who never improved an airplane part. In short this great and indispensable industry was greedily grabbed away from the control of those interested in aviation progress, and has been utilized by profiteers as a means for private gain through stock jobbing, speculation and monopoly.

He was no sooner finished with the investigation of mail-carrying subsidies than he became a chief participant in the assault upon the utility holding companies. Standing shoulder to shoulder with Senator Norris in behalf of public power, he fought zealously for the "death sentence" clause against large holding

371

companies in the bill then under debate. Along with other New Dealers he thought it outrageous for men like Samuel Insull and Howard Hopson to control and exploit the operating utility firms of the country by manipulating the voting stock at the highest level of a cleverly pyramided holding company.

The proponents of the bill were meeting with fierce resistance. The propaganda against it was ingenious, intensive, and extremely lavish financially. Members of Congress were overwhelmed with thousands of letters and telegrams, and the pressure upon them from influential lobbyists was tremendous. When the bill finally came to a vote it passed the Senate by the narrowest margin and in the House the "death sentence" clause was entirely eliminated.

While the bill remained deadlocked in conference, its proponents hit upon the idea of strengthening their position against the holding companies by an investigation of their enormous lobby. Black introduced the resolution and became chairman of the committee. With no time to lose, he worked fast and fervently. No respecter of the "best people" and knowing that he was to be opposed by the keenest lawyers in the country with unlimited expense accounts, he determined to ferret out the facts despite formal barriers and clever dodging. He ordered searches of files without permission, fought balky witnesses, and requisitioned letters and telegrams for "fishing" purposes.

His methods were severely criticized as roughshod and in violation of the Bill of Rights. At one point he was actually restrained by a court injunction on the ground that the Senate can subpoena certain papers but not an entire file. His retort was that this was the only way to obtain needed information from men of great power who held themselves above the law. "We've subpoenaed all the telegrams of these gentlemen who conceal themselves behind organizations and groups in order to determine the policies of the nation behind a mask." Somewhat later, in an article in *Harper's Magazine*, he maintained that the Congressional investigations were the primary weapon in the hands of the people against "the activities of powerful groups who can defy every other power."

372

The fact remains that his findings were definite and damning. He and his associates brought to light a vast amount of corrupt and unethical lobbying in connection with the holding-company bill. They showed that the Associated Gas and Electric Company spent $700,000 on fictitious letters and telegrams, and that a total of around $5,000,000 was disbursed by the several holding companies in fighting the bill—all of it charged to expenses. Thus in one Pennsylvania city all the telegrams sent to the local Representative were signed by names beginning with the letter B— taken from the town's telephone directory. In a radio talk Black disclosed that five million letters and telegrams against the measure were sent to members of Congress.

At the end of the investigation Black emerged as the stern prosecutor and ardent reformer, the public official who had matched wits with the shrewdest lawyers and industrialists in the land and got what he wanted out of them. Despite the shrill criticism against his methods of inquiry—mostly by industry partisans—he succeeded in reversing the tide of public opinion on the holding company bill and made possible the reform sought by the New Deal Administration.

Senator Black's nomination to the Supreme Court surprised certain liberals and shocked his detractors. The latter, still smarting from the "terrorism" of his investigations, felt that insult had been added to injury, that the nomination was a "defiant gesture." An editorial in the *Herald-Tribune* expressed the common reaction of his critics:

Senator Black's record at the bar offers not the slightest qualification for the high office to which the President would elevate him. His real qualification is plainly the intensity of his New Deal support. He is one of the few who stood by the Court packing plan to its grim death. . . . His subserviency to the New Deal gives a political cast to his candidacy which is highly unfortunate. Even more his services as chairman of the Senate Lobby Investigating Committee revealed such an utter lack of judicial spirit, such a complete scorn of constitutional restraints as would make ascent to the Supreme Court a national tragedy.

The unfairness of these slurs was patent to any who knew Black well and who had followed his part in the Court fight. The fact was that he had made a careful study of the Supreme Court and was intimately familiar with its history. As a conscientious liberal he had opposed the conservatism of the current majority of Justices and had favored President Roosevelt's reform bill. Speaking in its behalf in the Senate he had indicated his own dynamic view of the Constitution:

This prevailing dominant five-judge economic and social philosophy is becoming a part of our Constitution—not by amendments approved by our people but by the decisions of lifetime judges. With complete confidence in the integrity of the purposes of these dominant judges who are now following and expanding the economic philosophy of some of their predecessors in the Court, I believe with Justice Holmes and those other great Justices whose voices have been raised in protest, that their economic-social-constitutional philosophy is contrary to the letter and spirit of our Constitution.

The New Dealers rallied to his defense. Senator Norris, ill at home, expressed their resentment in a letter to Senator H. F. Ashurst, chairman of the Judiciary Committee:

I feel greatly grieved at the bitter, unreasonable and sometimes malicious attacks which are being made upon him. His work in the Senate must convince everyone that he possesses a superior ability and undaunted courage which are seldom equalled or surpassed. His nomination to that great tribunal expresses the wish and hope of the struggling citizens asking only for justice for all alike.

The question of Black's Klan connection was raised in the Senate debate, but he volunteered no information because he considered it irrelevant. Confirmation followed by a vote of 63 to 16. Soon thereafter he left for Europe on a long-postponed vacation.

On September 13 the Pittsburgh *Post-Gazette*, owned by a strong critic of the New Deal, began publishing Ray Sprigle's series of six articles on Black's association with the Klan. Although these articles offered little that was not widely known in Alabama, they were reprinted in many other newspapers, hailed as a remarkable journalistic coup, and later awarded a Pulitzer prize. Prominent citizens renewed their criticism of the appointment and leading editors again deplored its calamitous effect upon the Court's prestige. The demand for Black's resignation or impeachment became widespread. On his return from Europe he was confronted by an antagonism never before faced by a member of the Supreme Court. Determined to state his case in his own way and without distortion, he decided to address the nation over the radio. His first impulse was to expose the political nature of the attack upon him and to hit back at his enemies. Reflection, however, persuaded him to shun politics and to explain the situation with a dignity and objectivity befitting his judicial position. He said in part:

An effort is being made to convince the people of America that I am intolerant and that I am prejudiced against people of the Jewish and Catholic faiths, and against the members of the Negro race. . . . The insinuations of racial and religious intolerance made concerning me are based on the fact that I joined the Ku Klux Klan about fifteen years ago. I did join the Klan. I later resigned. I never rejoined. . . . I have no sympathy with any organization or group which, anywhere or at any time, arrogates to itself the un-American power to interfere in the slightest degree with complete religious freedom.

The speech did not satisfy his critics. So eminent a liberal as C. C. Burlingham of New York deplored "his lack of character" and called the address "a meeching, self-serving speech, unworthy of a judge or a gentleman." For weeks the clamor for his resignation continued to reverberate in the press and over the radio. Justice Black himself never again referred to the matter publicly. But the incisive liberalism of his opinions in the ensuing months, for and against the Court majority, served to silence his detractors. For his was indeed a fresh voice on the Court, a sharply reasoned, uncompromising, yet authoritative affirmation of the basic principles of the Constitution—backed by a philosophy of the social good which he considered above legal precedent and beyond mere privilege. At the end of his first term Paul Y. Anderson, the thoughtful journalist, expressed a not uncommon sentiment when he wrote in the *Nation*:

Time may prove that the most brilliant single stroke of the Roosevelt Administration was the appointment of Hugo L. Black to the Supreme Court. Laymen as well as lawyers are beginning to realize that Black's solitary dissents, instead of revealing a perverse temperament and a lack of "legal craftsmanship," may well guide the Court out of the metaphysical wilderness into which it has wandered. . . . Black is opposed to any compromise. He believes that the way to resume constitutional government is to resume.

For all its aura of lofty objectivity, the Supreme Court is essentially a political institution. Its Justices naturally and unavoidably deal with social and economic problems in the light of the personal prejudices and predilections developed during the years prior to their appointment. Its political complexion at any given time is determined not only by its dominant majority but also by the character of prevailing public opinion. Dissents, however, seemingly cries in the wilderness, not infrequently become what one writer termed "the most persuasive of precedents." Thus the sharply eloquent minority voices of Justices Holmes and Brandeis throughout the 1920's became only a decade later the judgments of the majority.

Justice Black joined a Court long dominated, if at last precariously, by a majority that respected the rights of property above the rights of the individual. For a half century it had interpreted the word "person" in the Fourteenth Amendment to include corporations—to the great profit of large-scale business organizations. For once the corporation became entitled to the "privileges and immunities" and to the "due process" guaranteed to persons by the Constitution, it was in a position to seek, and obtain, judicial protection against what its able lawyers termed arbitrary or unreasonable regulation on the part of government. Thus business-men, appealing to a sympathetic majority on the Court, managed to avoid paying certain taxes, or accepting limitations on rates for certain services or utilities, or yielding to labor demands for union recognition or improved working conditions. The rule during this half century was in effect: "Your property was what you made it, your liberty to make it your property."

Having made his reputation not as corporation lawyer, as did a good many of the Justices, but as an aggressive liberal Senator, and having fought hard for the defeated bill on Court reform, Black assumed his place on the Bench determined to follow what he believed was the original intent of the Constitution—that of furthering the general welfare. Tough-minded, courageous, and a persistent fighter, he felt no particular respect for the niceties of either legalistic precedent or accepted custom. As the first New Dealer on a conservative Court he was ready to challenge the reasoning of the majority in their interpretation of certain key phrases of the Constitution. He was particularly eager to question the rationalization which permitted the deviation of the traditional due process of law from formal procedure to doubtful substance.

In a sharp dissent against the rate claims of the Indianapolis Water Company he sought to expose the fallacy of the Court's reasoning in cases of this kind. The majority, he declared, ruled that states had the right to regulate the rates of intrastate utilities but not to make them confiscatory. In hearty agreement with the first part of the doctrine, he disagreed with the definition of the second. He was particularly critical of the "reproduction theory." To stress its fallacy he showed that the people of Indianapolis were being asked to pay 6 percent interest on $3,000,000 for a canal which originally had cost about $50,000 to dig. Courts and commissions, he contended, lost in the ambiguity of language— "too frequently invented for the purpose of confusing"—and listening to "conjectures, speculation, estimates and guesses, all under the name of 'reproduction costs,'" cannot well serve the public good. His basic argument, however, was that the Court majority was wrong in making use of the due process clause for the protection of utility corporations from state regulation. "I believe," he concluded, "the state of Indiana has the right to regulate the price of water in Indianapolis free from interference by federal courts."

In another strong dissent he maintained that a state had the right to impose a tax on outside firms doing business within it; specifically, that California had the right to tax Connecticut General Life Insurance Company. Here he made a frontal attack against the misuse of the due process clause. Unable to find in the Fourteenth Amendment "any hint that its adoption would deprive the States of their long recognized power to regulate corporations," he argued for a return to original meanings and a reconsideration of the doctrine that favored private enterprise to the great cost of the individual consumer.

This Court has many times changed its interpretations of the Constitution when the conclusion was reached that an improper construction has been adopted. . . . A constitutional interpretation that is wrong should not stand. I believe this Court should now overrule previous decisions which interpret the Fourteenth Amendment to include corporations. Neither the history nor the language justifies the belief that corporations are included within its protection. . . . The judicial inclusion of the word "corporation" in the Fourteenth Amendment has had a revolutionary effect on our form of government.

In still another dissent from a majority ruling that a state tax on gross income received by residents regardless of its source violated the commerce clause of the Constitution, Justice Black maintained that such a tax "is not a regulation of commerce, is valid and is within the powers of the State." He pointed out that the constitutional validity of the tax "does not turn upon whether the property is profitable to its owner." It was his view, moreover, that the majority ruling placed the burden of state taxes upon intrastate business, which he considered "unjust and unfair," since it was an obvious discrimination favoring interstate commerce. Finally, he believed that this was primarily a problem for

Congress and not for the courts. "The control of future conduct, the prevention of future inquiries and the formulation of regulatory rules in the fields of commerce and taxation, all present legislative problems."

By the end of his first term on the Court his courage and consistency, and even more his erudite resourcefulness, had disproved his detractors. There was a sharpness in his voice and a validity in his reasoning that put into clear focus the encrusted prejudices upon the original intent of the basic law.

In his solicitude for the rights of the states Justice Black was acting not so much the strict constructionist as the economic liberal. His prime aim was to check the growing power of corporate enterprises. It irked him to think that for the previous half century the Supreme Court had tended to curb the government regulation of business, and he sought to stop this favoritism at the expense of the public. Yet this concern was only a minor phase of his effort to safeguard the rights and privileges of the ordinary citizen; for by the late 1930's the Court majority was beginning to interpret the due process clause more cautiously.

The protection of civil rights has deeply concerned him throughout his judicial career. Recalling clearly his own experiences in the Alabama courts and no doubt mindful of the accusations arising out of his Klan membership, he has been particularly sensitive to the mistreatment of southern Negroes. In an early case he spoke out forcefully in favor of a jury trial for criminal defendants, insisting that a state should always prefer it to "judges or masters appointed by judges." This view he expounded further in *New York Life Insurance Co.* v. *Gamer*:

The *jury*—not the *judge*—should decide when there has been "substantial" evidence which overcomes the previous adequate proof. . . . I cannot agree to a conclusion which, I believe, takes away any part of the constitutional right to have a jury pass upon the weight of *all of the facts* introduced in evidence.

379

He also wanted defendants judged by a jury of their peers and contended that the exclusion of Negroes from jury panels was not in harmony with our traditional concepts of justice. In *Pierre* v. *Louisiana*, speaking for the Court, he pointed out that although one third of the parish population was Negro, no citizen of that race was on the jury to try the Negro defendant charged with murder. "Such an exclusion," he declared, "is a denial of equal protection of the laws, contrary to the Federal Constitution—the supreme law of the land."

In *Smith* v. *Texas* he wrote the majority opinion reversing the conviction of a Negro by a white jury. He showed that although the county in question had a 20-percent Negro population, with half of it poll tax payers, in eight years prior to the trial only five out of 384 grand jurors were Negroes. Juries thus chosen were in his view neither instruments of equal justice nor truly representative of the community. "The Fourteenth Amendment," he averred, "requires that equal protection to all must be given—not merely promised."

The liberalization of the Supreme Court in the late 1930's favored this view of equal rights. When in 1947 the legality of an all-white jury in Mississippi came up for consideration, Justice Black once more ruled for the majority that such a jury was in violation of the equal protection clause. He declared that the state had failed to act against "the very strong evidence of powerful racial discrimination" shown by the fact that for more than thirty years no Negro had served as a juror in the criminal courts of the county in which the petitioner was convicted.

When four Negroes from North Carolina, condemned to death, petitioned the Court in 1953 to reverse the verdicts on the ground of racial discrimination, the majority, reflecting the currently more conservative complexion of the Justices, held that the selection of juries in that state involved no racial bias since it was regulated by economic status and not by the color of the citizens. Justice Black, consistently the realistic liberal, took strong exception to this view, in which Justices Douglas and Frankfurter concurred. He insisted that racial discrimination in fact still prevailed in the selection of jury lists; in this instance "based not on race, but on wealth."

More recently, in *Michel* v. *Louisiana,* he again strongly dissented, along with Justices Warren and Douglas, from a majority ruling that favored the indictment of a Negro by a white jury. He maintained that the accused should have had the right to challenge the composition of the grand jury. "I would give every accused, regardless of his record, conduct, reputation or beliefs, the full benefit of the constitutional guarantees of due process." Later still he took a similar position in *Eubanks* v. *Louisiana.*

In the *Slaughterhouse* case in 1873 the Court majority had ruled that the Bill of Rights did not apply to the states. Justice Field, Bradley, and Swayne disagreed. Eleven years later Justice Harlan argued in his lone dissent in *Hurtado* v. *California* that due process included grand jury indictment, jury trial, and the other privileges of the Bill of Rights. In 1891 he and Justice Field wrote in dissent that since the adoption of the Fourteenth Amendment no state could deny or abridge the rights of life, liberty or property enumerated in the first eight Amendments. This view Justice Harlan restated even more firmly in 1900. And although the majority of Justices rejected this doctrine they, in their desire to expand the intent of the due process clause, interpreted it to embrace certain of the rights provided in the First Amendment.

Justice Black also believed that the background and wording of the Fourteenth Amendment served to incorporate the first eight Amendments. Opposed as he was to the natural-law doctrine used by earlier Court majorities to establish substantive due process in the economic field, he tended to utilize it in his defense of civil liberties. This logical discrepancy did not, however, invalidate his basic assumption that the Fourteenth Amendment, designed to provide the liberated Negroes with the "privileges and immunities" guaranteed by the Constitution to white citizens, incorporated the freedoms of the Bill of Rights. The Court majorities refused to follow this line of reasoning, yet acted upon it

381

indirectly in their reliance upon the First Amendment to bolster substantive due process. In a discussion of this point Professor Stanley Morrison stated:

If it is proper for the judges who believe in the great importance of the First Amendment to incorporate it in the Fourteenth, it is difficult to deny the propriety of the action of Mr. Justice Black, and those who concur in his views, in writing into the Fourteenth Amendment other provisions of the Bill of Rights which to them seem of equal, at least sufficient, importance.

Justice Black's opinion in *Chambers et al.* v. *Florida* in 1940 is perhaps his most celebrated defense of civil rights. The petitioners claimed that their confessions were obtained under duress—having been questioned intermittently for six days and nights and unceasingly for the last twenty hours. Moreover, during the period of interrogation they were not permitted to confer with counsel or to see any friends or relatives. From the time of their arrest until their final confession they were, during the questioning, surrounded by from four to ten men, all white officers bent on intimidating them. In a review of the evidence Justice Black affirmed that confessions elicited under such conditions violated the very essence of individual liberty. "To permit human lives to be forfeited upon confessions thus obtained," he stated, "would make of the constitutional requirement of due process of law a meaningless symbol." Yet he was not satisfied merely to reverse the convictions. He took this opportunity to speak out firmly and formally against the maltreatment of Negroes in the South and against the use of third-degree methods by police officials, and he did it with an impelling eloquence that made his opinion one of the great judicial decisions of our time.

Today, as in ages past, we are not without tragic proof that the exalted power of some governments to punish manufactured crime dictatorially is the handmaid of tyranny. Under our constitutional system, courts stand against any winds that blow as havens of refuge for those who might otherwise suffer because they are helpless, weak, outnumbered, or because they are nonconforming victims of prejudice and public excitement. Due process of law, preserved for all by our Constitution, commands that no such practice as that disclosed by this record shall send any accused to his death. No higher duty, no more solemn responsibility, rests upon this Court, than that of translating into living law and maintaining this constitutional shield deliberately planned and inscribed for the benefit of every human being subject to our Constitution—of whatever race, creed or persuasion.

The opinion was at once recognized as a charter of protection for all victims of oppression and intolerance. Father John A. Ryan, the eminent Catholic scholar and libertarian, wrote: "Every believer in human dignity and in essential human equality, every defender of the weak against the strong, every lover of justice should rejoice over this situation." Charles A. Beard stated that the opinion "asserted, with moderated eloquence, great American principles of civil liberty" and that it "will ring with power as long as liberty and justice are cherished in our country."

Justice Black's interpretation of the Fourteenth Amendment caused him two years later to dissent from the majority decision in *Betts* v. *Brady*. An unemployed farmhand, charged with robbery, was denied legal counsel by the presiding judge and sentenced to eight years in prison. Justice Roberts, speaking for the Court, rejected the petitioner's plea on the ground that the Fourteenth Amendment did not incorporate the specific guarantees of the Sixth Amendment. Justice Black, with Justices Douglas and Murphy concurring, strongly dissented from this view. Eager to argue his position on this point, he asserted:

If this case had come to us from a federal court, it is clear that we should have to reverse it, because the Sixth Amendment makes the right to counsel in criminal cases inviolable by the Federal Government. I believe that the Fourteenth Amendment made the Sixth applicable to the States.

To bolster his contention he maintained that fair and equal treatment inhered in our principles of government and should not be denied under any circumstances.

His broad interpretation of the Fourteenth Amendment was expressed most emphatically in 1947 in *Adamson* v. *California*. The petitioner, convicted of murder in the first degree, appealed on the ground that he was refused the right under the Fifth Amendment not to testify against himself. This appeal the Court majority denied. Justice Black, joined by Justice Douglas, took strong exception in a long and learned dissent. After relating in considerable detail the historical events that led to the adoption of the Fourteenth Amendment, he stated "that one of the chief objects that the provisions of the Amendment's first section, separately, and as a whole, were intended to accomplish was to make the Bill of Rights applicable to the States."

In a review of the Court's interpretation of this issue he was very critical of the majority's position. He explained that when the question was first breached in the *Slaughterhouse* case in 1873, no specific provision of the Bill of Rights was invoked but only the natural rights of a person to do business or engage in his trade or vocation. "These natural law arguments, so suggestive of the premises on which the present due process formula rests, were flatly rejected by a majority of the Court."

This refusal to invalidate states' legislative regulation of property rights or business practices under the Fourteenth Amendment was not reversed until 1889, when a state railroad rate regulation was stricken as a violation of the due process clause. The new doctrine was soon applied to other similar state statutes—an about-face from the *Slaughterhouse* interpretation and "a failure to carry out the avowed purpose of the Amendment's sponsors." The end product of this philosophy was reached in 1908 when the Court majority in the *Twining* case rejected the clause in the Fifth Amendment against self-incriminating testimony and consolidated its assumed power to invalidate state and federal regulatory legislation.

Thus the power of legislatures became what this Court would declare it to be at a particular time independently of the specific guarantees of the Bill of Rights such as the right to freedom of speech, religion

384

and assembly, the right to just compensation for property taken for a public purpose, the right to jury trial or the right to be secure against unreasonable searches and seizures.

Against this judicial arrogation Justice Black protested with all the force of his capable intellect. With a zeal that tended to favor the facts relevant to its purpose he insisted that the language of the first section of the Fourteenth Amendment was considered by its authors and sponsors "sufficiently explicit to guarantee that thereafter no State could deprive its citizens of the privileges and protections of the Bill of Rights." He argued therefore that the Court majority was wrong in disregarding the plain intent of the Amendment and that its decisions to the contrary endangered basic freedoms.

I cannot consider the Bill of Rights to be an outworn eighteenth-century "strait-jacket" as the *Twining* opinion did. Its opinion may be thought outdated abstractions by some. And it is true that they were designed to meet ancient evils. But they are the same kind of human evils that have emerged from century to century wherever excessive power is sought by the few at the expense of the many. In my judgment the people of no nation can lose their liberty so long as a Bill of Rights like ours survives and its basic purposes are conscientiously interpreted, enforced and respected so as to afford continuous protection against old, as well as new, devices and practices which might thwart those purposes. I fear to see the consequences of the Court's practice of substituting its own concepts of decency and fundamental justice for the language of the Bill of Rights as its point of departure in interpreting and enforcing that Bill of Rights.

In a series of cases involving the freedom of religion Justice Black spoke on the nature of its inviolability with firm clarity. Here, as in other similar instances, patriotism tended to become a factor. In June 1940 the *Gobitis* case, concerned with the refusal of children of Jehovah Witnesses to salute the flag in the class-room, came up for decision. Influenced by their sympathy with France, then being invaded by the Nazis, and by their consequent concern for American security, the majority ruled that the public school authorities had the right to inculcate patriotism by means of the flag salute. Justice Black concurred with the ruling that "the flag is the symbol of our national unity, transcending all internal differences, however large, within the framework of the Constitution." Only Chief Justice Stone disagreed, but his dissent reached to the heart of democratic faith and its insight and eloquence soon persuaded the liberal group of its error:

The Constitution expresses more than the conviction of the people that democratic processes must be preserved at all costs. It is also an expression of faith and a command that freedom of mind and spirit must be preserved, which government must obey, if it is to adhere to that justice and moderation without which no free government can exist.

Two years later, in *Jones* v. *Opelika*, Justices Black, Douglas, and Murphy recanted their error by joining Chief Justice Stone in dissenting from the majority opinion. They did more. As if in expiation of their patriotic aberration, they insisted on proclaiming their error:

Since we joined in the opinion in the *Gobitis* case, we think this an appropriate occasion to state that we now believe that it was also wrongly decided. Certainly our democratic form of government, functioning under the historic Bill of Rights, has a high responsibility to accommodate itself to religious views of minorities, however unpopular and unorthodox these views may be. The First Amendment does not put the right freely to exercise religion in a subordinate position. We fear, however, that the opinions in this and in the *Gobitis* case do exactly that.

By the time the *Barnette* case came up for decision the following year, the liberals, now joined by Justice Rutledge, were in a position of dominance. Justice Jackson, who had come to the Court after the *Gobitis* case, spoke for the majority in overruling the previous holding on the freedom of religion and hailed the broader freedom of the mind with great eloquence:

If there is any fixed star in our constitutional constellation, it is that no official, high or petty, can prescribe what shall be orthodox in politics, nationalism, religion, or other matters of opinion or force citizens to confess by word or act their faith therein. If there are any circumstances which permit an exception, they do not now occur to us.

Justice Black, holding the freedom of conscience synonymous with religious liberty, dissented from the majority opinion in *In re Summers*, which upheld an Illinois law barring a license to practice law to a conscientious objector. He felt that this statute would not only exclude Quakers from the legal profession but could also be applied to other professions and vocations and was therefore unconstitutional. No qualified man of good character, he asserted, could be lawfully barred from practicing his profession merely "because he entertains a religious belief which might prompt him at some time in the future to violate a law which has not yet been and may never be enacted." And he added: "Freedom to think, to believe, and to worship, has too exalted a position in our country to be penalized on such an illusory basis."

Another perplexing problem on the question of religious freedom was presented to the Court in 1947 in the case of *Everson v. Board of Education*. The township of Ewing, New Jersey, had passed an ordinance permitting the repayment to parents of their children's bus fare to and from public and parochial schools. Justice Black held for the majority that this law did not violate the First Amendment. Free bus rides were no different in intent from traffic and fire protection, since they served to bring children to schools chosen by their parents. "The First Amendment," he averred, "has erected a wall between church and state. That wall must be kept high and impregnable. We would not approve the slightest breach. New Jersey has not breached it here."

A year later Justice Black, again the Court's spokesman, detected such a breach in *McCullum v. Board of Education* and invalidated an Illinois law permitting "released time" from school for religious instruction. He pointed out that here tax-supported property was being used for religious education and school authorities were cooperating closely with the churches:

This is beyond all question a utilization of the tax-established and tax-supported public school system to aid religious groups to spread their faith. And it falls squarely under the ban of the First Amendment (made applicable to the States by the Fourteenth Amendment) as we interpreted it in *Everson* v. *Board of Education*.

With the Court having again altered its political complexion by 1952, the majority found in *Zorach* v. *Clauson* no constitutional violation in the New York regulation permitting the release of students for religious instruction. Justice Douglas maintained for the Court that the rule was not compulsory, and that it neither prohibited the free exercise of religion nor favored any one religion over others. Justice Black, jealous of any weakening of the wall between church and state, refused to concur in this view and insisted that, except for the use of the school buildings, there was no difference between this and the *McCullum* cases. He wrote:

State help to religion injects political and party prejudices into a holy field. It too often substitutes force for prayer, hate for love, and persecution for persuasion. Government should not be allowed, under cover of the soft euphemism of "cooperation," to steal into the sacred area of religious choice.

In keeping with his strong concern for the weak and the oppressed, Justice Black maintained a watchful eye for the welfare of the worker and the rights of the small businessmen. Yet he had relatively little opportunity to speak memorably in either field, since by the time he joined the Court the Wagner Act had already initiated the spectacular development of organized labor and a number of other New Deal laws were curbing the former unrestraint of powerful corporations. His record is nevertheless impressive.

In 1940 he held for the Court, in *Drivers' Union* v. *Lake Valley Co.*, that milk drivers were within their rights under the Norris-La Guardia Act in picketing milk dealers who refused to maintain union standards. A year later, when the majority, in *Drivers' Union* v. *Meadowmoor Co.*, did grant an injunction on the ground that the pickets had committed acts of violence, he dissented with the statement that the Illinois action was "too broad and sweeping" and therefore in violation of free speech. He insisted, moreover, that although lawless conduct must be punished to safeguard "the peace and tranquillity of society," it was far from just to curb the freedom of expression of six thousand members because of the unlawful acts of a few.

This concern for free expression he stated forcefully in *Bridges* v. *California*. Harry Bridges, leader of the Pacific Coast longshoremen, and the Los Angeles *Times* had made statements prior to court decisions which the judge considered efforts at intimidation and therefore contemptuous. Justice Black, in behalf of the Court, held that the defendants had the right under the First Amendment to express their views at the time they did. "No suggestion can be found in the Constitution," he declared, "that the freedom there guaranteed for speech and press bears an inverse ratio to the timeliness and importance of the ideas seeking expression."

In a number of dissents Justice Black stressed the rights of labor over property rights, cavalierly disregarding the legalisms and precedents which served the majority. He took the position that a worker was entitled to compensation in accidents even when he was partly at fault; that employers had no right to consider tips given to redcaps as part of wages; that a union could picket against nonunion workers even when such picketing was detrimental to their employers; that since the "slack movement" on long freight trains was dangerous to railroad employees, a state had the right to shorten them; and that railroad companies could not shirk their responsibilities by specifying exemption on passes given to employees. An active sponsor of the Wagner Act when in the Senate, he twice expressed disapproval of provisions in the Taft-Hartley Act—once when three other Justices and he concurred in invalidating the prohibition against political expenditures by labor organizations and again in a lone dissent denouncing the noncommunist affidavit for union officials as contrary to the First Amendment.

He spoke for the Court majority in maintaining that states could provide that no man should be deprived of a job because he was not a member of a union; that the Pacific Coast Fishermen's Union, though affiliated with the CIO, was not a labor but a business union and was not entitled to the benefits of the Norris–La Guardia Act; that an injured worker was entitled to full compensation even though he was induced to sign a deceptive settlement; that it was illegal to discriminate against Negroes because of a union agreement; that the United Mine Workers disobeyed the law when it refused to call off a strike after the mines were taken over by the government; that Petrillo's "featherbedding" tactics were in violation of the Lea Act; that a union violated a state law in restraint of trade when it induced an ice manufacturer not to sell ice to nonunion peddlers. He also joined the majority in invalidating a Texas law prohibiting union organizers to speak without a license. In all these cases he sought to effect justice and assure fair play to the individual worker, the weak union, and the petty merchant.

His insistence on fair treatment and the public good was evident in his majority opinions and dissents in a number of cases pertaining to business practices, patents, taxes, insurance, and other similar matters. In 1942 he ruled against the government when it sued for the return of the excess profits made by the Bethlehem Steel Corporation on legal contracts in World War I. He stated that although these profits amounted to 22 percent, government policy could not be nullified by declaring "these contracts unenforceable on the ground that profits granted under Congressional authority were too high." In *Goodyear Co.* v. *Ray-o-Vac Co.* he struck out, in a dissent, against the practice of patenting minor mechanical improvements in order to obtain "unearned special privileges which serve no purpose except unfairly to harass the honest pursuit of business." He held for the Court in *I. C. C.* v. *Mehling* against rates which favored grain shipments made to Chicago by rail over those using barges part of the way. Maintaining that Congress wanted shippers to receive the full benefit of the lower rates, he did not give the Commission power to nullify that benefit by equalizing rail and barge rates. If reshipping barge grain to the East required extra services, the railroads should charge for that, but for no more than that.

In 1948 Justice Black devoted several months to the study of many thousands of pages of transcript in *Trade Commission* v. *Cement Institute*. Speaking for the Court, he held that the cement companies were guilty of unfair competition and restraint of trade when they agreed to charge the same price for cement in every part of the United States and to stop competition by means of underselling tactics. He again acted for the majority in *Trade Commission* v. *Morton Salt Co.* when he adjudged the firm guilty of unfair pricing. The company charged $1.60 per case on orders less than carloads and $1.35 per case when the purchaser bought 50,000 cases a year. Since only the few largest chain stores were able to take advantage of the lower price, they were helped to compete unfairly with the small independent grocer. Congress, however, had enacted the Robinson-Patman Act to protect the weak merchant from just such unfair competition.

Another type of restraint of trade came to the Court's attention in *Associated Press* v. *United States*. A by-law of the Association conferred upon a member the power to deny admission to a competing newspaper. This privilege was exercised by the *Chicago Tribune* when the *Chicago Sun*, established by Marshall Field, applied for membership. When the suit reached the Supreme Court, Justice Black held for the majority that this by-law of the Association served to curb the initiative which brought new newspapers into existence and therefore curtailed the system of free enterprise protected by the Sherman Act. Nor did he accept the contention of counsel that such application of the Act abridged the freedom of the press. This assumption, he declared, would leave the government without power to protect that freedom.

The First Amendment, far from providing an argument against application of the Sherman Act, here provides powerful reasons to the contrary. That Amendment rests on the assumption that the widest possible dissemination of information from diverse and antagonistic sources is essential to the welfare of the public, that a free press is a condition of a free society. Surely a command that the government itself shall not impede the free flow of ideas does not afford non-government combinations a refuge if they impose restraints upon that constitutionally guaranteed freedom. Freedom to publish means freedom for all and not for some. Freedom to publish is guaranteed by the Constitution, but freedom to combine to keep others from publishing is not.

In favor of state regulation of business for "the protection of the small enterprisers," he in 1949 dissented from a majority opinion invalidating a New York law which stopped a large milk company from opening a new plant in competition with local milk distributors. The gravity of such action, he argued, "is immeasurably increased when it results as here in having a no-man's land immune from any effective regulation whatever." He considered such a situation dangerous because it created the assumption "that the aggressive cupidity of some need never be checked by government in the interest of all." He also took the opportunity to criticize the Court's regressive attitude toward government regulation.

The judicially directed march of the due process philosophy as an emancipator of business from regulation appeared arrested a few years ago. That appearance was illusory. That philosophy continues its march. The due process clause and commerce clause have been used like Siamese twins in a never-ending stream of challengers to government regulation. . . . A stretching of either outside its sphere can paralyze the legislative process, rendering the people's legislative representatives impotent to perform their duty of providing appropriate rules to govern this dynamic civilization.

The next year, in *United States* v. *Commodities Corporation*, he spoke for the Court in upholding the government's wartime control of prices. In 1944 the War Department had requisitioned the firm's stock of whole black pepper—accumulated prior to the war in order to profit from the expected scarcity of the condiment. The government paid the ceiling price of 6.63 cents per ounce. After the war the corporation sued for an additional 15.37 cents—considering itself entitled to 22 cents per ounce. The Court of Claims allowed a total of 15 cents in view of the "retentive value" of the pepper in the postwar market. The government then brought the case to the Supreme Court. In reversing the judgment of the lower court, Justice Black stated that in time of war the government had the right to requisition needed goods at a fair price without regard to peacetime potential profits. He maintained that the word "just" in the Fifth Amendment was taken fully into account when ceiling prices were prescribed under the Emergency Price Control Act. Nothing in the Constitution required that "the Government must pay Commodities for potential profits lost because of war and the consequent price controls."

In his belief that the general welfare was best served by the federal government, Justice Black tended to favor it over private enterprise or state claims. When certain individuals sought to stop the Tennessee Valley Authority from acquiring private lands which it needed for the development of its projects, he ruled for the Court that the law creating the Authority empowered it to transact all the business necessary in the building and operation of "dams, reservoirs, transmission lines, power houses, and other structures." These provisions imply the power "to acquire lands by purchase or by condemnation."

When certain seacoast states sued for title to their tideland oil, Justice Black took the position that in matters of vital importance to the nation the claims of states were inferior to those of the federal government. In a well-written and cogently reasoned majority opinion he favored the government's claim to these tidelands because of its paramount responsibilities in protecting the nation's shores and in regulating its international commerce. "The ocean, even its three-mile belt, is thus of vital consequence to the Nation in its desire to engage in commerce and to live in peace with the world." He contended that in this and other instances the government held its interests in trust for all the people, "and was not to be deprived of those interests by the ordinary court rules designed particularly for private disputes over individually owned pieces of property."

In 1949 he again held for the Court against the allegation that the government could not appeal a ruling of the Interstate Commerce Commission. This body rejected its request that certain railroads pay for wharfage services which it supplied. The lower courts upheld the Commission on the ground that since it was a federal agency the government was in effect suing itself. Rejecting this line of reasoning, Justice Black insisted that it was necessary to look behind names and see the real claims in question.

Shortly thereafter, in *Power Commission* v. *Panhandle Co.*, Justices Douglas and Rutledge joined him in a sharp dissent from the majority opinion favoring the transfer of a natural gas concern. Such permission, he argued, went far "toward scuttling the Natural Gas Act." Indeed, in this instance the transfer actually inflated the valuation of the property from an original $160,000 to $10,000,000.

Thus the unwholesome practices that the Natural Gas Act was primarily designed to prevent are given a new lease on life. For a purpose of the Act was to protect consumers and one of the evils it was aimed to prevent was the holding company technique of transfers and retransfers between parent corporations, their offspring and affiliates.

Although Justice Black tended to favor the government when its objectives appeared to serve the general welfare, he required substantiation in the Constitution or an Act of Congress. When President Truman sought in 1952 to avert a nationwide steel strike by an Executive Order directing the Secretary of Commerce to take over the affected steel plants, Justice Black held for the Court that the President had no power to issue such an order and that Congress had in fact specifically denied him such power in labor disputes.

There is no statute that expressly authorizes the President to take possession of property as he did here. Nor is there any Act of Congress to which our attention has been directed from which such a power can fairly be implied. . . . The Founders of this Nation entrusted the law-making power to the Congress alone in both good and bad times. It would do no good to recall the historical events, the fears of power and the hopes for freedom that lay behind their choice. Such a review would only confirm our holding that the seizure holding cannot stand.

A genuine patriot, Justice Black regards national security of paramount importance. In time of war he was ready to bend freedom to the country's safety and to allow government restrictions not permissible when the nation is at peace. All through World War II he evidenced such patriotism. He went along with the majority of the Court, more than once acting as its spokesman, in condemning spies and Nazi adherents and in upholding military restrictions against citizens of Japanese origin on the Pacific Coast. In several instances, when the majority was inclined toward leniency, he insisted that no fine distinctions be made in cases of treason or disloyalty.

When the majority held in *Viereck* v. *United States* that Viereck did not have to make known the propaganda activities he initiated in his own behalf even though they served his German masters, Justice Black dissented. "As a practical matter," he argued, "the very fact that in the instant case it is extremely difficult to determine with conviction which activities the petitioner carried on in his own behalf and which he carried on in behalf of Germany is reason enough for requiring him to report on both." In another dissent he stated that Cramer, the young German who remained a Nazi sympathizer despite his American citizenship, was guilty of treason because he had given aid and comfort to his friend Thiel, one of the Nazi saboteurs who had stolen into this country from a German submarine.

He concurred with the majority opinion in *Knauer* v. *United States* on the ground that the petitioner's admissions left him "in no doubt at all he was, even in obtaining naturalization, serving the German Government with the same fanatical zeal which motivated the saboteurs sent to the United States to wage war."

Conscious nevertheless of "the dangers inherent in denaturalization," he made clear that he would have taken a contrary position if only matters of belief were involved. In 1948, however, with the war long ended, he again became the sensitive guardian of the Bill of Rights, ruling for the majority that Mrs. von Moltke, accused of aiding the enemy, was denied the right to counsel. He rebuked the trial judge for not making sure that the defendant had "that full understanding and comprehension of her legal rights indispensable to a valid waver of assistance of counsel."

Speaking for the Court in two cases involving Japanese in wartime, Justice Black balanced his sympathy for the minority groups with his unswerving patriotism. In *Ex Parte Kawato* he overruled the judgment of the lower court barring a Japanese sailor from suing for damages because of his status as an enemy alien. "Harshness toward immigrants," he stated, "was inconsistent with that national knowledge . . . of the contributions made in peace and war by the millions of immigrants who have learned to love the country of their adoption more than the country of their birth." In *Korematsu* v. *United States* he was critical of racial discrimination while upholding the right of the military to declare a curfew or to exclude certain elements of the population from areas considered in danger of invasion. Korematsu, a loyal American citizen, was charged with remaining in an area forbidden to those of Japanese descent. In ruling against him Justice Black admitted his abhorrence of "legal restrictions which curtail the civil rights of a single racial group," but asserted that dire necessity sometimes required them. Though this undeniably imposed hardships on loyal Americans, all citizens, in or out of uniform, were subject to hardships in wartime.

Once the danger of invasion was past, Justice Black held that the law of the land was again supreme. Speaking for the Court in *Duncan* v. *Kahanamoku* and *White* v. *Steer*, he reversed the sentences of two civilians by provost court on the ground that the martial law declared at Pearl Harbor after the Japanese attack "was not intended to authorize the supplanting of courts by military tribunals." Our system of government, he declared, made courts and their procedural safeguards indispensable. He was especially averse to the potential evils of summary criminal trials. Consequently he maintained that the Hawaiian Organic Law, passed by Congress, was "part of our political philosophy and institutions" and favored civil rule as soon as the invasion emergency had passed.

When California sought to discriminate against the Japanese returning from wartime internment, Justice Black asserted their rights in vigorous opinions. In *Oyama* v. *California* he voided a state statute prohibiting the ownership of land by aliens who were ineligible for citizenship in that it violated the equal-protection clause of the Fourteenth Amendment. He also held in favor of a Japanese commercial fisherman, licensed in that state from 1915 to 1942, who was refused a license on his return in 1945. "We are unable to find that the 'special public interest' on which California relies provides support for this state ban on Takahashi's commercial fishing."

After 1945, when government agencies began to take a hostile attitude toward dissident aliens, Justice Black sought to prevent their unfair treatment. In 1948 he dissented from a majority ruling in *Ludecke* v. *Watkins* which permitted the deportation of an enemy alien without a hearing. He contended that as a result of this action "individual liberty will be less secure tomorrow than it was yesterday"; that the security of aliens was lessened where "their ideas happen to be out of harmony with those of the governmental authorities." Not long after, he was able to speak for the Court in *Klapprot* v. *United States* when he insisted on a fair trial for a Nazi threatened with denaturalization.

This Court has long recognized the plain fact that to deprive a person of his American citizenship is an extraordinarily severe penalty. . . . Furthermore, because of the grave consequences incident to denaturalization proceedings we have held that a burden rests on the Government to prove its charges in such cases by clear, unequivocal or convincing evidence which does not leave the issue in doubt.

When the Court majority, affected by the "cold war" psychology, ruled in *Carlson* v. *Landon* that a communist alien could be kept in jail until his deportability was established, Justice Black wrote a trenchant dissent. To him this opinion revealed "a shocking disregard" of such provisions in the Bill of Rights as the bans against excessive bail, abridgment of free speech, and deprivation of liberty without due process of law. What it made possible, he stressed, was the holding in jail indefinitely of law-abiding persons who were neither charged with nor convicted of any crime—"if a subordinate Washington Bureau agent believes they are members of the Communist party, and therefore dangerous to the Nation because of the possibility of their 'indoctrination of others.'" And he concluded: "I can only say that I regret, deeply regret, that the Court now adds the right to bail to the list of other Bill of Rights guarantees that have recently been weakened to expand governmental powers at the expense of individual freedom."

With three of his colleagues concurring, he again dissented vigorously when the Court on March 16, 1953, guided by the intent of the McCarran Act of 1950, ruled that an alien barred from this country because of his communistic connections could be held indefinitely on Ellis Island and be deported without a hearing and without disclosing the reasons for his deportation order.

In *Jay* v. *Boyd* he once more strongly dissented when the majority approved the deportation of alien Jay because of his alleged communist membership in the 1930's. What perturbed him was that "membership at that time did not violate any law" and that the majority decision was based on anonymous information. He stated:

No nation can remain true to the ideal of liberty under law and at the same time permit people to have their homes destroyed and their lives blasted by the slurs of unseen and unsworn informers. There is no possible way to contest the truthfulness of anonymous accusations. . . . No amount of legal reasoning by the Court and no rationalization that can be devised can disguise the fact that the use of anonymous information to banish people is not consistent with the principles of a free country. Unfortunately there are some who think that the way to save freedom in this country is to adopt the techniques of tyranny.

During the "cold war" years in the early 1950's Justice Black was severely critical of the Court's numerous holdings in which its traditional jealous concern for the Bill of Rights was relaxed in cases involving communists and dissidents. Like many other Americans the majority of Justices, apprehensive of Soviet Russia's growing military might, acted on the assumption that members of the American Communist party were in effect Russian agents and therefore disloyal. A Jeffersonian to the core, cherishing liberty wholeheartedly and eager to preserve it unblemished and unimpaired, Justice Black has no fear of political radicals and is inclined to give alleged subversives the benefit of the doubt. He is sincerely convinced that it is far better to risk the danger of disloyalty on the part of the communist minority than to scotch this threat at the cost of the Bill of Rights. For he knows, in the ripeness of wisdom, that in the long run the struggle between democracy and communism—the two philosophies now sparring for world control—will be resolved not on the field of battle but in the hearts of men—and there the appeal of the Bill of Rights is far more potent than any communist dogma.

An early and therefore ineffective instance of intolerance emerged in the case of *United States* v. *Lovett*. Here Justice Black, speaking for the Court, invalidated an amendment to an appropriation bill which sought to eliminate three well-known liberal officials who had incurred the displeasure of Representative Martin Dies, then chairman of the Committee on Un-American Activities. In a House speech on February 1, 1943, he attacked these and other New Dealers as "irresponsible, unrepresentative, crackpot, radical bureaucrats." Four days later the rider to rid them from office was approved, a procedure referred to by some Representatives as "legislative lynching." Although the Senate again and again voted unanimously to eliminate the rider in the conference report, it capitulated the fifth time when the House members insisted on retaining it. President Roosevelt signed the bill in order to validate the appropriations, but he protested that the amendment was "not only unwise and discriminatory but unconstitutional." Justice Black agreed:

When our Constitution and Bill of Rights were written, our ancestors had ample reason to know that legislature trials and punishments were too dangerous to liberty to exist in the nation of free men they envisioned. And so they proscribed bills of attainder. Section 304 is one. Much as we regret to declare that an Act of Congress violates the Constitution, we have no alternative here.

The Court majority evidenced no such scruple in the cases of open or alleged communists. In *Dennis* v. *United States* the petitioner, general secretary of the Communist party, was tried in Washington for contempt of Congress because he had refused to appear before the Committee of Un-American Activities and was found guilty by a jury of which seven members were government employees. The Court majority dismissed the allegation that the jurors in government service could not be impartial in view of the reflection upon their loyalty in case of acquittal. Justice Black disagreed. He believed it was very difficult for a jury of this kind to act objectively, as was evidenced by the number of prospective jurors who were excused because of their prejudice against communism. To expect government employees, influenced by "the prevailing pattern of loyalty investigations and threatened purges," to serve as impartial jurors in the trial of a communist, was to him an unrealistic assumption.

Probably at no period of the Nation's history has the "loyalty" of government employees been subjected to such constant scrutiny and investigation by so many government agents and secret informers. . . . Government employees have good reason to fear that an honest vote to acquit a communist or anyone else accused of "subversive" beliefs, however flimsy the prosecutor's evidence, might be considered a "disloyal" act which could easily cost them their job.

400

His reasoning prevailed in another similar case. In *Morford* v. *United States* a unanimous Court reversed the conviction of the director of the National Council of American-Soviet Friendship on the ground that, unlike in the Dennis case, the petitioner was not permitted to question prospective jurors who were government employees as to the effect of the Loyalty Order on their impartiality.

The years of the "cold war" brought both known communists and suspected dissidents under the scourge of Congressional investigations, inimical laws, and judicial bias. The Supreme Court had to deal with the more important of these cases. After refusing certiorari to the board of directors of the Joint Anti-Fascist Refugee Committee, convicted on the charge of refusing to produce its financial records before the Committee of Un-American Activities, the Court sustained the convictions of two of the organization's officials (*United States* v. *Bryan* and *United States* v. *Fleischmann*). Justice Black dissented in each instance, maintaining that Miss Bryan did not violate any law in refusing to submit documents which were not hers and that Miss Fleischmann could not act without the concurrence of the majority of the board.

He similarly disagreed with the ruling of the majority, in *Rogers* v. *United States*, that a refusal to answer questions was valid only when self-incrimination was involved. To his thinking the answers to the questions asked the petitioner would have incriminated her. "Today's holding," he claimed, "creates this dilemma for witnesses: On the one hand, they risk imprisonment for contempt by asserting the privilege prematurely; on the other, they might lose the privilege if they answer a single question." He again dissented from the Court ruling in *Feiner* v. *New York*, that the Syracuse student was properly convicted for making an unpopular political speech during the 1948 presidential campaign. Such a judgment, he declared, "makes a mockery of the free speech guarantee of the First and Fourteenth Amendments." It subjected with impunity all speeches to the censorship of local police. In this instance it was the duty of the policeman on the spot to protect Feiner against his detractors rather than to arrest him because of them. "I will have no part or parcel in this holding which I view as a long step toward totalitarian authority."

The majority joined him in invalidating the separate convictions of Mr. and Mrs. Blau for refusing to answer questions that might incriminate them. "The attempts of the courts below," he said in Mrs. Blau's case, "to compel petitioner to testify runs counter to the Fifth Amendment as it has been interpreted from the beginning." He also held that in convicting Mr. Blau the lower courts erred in failing "to sustain the claim of privilege against self-incrimination." This double ruling made it possible for witnesses thereafter to refuse to testify on the ground of self-incrimination without being cited for contempt. Ironically, such refusal to answer questions has come to signify guilt and has caused many the loss of their jobs.

When the noncommunist affidavit for union officials provided for in the Taft-Hartley Act came to the Supreme Court for decision in 1950, Chief Justice Vinson upheld it on the ground that Congress intended it as a protection against possible sabotage in vital industries. Justice Black, in a lone dissent, argued that the ruling rejected the First Amendment. What concerned him was not that the opinion barred communists from becoming union officials. More important was their possible exclusion from union membership, even from political office, "and in fact from getting or holding any job whereby they could earn a living." Such a condition, he insisted, was arbitrary, discriminatory, and contrary to democratic principles.

Like anyone else, individual Communists who commit overt acts in violation of valid laws can and should be punished. But the postulate of the First Amendment is that our free institutions can be maintained without proscribing or penalizing political belief, speech, press, assembly, or party affiliation. This is a far bolder philosophy than despotic rulers can afford to follow. It is the heart of the system on which our freedom depends.

In 1951 the Supreme Court, in the second *Dennis* v. *United States*, sustained the Smith Act prohibiting the advocacy of overthrowing the government by force or violence. Chief Justice Vinson, delivering the opinion, reasoned that the "clear and present danger" doctrine was valid in isolated instances of subversion but not "in the context of world crisis after crisis." The convicted eleven Communist party leaders were obviously prepared forcefully to overthrow the government "as speedily as circumstances would permit" and this threat "justifies such invasion of free speech as is necessary to avoid the danger." Justices Black and Douglas dissented spiritedly. They argued that this case pertained primarily to a question of free speech and not of action or violence. Even if communist doctrine did endanger the republic, the Founders of this nation believed that "the benefits derived from free expression were worth the risk." As construed by the majority, however, the First Amendment would henceforth protect only those orthodox views which rarely need its protection. The charge against the petitioners was in fact "a virulent form of prior censorship of speech and press." They would therefore hold the Smith Act "authorizing this prior restraint unconstitutional on its face and as applied." And Justice Black concluded wistfully:

Public opinion being what it now is, few will protest the conviction of these Communist petitioners. There is hope, however, that in calmer times, when present pressures, passions and fears subside, this or some later Court will restore the First Amendment liberties to the high preferred place where they belong in a free society.

The majority joined him in the next of these cases, *Anti-Fascist Committee* v. *McGrath*, holding that the Attorney-General could not list any organization as communist-controlled without establishing the proof for it. In his concurrence he added that no executive official had the constitutional right, with or without a hearing, to prepare and publish such lists. These official acts in the present climate of opinion, he stated, were "the practical equivalent of confiscation and death sentences for any blacklisted organization not possessing extraordinary financial, political or religious prestige and influence."

When the Court upheld the validity of the New York Feinberg Law prohibiting the employment of teachers who were members of "subversive" organizations, Justices Black, Douglas, and Frankfurter strongly dissented. The sharpest criticism was expressed by Justice Douglas, who argued that it "proceeds on a principle repugnant to our society—guilt by association . . . is certain to raise havoc with academic freedom . . . [and] inevitably turns the school system into a spying project." Furthermore, "the guilt of a teacher should turn on overt acts." As long as she meets professional standards her private beliefs "should not be the cause of reprisals against her." Justice Black, concurring, added:

This is another of those rapidly multiplying legislative enactments which make it dangerous—this time for school teachers—to think or say anything except what a transient majority happen to approve at the moment. Basically these laws rest on the belief that government should supervise and limit the flow of ideas into the minds of men. . . . Public officials with such powers are not public servants; they are public masters.

Consistent in his position on civil rights, he also dissented from the majority ruling, in *Sacher* v. *United States*, against the lawyers convicted of contempt in connection with the trial of the eleven Communist leaders. He held that Judge Harold Medina should not have passed on his own charges and that the defendants were entitled to a jury trial. He was particularly critical of the judge's behavior in the courtroom.

From the very parts of the record which Judge Medina specified, it is difficult to escape the impression that his inferences against the lawyers were colored, however unconsciously, by his natural abhorrence for the unpatriotic and treasonable designs attributed to their Communist leader clients.

Justice Frankfurter's dissent was equally powerful and forthright.

Both Justices Black and Douglas vigorously dissented from the majority in *Rosenberg* v. *United States.* They maintained that "there were substantial grounds to believe the death sentences of these two people were imposed by the district judge in violation of law." Black added:

It is not amiss to point out that this Court has never reviewed this record and has never affirmed the fairness of the trial below. Without an affirmance of the fairness of the trial by the highest court of the land there may always be questions as to whether these executions were legally and rightfully carried out.

Shortly after the Korean fighting had ended the intensity of the "cold war" hysteria began to relax. With the United States and Russia having reached an atomic stalemate and with Senator McCarthy's demagogic aggressiveness deflated by the Senate's censure, the political atmosphere became less oppressive. Under the leadership of the newly appointed Chief Justice Earl Warren the Supreme Court also took a more liberal position. Justice Black nevertheless remained vigilant in his concern for the sanctity of the Bill of Rights. He dissented in *Barsky* v. *Board of Regents* when the majority validated the legality of the Attorney-General's subversive list. "My view was and is," he insisted, "that the list was the equivalent of a bill of attainder which the Constitution expressly forbids."

When Congress, prodded by McCarthy and his sympathizers, enacted the Immunity Act as a means of circumventing the Fifth Amendment clause permitting witnesses not to testify against themselves, Justices Black and Douglas spoke out against the law in a sharp dissent the first time it came up for a ruling in the Supreme Court in *Ullmann* v. *United States.* They argued "that the right of silence created by the Fifth Amendment is beyond the reach of Congress. . . . The Fifth Amendment protects the conscience and the dignity of the individual, as well as his safety and security against the compulsion of government."

405

In 1957 a series of rulings by the liberalized majority favored the strict interpretation of the Bill of Rights that Justices Black and Douglas had advocated so eloquently and so persistently, especially in their numerous dissents. In the *Jencks, Sweezy, Watkins, Shware, Yates,* and other cases the Court effectively, if informally, modified or reversed its former holdings in instances affecting the freedoms under the Bill of Rights. The two dissenters, while eagerly voting with the majority, persisted in stressing the inviolable nature of our constitutional liberties. Thus in the *Yates* case they argued for the reversal of the conviction of all fourteen petitioners on the ground that the statutory provisions on which their prosecutions were based abridged the freedoms of the First Amendment. Refusing to compromise with principle, Justice Black added:

Government suppression of causes and beliefs seem to me to be the very antithesis of what our Constitution stands for. . . . Unless there is complete freedom of expression of ideas, whether we like them or not, concerning the way government should be run, and who shall run it, I doubt if any views in the long run can be secured against the censor. The First Amendment provides the only kind of security system that can preserve a free government.

This spurt of liberalism on the part of the Court majority quickly antagonized the reactionaries in Congress and out. Because a unanimous Court had ruled against Negro segregation and a majority held against the "cold war" fears, the Southern demagogues allied with the dogmatic anticommunists in an effort to curb the Court by legislative measures. The attempt failed in Congress, but its effect on some of the Justices showed up in subsequent holdings. Thus in 1958 Justice Black, joined by Chief Justice Warren and Justice Douglas, was again the spokesman for the liberal minority in several cases pertaining to the rights of individuals. He was particularly critical of the majority's ruling that treated criminal contempt by communists differently from other criminal cases. The summary trial of criminal contempt, he maintained, makes the judge "lawmaker, prosecutor, judge, jury and disciplinarian." No person, he insisted, "should be granted such autocratic omnipotence."

When the Court majority in *Barenblatt* v. *United States* flagrantly negated its liberal position taken in 1957, Justice Black dissented with resolute eloquence. He argued that it was "unconscionable" to make the defendant choose between the right to keep silent and the need to speak when the statute in question "is too vague to give him guidance." He further averred that our strength as a nation is founded on "the right to err politically." No law against communism, he asserted, can be as effective as "the personal conviction which comes from having heard its arguments and rejected them, or from having once accepted its tenets and later recognized their worthlessness."

Finally, I think Barenblatt's conviction violates the Constitution because the chief aim, purpose and practice of the House Un-American Activities Committee, as disclosed by its many reports, is to try witnesses and punish them because they are or have been Communists or because they refuse to admit or deny Communist affiliations. . . . Ultimately all questions in this case really boil down to one—whether we as a people will try fearfully and futilely to preserve democracy by adopting totalitarian methods, or whether in accordance with our traditions and our Constitution we will have the confidence and the courage to be free.

The foregoing account of Justice Black's career in the Senate and particularly on the Supreme Court testifies to his being eminently a twentieth-century Jeffersonian: like Justice Brandeis a passionate activist in the fight for the rights of the individual, a firm defender of the weak against the powerful, a strong advocate of justice and equality. A ready supporter of government regulation for the common good, he is an intrepid opponent of any kind of governmental tampering with the basic freedoms established by the Bill of Rights. His gracious and urbane personality shelters an inflexible will. Acutely intelligent, highly democratic, warmly idealistic, he is also intensely self-confident, almost earthily realistic, impatient with legalism and precedent, and forthright in his critical reactions. He seems intractable in his judgments because more than any of the other Justices he adheres strictly, almost rigidly, to the fundamental principles of our basic freedoms; yet in time of war his strong patriotism made him yield to the majority of his brothers on the Court in matters pertaining to the nation's security.

No chauvinist, he cherishes the American form of government because he considers it the highest phase of political development. Because he wants America to remain a beacon of liberty for all mankind, he is jealous of any weakening of our democratic principles. He firmly believes that if we do not swerve from the path laid out for us by the Constitution we shall remain beyond the reach of either communist or fascist aggressors. Furthermore, he wants the United States to lead in making an end to war and aggression. In 1942, shortly after we entered World War II, he stated in an article in the *New Republic*:

We must not lose the opportunity this time to win peace for our children. As a nation we have tried isolation, neutrality, bipartisan pacts, tripartisan pacts, balance of power and all the other practices of traditional diplomacy. None of these has averted war. The only thing the world has failed to try is unselfish cooperation among nations. A people with the boldness, imagination and pioneering spirit which gave birth to the United States should be more than willing—and more than able—to take the lead in a cooperative program for permanent peace, a peace which will give reality to the four fundamental freedoms set forth in the Atlantic Charter already adopted as the fighting faith of the United Nations.

Justice Black's achievement on the Supreme Court ranks him with the most eminent Justices in the history of the high tribunal. Despite his inauspicious start, he established himself in his very first term as a vigorous and valiant interpreter of the Constitution. Fully aware that in fact the law is what the Supreme Court says it is, he upheld the weak and oppressed in asserting their right to equity and justice. He rejected arrogated privileges in his effort to alter the conditions that favored the powerful corporation over the small businessman and the governmental attempts at regulation. With an erudition that impressed even his harshest critics he disregarded encrusted precedent and asserted the original intent of the basic law; even in his rationalized thesis on the historic background of the Fourteenth Amendment he marshaled his arguments with a learning that carried conviction. Both an altruist and a democrat, he has sought to win for the Negro and the alien, the communist and the political dissident, the justice and protection which were their right under the Constitution but which prejudice had withheld from them. And although he often found himself in the minority—many times the sole dissenter—the forcefulness and validity of his protests had the impact of eventual triumph.

Justices Harlan, Holmes, and Brandeis were great and influential dissenters, but none was as insistent or as radical as Justice Black. He came to the Court as a New Deal legislator among conservative jurists, with a full knowledge of what the law meant and how it had long been interpreted—and he argued for a return to what he considered its original intent in order to place the general good above property or precedent. In his dissents he appealed from majority decisions with a power and perspicuity not often heard by his brothers on the Bench. And more than once the effect of these dissents became evident in the manner described by Chief Justice Hughes: "A dissent in a court of last resort is an appeal to the brooding spirit of the law, to the intelligence of a future day, when a later decision may possibly correct the error into which the dissenting judge believes the Court to have been betrayed."

President Roosevelt's other appointees helped to give his voice frequent dominance, and for several years his dissents were few and casual. But the Justices chosen by President Truman again made the court largely conservative, and this attitude became pronounced with the aggravation of the "cold war" against Soviet Russia and the consequent increased fear of communism. Thus Justice Black had once more to resume the role of the dissenter.

Because he was frequently joined by Justice Douglas, their dissents recalled the minority opinions of Justices Holmes and Brandeis; only their protests were sharper in tone and even more zealous for the sanctity of the Bill of Rights.

As the dread of communism, instigated by a strident McCarthyism, tended to force intellectual conformity and political compliance upon a frightened public, the Court majority began to bend the Bill of Rights to the prevailing panic. With communism considered synonymous with disloyalty or even treason, the Court permitted the government to whittle away the civil rights of those associated with alleged or likely subversion. Not so Justice Black. Repugnant as communist dogmas are to him, he refused to be intimidated by propagandistic clamor against them. In case after case he stood his ground as the defender of the Bill of Rights with notable tenacity. He knew that as a Justice of the Supreme Court he was in a commanding position to caution the country against actions which seemed to him to endanger our democratic form of government, and his dissents pleaded eloquently for the preservation of our great heritage.

He voiced his defense of this heritage with moving effectiveness in his James Madison lecture on the Bill of Rights, delivered at the New York University School of Law on February 17, 1960. Delving into the historical origins of the freedoms incorporated in the first eight Amendments and quoting freely from the debates leading to their enactment, he made incontrovertibly clear that the Founding Fathers were fully aware of the words they used and "meant their prohibitions to be 'absolutes.'" He explained that they wanted no violations of individual rights as previously practised in England against such dissenters as John Lilburne and in our own country during Colonial times and therefore agreed "to give the people of America greater protection against the powerful Federal Government than the English had against their government." He pointed out forcefully that the Fathers fully appreciated the risks involved but "decided that certain rights should be guaranteed regardless of these risks."

Justice Black looks upon the world with the vision of the philosopher—being moved neither by personal ambition nor by transient events. He works long hours to assure thorough attention to the duties of his office. An insatiable reader, he keeps abreast of world affairs and national trends and observes the follies and foibles of men with an anxious wistfulness. Withal he remains a passionate libertarian, the forthright defender of Jeffersonian democracy, the perspicacious and incisive man of law—in truth one of our most distinguished living Americans.

Harry S. Truman

THE NEW DEAL IN ECLIPSE

T HE TRAGEDY OF PRESIDENT ROOSEVELT'S sudden death was
highlighted by the inexperience and seeming inadequacy
of his successor. Harry S. Truman was an honest office-
holder, a man of good will and stanch loyalties. As chairman of
the Senate Committee to Investigate the National Defense Program he had labored hard in the nation's interest and prodded
both government agencies and private corporations toward greater
efficiency and increased economies. So fully had he familiarized
himself with the details of the war effort that he soon knew more
about the "arsenal of democracy" than any other man in Washington with the exception of President Roosevelt. It was this
notable achievement, widely publicized and fully appreciated,
that had made him first choice as candidate for the Vice-Presidency
in 1944.

Success as chairman of a Senate investigating committee did
not, however, prepare him for the tremendously complex office
of the Presidency. With a mind governed by copybook maxims,
he lacked the broad world view on international problems; at
times either impulsive or mulishly stubborn, he on occasion acted
tactlessly or out of personal pique. Yet he strove valiantly, if not
often successfully, to emulate the sagacity and liberalism of his
distinguished predecessor. Time and again his words and sentiments approximated the aims of the New Deal; yet equally frequently they emerged blurred and even distorted in application.

412

Unfortunately for Truman, he assumed office in a time of severe crisis. In a time of "normalcy," such as the one in which Calvin Coolidge succeeded President Harding, he would no doubt have served eminently well. But he began his Presidency toward the end of a cataclysmic world war which, in achieving the defeat of Hitlerism, ushered in the atomic age and brought to the fore a strengthened and aggressive Soviet Union. The extraordinary situation required of the United States, the most powerful nation in the world, a leadership capable of coping with the emergent complexities. President Truman stretched his considerable talents to the utmost, but he lacked the astuteness and the imagination to ease the tensions of a war-shocked society—assuming that such easement was at all possible.

Unlike Roosevelt, who was a born-and-bred patrician, Truman was truly a man of the people. He came of good pioneer stock—Democrats and later Confederates who left Kentucky in the 1840's to carve out farms for themselves on the virgin Missouri prairie. His father, John Truman, was a dealer in horses and mules. He married a daughter of a well-to-do farmer and on May 8, 1884, she gave birth to Harry, the first of their three children. Honest and not as shrewd as some of his competitors, John sometimes failed to profit from his investments. Around 1890 he moved from a farm in Grandview to Independence, where he hoped to give his children the benefits of urban culture.

Harry's myopia caused him to begin wearing glasses when he was eight years old. Bespectacled boys were rare in those days, and his playmates considered him handicapped and excluded him from rough games. His mother kept him out of school till his ninth year but she taught him at home and encouraged him to become an assiduous reader. Like so many boys of his time, he devoted himself to the study of the Bible and had read it through twice before he reached his tenth birthday. Many other books were made available to him by his mother, and he was especially fond of those dealing with historic events and military heroes. It was this habit of reading that later provided him with a ready knowledge of past wars.

His mother also stimulated him to study music. By the time he was thirteen he had begun to play the piano in "dead earnest." He rose early every morning and practiced two hours. Twice weekly he went for a music lesson. After several years, despite encouragement from his teacher, he gave up the thought of becoming a professional musician, having come to regard it as a "sissy" occupation.

Much reading of books on military exploits made him wish to become an army officer, and he prepared himself for West Point, but his poor eyesight made naught of his ambition. His father having suffered serious financial losses in "grain market futures," Harry went to work on graduating from high school at the age of seventeen. He held jobs briefly as timekeeper on a railroad construction project, as a mailer on a newspaper, and as a ledger clerk in a bank. During this period he joined the Baptist church and the National Guard. For amusement he attended vaudeville shows regularly.

In 1906 he left the city to work on the family farm. For the next ten years he devoted himself to its operation, relieving his ailing father of many chores. In time he learned to make the straightest furrow in the vicinity. All the while he courted Bess Wallace, whom he loved from the age of six, and visited her nearly every week-end. To expedite these excursions to town and to enjoy the fruits of his successful farming, he bought a used automobile in 1913—and thus was one of the first in his county to purchase a "horseless carriage."

He was becoming a man of solidity and substance. Every year he went for a fortnight to the National Guard encampment and greatly relished the activity and companionship. A Mason since 1909, he strove to make himself worthy of the organization—and received his reward in 1940 when he was elected grand master of Missouri. When his father died in 1915 he succeeded him as road overseer. For six months he was postmaster of Grandview. He also

414

took fliers in mining stock, on which he lost $7500, and in oil lands which began to produce after he had sold his share to enlist.

When it appeared certain that the United States would declare war on Germany, Truman was among the first to volunteer. He was made a first lieutenant and given the task of helping to build up a field artillery regiment of the National Guard. Because of his knowledge of bookkeeping he was placed in charge of the canteen. With the help of Eddie Jacobson, a sergeant who was a skilled salesman, he was able to show a profit of $15,000 after six months of operation. This remarkable success brought him to the favorable notice of his superior officers. Promoted to a captaincy and chosen as one of the advance group to receive special training in France, he was a zealous student and put his knowledge of artillery to good use when made the head of a company of hardy Missourians. His tough yet tolerant manner gained him their respect and a number of them became his lifelong friends and did yoeman work in furthering his political advancement. Later he said, "My whole political career is based upon my war record and war associates."

Truman returned to the United States in April 1919 and was discharged the following month. He was now ready to marry Bess Wallace and did so on June 28. The honeymoon over, he began thinking of how to earn his living. The life of a farmer seemed to him circumscribed. Having inherited $15,000 and an 80-acre farm from an uncle, he was strongly tempted to enter business. A chance meeting with Eddie Jacobson reminded him of their successful canteen operation and the two arranged to open a haberdashery store, with one providing the capital and the other the experience. At first they prospered. Wages were high and workers had the money to buy silk shirts. But the sudden and sharp depression of 1921 played havoc with the value of the partners' inventory and forced them into bankruptcy. Truman insisted, however, on paying all debts in full and discharged them about fifteen years later.

Without capital and at loose ends, he readily accepted Michael

J. Pendergast's offer of nomination as county judge—in Missouri the equivalent of a county supervisor. Michael, brother of Boss Tom Pendergast, was moved to this action by his son Jim, who had served under Truman and wished to help him. The shrewd politician was of course aware of Truman's fine war record and good family background. Campaigning hard and aided by numerous friendly veterans, Truman won the election by 282 votes.

Although he performed his duties honestly and efficiently, he failed of re-election in 1924 owing to a split in the local Democratic machine and the opposition of the Ku Klux Klan. To earn a living he began to sell memberships in the Kansas City Automobile Club. He also dealt in building loans and managed the Community Savings and Loans Association of Independence.

In 1926 he asked Tom Pendergast for the office of county collector, which yielded an annual income of around $25,000. Having already promised the political plum to another, Tom offered him the presiding judgeship of the county court. With the party again united, Truman won the office by a large majority. Two years later he was not only re-elected but given the right to float a $6,500,000 bond issue by pledging "that every cent of contracts for roads will be let to the lowest bidder in open bidding." He could do this because of his understanding with Pendergast that he would use his office honestly and for the benefit of the county. Years afterwards he remarked:

Tom Pendergast never asked me to do a dishonest thing. He knew I wouldn't do it if he asked it. He was always my friend. He was always honest with me, and when he made a promise he kept it. If he told me something, I knew it was the truth.

Truman's efficiency as a director of road building soon became favorably known over the entire state. In 1930 he was easily re-elected and another bond issue was approved—a notable feat in a time of depression. As good as his word, he succeeded in reducing the interest rate on county notes from 6 to 4½ percent and in placing the financial affairs of the county on a solid foundation.

He also provided it with a modern road system, two new court-houses, and a hospital for the aged. So well established had he become both as a public-spirited citizen and as a successful politician, that when Michael Pendergast died in 1929 Truman replaced him as leader of the county political organization. On election day he claimed control of 11,000 legitimate votes. "I looked out for the people and they understood my leadership."

In 1934 Truman felt he deserved a promotion. Having taken part in the redistricting which gave Missouri an additional seat in the House, he asked Pendergast's backing for this office. Again Tom told him that he had already promised it to another stalwart. Instead, unable to find a suitable opponent against Jacob Milligan of the St. Louis machine for the Senate nomination, he offered to support Truman's candidacy. The latter accepted gratefully, although he doubted his chances of success on a statewide basis.

Few politicians thought he had a chance. Although he was then Federal Re-employment Director for Missouri and thus associated with the New Deal, he was considered unsuitable for the high office. Congressman Joseph B. Shannon said: "Truman's too light. He's a good mixer, a very pleasant sort of fellow. And he's clean. I suspect that was one of the chief reasons Tom wanted him. The *Star's* been hammering Tom hard and he naturally wants to make sure his man's all right." Late in the campaign Truman benefited from an unexpected piece of good fortune when Congressman John J. Cochran entered the race. His popularity in St. Louis made possible Truman's nomination. It is interesting to note that in Kansas City the Pendergast machine was able to skyrocket a vote of 137,529 for Truman as against 10,437 for the two rival candidates, while in St. Louis the Bennett C. Clark machine gave Cochran 104,265 votes and only 10,412 to the others.

In 1934 it was easy for a New Deal candidate to win at the polls, and Truman, announcing himself "heart and soul for Roosevelt," had no difficulty in being elected as the state's junior Senator. Not a few considered the success of this "obscure man" as evidence of "the power of machine politics." Others, familiar with his work as county judge, were less critical—taking comfort in the thought that he was "a capable and honest public official."

The new Senator went to Washington weighted with the feeling of his own inferiority. He was in awe of the seasoned and sophisticated politicians around him and dared not assume equality with them during his long period of initiation. The stigma of being regarded as Pendergast's "office boy" stung him to the quick. "I don't follow his advice on legislation," he insisted. "I vote the way I believe Missourians as a whole would want me to vote." Yet his votes in favor of New Deal legislation did serve Pendergast's claim on federal patronage.

During his first six months in office Truman remained timidly passive, never once raising his voice in debate. All the while, however, he listened attentively to others and spent many hours studying reports and documents. His faithful attendance at committee meetings influenced Senator Burton K. Wheeler, chairman of the Committee on Interstate Commerce, to appoint him as vice-chairman. In this capacity he conducted hearings on aviation that led to the preparation of the Civil Aeronautics Act. Even more important were the hearings on railroad finance which brought about the Transportation Act of 1940. Although he knew nothing about the subject at the outset, he devoted many evenings to a perusal of reports and background studies of railroad operation. Quietly yet persistently he dug into shady financial manipulations and brought up incriminating evidence. With the aid of Max Lowenthal's expert questioning he made public the various ways in which leading banking firms exploited their railroad properties. Nor did he spare the Missouri Pacific despite pleas from his home state to go easy on that railroad. By the time the hearings ended he had become a popular and respected member of the Senate.

Success bolstered Truman's self-confidence. He shed his timidity on the Senate floor. Imbued with middle-western prejudices against "Wall Street" and influenced by the high popularity of the New Deal, he spoke and voted like a seasoned liberal. Several visits to the home of Justice Brandeis strengthened his distaste for big business. In December 1937 he expostulated in the Senate:

We worship Mammon. . . . It is a pity that Wall Street with its ability to control all the wealth of the nation and to hire the best brains of the country has not produced some statesmen, some men who could see the dangers of bigness and of the concentration of the control of wealth. Instead of working to meet the situation, they are still employing the best law brains to serve greed and selfish interests.

When Pendergast succumbed to his gambling mania and became reckless in his desperate scramble for large sums of money, Truman persisted in his refusal to believe that his political mentor was crooked. As a mark of loyalty he vehemently opposed the re-appointment of Maurice Milligan as United States District Attorney for Missouri because he was an enemy of the Pendergast machine. Nor did he lessen his allegiance to the corrupt boss when Milligan succeeded in indicting and convicting him for tax evasion. "Pendergast has been my friend when I needed it. I am not one to desert a ship when it starts to go down." This devotion reflected adversely on Truman, but only on the basis of guilt by association. Milligan, no friend, found nothing against him when he investigated Pendergast's venality. And he was found equally blameless by Senator Norris, who thus characterized him in a letter to Secretary Henry Wallace: "I must say that in all the time I know him, I never knew of an instance, I knew of no time that the bosses or the machine controlled his official work. I think he has done some very good work."

When he announced his candidacy for re-election in 1940 he was decried as Pendergast's "stooge" and opposed by many leading citizens of Missouri. With the Kansas City machine badly broken, with most of his political friends shying away from any contact with him, and with such strong candidates as Maurice Milligan and Governor Lloyd C. Stark opposing him, his chances of nomination appeared nil.

With the help of a few loyal supporters Truman set up cam-

419

paign headquarters and began a speaking tour across the state to discuss his Senate record. A quartet of prominent Senators came to Missouri to promote his candidacy. Senator Clark also spoke favorably of him. Farmer, Negro, and labor organizations, recalling his good work in their behalf, exerted themselves to help him. The railroad unions, led by Alexander Whitney of the trainmen, were particularly active and blanketed the state with a special issue of *Labor*. Robert Hannegan, an influential member of the St. Louis machine, broke with the Stark backers to work for Truman. A good organizer, he succeeded in swaying a large number of voters. Truman himself worked day and night to advance his candidacy. As the campaign progressed, his refusal to repudiate the sick and imprisoned Pendergast, viewed in the light of his own probity and liberalism, won the sympathy of many citizens. The combination of these factors lifted his chances of victory and finally yielded him the nomination by 8000 votes. In the election on the same ballot with Roosevelt he ran far ahead of his Republican rival—though considerably behind the President.

When Truman returned to Washington in 1941 for his second term, the country was engaged in a feverish defense program. The heads of the Army and Navy were strenuously enlarging staffs and accumulating every type of military equipment. They arranged for the construction of camps, tool shops, and airplane factories. Both industrialists and labor leaders were besieging the Capital—the first in quest of orders and favors, the second to promote union interests. Billions of dollars were obtained in contracts for goods and services and thousands of agents were collecting commissions for exerting "influence" in the proper places. The attitude of urgency coupled with inexperience on the part of key officials created a bumbling inefficiency that resulted in much waste and extravagance. Moreover, favoritism was rampant. Large corporations through their well-placed agents received large orders, while small manufacturers without political backing sought contracts in vain.

Truman was disturbed by what he observed. Struck by the waste and incompetence he had seen at Fort Leonard Wood in Missouri, he visited several other camps in different sections of the country. Everywhere he found the same situation. Cost-plus contracts, poorly supervised, led to inexcusable prodigality. He discussed his findings with several friendly colleagues and with their encouragement he offered a resolution that the Senate appoint a committee to investigate the defense program with a view to stopping waste and inefficiency. On March 1 the resolution was approved and Truman was made chairman of the new committee.

Still the county judge eager to give the people the most for their money, he made the nation's interest his prime concern. He studied the history of the Civil War Committee on the Conduct of the War to avoid repeating its damaging mistakes. He wanted neither a witch-hunt nor a whitewash. After consulting with Attorney-General Jackson he engaged as counsel Hugh Fulton, a shrewd and dynamic lawyer who had recently sent to jail a corrupt federal judge and the unscrupulous head of a large public utility corporation. Given a free hand and assured of the Committee's support, Fulton shunned politics, disregarded rumor and hearsay, and acted fairly on the evidence. Witnesses were allowed counsel and treated respectfully. Businessmen were served without fear or favor: their grievances were investigated as readily as the complaints against them. With the aid of numerous youthful and ardent assistants and with the ready support of the Committee, Fulton studied shortages of raw materials, new inventions, plant adequacy, and other aspects of defense needs and activities.

The Committee first concentrated on "the appalling waste" in the building of army camps. In a tempered report on its findings Truman stated:

I am sorry to say that I do not think the Army has done a good job on camp construction. There has been a lack of foresight and planning and a large amount of inefficiency, as a result of which I believe that several hundreds of millions of dollars have been wasted. . . . If our plans for military campaigns are no more extensive and no better than those for construction, we are indeed in a deplorable situation.

The report made a good impression and the favorable publicity established the Committee on a solid and popular basis.

Truman was completely absorbed in the work of the Committee. He traveled more than 30,000 miles to follow up leads given by Fulton and his staff investigators. Everywhere he insisted on efficiency and fair-dealing. Late in 1941 he made public his sharp criticism of the Office of Production Management headed by William Knudsen and Sidney Hillman and declared that the chaos and confusion bedeviling the agency could be eliminated only by placing responsibility in a single head. This soon led Roosevelt to appoint Donald Nelson as sole chief of the new War Production Board. Another of Truman's achievements was to help resolve the deadlock between the United Mine Workers and the southern mine operators. His statement that unless the strike was settled quickly he would call some of the wealthy mine owners to testify caused them to agree to a settlement.

Success and popularity imbued Truman with increased confidence. He spoke boldly and aggressively. When he found that the building unions were turning favorable rulings into self-serving rackets, he condemned the practice and had it stopped. Nor did he hesitate to expose the flagrantly favorable terms in defense contracts offered to large corporations and the part played by dollar-a-year officials in helping their firms obtain major contracts.

When the United States entered the global war in December 1941, the Committee urged an all-out war effort in its forthright annual report. Among other recommendations it advised the conversion of the gigantic automobile industry into a munition arsenal, the construction of steel plants on the Pacific Coast, the expansion of the machine tool program, the acceleration of airplane production, the reduction of metal shortages, the correlation of housing with war plants, and the constant review of all major contracts.

The fact that the entire future of the nation is at stake makes it imperative that there should be a constant check to ascertain that the program is actually being carried out efficiently, economically, and fairly so that the necessary sacrifices are apportioned to all without favoritism.

For forty months Truman actively headed the work of this important Committee. Although he received superb assistance from an intelligent and enthusiastic staff and the ready cooperation of his Senate colleagues, the enormously successful results of the Committee's efforts—a total saving of millions of dollars and the acceleration of war production—were due largely to his watchful and energetic initiative. Of particular significance was his demonstration that a Committee of Congress managed to carry on a highly effective inquiry without resorting to either political demagoguery or a heresy hunt. That his work was widely appreciated appeared in a poll conducted by *Look*, when he was voted the most valuable man in Washington. And President Roosevelt, speaking at a political rally in Philadelphia on October 27, 1944, said: "The Truman Committee has done a job which will live in history as an example of honest, efficient government at work."

In 1944, with the Vice-Presidency a possibility, destiny was beckoning Truman. He knew that there was stubborn opposition to the renomination of Vice-President Wallace—on the part of both the southern conservatives and the city bosses. He was also aware that organized labor and a good many influential Catholics would never accept Byrnes. Nor was it a secret to him that his popularity with liberals and labor leaders made him a potent candidate. His biographers have of course maintained that he did not seek the nomination and was in fact helping Byrnes to achieve that honor. On its face this assertion is valid enough. Truman did express his disinterest in the office and did speak up for his colleague. In politics, however, such behavior is often "good politics." For while he was reiterating his complete devotion to his Committee, Robert Hannegan, whom he had helped become chairman of the Democratic National Committee in gratitude for aiding him

423

in the 1940 election, lay the groundwork for the nomination with the important leaders of the party.

It was Truman's good fortune that in 1944 Roosevelt was already preoccupied with the establishment of the United Nations. Ever aware of Woodrow Wilson's tragic political blunders in connection with the League of Nations, he now leaned backward in his effort not to antagonize the powerful men in the Senate. Much as he still preferred Wallace as his "teammate" in the approaching campaign—and he assured him of this more than once—he was only too cognizant of the antagonism against his associate. For Wallace was sometimes too forthright in speech and manner and too much the uncompromising New Dealer to get along with hard-boiled politicians. Yet more than in previous years Roosevelt needed a Vice-President who could cajole Senators—especially the Southerners of his own party—and keep them in line during the epochal months of peacemaking.

In his talks with Roosevelt, Hannegan kept magnifying the political objections to Wallace and offering Truman as the logical running mate. The President knew the Missouri Senator only casually, having met him in a routine way and having followed his good work on the Committee bearing his name. Now that he considered the pragmatic need for a popular teammate, however, he found Truman coming closest to the kind of Vice-President he required: a mild New Dealer, friendly with labor, and a practical politician who had the ready ear of many of his fellow Senators. In typical fashion, therefore, Roosevelt continued formally to favor Wallace but told Hannegan that he would accept Truman as his running mate.

Truman, once nominated, resigned his Committee chairmanship and worked conscientiously for the success of the Democratic ticket. He made the assigned speeches, met people of political prominence, and urged local bosses to get the voters to the polls. Roosevelt did not take him into his intimate circle—indeed he saw little of him during and after the campaign—but in his speeches he praised his Committee's work and generally accepted him as a member of his team.

After the inauguration the following January Truman worked faithfully to keep the Senate friendly to the Administration. When Roosevelt, wishing to placate Wallace by appointing him Secretary of Commerce, ran afoul of Senatorial opposition, Truman exerted himself to obtain the necessary votes for confirmation and succeeded only by breaking a tie with his own vote. He also helped to strengthen the prevailing favorable atmosphere for the approval of the United Nations organization. Though now a leading member of the Administration, he remained on intimate terms with members of Congress and frequently joined them in "striking a blow for liberty"—a euphemism for imbibing bourbon—and in a friendly game of poker.

At five o'clock on April 12, 1945, Truman left the Senate chamber to join several of his Congressional cronies. On reaching his destination he was told that a Presidential secretary was frantically trying to talk with him. He telephoned the White House and was urged to hurry over. At the door he was asked to go directly to Mrs. Roosevelt and from her he learned that the President had died that afternoon.

"What can I do?" were his first words. Her response was, "Tell us, what can we do for you?" Two hours later he was sworn in as President.

Never before was a President confronted with so many crucial and complex problems—especially one as inexperienced and as unprepared as Truman. Although Truman had at first only a vague notion of the stupendous tasks ahead of him, he approached them prayerfully and with the determination to do his very best. An hour after reaching the White House he convened the shocked and grief-laden members of the Cabinet and told them: "I shall only say that I will try to carry on as I know he would have wanted me and all of us to do. I should like all of you to remain in your

Cabinet posts and I shall count on you for all the help I can get."

Roosevelt's advisers remained to provide background information and to guide his immediate actions. His first decisions were indeed an earnest effort to carry on his predecessor's policies. He insisted that the organizational meeting of the United Nations be opened in San Francisco as scheduled. When he learned that Molotov, the Soviet Foreign Minister, was not to head the Russian delegation, thereby deflating the importance of the conference, he persuaded Stalin to send him to the opening session.

Sincere and well-intentioned, Truman lacked finesse and insight. A feeling of inadequacy caused him on occasion to act impetuously, almost bluntly, when the situation required diplomatic tactfulness. Walter Lippmann described his manner quite aptly when he said, "I never thought his quick way of shooting from the hip was the way the Presidency should be conducted." Even before Truman assumed the Presidency there was evidence of difficulty in our relations with the Russians. Victory over the Nazis had made the Soviet Union the most powerful nation in Europe. The confidence of great strength had released in the Politburo leaders a latent aggressiveness—a desire to capitalize on their opportunities to widen the orbit of their political influence. They also were traumatically aware of their fearful losses during the war and were bent on safeguarding Russia against its potential enemies. The United States and Great Britain, the only other world powers in 1945, were just as eager to curb the spread of communist dominance. This clash of aims was of course aggravated by misunderstandings owing to radically different cultural backgrounds and world views. President Roosevelt, keenly aware of the danger to world peace resulting from a rift between the two major powers, had exerted his great personal charm and his extraordinary diplomatic finesse to win and retain Stalin's good will. Truman, however, became so irritated by specific Soviet trespasses that he overlooked the major aim of establishing world peace.

When Molotov stopped off in Washington on his way to San

Francisco, Truman, ten days in the White House, received him with the bluntness of an annoyed neighbor. "I made up my mind that I would lay it on the line with Molotov." Going on the assumption that "the Russians needed us more than we needed them," he told Molotov that if Russia breached any part of the Yalta agreement the United States would consider it no longer binding; that the United Nations would organize with or without the Soviet Union. On leaving, Molotov remarked angrily, "I have never been talked to like that in my life." And so intent was our delegation at San Francisco on keeping the Russians to the American interpretation of the Yalta provisions that Lippmann warned of our relations with them becoming hopeless "if we yield to all those who, to say it flatly, are thinking of the international organization as a means of policing the Soviet Union."

On his twenty-sixth day in office President Truman accepted Germany's unconditional surrender. Four days later he signed an order that at once terminated all Lend-Lease to the Soviet Union, so that ships already sailing with supplies for that country were called back to port. The haste with which this important action was carried out greatly irritated the Russians, coming as it did soon after our refusal of a postwar loan which President Roosevelt's advisers had ostensibly favored. Then, unaware of the cause but conscious of the increasing tension between the two countries, Truman sent the ailing Harry Hopkins to Russia in order to learn what might be done to lessen the strain. Stalin was not slow in telling Hopkins how strongly he resented the "scornful and abrupt manner" in which Lend-Lease was stopped but agreed to meet with Truman and Churchill at Potsdam. The President had at first insisted that the meeting take place in Washington, but he yielded when Stalin maintained that his doctors would not permit him to take the long trip.

With the fighting in Europe at an end and with Japan clearly on the defensive, the occasion demanded extraordinary leadership on the part of the United States if real universal peace were to be established. Truman was a conscientious and able executive but he lacked the imaginative statesmanship to calm and control the aggressively selfish forces eager for postwar spoils. Nor did it help him to surround himself with relatively mediocre advisers—most of them cronies from Missouri and Washington. Two days after assuming the Presidency, his conscience troubled by the thought that Byrnes might have been in his place, he offered his friend the headship of the Department of State. A man of administrative ability and considerable experience, he too lacked the sagacity to deal successfully with so alien and inimical a political force as Russian communism. Nor could both be unaffected by the knowledge that they had sole possession of the atom bomb—which was satisfactorily demonstrated at Alamogordo on the opening day of the Potsdam conference.

Truman and his advisers came to Potsdam intent on communist containment. Admitting Russia's right to assure herself of friendly neighbors, they nevertheless insisted on democratic procedures which were not only novel in those countries but which would certainly produce governments inimical to the Soviet Union. This concession the Russians could not and would not make. Stimson pointed out that outside of the United States and Great Britain few other countries understood or cared for free elections. He added that "the Russians perhaps were more realistic than we were in regard to their own security." When Truman nevertheless insisted on free elections in Poland, Stalin reminded him that Poland bordered on Russia and not on the United States or Great Britain. He added, "You demand too much of me. In other words, you demand that I renounce the interests of security of the Soviet Union, but I cannot turn against my country."

When Truman informed Stalin of the successful detonation of the atom bomb, the Russian's reaction was outwardly unappreciative of the dread weapon. Yet he no doubt must have wondered why he had not been informed of it earlier. Added to other American slights, real and fancied, it must have seemed to him ominous of our growing unfriendliness. Nevertheless the conference ended on a seemingly amicable basis and Stalin agreed to throw the Red Army against Japan as originally scheduled.

On his way back from Potsdam Truman consulted with his top military and civil advisers and decided to use the atom bomb against Japan. Later he said, "I had reached a decision after long and careful thought. It was not an easy decision to make. I did not like the weapon. But I had no qualms if in the long run millions of lives could be saved." When he learned, while still on the *Augusta* in mid-Atlantic, that the bomb had caused frightful destruction in Hiroshima, he felt highly exhilarated. He insisted on immediately announcing the news to the men on the ship and to the captain he exclaimed, "This is the greatest thing in history!"

For all their excitement over the new weapon, which had caused Japan's quick capitulation after a second bomb had exploded over Nagasaki, Truman and his chief advisers failed to envisage its deteriorating effect on world peace. With society in the control of two great powers of unlike cultural backgrounds and antagonistic economic philosophies, amity between them was precarious and infirm so long as one of them had cause to fear the other's possession of a secret, menacing weapon. Secretary of War Henry L. Stimson, one of our wisest leaders, clearly perceived this danger and urged in a memorandum to President Truman on September 11, 1945, that we do our utmost to establish "relations of mutual confidence" with the Soviet Union.

Those relations may be perhaps irretrievably embittered by the way in which we approach the solution of the bomb with Russia. For if we fail to approach them now and merely continue to negotiate with them, having the weapon rather ostentatiously on our hip, their suspicions and their distrust of our purposes and motives will increase. . . . The chief lesson I have learned in a long life is that the only way you can make a man trustworthy is to trust him; and the surest way to make him untrustworthy is to distrust him and show your distrust.

At a Cabinet meeting ten days later the question of how to deal with the bomb was discussed at length. Stimson urged that we agree to "limit the use of the atomic bomb as an instrument of war and so far as possible to direct and encourage the development of atomic power for peaceful and humanitarian purpose." He added that scientific secrets were not secrets. Secretary Wallace, also eager for friendly relations between the United States and the Soviet Union, backed Stimson and agreed that we should share atomic energy information with the Russians. James Forrestal, however, opposed this conciliatory step—insisting that the bomb was "the property of the American people" and could not be given to another nation.

Meantime Truman and his close advisers proceeded to act unilaterally in Japan and the Pacific, thereby further deteriorating our relations with the Russians. Our cavalier treatment of the Soviet representative caused him to be withdrawn altogether. But the slight rankled and made our negotiations with the Russian leaders all the more difficult. Although the State Department opposed the demand of the military chiefs that we keep the Pacific islands, arguing that such arbitrary behavior would set a bad example to the Soviet Union and give validity to the claim that its aggressive actions in Eastern Europe were defensive measures, Truman sided with the admirals. In a statement to Congress three days after the bombing of Hiroshima he declared: "Bases which our military experts deem to be essential to our protection, and which are not now in our possession, we will acquire."

In the meetings of the Council of Foreign Ministers during the next year, the impasse between Byrnes and Molotov thwarted all attempts at peacemaking. The first continued to insist that the governments of the countries adjoining the Soviet Union be based on democratic elections. "Our objective," he claimed, "is a government both friendly to the Soviet Union and representative of all the democratic elements of the country." Molotov considered this insistence an unrealistic and therefore unfriendly request. Impassively persistent and provokingly stubborn, he strongly irritated Byrnes and caused him to act with even more unyielding firmness. With little good will between them, at times with even less understanding, and with their points of view and immediate aims obviously irreconcilable, the sessions ended in frustrating futility.

Truman's impetuous leadership was not helpful. To please one of his cronies he persuaded Winston Churchill, on vacation in Florida, to deliver an address at little Westminster College in Missouri. His benign presence at this "Iron Curtain" speech served only to widen the rift between the United States and the Soviet Union.

Aware that he could expect little assistance from the President, Byrnes tended to act independently. When in Moscow at the end of 1945, desperately trying to reach an agreement with Molotov and more than once appealing to Stalin to break the deadlock, he did not trouble to send daily reports to the White House. Truman, instigated by some of his cronies and influenced by the criticism of those who feared that Byrnes might compromise on some issue, strongly resented the latter's silence. He assumed, contrary to fact, that "Byrnes had lost his nerve in Moscow." While in this mood he wrote him a memorandum urging that the Soviet Union be "faced with an iron fist."

I do not think we should play compromise any longer. We should refuse to recognize Rumania and Bulgaria until they comply with our requirements; we should let our position on Iran be known in no uncertain terms and we should continue to insist on the international-ization of the Kiel Canal, the Rhine-Danube waterway and the Black Sea Straits and we should maintain complete control of Japan and the Pacific. . . . I'm tired babying the Soviets.

Truman claimed in 1952 that he read this memorandum to Byrnes to put him in his place. The latter insisted that this was contrary to fact. "Mr. Truman's statement that he read the letter to me is absolutely untrue. Had he done so, he would have had to write another letter accepting my resignation." A year later, after strenuous but ultimately futile efforts at further negotiation, Byrnes did resign and returned to South Carolina a fractious and frus-trated politician. Truman was equally bitter. "He failed miserably as Secretary of State, and ran out on me when the going was very rough and when I needed him most."

In domestic affairs President Truman's efforts were no more successful. He assumed office with the promise to carry out Roosevelt's liberal policies. In great awe of his predecessor, he sought to adapt New Deal principles to postwar conditions. Of his message to Congress on September 6, 1945, be observed later, "I first spelled out the details of the program of liberalism and progressivism which was to be the foundation of my administration." These are the main planks:

The right to a useful and remunerative job.
The right to earn enough to provide adequate food and clothing and recreation.
The right of every farmer to raise and sell his products at a return which will give him and his family a decent living.
The right of every businessman, large and small, to trade in an atmosphere of freedom from unfair competition and domination by monopolies at home and abroad.
The right of every family to a decent home.
The right to adequate medical care and the opportunity to achieve and enjoy good health.
The right to adequate protection from the economic fears of old age, sickness, accident, and unemployment.
The right to a good education.

To implement these rights he proposed extension of unemployment compensation, a higher minimum wage, price supports for farm products, private and public housing, a scientific research program, greater water control, and civil rights legislation. However liberal this program appeared in print, it was delivered with a pragmatic implication of compromise. With the complexion of the Congress becoming increasingly conservative, these progressive sentiments made little impression on its leaders and only a watered-down portion of the program was enacted into law.

Not at ease with Roosevelt appointees, Truman soon replaced

them with men more to his liking but egregiously inferior. One of his first Cabinet changes was the selection of the mediocre but ambitious Tom Clark of Texas to succeed Francis Biddle as Attorney-General. Other newcomers, such as John Snyder, George Allen, J. K. Vardaman, Jr., Harry Vaughan, John Steelman, and Edwin Pauley, would have proved congenial to President Harding's circle—and their inadequacy was all the more manifest because of the high caliber of the men they superseded.

Truman's wish to repay Pauley for past favors by nominating him as Under-Secretary of the Navy caused consternation among loyal New Dealers. A successful fund-raiser for the Democratic party, Pauley was also known as an aggressive lobbyist for the oil men seeking the transfer of tidelands from federal to state control. Since the liberals, headed by Secretary of the Interior Harold Ickes, had long fought this move as a prodigal concession to the oil companies, they saw themselves betrayed by Pauley's appointment and were determined to oppose his confirmation at the Senate hearings. Truman asked Ickes to be "as gentle as you can with Ed. Pauley," but the forthright "curmudgeon" spoke out sharply against the nominee and resigned. At a press conference he said acidly: "I don't care to stay in an Administration where I am expected to commit perjury for the sake of a party."

A series of strikes, normal in a period of postwar inflation, plagued Truman shortly after the fighting in the Pacific had ended. Aware of the high corporation profits and the increased cost of living, he sympathized with labor's demand for higher wages and obtained increases by permitting rises in prices—thus furthering a vicious inflationary cycle. He lost patience with John L. Lewis of the coal miners and with Alexander Whitney and Alvenly Johnston of the railroad brotherhoods for insisting on more than his advisers recommended. A crisis was averted in the coal strike when the government took over the mines and negotiated a settlement. Whitney's and Johnston's "obstinate arrogance" deeply angered Truman. Ignoring their last-minute compliance, he went before the Congress to ask for the severest antilabor legislation ever requested by a President—the power to draft essential-industry strikers into the armed forces. In 1950, referring to these two labor leaders and their ill-fated strike, he remarked: "I sent for them and talked to them like a Dutch uncle. 'If you think I'm going to sit here and let you tie up this country, you're crazy as hell.' "

Fortunately cooler heads prevailed. Even Senator Robert A. Taft, whose own bill to curb labor unions was to gain strength from Truman's intemperate outburst, was shocked by the request. "The idea of drafting men to work," he declared, "is the most extreme form of slavery." The conservative *Wall Street Journal* likewise gagged at the spiteful proposal:

President Truman's Strike Control bill, passed by the House in thoughtless haste, is in several respects offensive to our every instinct of political safety and impossible to apply in practice. The country is consequently relying upon the Senate to nullify the President's erratic and probably unconscious plunge in the direction of dictatorship.

The Senate, with Taft's help, refused to act on the bill. But the damage was done and was to become a factor in the election of a Republican and highly conservative Congress.

Concurrently the place of the New Dealer in the Truman Administration was becoming increasingly untenable. Eager as they were to serve it, they were discouraged and thwarted at every turn. There was no real sympathy for them at the White House, and the Congress was openly inimical. One by one the prominent liberals either resigned or were dismissed. Chester Bowles, Wilson Wyatt, William H. Davis, James Landis, Henry Morgenthau, Harold Ickes, Paul Porter—these and numerous others who had given color and character to the New Deal swelled the exodus from government service.

Henry Wallace, leader of the New Dealers, was cashiered with an abruptness that emphasized Truman's impulsive leadership. In the summer of 1946 Wallace was deeply disturbed by the "get tough" policy toward the Soviet Union and the loose talk about

434

the use of the atom bomb on Russian cities. He felt that unless the two great powers reached an understanding and developed friendly relations they would sooner or later engage in another disastrous war and endanger the survival of civilized society. Knowing that mutual confidence required compromise and good will, he held that Byrnes's policy of "firmness and patience" was in fact so laden with suspicion and toughness as to aggravate the existing antagonism between the two countries.

President Truman, condoning the "tough" policy of Byrnes and Forrestal, nevertheless led Wallace to believe that he really agreed with his "soft" approach. Canny politician that he was, he reassured him of this in the hope of retaining the decisive liberal vote in the fall elections. It was with his encouragement that Wallace went to New York to speak before the progressive groups at the Madison Square Garden. Both of them went over the speech together, and Truman approved the controversial passages despite their criticism of official policy—although he subsequently denied that he had seen them. When the address was delivered on September 12 in the packed arena, the remarks unfavorable to the Soviet Union were booed by the communist sympathizers, while those urging sympathy and compromise with the Russians were cheered to the echo. The next morning, however, the newspapers headlined only the remarks disparaging the policy of the State Department.

At that very time Secretary Byrnes and Senators Connally and Vandenberg were in Paris in angry deadlock with the Russian delegation. When the report of Wallace's speech reached them, their frustrated efforts at the conference table made them all the more sensitive to such opposition. The Secretary at first kept silent, but both Senators condemned the speech as irresponsible. Perplexed and disturbed by the unexpected reaction to the address, Truman consulted with Wallace and had him announce that he would make no more speeches until after the end of the Paris Conference. Yet Byrnes remained dissatisfied. Goaded by Vandenberg's taunt that there were two Secretaries of State, he told the President over teletype that Wallace must never again speak on foreign policy while a member of the Administration.

If it is not completely clear in your own mind that Mr. Wallace should be asked to refrain from criticizing the foreign policy of the United States while he is a member of your Cabinet, I must ask you to accept my resignation immediately. At this critical time, whoever is Secretary of State must be known to have the undivided support of your Administration and, so far as possible, of the Congress.

The next morning Truman telephoned Wallace to ask for his resignation. To reporters he said blandly that "there was a fundamental conflict" between Wallace's views on foreign policy and that of his Administration and that "the Government of the United States must stand as a unit in its relations with the rest of the world."

Apprehensive of the conservative legislation to be passed by the incoming Republican Congress, Truman requested the outgoing body on December 3, 1946, to pass a new labor law designed "to provide adequate means for settling industrial disputes and avoiding industrial strife." No action was taken at the time, but the new Congress, sparked by the lobbyists of the National Manufacturers Association and other business groups, labored for months to produce the Taft-Hartley Act. Aiming to weaken certain important provisions in the earlier Wagner Act, it outlawed the closed shop, permitted limited use of the injunction, gave employers certain rights in dealing with workers, and specified a noncommunist oath for union officials.

Although in his anger Truman was ready to draft labor, he and his advisers considered the bill presented to him for his signature an obnoxious piece of legislation. Spurred by liberals and organized labor and guided by the intelligent analysis of his counsel Clark Clifford, he vetoed it in a message notable for its bold spirit and incisive criticism. He pointed out that the bill discriminated against employees, favored employers, raised "serious issues of public

436

policy," and "would substantially increase strikes." "The bill, as a whole," he continued, "would reverse the basic direction of our national labor policy, inject the Government into private economic affairs on an unprecedented scale, and conflict with important principles of our democratic society." But he had no control over the members of his own party and his veto was overridden by large majorities in both Houses of Congress.

Long before Secretary Byrnes resigned in January 1947, President Truman told General George C. Marshall that he wanted him as his next Secretary of State. With this in mind he sent him to China for the purpose of uniting the government of Chiang Kai-shek with the powerful communist faction. Marshall left nothing undone toward this end, but futility met him everywhere. He had little patience with the corrupt and incompetent Nationalist government and he did not trust the Communists. Accusing both sides of fomenting hate campaigns, he sought to bring about, perhaps naively under the circumstances, a democratic coalition government under the aegis of a "third force"—the Chinese liberals, whom he considered "a splendid group of men." But Chiang Kai-shek not only refused to cooperate but outlawed the liberal organizations and imprisoned their leaders. The Communists, on their part, scorned cooperation with Chiang Kai-shek and urged the United States to halt military aid to the Nationalists. Despite our enlarged flow of military supplies to Chiang Kai-shek, his armies continued to deteriorate. Later, when the Communists gained control of China, Marshall was unfairly criticized by apologists of the Chiang Kai-shek regime.

On his return to this country Marshall took charge of the State Department. He was immediately confronted by the suddenly aggravated crisis in Greece. Great Britain, strained financially to the breaking point, was no longer able to keep the conservative Greek government in power by maintaining an army in that country. The English leaders declared bluntly that unless we took over the task of bolstering the existing regime the communist rebels would certainly overthrow it shortly. This, they pointed out, would add Greece to the Soviet orbit and surround Turkey with communist enemies. On February 27, 1947, Truman and Marshall conferred with the leaders of Congress and persuaded them to agree to a strict policy of communist containment.

This radical departure in foreign affairs, begun tentatively the previous year, was formalized by the President in an address to Congress on March 12 and later became known as the Truman Doctrine. In this speech he declared that the United States must not permit any further violation of the existing status quo "by such methods as coercion, or by such subterfuges as political infiltration."

One of the primary objectives of the foreign policy of the United States is the creation of conditions in which we and other nations will be able to work out a way of life free from coercion. . . . I believe that it must be the policy of the United States to support free peoples who are resisting attempted subjugation by armed minorities or by outside pressures. . . . I believe that our help should be primarily through economic and financial aid which is essential to economic stability and orderly political process.

A bill to grant $300,000,000 to Greece and $100,000,000 to Turkey for economic and military support was introduced in the House. Senator Vandenberg, Republican leader of the bipartisan policy in Congress, at once noted that the draft bypassed the UN and declared, "The Administration made a colossal blunder in ignoring the UN." In the Senate Committee he redrafted the preamble to make clear that the United States was acting within the world organization and was subject to its approval.

Let us be totally plain about it. It is a plan to forestall aggression which, once rolling, could snowball into a global danger of vast design. It is a plan for peace. It is a plan to sterilize the seeds of war. We do not escape war by running away from it. No one ran away from war at Munich.

438

Despite this bipartisan support, the bill had hard sledding in Congress. Many members were fearful of the consequences of this deep plunge toward policing the world. But the exertion of much pressure finally forced its passage by large majorities.

If Greece occupied the center of the international stage early in 1947, the other countries of Europe were also in dire straits and too disturbed politically to be left to themselves. People everywhere were hungry and restive. American emergency relief was temporarily helpful but it did not remove the economic distress upon which communism thrived. Exceptionally bad weather served to aggravate both unemployment and unrest. In May 1947 Congress voted another $350,000,000 for relief. It also approved large loans to Britain and France. American leaders realized, however, that a bolder, more positive program was needed to stop the spread of communism. They perceived the futility of containing it in Greece if it were permitted to overwhelm France and Italy. On May 8 Under-Secretary Dean Acheson, using Cleveland, Mississippi, as a sounding board for the implementation of the Truman Doctrine, declared "that totalitarian regimes imposed on free people, by direct or indirect aggression, undermine the foundations of international peace and hence the security of the United States." Other Administration spokesmen reiterated and emphasized the danger of potential communist aggression to the safety of the United States.

On June 5 Secretary Marshall climaxed this discussion of communist containment in an address at Harvard University. He proposed to build up the economies of the European nations by a combination of American aid and self-help, with the initiative to come from the countries themselves and with the United States providing friendly assistance toward the realization of an economic program agreeable to all concerned.

The truth of the matter is that Europe's requirements for the next three or four years of foreign food and other essential products— principally from America—are so much greater than her present ability to pay that she must have substantial additional help, or face economic, social, and political deterioration of a very grave character. . . . It is logical that the United States should do whatever it is able to do to assist in the return of normal economic health in the world, without which there can be no political stability and no assured peace. Our policy is directed not against any country or doctrine but against hunger, poverty, desperation, and chaos. Its purpose should be the revival of a working economy in the world so as to permit the emergence of political and social conditions in which free institutions can exist.

Governmental leaders in Western Europe hailed the Marshall Plan. England and France took the initiative and invited all European nations to Paris to confer on the ways and means of its realization. The Soviet Union and her satellites agreed to participate and Molotov headed the Russian delegation. He was not very long, however, in criticizing the proposed means. Asserting that the plan was in effect a disguised form of "capitalist imperialism," he departed in a huff and took the representatives of Eastern Europe with him. The countries that remained proceeded to accommodate themselves to American requirements and to benefit from the proffered assistance. The communist-controlled countries met separately to organize the Cominform and to arrange for mutual economic assistance. Nor did they fail to take advantage of their fortuitous opportunity to bring Czechoslovakia, the only relatively democratic nation in Eastern Europe, within their orbit.

A number of New Dealers joined the conservative isolationists in criticizing the Truman Doctrine of policing the world against communism. Although they too opposed the forcible extension of communist power, they were deeply troubled by American actions that served to sharpen the antagonism between the Soviet Union and the capitalist democracies. They felt that the danger of communism was best fought not by financial and military intervention but by a practical demonstration of the unequivocal advantages of democracy. Fiorello La Guardia, New York's peppery mayor, expressed this attitude when he stated:

Let us not do anything that will create the impression that we want to rule the whole world, that any government that doesn't please us will be put out of business. . . . We can lick communism in the world by making democracy work, by proving to the world that people can live properly and decently.

If the Truman Administration acted positively, if not always astutely, in foreign affairs, on domestic issues it continued to bluster and blunder. Opposed by a conservative Republican Congress, unable to control the members of its own party, confronted by an anticommunist hysteria somewhat of its own making, plagued by postwar social strains and economic discontents, and yet conscious of its moral obligations to the New Deal, it strove fitfully and ineffectually to satisfy all factions at once. Oscillating between high-minded liberalism and personal petulance, President Truman unwittingly furthered the purposes of reactionary demagogues and alienated the liberal groups upon whom he depended for support. Walter Lippmann, writing critically of his foreign policy, indicated as well the cause of his domestic failure:

At the very center of the Truman Administration, at the critical point where the fateful decisions of the highest diplomatic and military consequence are made, there is a vacuum of authority and responsibility. There is, that is to say, no one who guides, directs, coordinates, and disciplines the actions by the government.

The direction of the loyalty program was a significant example of this muddled leadership. A number of conservative opponents of the Administration, in and out of Congress, took advantage of the deepening "cold war" to denounce not only known communists but also those whom they considered "fellow travelers." They decried particularly the presumed presence of "subversives" in government service. The House Committee on Un-American Activities, headed by the notorious Parnell Thomas who was later convicted of office "kickbacks," became host to repentant communists, professional informers, hysterical patriots, and all others who cared to make public their factual or fancied knowledge of subversive

441

activities. As Senator Denis Chavez, no radical, declared in this connection, "Ex-Communists are treated as heroes of the Republic. They are rushed to forums from which they denounce good citizens who always opposed communism but refused to make merchandise of their patriotism." A number of sensation-mongering syndicated columnists and radio commentators helped to spread the alarm to the point of panic. Evidence of espionage in connection with the atom bomb, uncovered in Canada and England, served to accelerate the growing dread of disloyalty.

President Truman was as anxious as anyone to drive out the disloyal from government employment. Yet he was certain that the overwhelming majority of federal workers were genuinely patriotic and that the slur upon their loyalty was hurting their morale. Eager to protect them from harassment by demonstrating the truth of his contention, he in March 1947 issued an Executive Order to investigate the loyalty of all employees of the administrative branch of the government. He also hoped thereby to forestall publicity-seeking Committees of Congress by placing the probe in the hands of a professional and impartial agency.

Critics of the Order were quick to indicate its ill effects. They argued that the very idea of investigating the loyalty of millions of federal employees was an insult to their integrity and that many thoughtful and able officials would be driven away from government service. They also pointed out that the loyalty check would hamper the efficiency of those who remained. Even more damaging, they maintained, would be the intensification of the witch-hunt, since the investigation would be interpreted as an admission of doubt and would only encourage the efforts of demagogic politicians.

These fears were soon justified. Despite the fact that after six years of assiduous investigation, involving the zealous screening of over four million federal employees, only 490 were ousted or rejected, the campaign against subversion in government continued unabated. The discovery of alleged disloyalty on the part of Alger Hiss encouraged the opportunistic anticommunists to cast doubt upon the top members of the Truman Administration. After February 1950 Senator Joseph McCarthy's reckless charges and adroit insinuations persuaded millions of Americans that the State Department was infested with communist sympathizers.

Truman seriously resented this hysterical agitation. More than once he spoke out against it sharply and unequivocally. He insisted that the measures he had taken guarded "the internal security of the United States" and that there were fewer communists in America than in any other large country in the world. On May 29, 1950, speaking to the head of the Veterans of Foreign Wars, he ridiculed the stigma being attached to membership in certain organizations. "I'd be willing to bet my right eye that you yourself and I have joined some organizations that we wish we hadn't. It hasn't hurt me any and I don't think it has hurt you any."

Despite these efforts to calm the noisy turbulence, in 1951 he again yielded to demagogic clamor by promulgating a new loyalty order requiring an adverse finding "if reasonable doubt exists as to [an individual's] loyalty to the United States." Thus employees could be dismissed if they held "membership in, affiliation with or sympathetic association with any foreign or domestic organization, association, group or combination of persons designated by the Attorney-General as totalitarian, Fascist, Communist, or subversive." Under this order disloyalty no longer had to be proved as a tangible and current fact; all that was necessary was mere suspicion, easily aroused by the irresponsible charges made by fanatics and informers.

Even this dangerously lax procedure uncovered very few officials against whom the charge of disloyalty could be made. Nor did it silence the Administration critics, who knew only too well the value of propaganda reiterated over and over. On May 3, 1952, addressing the National Civil Service League, President Truman took the opportunity again to strike back at the "political gangsters." He declared that their tactics, containing "the seed of tyranny," were undermining the Bill of Rights and were thus betraying "our country and all it stands for." On the loyalty of federal employees he stated:

I say, with all the emphasis at my command, that there is no more cancerous, no more corrosive, no more subversive attack upon the great of our Government today than that which seeks to undermine confidence in Government by irresponsible charges against the loyalty and integrity of Government employees. . . . The truth is that Government service, in the light of its tremendous size and scope, has a remarkable record of honesty and integrity. I firmly believe that its ethical standards are as high as those of any Government in the history of the world.

Early in 1948 there was strong resistance among Democrats to the nomination of Truman for President. His popularity, oscillating sharply during his years in office, appeared to be minimal. The conservatives were antipathetic to his Fair Deal coloration, many powerful Southerners were antagonized by his insistence on civil rights legislation, and the liberals were alienated by his inability to stem the tide of postwar reaction. All factions felt, moreover, that he simply had no chance against a strong Republican opponent.

One of his sharpest critics was Michael Straight, publisher of the *New Republic*, then edited by Henry Wallace. In a front-cover editorial, headed in large type "Truman Should Quit," he said, "Great leadership is demanded of America now in securing peace. It is not within Truman's power to give." In another editorial he asserted, "Truman cannot be re-elected. The overriding interest of liberal Americans demands that he should not be renominated." Southern politicians, spurred by such leaders as Byrnes, now governor of South Carolina, were equally vocal in their opposition.

These critics made little headway against Truman's nomination. In his favor was the fact that as President he had control of the party machinery and the active backing of numerous political appointees. An even more powerful factor was the lack of a strong rival candidate. None of the eligible Democrats wanted either to oppose the incumbent or to enter a campaign with the odds favoring the Republicans. When the convention opened, Truman's backers were in control. The left New Dealers were absent, but the Southerners were present and irreconcilable. In the balloting their standard-bearer, Senator Richard Russell, received 263 votes and Truman 947½.

The cleavage in the Democratic party, for sixteen years held together to make a dominant majority by the political genius of Franklin D. Roosevelt, opened wide in July 1948. The "Dixiecrats" were rallying the conservatives in the South around Senator Russell—acclaiming white supremacy, denouncing civil rights legislation, the FEPC bill, and the Truman Administration. To the very end of the campaign they remained firm and embittered, and succeeded in garnering a sizable number of electoral votes.

The threat from the left was at first even more serious. The zealous New Dealers, having been alienated by Truman's lapses from liberalism and the conservative effect of his policies, rallied around Wallace. The gulf between them and Truman widened when Administration spokesmen denounced Wallace's speeches favoring amity with the Soviet Union as harmful meddling and when Forrestal proposed the cancellation of his passport. Certain they could not make themselves heard in the councils of the National Democratic Committee, these disgruntled New Dealers decided to form a political party of their own under Wallace's leadership.

Arrayed in the prophet's mantle, the modern Gideon issued a call for sturdy and intrepid recruits. Thousands of earnest liberals, craving world peace and freedom from fear, rushed to his standard —exhilarated once more by the lure of the progressive quest. Some of them were unreconstructed Bull Moosers, who had been battling for social reform since early in the century, and their hallelujah spirit pervaded the meetings of the new party. But with them, equally zealous and actively in command, were a number of communists and their sympathizers. They sparked the popular-front policies and stopped the coupling of the Soviet Union with the United States in the party's critical stand on foreign policy. At its convention in Philadelphia Wallace was more the political visionary than the practical politician. Only dimly aware of the role played by his communist followers, he made no effort to curb their aggressiveness at the outset—thereby forfeiting millions of votes.

As late as May 1948 astute politicians predicted that the Progressive party might attract as many as ten million voters. In his own considered estimate during the campaign Wallace expected at least a third that many. But his blundering leadership at the Philadelphia convention blighted the party's prospects. The first to attack the Progressives were the anticommunist liberals who had formed the Americans for Democratic Action. Opposed to Truman's candidacy, they nevertheless refused any contact with the communists and rejected Wallace because of his unwillingness to drive the latter out of the party. Their charge of Progressive subservience to the Soviet Union, repeated and perverted and hyperbolized by Democratic speakers and writers throughout the campaign caused intimidated Wallacites to fall away like leaves in a late autumn storm. By Election Day only a little more than a million voters cast their ballots on the Progressive ticket.

With sizable defections in the South and among Progressives, Truman's chances of victory in the face of an invigorated and determined Republican party appeared poor indeed. As eight years previously, however, he was confident of election. And luck was with him. Again fortuitous circumstances turned millions of voters in his direction. First was his "secret weapon"—the conservative Republican Congress, with such unpopular measures as the Taft-Hartley Act debited against it. In his acceptance speech at the Democratic convention he took advantage of this situation by announcing that he was calling a special session of Congress to deal with such liberal measures as the excess-profits tax, consumer-credit controls, stronger rent controls, price controls, and housing. He asserted that action on these reforms would demonstrate the sincerity of the Republican party. Congressional leaders, considering this move a cheap political gesture, angrily rejected these legislative proposals—thereby giving weight to his accusation that the Eightieth was "the worst Congress in history." During the campaign he traveled 30,000 miles and made 351 speeches—most of them denouncing the "do-nothing, good-for-nothing, worst Eightieth Congress."

A second factor favoring his election was his decision to capitalize on the liberal platform adopted at the Democratic convention. In his campaign speeches he reiterated his promise to urge the repeal of the Taft-Hartley Act, and to further legislation curbing inflation and promoting low-cost housing, civil rights, health insurance, social security, education, and a higher minimum wage. Although his was hardly the "intellectually honest campaign" he claimed, it did appeal to independent voters. So liberal indeed were Truman's campaign promises on domestic issues that in the end they differed little from Wallace's—thus attracting many uneasy Progressives to the safer Democratic fold.

Perhaps the most important determining factor was the overconfidence of the Republican candidate. Governor Thomas E. Dewey was so sure of victory that he limited his campaign to ambiguous generalities and vague promises. Insensitive to the inner conflicts of the millions of independent voters—many of whom had never cast a ballot for anyone but Roosevelt and still felt attached to New Deal policies—he made little effort to wean them from the Democratic party. Nor did he possess the easy, warm personality that aroused political enthusiasm among the mass of voters. By way of contrast many Americans came to admire the hard, uphill fight put up by his embattled rival.

When the ballots were counted on election night, Truman stumped the expert pollsters by winning decisively despite his losses in the South and among the New Dealers. The next day Senator Vandenberg expressed a common reaction when he remarked, "You've got to give the little man credit. There he was flat on his back. Everyone had counted him out but he came up fighting and won the battle. He did it all by himself. That's the kind of courage the American people admire."

James P. Warburg, a keen student of international affairs, wrote that the Truman containment policy forced the United States to fight a windstorm with bayonets—and not enough of them at that. Suggested by Winston Churchill and developed by George Keenan, it was essentially a negative and therefore fallacious doctrine based on the devil theory that the Soviet leaders were not Anglo-Saxon gentlemen but infernal barbarians. What neither Truman nor his advisers realized was that communism is not a Stalin invention but a social force rooted in discontent, nurtured by economic and political inequality, and brought to flower by cleverly fomented uprisings against callous oppressors. To prevent its spread among underprivileged peoples it is necessary to demonstrate the superiority of democracy in tangible form. Not armaments but abundance, not loans to the wealthy but food to the hungry, not alliance with timeserving reactionaries but the promotion of individual freedom—by these means only could the roots of communism be dried up.

Definitely committed to the policy of containment, the Truman Administration developed the idea of "situations in strength": To resist every expansive effort of the communists and to build up the military strength of the United States and its allies as quickly and as intensively as possible. In the process the government spent many billions of dollars without lessening world tension. It remains questionable whether our uneasy peace with the Soviet Union is the result of our costly containment policy or the consequence of the communist assumption that ultimate victory lay not on the field of battle but in the bursting discontent of dependent and exploited peoples.

Even before the election campaign of 1948 the implementation of the Marshall Plan with the European Recovery Program had brought our relations with the Soviet Union to a critical juncture.

448

In retaliation the Red Army blockaded the land routes leading into and out of Berlin, thus virtually isolating nearly two million people living in the Allied zones of the German metropolis. When the Defense Chiefs, called to the White House for consultation, began to discuss the question of whether Americans should remain in Berlin or be evacuated, President Truman stopped the talk with the declaration, "We are going to stay period." Three weeks later, with the problem again under debate, he once more insisted that "we would stay in Berlin until all diplomatic means have been exhausted." Not long after, at another meeting, he told his military advisers that although he prayed he would never have to decide on the use of the atom bomb in case of war, he would not hesitate to do so. Thus began the airlift from the American zone to Berlin, which for nearly a year supplied food and coal and other needs to the blockaded population at tremendous cost. When the friction was eased without war and the blockade was lifted in May 1949, agreement brought no international easement. The tension of "cold war" remained.

In his inaugural message on January 20, 1949, President Truman proposed to further his containment policy by uniting the North Atlantic nations into a defensive organization and by helping them develop military strength sufficient to discourage any attempt at aggression on the part of the Soviet Union. This step was prepared in 1948 by the passage of the Vandenberg Resolution which empowered the President to enter into military alliances with countries of Western Europe. On March 18 the Administration made public the North Atlantic Treaty, and seventeen days later representatives of twelve nations signed it in a Washington cere‑ mony. After weeks of debate the Senate approved the Treaty and thus initiated the development of a European army with Ameri‑ can help and guidance and with General Eisenhower as its first head.

In the same address Truman made a much more positive proposal—his Point Four program to make our scientific and technological advances "available for the improvement and growth of undeveloped areas." He pointed out that more than half of the world's population was "living in conditions approaching misery," and that "for the first time in history humanity possesses the knowledge and the skill to relieve the suffering of these people." Since the United States was industrially and scientifically the most developed of nations, it behooved us to take the initiative.

I believe we should make available to peace-loving peoples the benefits of our store of technical knowledge in order to help them realize their aspiration for a better life. . . . The old imperialism—exploitation for foreign profit—has no place in our plans. What we envisage is a program of development based on the concepts of democratic fair dealing.

To him Point Four was "a practical answer to a growing crisis in a world torn between aggression and peace," another step in the effort to contain communism. He saw no other alternative. When Senator Brien McMahon in 1950 offered him the idea of proposing general disarmament and using part of the saving for economic and social advancement of mankind—an expansion of Point Four—Truman refused to lend his name to it. (Three years later President Eisenhower did make the proposal, although he too did little thereafter to give it reality.) Consequently, instead of capitalizing on this noble gesture by our accustomed largesse and making evident to peoples suspicious of Western imperialism that our generosity was genuinely altruistic, we offered it only casually and with an anticommunist proviso. Although the experts and the material help we did send to the backward areas definitely improved living conditions, we made little headway against communist propaganda that our aims are imperialistic.

On January 7, 1949, Truman appointed Dean Acheson Secretary of State. The two men made a harmonious team. The President respected Acheson's high intelligence and moral fervor, and the latter greatly appreciated Truman's loyalty and served him devotedly. Despite accusations to the contrary, Acheson was profoundly distrustful of the Soviet Union—as he made it perfectly clear in the Senate Committee hearings on his appointment.

450

"Communism as a doctrine is fatal to free society and to human rights and fundamental freedom. Communism as an aggressive factor in world conquest is fatal to independent governments and to free peoples." So formidable a leader of the opposition as Senator Vandenberg was thoroughly persuaded of Acheson's anti-communist position and was even fearful that it might preclude any agreement with the Russians. When the Secretary went to Paris in May 1949 to attend the Foreign Ministers Conference, Vandenberg expressed his apprehension in a letter to his wife: "As a matter of fact he is so *totally* anti-Soviet and is going to be so *completely* tough that I really doubt whether there is any chance *at all* for a Paris agreement."

After a year in office Acheson concluded that the only way to deal with the Soviet Union was to match strength with strength, toughness with toughness, aggression with aggressiveness. He believed that the Russian leaders were ruthless but realistic, hostile but opportunistic—and he determined to thwart them by building up anticommunist power. "The only way to deal with the Soviet Union, we have found from hard experience, is to create situations of strength. Whenever the Soviet detects weakness or disunity—and it is quick to detect them—it exploits them to the full." In dealing with the Russian leaders, therefore, he insisted that no agreement was possible until they gave up "the idea of aggression." And in his definition that included not only military attack but also "propaganda warfare and the secret undermining of free countries from within."

Since it was not possible for the United States to strengthen weak spots in every part of the world and since even those countries which accepted American assistance were not always fully cooperative, the Truman-Acheson policies succeeded in preventing World War III largely because the Soviet Union sought to further its aggressive aims without military involvement. And world communism became immeasurably stronger when the Communist Mao Tse Tung gained control of the Chinese mainland. By this single stroke of good fortune Russia gained a powerful ally. The United States, on the contrary, having supported Chiang Kai-shek, lost face and influence throughout Asia. American assistance to warlords and landlords backfired—as we should have known if our political vision had not been limited by anticommunist blinders.

The outbreak of war in Korea in June 1950 was a logical sequel. When Japan capitulated, the occupation of Korea was divided between the United States and the Soviet Union. The latter concentrated on forming a friendly government in North Korea. By instituting land and other reforms and by placing Russian-trained Koreans in office it soon succeeded in developing a loyal leadership. By 1948 it was able to withdraw its occupational troops and to call on the United States to evacuate the southern part of Korea. Our own position, however, was far less secure. Our dichotomous policy of stopping communism at all costs and yet abiding by formal democratic procedures caused us to favor a political feudalist like Syngman Rhee and to permit him to establish his power by arbitrary and despotic methods. When American troops departed in 1949 they left behind a reactionary government at Seoul that yearned for the control of the entire country as aggressively as did the communist dictatorship to the north. A flare-up between the divided halves of Korea became inevitable.

When the North Korean troops did begin to march on Seoul, the American policy of containment was immediately put into action. Earlier we had maintained that the orbit of our strategy did not include Korea. On May 7, 1947, Forrestal noted that Secretary Robert Patterson "reiterated that we should get out of Korea at the earliest possible time. He stressed the expense to the United States and the insignificance of the strategic and economic value of Korea." Nearly three years later Acheson, expressing the views of the military chiefs at the Pentagon, again stressed our disinterest in that hapless country. Once the fighting began, however, President Truman acted quickly and boldly. Faced with a concrete situation, an act of communist aggression, he at once ordered our mighty military forces to drive the North Koreans back across the 38th Parallel. With the Russian delegate absenting himself from the UN Security Council, it was a simple matter to persuade the other representatives to denounce the invasion and to give the repelling army UN blessing.

The "police action" in Korea greatly accelerated our rearmament program. Our military expenditures multiplied, amounting to tens of billions annually. Congress, at the urging of the Administration and the Chiefs of Staff, re-enacted the draft—refusing, however, to pass the bill instituting universal military training. The nation as a whole accepted the war as a necessary evil, without enthusiasm but also without much disgruntlement. Even so outspoken a critic of the Administration as Henry Wallace approved of it and took the opportunity to disavow his formerly friendly position toward the Soviet Union. "Russia," he claimed, "could stop the fighting now if she wished to do so." And in November, after Chinese "volunteers" began to cross the Yalu River, he declared: "When Russia incites China to bloody conflict with the United States she is committing a criminal act."

Meantime General Douglas MacArthur had succeeded in stopping the North Koreans near Pusan and then drove them steadily northward. When the fighting neared the 38th Parallel, a number of voices in and out of the UN cautioned the Americans against crossing the boundary line. The argument was that the UN police action was instituted to stop aggression and not to destroy North Korean independence. To cross the 38th Parallel and to drive the enemy to the Yalu River would not only antagonize Asians fearing American domination but would force the Chinese to join the fighting. In the UN, however, the American delegate persuaded a majority to approve the drive north and General MacArthur proceeded toward the highly sensitive Yalu area. It was his belief that the Chinese communists would not dare openly to take over the front. If they did, he maintained, "only 50,000 to 60,000 could be gotten across the Yalu River" and these would be exposed to "the greatest slaughter." Acheson likewise assumed that for the Chinese to enter the war against the UN forces "would be sheer madness."

When victory appeared imminent late in 1950, the Chinese attacked. Their large armies forced the UN troops to retreat pell-mell and to suffer considerable losses in both men and matériel. After months of indecisive but costly fighting General MacArthur tried to force his military and civilian superiors into permitting him to bomb Manchurian bases and thus destroy Chinese opposition at its source. Leaders in the UN and in the Truman Administration opposed extension of the war on the ground that it would surely provoke Russian participation and thus explode into World War III. When MacArthur persisted in his efforts and brought his plea before the Republican leader in Congress Joseph Martin, President Truman relieved him of his command—causing a political storm over the nation and great agitation in Congress. The day before he signed the order he wrote in a letter: "Under the circumstances I could do nothing else and still be President of the United States. Even the Chiefs of Staff came to the conclusion that civilian control of the military was at stake and I didn't let it stay at stake long."

Shortly thereafter, acting on a suggestion of the returned Russian UN representative, cease-fire negotiations were initiated at Panmunjom. Session after session brought no meeting of minds. After months of discussion agreement was reached on a number of issues, but the talks came to a dead-end on the repatriation of prisoners. The North Koreans and Chinese insisted that all prisoners be returned to their countries of origin and the Americans maintained that none be forced to go back against his will. For nearly two years this issue remained a stumbling block. Meanwhile the fighting continued and many thousands on both sides suffered injury and death. The civilian population endured brutal punishment and the land was devastated. In the spring of 1953 agreement was reached on the exchange of wounded prisoners. Soon truce negotiations were resumed and were on the verge of completion when Syngman Rhee unilaterally arranged for the release of around 27,000 North Korean prisoners of war—thereby temporarily disrupting the discussions. Both sides, however, were anxious to put an end to the fighting and a cease-fire agreement was signed late in July. There was no jubilation at the news. Men everywhere realized that there was little good will in the hearts of those who were to negotiate the final settlement.

In the 1948 campaign President Truman promised numerous reforms tending toward the welfare state. And he meant what he said: he did not consider these promises mere "campaign oratory." In his messages to Congress he faithfully recommended the repeal of the Taft-Hartley Act and legislation on low-cost housing, civil rights, fair employment practices, extended social security, and other social welfare reforms.

The time, however, was unpropitious for his Fair Deal. He had to treat with a Congress that was entangled in factionalism, easily intimidated by demagogic reactionaries, and generally devoted to conservative policies. Although it was forced in the national interest to approve the Administration's diplomatic activities and to vote the required funds, it refused to follow Truman's leadership on domestic issues. Unable to control members of his own party, lacking the imagination and the ingenuity to arouse the nation in favor of his reform measures, he made little impression on a Congress that chose to ignore some of his proposals, such as action on labor legislation and civil rights, and to enact others into law in so garbled or attenuated a form as to impair their original purpose.

Emphasis on loyalty investigations of federal employees and resort to the Smith Act in jailing Communist party leaders encouraged intolerance of individual dissidence and growing antagonism against communism. The appointment of commonplace conservatives like Tom Clark and Harold Burton to the Supreme Court to replace such eminent liberals as Frank Murphy and Wiley Rutledge weakened the position of the Court on civil rights in a time of crisis and caused it to validate legislation tending to curb the Bill of Rights. Professor Fred Rodell of Yale University observed at the time that "the Truman-Vinson Court, judged by both the quantity of work it takes on and by the quality of its work, has branded itself—conservatism aside—as incompetent, indolent, and irresponsible." Another factor creating much confusion and wide intimidation was the publication of a list of so-called subversive organizations—drawn up by the Attorney-General from information provided by government-paid informers serving the FBI and Congressional committees. This list included numerous antifascist groups that had flourished in the 1930's and had attracted many liberal Americans.

Although President Truman publicly deplored this acceleration of intolerance, for which he was in some measure responsible, he had neither the will nor the strength to curb it. One of the bitter fruits of this hysteria was Senator Pat McCarran's Internal Security Act of 1950. This law combined the worst features of the Republican Mundt-Ferguson-Nixon bill, which even the Eightieth Congress dared not pass, with provisions against foreign agents and aliens. The Act created a Subversive Activities Control Board for the purpose of providing a list of "Communist-action" and "Communist-front" organizations arbitrarily termed conspiratorial and disloyal. These groups, once listed, were to register with the Attorney-General and file periodic reports. Their activities were to be labeled communist propaganda and their members became subject to harsh disabilities. The Attorney-General was also empowered to imprison aliens indefinitely pending determination of their deportability. In time of war the President was enabled to declare an Internal Security Emergency and the Attorney-General was thereupon to confine in "places of detention"—concentration camps—all persons likely to engage in disloyal activities.

The passage of the bill alarmed many distinguished Americans and prominent civic groups. Their protests were anxious and urgent. President Truman termed it a vicious bill in a forthright veto and pointed out that "the application of the registration

requirements to Communist-front organizations can be the greatest danger to freedom of speech, press, and assembly since the
Alien and Sedition laws of 1798." Like Frankenstein, however,
he was helpless. A callous and contemptuous Congress overrode
his veto by a wide margin. Two years later the same combination
of Congressmen passed the McCarran-Walter Immigration and
Naturalization Act, ostensibly a law to codify and combine existing legislation, but in effect a restrictive and iniquitous attempt
to close the United States to persons of liberal as well as communist associations. Both of these laws have since made America
appear ridiculous and reactionary by its refusal to admit distinguished foreigners on even temporary visas.

Many thoughtful Americans no doubt deeply regretted this
reactionary trend, but few had the courage to oppose it openly
and trenchantly. Always in the past, during periods of repression
and intolerance, there was an influential group ready to protest
against inequities and to protect the Bill of Rights at great personal risk. In our own time such an occasion occurred in 1920,
when twelve of the country's most eminent lawyers, headed by
former President Taft and Charles Evans Hughes, severely criticized the anti-Red hysteria of the time and helped to put an end
to it. Now there appeared no such combination of influential
citizens willing to breast the tide of intolerance in the face of
unscrupulous and demagogic intimidation.

A few brave spirits did speak out, providing oases of comfort
to liberty-loving citizens. One of these critics was the venerable
Judge Learned Hand, who declared that he would rather chance
the escape of a traitor than detect him by means of spreading
abroad "a spirit of general suspicion and distrust." And he warned
against the dire effects of such bigotry:

I believe that that community is already in the process of dissolution
where each man begins to eye his neighbor as a possible enemy; where
nonconformity with the accepted creed, political as well as religious,
is a mask of disaffection; where denunciation, without specification or
backing, takes the place of evidence; where orthodoxy chokes freedom

of dissent; where faith in the eventual supremacy of reason has become so timid that we dare not enter our convictions in the open lists to win or lose.

Justices Black and Douglas expressed similar views in a number of dissenting opinions, but unfortunately these admonitions received little public attention. Douglas also made use of the radio and popular periodicals to broadcast his critical reactions to the current disregard of the Bill of Rights. In a candid article published in the New York *Times* Magazine he cautioned against the prevailing tendency to cling to the orthodox and to tolerate the philosophy of fear.

The Communist threat inside the country has been magnified and exalted far beyond its realities. Irresponsible talk by irresponsible people has fanned the flames of fear. . . . Innocent acts become tell-tale marks of disloyalty. The coincidence that an idea parallels Soviet Russia's policy for a moment of time settles an aura of suspicion around a person. . . . Our real power is our spiritual strength, and that spiritual strength stems from our civil liberties. . . . Our weakness grows when we become intolerant of opposing ideas, depart from our standard civil liberties, and borrow the policeman's philosophy from the enemy we detest.

President Truman also cautioned against the corroding effects of unbridled fear. In his final message to Congress on January 8, 1953, speaking with the voice of Jacob and conveniently disregarding his earlier Esaulike actions, he expressed these noble sentiments:

To beat back fear, we must hold fast to our heritage as free men. We must renew our confidence in one another, our tolerance, our sense of being neighbors, fellow citizens. We must take our stand on the Bill of Rights. The inquisition, the star chamber, have no place in a free society.

Yet words alone, however sincerely uttered by a President, if not implemented by determined deeds, have little effect on the insensitive and cynical minds of a McCarran or a McCarthy. These and other warped politicians continued their damaging work unchecked, impugning the loyalty of government officials from Secretary Acheson down, of teachers, writers, preachers, actors, and others who were suspect of communistic views by association. The conviction of perjury of Alger Hiss and of espionage of Julius and Ethel Rosenberg encouraged the spread of intolerance against every form of dissidence. For what these self-appointed guardians of the nation's security really wanted was not so much to eradicate communist disloyalty as to silence liberalism and nonconformity.

The moral laxness normally manifested in postwar periods, combined with the mediocre caliber of many of Truman's appointees, resulted in a certain amount of "five-percentism" and plain corruption. The Republicans in Congress at once magnified this malfeasance and made many headlines by their sensational charges. President Truman, ever the conscientious county judge, was genuinely distressed by this evidence of dishonesty. Torn between his strong loyalty to friends and his antipathy to improbity in office, he vented his anger against the businessmen who made these deceitful acts possible.

There is nothing I detest so much as a crooked politician or a corrupt government official. But the type of businessman who is a fixer is even lower in my estimation. These are the termites that undermine respect for government and confidence in government and cast doubt on the vast majority of honest and hard-working public officials.

When the end of his term approached he had the good sense to refuse again to become a candidate. He believed he had served his country well and wanted to be relieved of the tremendous responsibility of his high office. What concerned him deeply was his place in American history. He took strong satisfaction in the thought that he had helped to prevent World War III and that he had kept the American economy at its most prosperous level. In his valedictory message to Congress he stressed the fact that "the dread consequences of atomic warfare" had outdated the communist doctrine that war between communist and capitalist countries was inevitable. And he ended his view of the future on an optimistic note:

As we continue to confound Soviet expectations, as our world grows stronger, more united, more attractive to men on both sides of the Iron Curtain, then inevitably there will come a time of change within the Communist world. . . . If the Communist rulers understand they cannot win by war, and if we frustrate their attempts to win by subversion, it is not too much to expect their world to change its character, moderate its aims, become more realistic and less implacable, and recede from the "cold war" they began.

In the heat of the 1952 campaign President Truman, assisting the Democratic candidate Adlai Stevenson, used the same homely tactics he had employed in his own behalf four years earlier. He attacked the Republicans with a ferocity and invective that had served him well against Dewey but that boomeranged when directed against the popular Eisenhower. Since the election, however, he has assumed the role of sagacious yet peppery statesman, exuding good will and confusing popularity with political power. He is actively interested in politics and world events and frequently expresses his views in newspaper articles, books, and interviews. Openly anxious about his proper niche in history, and incidentally capitalizing financially on his prestige as former President, he has recorded what in his view is the unvarnished and veracious history of his Administration. He has also taken great pains to erect a permanent library of his papers and documents for future study.

He need have no concern on this score. His place in history is assured. Fate has given him an eminence he neither expected nor merited. Fortuitous circumstances have placed him at the head of the world's mightiest nation in a time of deep crisis and revolutionary upheaval. With little preparation, either by experience or training, for the high and exacting office which was suddenly thrust upon him at Roosevelt's death, he was immediately forced to make decisions affecting the fate of all mankind. He had to bring the greatest world war in history to a dramatic close, to make up his mind concerning the use of the new and terrible atom bomb, to lead the victorious allies into the United Nations and give the organization a strong lease on life, and to negotiate the terms of peace with Great Britain and the Soviet Union. Like Christian before the hill Difficulty, he dutifully and prayerfully took the steep and narrow path leading to what seemed to him good and proper ends. That he faltered and floundered was neither surprising nor wholly to his discredit; under the very trying circumstances he did the best he could.

The pity was that the time called for an American leader of political genius and Truman was only a middling, if well-intentioned politician. Endowed with normal competence, if occasionally impetuous or even petulant, he evaluated men and events without the insight and imagination that make for greatness. When he came up against the toughness of Stalin and Molotov, he too acted tough. Unlike Roosevelt he did not look ahead far enough nor consider the inevitability of having to live with the Russians in the same world. When the Soviet leaders refused to accede to American demands and countered with terms favorable to themselves, Truman invoked his doctrine against aggression and disbursed many billions to build up a wall of containment against them. To force acquiescence upon Congress he based his requests on urgent alarms and agitated fears. James Reston, discerning political analyst for the New York *Times*, well summed up this procedure when he wrote in a review of Adlai Stevenson's collection of campaign speeches:

One of the tragedies of the postwar era in America is that nobody at the top of our Government has been able to speak with the clarity and eloquence which the times demand. For the past eight years we have been engaged in historic and even noble ventures, but they have been surrounded by such complexity, and discussed with such mediocrity, that vast numbers of our people have never been made conscious of anything but the dangers of not going along with the Government policy.

The two achievements of which Truman was most proud were the prevention of World War III and the record of full employment. That he did strive to keep the world at peace was certainly true. Yet his actions did not always square with his sentiments. More than once he behaved with a belligerence that would have provoked war if the Russians had been ready for it. Fortunately for him, and for mankind, Stalin was enough of a Marxist to believe in the communist doctrine that the inner contradictions of capitalism would sooner or later cause its own collapse. Moreover he was canny enough to realize the danger of exposing Russian cities to the devastation of atom bombing—especially since he knew that it would be many years before his own stockpile of atom bombs would serve to nullify the awful threat to his country. Yet if the Russians avoided direct involvement in war, they were actively engaged in provoking us without hurt to themselves. Thus, although they did not enmesh the United States in a worldwide conflict, they did force her to rearm on a gigantic scale and to become embroiled in the "police action" in Korea that cost more than 142,000 American casualties.

Nor was full employment achieved by a formula unknown to Roosevelt in the 1930's. If the latter had pumped into the economy the tens of billions of dollars which Truman had annually disbursed abroad and spent on armaments, he too would not have had to wait till the imminence of war before abolishing unemployment relief. The fact is that since 1940 the United States has been in either a hot or cold war—and there is no lack of work in a highly industrialized nation when millions of men are in uniform and billions of dollars are devoted to destructive uses. In keeping the nation's population employed, Truman had not performed an economic feat but merely benefited from the fortuitous circumstances that have characterized his years as President.

In retrospect this might be said of him: He was a shrewd minor politician, honest, hardworking, well-intentioned, yet without the qualities that make for eminence, whom chance had catapulted into world leadership. He did the best he could—better than some had feared—yet not nearly as well as the critical conditions demanded.

The Dynamism of Democracy

O N ITS FACE the inauguration of President Dwight D. Eisenhower in January 1953 signified a political relapse. Conservative Republicans assumed the seats of power and proceeded to nullify or at least to modify some of the liberal laws enacted during the previous twenty years. Heads of large corporations, in the Cabinet or on intimate terms with the new Administration, reasserted the idea of free enterprise and sought the return to businessmen of the benefits and opportunities taken from them by the New Deal.

As the 1950's have shown, however, this was hardly the situation. The Eisenhower Administration had, for instance, frowned upon TVA as "creeping socialism" and sought to retard the development of public power over the country; yet it was unable to ignore the irrepressible need to harness overflowing rivers and to irrigate the dry lands—a need which private enterprise cannot well meet to its profit. Similarly, although President Eisenhower did not urge the repeal of the Taft-Hartley Act and approved of the more drastic provisions in subsequent labor legislation, he nevertheless could not but pay lipservice to the legitimacy of labor unions and approve of greater social security benefits. Indeed, one of his Administration's early acts was the establishment of the Department of Health, Education, and Welfare. And in the 1960 campaign both Nixon and Kennedy talked as if they were advocates of the welfare state. Thus, however the conservatives might deplore it, they can no longer revive the free-enterprise barbecue of the previous century.

Ours is indeed a dynamic society, constantly growing and changing, definitely rejecting the very idea of a static economic system. To freeze the *laissez-faire* principle in the American economy would mean to encourage social inequality and political stagnation—practices incompatible with our democratic form of government. From the very beginning of our national existence the Founding Fathers stressed the proposition that in a democracy everyone was entitled to life, liberty, and the pursuit of happiness. Jackson and Lincoln, Emerson and Thoreau, and a host of Americans of good will preached this gospel throughout the nineteenth century. Inspired by this ideal, countless pioneers from the eastern states and from every part of Europe suffered the hardships and dangers of an inimical frontier in order to establish their economic independence and enjoy the personal dignity of political freedom. In this sense the United States was in truth the land of promise—a bright beacon for the world's oppressed. With the frontier beckoning them, and with opportunity obtained for the asking, each man was for himself and the rewards of enterprise were dependent almost as much on chance as on ability.

Conditions in the nineteenth century favored liberty of action rather than personal security. So long as free land was available and every man could fend for himself as a farmer or tradesman, there appeared little need for the federal government to protect the weak from exploitation by the strong or to succor the few destitute. So essential was aggressive enterprise to the development of our continental expanse that it became the measure of personal success. Hard work and shrewd dealing were prized virtues. Those who failed to provide adequately for themselves—whether because of their own shortcomings or because of their inability to cope with the ruthlessness of the marketplace—were considered ne'er-do-wells and left to the casual charity of their neighbors.

In the latter decades of the century the rapid development of industrialism was accompanied by social excrescences that cried for remedy. As Henry George and other men of conscience saw it, great wealth gave rise to extreme poverty. The vanishing of the frontier and the decline of agricultural dominance made millions of workers in industrial centers completely dependent on their jobs for a livelihood. The victims of oppressive factory conditions, a high accident rate, low wages, and periodic unemployment, they were increasingly disgruntled and restive. Their strikes and rioting were beaten down brutally by the army and the constabulary, but their wretchedness made a blotch on the annals of the period. More vociferously rebellious were the farmers. Proud of their democratic prerogatives, they strongly resented being squeezed on the one hand by a constantly falling market and on the other by excessive interest and freight rates. Independent to the core, they joined forces at their granges and at Populist meetings to express their exasperated anger.

Men and women of conscience—ministers, social workers, journalists, and reformers—distressed by this nationwide maladjustment and aware of the altered nature of our economy, began to advocate a more equitable distribution of the benefits of industry. For a long time their voices were cries in the wilderness—unheard by a nation lulled by the cultural lag of its *laissez-faire* philosophy. Gradually, however, the ears of more and more Americans became sensitive to the rising clamor for social reform. The wheels of democracy accelerated their pace. From pulpit and platform and in periodicals the nation was reminded of its liberal legacy. A group of young, enterprising journalists, named muckrakers by President Theodore Roosevelt, began to write sensationally about the ills and blemishes of industrialism. Eminent citizens denounced the conspicuous malpractices of gigantic corporations. Soon the trusts became execrated symbols of selfish business combinations and their powerful heads were condemned as malefactors of great wealth.

Theodore Roosevelt's assumption of the Presidency gave him the opportunity and the power to take legal action against these monopolistic corporations. He was a man of great energy and vivid phrasing, but he was too divided in his loyalties to serve the cause of reform effectively. Forgetful of his formula in foreign affairs, he talked almost shrilly of business aggrandizements and made only feeble use of his presidential big stick. His political rival, Senator Robert M. La Follette, was a truer and more forthright liberal. Nurtured on Jeffersonian ideals and a product of mid-western Populism, he fought for the public good with battle-axe and bludgeon—a zealous crusader determined to muzzle the leviathan corporations. Another outstanding liberal leader of the time was Louis D. Brandeis. Possessed of exceptional intellectual ability, dedicated to the protection of the public from aggressive businessmen, he became the relentless critic of bigness and insisted that the large-scale concentration of industry was bringing about the degradation of democracy. Later, as Justice of the Supreme Court, he struck mighty blows in behalf of our basic freedoms.

In 1912 democracy in America was bursting with renewed vigor. A decade of concentrated effort was bearing fruit. There was a sense of political release in the minds of men. They became strongly conscious of their American birthright, of their sovereign privilege to choose a government to their own liking. While the conservatives were discouraged and on the defensive, the radicals were envisioning the millennium; nearly a million voters cast their ballots for Eugene V. Debs—a record never again equalled by the Socialist party. The mass of Americans had the rare opportunity of expressing a preference for one of two conspicuous liberal candidates for the Presidency. That autumn democracy was indeed entrenched at Armageddon.

Many progressives hailed the victorious Woodrow Wilson. Certainly the New Freedom platform gave promise of a return of the government to the people. Nor did Wilson at first fail in his pledge again to make America the land of democratic promise. Laws were passed to curb monopolistic corporations, to further opportunities for independent and small businessmen, to enable workmen to organize as a matter of right. And if these laws looked better on the statute books than in daily practice, the power of amendment was available to Congress. But the outbreak of war in Europe at first deflected the march of the New Freedom and later completely halted it. President Wilson became a tragic victim of political adversity. Essentially a self-righteous Covenanter, obstinate in the pursuit of his laudable aims, in effect a liberal and idealist lacking the politician's "common touch," he in the end failed not only to make the world safe for democracy but also to establish a genuine peace. The armistice in November 1918 brought no efflorescence of freedom and reform; on the contrary, only the notorious Palmer raids, intolerance of nonconformists, and race riots.

For the next dozen years political liberalism was in eclipse. Conservative Republicans were in the saddle and Harding "normalcy" prevailed over the land. A brief, though intense depression in 1921 was followed by eight years of hectic and meretricious prosperity. The lure of easy money caused millions to speculate with their modest savings; Secretary of the Treasury Andrew Mellon and leading bankers strongly encouraged the purchase of foreign bonds of doubtful merit; the economic spiral was paced at a giddy rate. The stockmarket ticker became the exalted oracle of millions of investors. The high priests of business, intoning their chant of everlasting economic weal, lulled the people into an acceptance of their grimy fleshpots.

The shrunken group of liberals, as zealous as ever, strove valiantly in 1924 to shake the nation out of its hypnotic lethargy. Their veteran leader La Follette appealed forcefully to the social conscience of his fellow Americans. Yet only a small fraction of the voters heeded his call; the large majority preferred President Coolidge and his gewgaws of economic plenty.

After La Follette's death in 1925, Senator George W. Norris stood out among the handful of progressives in Congress. He persisted in the fight for the public good with a dignified determination that withstood both the blandishments and the blastings of the dominant politicians ministering to the business barbecue.

Almost alone he kept Muscle Shoals from assignment for private exploitation. Despite vetoes by Presidents Coolidge and Hoover, he maneuvered to keep the issue alive and to persuade more and more of his fellow Congressmen that the proper harnessing of an unruly river would turn a wasted region into a fertile and flourishing valley. For years this project seemed only a tenuous daydream—a vague vision of dynamic democracy in action—till one day in 1933 the Tennessee Valley Authority became a reality and soon established itself as the world's largest industrial undertaking devoted solely to the public benefit.

In 1929 worshipers of the golden calf saw their idol crashing at their feet. The era of reckless business enterprise and spurious foreign investment came to a sudden halt. It was a day of reckoning for the sharp, scheming manipulator as well as for the petty speculator—and few escaped. In time the distress of insecurity, unemployment, and physical want caused many Americans fondly to recall the precepts and principles of the Founding Fathers. More and more of them began to pay heed to the liberals who were preaching the ideals of Jeffersonian democracy. Chastened and anxious, millions of voters went to the polls in November 1932 and cast their ballot overwhelmingly for Franklin D. Roosevelt and the New Deal.

Desperate conditions require radical remedies, and Roosevelt had both the imagination and the courage to fight the depression with new and unconventional weapons. He was eager to save capitalism by stopping its egregious abuses and by fostering greater freedom of enterprise—and he succeeded in both respects far better than his opponents would admit. Of course he made mistakes; but he drove away fear from millions and inspired them with fresh confidence in themselves. Although multitudes remained unemployed and on the verge of want, they took comfort in the thought that the government was trying hard to keep them fed and housed—and not as paupers but as worthy citizens in distress. Most important was Roosevelt's readiness to experiment, his strong faith in the dynamism of democracy. More liberal legislation was enacted in the early years of his Administration than in all the generations since the adoption of the Constitution. In these laws men's sense of freedom was given full play, liberals enjoyed letting their minds range far and high in the realm of ideas.

The canker of fascism, slowly corroding political life in Europe for a generation, finally attacked society at large. The lowering clouds of war darkened the world in 1939 even more ominously than in 1914. Again the enemy was Germany, more ruthless and more brutal than before. President Roosevelt, like his predecessor a quarter of a century before, readily perceived the danger and struck the alarm. Unlike Wilson, however, he proceeded to forge the arsenal of democracy without at the same time endangering the nation's cherished freedoms. "Dr. Win-the-War" was of necessity given full sway but limited to the war effort; "Dr. New Deal" was not sent packing but kept in readiness for renewed activity immediately after the fighting ceased. Roosevelt also exerted his depleted energy to achieve universal peace as an extension of the democratic effort—making sure politically to succeed where Wilson had failed. His sudden death and Russian recalcitrance served tragically to nullify his valiant efforts.

When President Truman assumed office in 1945 the political world was in delicate balance. The fascist enemy was routed and about to collapse. The chief victors, democratic United States and communistic Russia, were allied in war but in fundamental conflict otherwise. Keenly aware of this sharp difference between the two great powers, Roosevelt had hoped and worked for their peaceful coexistence. And to the day of his death—despite Stalin's obstinacy—the outlook appeared auspicious. Inept diplomacy on our part, however, accelerated Russian aggressiveness. The resulting impasse brought about the "cold war" which has plagued mankind ever since with its crushing burden of rearmament, intense hostility between the two worlds, and inflamed fear within each nation.

For the first time in its history the United States became almost completely preoccupied with foreign affairs. The dread of communism, fomented and intensified by zealous patriots and ambitious demagogues, has assumed hysterical proportions. Veteran organizations, Congressional Committees, old-style reactionaries, and common cranks have exploited this fear for their own devious ends. American communists, accused of advocating violent revolution and of acting as agents of an enemy power, became the formal scapegoats. The attack upon them, however, tended not so much to eliminate potential disloyalty as to stifle dissenting opinion—reducing the traditional American freedoms to a mere shadow of their noble substance.

Always in the past there were audacious spirits who, cherishing liberty more than life, risked imprisonment and worse to safeguard the threatened rights of unpopular minorities. As already stated, however, since 1945 there have been relatively few who dared cry halt to those who confused dissidence with subversion. In their notable dissents from majority opinions that in their judgment served to weaken the Bill of Rights, Justices Black and Douglas, and occasionally Frankfurter, were conspicuously alone among public men who influence public opinion. Frank P. Graham, a North Carolinian of national eminence, declared entreatingly that "in the days of its weakness America was the haven of heretics and should not in the days of its power become the stronghold of bigots." Judge Learned Hand also spoke out nobly against the abusers of liberty. Eminent churchmen and learned scholars likewise cried halt to the hysteria. These and other sporadic voices, however, remain little heard in the persistent clamor of our contemporary Yahoos. As a consequence peoples in other parts of the world confused McCarthyism with Americanism, to our serious disadvantage in the real struggle against communism. It was because of this unhappy situation that the New York *Times* was moved to editorialize on May 6, 1953:

Today there are too many among us, with wits dulled by ignorance or by fright, who seek safety and security only in what they think is the narrow pattern of the past. It isn't the pattern at all; if our ancestors taught us anything, they taught us to dare, to experiment, to explore and not to fear. It is contrary to the best of our tradition to equate nonconformity with treason, unorthodoxy with disloyalty. Yet that is the state of mind to which some of our public figures seem to be trying to lead us. Nothing could be more unimaginative or "un-American."

These few defenders of individual liberty made little impact upon the zealots who considered the Bill of Rights inapplicable to those accused of having communist associations. It was clear that the condition of fear and reaction, favorable to McCarthyite demagogues but deleterious to the basic freedoms, would endure as long as the "cold war" remained acute. It was also obvious that this international tension could not continue indefinitely. Human endurance is not unlimited and sooner or later reaches a breaking point. With both sides in possession of infernal missiles and hydrogen bombs that make war too horrible to contemplate, American and Russian diplomats will be forced to devise a formula for peaceful, if not peaceable, coexistence. On November 23, 1960, the Khrushchev leadership stated its position in a *Pravda* editorial: "The Soviet Communist party has regarded and regards the Leninist principle of peaceful coexistence of states with different social systems as the general line of U.S.S.R.'s foreign policy." It is to be hoped newly elected President Kennedy will approach matters in the same light.

With the end of the "cold war" will come a more realistic attitude toward communism in the United States. Democracy, languishing in an atmosphere of either hot or cold war, will resume its dynamic march. The advocacy of ideas will cease to be a crime; subversive or violent political acton will be dealt with not by demagogues but by the local or federal police power. Once more the good of all the people will become the paramount aim of government.

The efficacy and pertinence of New Deal policies will be re-established. For with billion-dollar corporations multiplying in number and in power—industry doubled production in the past twenty years—no Administration can shirk its duties of supervision and control. Indeed the complex network of modern technological development has made every element of the economy interdependent and affected by a blockage anywhere. How essential government regulation becomes in these circumstances may be imagined if, say, the exploitation of the radio and television were carried on without federal allotment of the available channels and without control of their proper utilization. Enlightened businessmen accept this government supervision of vital industries as necessary to their successful functioning.

Yet the purpose of government in our economy is conditioned not merely by the general need to safeguard and stimulate business enterprise. From the standpoint of the mass of the people an even greater need is that of assuring those who work an adequate livelihood. No matter how much certain politicians and industrialists may impugn and deprecate the idea of the welfare state, its basic purpose has become an inseparable part of modern industrial society. The truth is, of course, that the welfare state is not at all what its critics accuse it of being. In a real sense it is the antithesis of the communistic community. For it not only assures workers and farmers a minimum level of subsistence but also equalizes opportunity for investors and enterprisers. The idea is well stated by Professor Robert M. MacIver, one of our eminent sociologists:

In the welfare state the goal is the adequate provision of protection against want and insecurity and the safeguarding of health and the general well-being of the people. All modern states are increasingly welfare states. The trend in that direction is irresistible. Therefore it is particularly unwise to identify it with the coming of communism. If we do not welcome it as the most fundamental of all economies we should at least recognize in it the surest protection against the peril of communist infiltration.

Those who oppose the purposes of the welfare state and condemn government regulation as an unnecessary evil fail to realize that they are weakening the strongest bulwark against communism.

Moreover, there is no turning back the hands of history. Classical *laissez-faire* methods are simply not applicable to modern industrial conditions; nor is the state of economic anarchy in which the life of most men was described by Hobbes as "solitary, poor, nasty, brutish, and short." Contemporary society must choose between the totalitarian state and welfare democracy. And Americans, having long ago established their preference, will continue to uphold and strengthen their cherished political and economic principles.

BIBLIOGRAPHY *

I. THE REVOLT AGAINST *LAISSEZ FAIRE*

Buck. Solon J., *The Granger Movement*, Cambridge, Mass., 1913.
Gabriel, Ralph H., *The Course of American Democratic Thought*, New York, 1940.
Hacker, Louis M., *The Triumph of American Capitalism*, New York, 1940.
Hicks, John D., *The Populist Revolt*, Minneapolis, 1931.
Hofstadter, Richard, *The American Political Tradition and the Men Who Made It*, New York, 1948.
Lloyd, Henry D., *Wealth Against Commonwealth*, New York, 1894.
Peck, Harry T., *Twenty Years of the Republic*, New York, 1906.
Starr, H. E., *William Graham Sumner*, New York, 1925.
Turner, Frederick J., *The Frontier in American History*, New York, 1920.
Veblen, Thorstein, *Absentee Ownership and Business Enterprise in Recent Times*, New York, 1923.

II. THEODORE ROOSEVELT: THE BULLY CRUSADER AT ARMAGEDDON

Abbott, Lyman F., *The Letters of Archie Butt*, New York, 1924.
Baker, Ray Stannard, *American Chronicle*, New York, 1945.
Bishop, Joseph B., *Theodore Roosevelt and His Time*, 2 vols., New York, 1920.

* The following listings refer to books, articles, and periodicals useful in the preparation of this book.

Croly, Herbert, *The Promise of American Life*, New York, 1912.

Davis, O. K., *Released for Publication*, Some Inside Political History of Theodore Roosevelt and His Times, Boston, 1925.

DeWitt, Benjamin P., *The Progressive Movement*, New York, 1915.

Duncan-Clark, S. J., *The Progressive Movement*, Boston, 1913.

Einstein, Lewis, *Roosevelt: His Mind in Action*, Boston, 1930.

Filler, Louis, *Crusaders for American Liberalism*, Yellow Springs, O., 1950.

Hansbrough, H. C., *The Wreck*, New York, 1913.

Howland, Harold, *Theodore Roosevelt and His Times*, New Haven, 1921.

Ickes, Harold L., "Who Killed the Progressive Party?" *Am. Hist. Rev.*, Jan. 1941.

Irwin, Will, ed., *Letters to Kermit from Theodore Roosevelt*, New York, 1946.

Johnson, Walter, ed., *Selected Letters of William Allen White*, New York, 1947.

——, *William Allen White's America*, New York, 1947.

Lewis, William D., *The Life of Theodore Roosevelt*, Philadelphia, 1919.

Longworth, Alice R., *Crowded Hours*, New York, 1923.

Looker, Earl, *Colonel Roosevelt: Private Citizen*, New York, 1932.

Merriam, Charles E., *Four American Party Leaders*, New York, 1926.

Mowry, George E., *The Era of Theodore Roosevelt, 1900–1912*, New York, 1958.

——, Theodore Roosevelt and the Progressive Movement, Madison, Wis., 1946.

Pringle, Henry F., *Theodore Roosevelt*, New York, 1931.

Roosevelt, Theodore, *A Square Deal*, Allendale, N. J., 1906.

——, *American Ideals*, New York, 1900.

——, *American Problems*, New York, 1925.

——, *An Autobiography*, New York, 1920.

——, *Campaigns and Controversies*, New York, 1926.

——, *Citizenship, Politics and the Elemental Virtues*, New York, 1925.

——, *Fear God and Take Your Own Part*, New York, 1916.

——, *The Letters of Theodore Roosevelt*, ed. by E. E. Morrison, et al., 8 vols., Cambridge, Mass., 1951–1954.

——, "The Progressive Party," *The Hibbert Jour.*, Oct. 1913.

——, *Progressive Principles*, ed. by E. H. Youngman, New York, 1913.

Theodore Roosevelt, Jr., *Average Americans*, New York, 1920.

Selections from the Correspondence of Theodore Roosevelt and Henry Cabot Lodge, 1884–1918, 2 vols., New York, 1925.

Thayer, William R., *Theodore Roosevelt: An Intimate Biograpahy*, Boston, 1919.

Washburn, Charles G., "Roosevelt and the 1912 Campaign," *Proceedings of the Mass. Hist. Soc.*, May 1926.

——, *Theodore Roosevelt: The Logic of His Career*, Boston, 1916.

Winter, Ella and G. Hicks, eds., *The Letters of Lincoln Steffens*, vol. 1, New York, 1938.

Wister, Owen, *Roosevelt: The Story of a Friendship*, New York, 1930.

III. WOODROW WILSON: THE NEW FREEDOM— A WAR CASUALTY

Bailey, Thomas A. *Wilson and the Peacemakers*, New York, 1947.

——, *Woodrow Wilson and the Great Betrayal*, New York, 1949.

Baker, Ray Stannard, *American Chronicle*, New York, 1945.

——, *Woodrow Wilson—Life and Letters*, 8 vols., 1927–1939.

——, *Woodrow Wilson and World Settlement*, 3 vols., New York, 1922.

——, and W. E. Dodd, *The New Democracy*, 2 vols., New York, 1926.

——, ——, *War and Peace*, Presidential Messages, Addresses, and Public Papers (1917–1924), New York, 1927.

Bell, H. C. F., *Woodrow Wilson and the People*, Garden City, 1945.

Black, H. G., *The True Woodrow Wilson*, New York, 1946.

Blum, John M., *Joe Tumulty and the Wilson Era*, Boston, 1950.

——, *Woodrow Wilson and the Politics of Morality*, Boston, 1956.

Cranston, Ruth, *The Story of Woodrow Wilson*, New York, 1945.

Creel, George, *The War, the World and Wilson*, New York, 1920.

Daniels, Josephus, *The Life of Woodrow Wilson*, New York, 1924.

Diamond, William, *The Economic Thought of Woodrow Wilson*, Baltimore, 1943.

Dillon, E. J., *The Inside Story of the Peace Conference*, New York, 1920.

Dodd, W. E., "The Social and Economic Background of Woodrow Wilson," *Jour. of Pol. Econ.*, March 1917.

Harden, Maximilian, *I Meet My Contemporaries*, New York, 1925.

Hendrick, Burton J., *The Life and Letters of Walter H. Page*, New York, 3 vols., 1922–1925.

Houston, David F., *Eight Years with Wilson's Cabinet*, 2 vols., New York, 1926.

Hugh-Jones, E. M., *Woodrow Wilson and American Liberalism*, New York, 1948.

Johnson, Walter, *William Allen White's America*, New York, 1947.

Josephson, Matthew, *The President Makers, 1896–1919*, New York, 1940.

Keynes, J. M., *The Economic Consequences of the Peace*, New York, 1921.

Lane, Franklin K., *Letters*, Personal and Political, Boston, 1922.

Lansing, Robert, *The Peace Negotiations*, A Personal Narrative, New York, 1921.

Latham, Earl, *The Philosophy and Policies of Woodrow Wilson*, Chicago, 1958.

Link, Arthur S., *Wilson: The Road to the White House*, Princeton, 1947.

——, *Woodrow Wilson and the Progressive Era*, New York, 1954.

——, *Wilson*, Princeton, 1956.

Lippmann, Walter, *Drift and Mastery*, New York, 1917.

Lowenthal, Max, *The Federal Bureau of Investigation*, New York, 1950.

Merriam, Charles E., *Four American Party Leaders*, New York, 1926.

Millis, Walter, *Road to War*, America 1914–1917, Boston, 1935.

McCombs, William F., *Making Woodrow Wilson President*, New York, 1921.

Myers, W. S., ed., *Woodrow Wilson:* Some Princeton Memories, Princeton, 1946.

Perry, Bliss, *And Gladly Teach*, Boston, 1935.

Seymour, Charles, *The Intimate Papers of Colonel House*, 4 vols., Boston, 1926–1928.

Smith, A. D. H., *The Real Colonel House*, New York, 1918.

Steffens, Lincoln, *Autobiography*, Vol. II, New York, 1932.

Tumulty, Joseph P., *Woodrow Wilson As I Knew Him*, New York, 1921.

White, William Allen, *Woodrow Wilson*: The Man, His Times, and His Task, Boston, 1924.

Williams, Harley, *Men of Stress*, London, 1948.

Wilson, Edith Bolling, *My Memoir*, Indianapolis, 1938.

Wilson, Woodrow, *Congressional Government*, Boston, 1885, 1900.

——, *Constitutional Government of the United States*, New York, 1908.

——, *The New Freedom*, New York, 1913.

——, *Great Speeches and Other History Making Documents*, Chicago, 1919.

——, Selected Literary and Political Papers and Addresses, 3 vols., New York, 1926–1927.

——, *State Papers and Addresses*, New York, 1918.

Winkler, John K., *Woodrow Wilson*, The Man Who Lived On, New York, 1933.

IV. ROBERT M. LA FOLLETTE: UNCOMPROMISING PROGRESSIVE

Allen, Philip L., *America's Awakening*, New York, 1906.

Barton, A. O., *La Follette's Winning of Wisconsin*, Madison, Wis., 1922.

Bliven, Bruce, "Robert M. La Follette's Place in Our History," *Cur. Hist.*, August, 1925.

Commons, John R., *The Industrial Commission*, Its Organization and Methods, Madison, Wis., 1913.

——, "La Follette and Wisconsin," *The New Republic*, Sept. 17, 1924.

——, *Myself*, New York, 1934.

Crabtree, L. T., *The Wayback Club*, A Textbook in Progressivism in Wisconsin, Crandon, Wis., 1912.

Doan, E. N., *The La Follettes and the Wisconsin Idea*, New York, 1947.

Ely, Richard T., *Ground Under My Feet*, New York, 1938.

The Facts about La Follette and Wheeler, New York, 1924.

Fitzpatrick, E. A., *McCarthy of Wisconsin*, New York, 1944.

Gilbert, C. W., *You Takes Your Choice*, New York, 1924.

Holmes, Fred L., *Badger Saints and Sinners*, Milwaukee, 1939.

Howe, F. C., *Wisconsin*, An Experiment in Democracy, New York, 1912.

Jackson, Robert H., Address on Robert M. La Follette, June 23, 1940.

Johnson, Walter, *William Allen White's America*, New York, 1947.

La Follette, Belle C. and Fola, *Robert M. La Follette*, 2 vols., New York, 1953.

La Follette, Robert M., The Armed Ship Bill Meant War, New York, 1917.

——, *Autobiography*, Madison, Wis., 1913.

——, Government by Private Monopoly, Washington, 1924.

——, Inaugural Messages to the Wisconsin Legislature, 1901–1905, Madison, Wis., 1905.

——, A New Declaration of Independence, Chicago, 1924.

——, War with Germany, Speech in the U. S. Senate, April 4, 1917, Washington, 1917.

La Follette's Weekly Magazine, 1909–1924.

Lovejoy, A. F., *La Follette and the Establishment of the Direct Primary in Wisconsin*, 1890–1904, New Haven, 1941.

McCarthy, Charles, *The Wisconsin Idea*, New York, 1912.

McKay, K. C., *The Progressive Movement of 1924*, New York, 1947.

Nation, The, 1918–1920, 1924–1925.

New Republic, The, 1916–1919, 1922–1925.

Nye, Russell B., *Midwestern Progressive Politics*, East Lansing, Mich., 1951.

Ogg, Frederick A., "Robert M. La Follette in Retrospect," *Cur. Hist.*, Feb. 1931.

Platt, C. C., *What La Follette's State Is Doing*, Batavia, N. Y., 1923.

Steffens, Lincoln, *The Struggle for Self-Government*, New York, 1906.

Stirn, E. W., *An Annotated Bibliography of Robert M. La Follette*, The Man and His Work, Chicago, 1927.

Sullivan, Mark, "Looking Back on La Follette," *World's Work*, Jan. 1925.

Torelle, Ellen, ed., *The Political Philosophy of Robert M. La Follette*, Madison, Wis., 1920.

Villard, O. G., *Prophets True and False*, New York, 1928.

Warren, Charles, Borah and La Follette and the Supreme Court of the U. S., New York, 1923.

White, William Allen, *Politics, The Citizen's Business*, New York, 1924.

V. LOUIS D. BRANDEIS: "COUNSEL FOR THE PEOPLE"

Bickel, A. M. *The Unpublished Opinions of Mr. Justice Brandeis: The Supreme Court at Work*. Cambridge, Mass., 1957.

Brandeis, Louis D., *Business—A Profession*, Boston, 1914, 1933.

——, *The Curse of Bigness*, ed. by Osmond K. Fraenkel, New York, 1934.

——, *Other People's Money and How the Bankers Use It*, New York, 1914, 1932.

——, *The Brandeis Reader*, ed. by Erwin H. Pollock, New York, 1956.

Brief on Behalf of the Opposition to the Confirmation of Louis D. Brandeis as Associate Justice of the Supreme Court of the United States, U. S. Senate, Washington, D. C., March 25, 1916.

De Haas, Jacob, *Louis D. Brandeis*, New York, 1929.

Dilliard, Irving, ed., *Mr. Justice Brandeis, Great American*, St. Louis, 1941.

Flexner, Bernard, *Mr. Justice Brandeis and the University of Louisville*, Louisville, 1938.

Frankfurter, Felix, ed., *Mr. Justice Brandeis*, New Haven, 1932.

Goldman, Solomon, ed., *Brandeis on Zionism*, Washington, D. C., 1942.

Goldmark, Josephine C., *Fatigue and Efficiency, A Study in Industry*, New York, 1912.

——, *Pilgrims of 1848*, New Haven, 1930.

Hard, William, "Brandeis," *The Outlook*, May 31, 1916.

Harvard Law Review, Nov. 1931; Dec. 1941.

Kallen, Horace M., *The Faith of Louis D. Brandeis, Zionist*, New York, 1943.

Konefsky, Samuel J., *The Legacy of Holmes and Brandeis*, New York, 1957.

Levine, Louis, *The Women's Garment Workers*, New York, 1924.

Levy, Beryl H., *Our Constitution:* Tool or Testament? New York, 1941.

Lief, Alfred, *Brandeis:* The Personal History of an American Ideal, New York, 1936.

——, ed., *The Brandeis Guide to the Modern World*, Boston, 1941.

——, ed., *The Social and Economic Views of Mr. Justice Brandeis*, New York, 1931.

Majority Reports of the Committee on the Judiciary, U. S. Senate, Washington, D. C., 1916.

Mason, Alphaeus T., *Brandeis: A Free Man's Life*, New York, 1946.

——, *Brandeis: Lawyer and Judge in the Modern State*, Princeton, 1933.

——, *The Brandeis Way:* A Case Study in the Workings of Democracy, Princeton, 1938.

New Republic, The, Feb.–June, 1916.

Nomination of Louis D. Brandeis Hearings before the Subcommittee of the Committee on the Judiciary, U. S. Senate, Document No. 409, Washington, D. C., 1916.

United States Reports, Cases Adjudged in the Supreme Court, 1916–1939, vols. 243–304, Washington, D. C.

VI. FRANKLIN D. ROOSEVELT—PROTAGONIST OF THE NEW DEAL

Adamic, Louis, *Dinner at the White House*, New York, 1946.

Beard, Charles A., *Midpassage*, New York, 1940.

——, *President Roosevelt and the Coming of War, 1941:* A Study in Appearances and Realities, New Haven, 1948.

——, and G. H. E. Smith, *The Old Deal and the New*, New York, 1940.

Bemis, S. F., *The United States as a World Power*, New York, 1950.

Brogan, Denis W., *The Era of Franklin D. Roosevelt*, New Haven, 1950.

Busch, Noel F., *What Manner of Man?* New York, 1944.

Byrnes, James F., *Speaking Frankly*, New York, 1947.

Chase, Stuart, *A New Deal*, New York, 1932.

Day, Donald, ed., *Franklin D. Roosevelt's Own Story*, Boston, 1951.

Farley, James A., *Jim Farley's Story:* The Roosevelt Years, New York, 1949.

Feis, Herbert, *Churchill, Roosevelt, Stalin:* The War They Waged and the Peace They Sought, Princeton, 1957.

Flynn, John T., *Country Squire in the White House,* New York, 1940.

———, *The Roosevelt Myth,* New York, 1948.

Freidel, Frank B., *Franklin D. Roosevelt,* 3 vols., Boston, 1952–1956.

Gunther, John, *Roosevelt in Retrospect,* New York, 1950.

Hardman, J. B. S., ed., *Rendezvous with Destiny,* New York, 1944.

Hassett, W. D., *Off the Record with FDR,* New Brunswick, N. J., 1958.

Hull, Cordell, *Memoirs,* 2 vols., New York, 1948.

Jackson, Robert H., *The Struggle for Judicial Supremacy,* New York, 1941.

Johnson, Gerald W., *Roosevelt: An American Study,* New York, 1941.

Kiernan, R. H., *President Roosevelt,* London, 1948.

Langer, William L., and S. E. Gleason, *The Challenge to Isolation, 1937–1940,* New York, 1952.

Leahy, William D., *I Was There,* New York, 1950.

Lindley, Ernest K., *Franklin D. Roosevelt: A Career in Progressive Democracy,* Indianapolis, 1931.

———, *The Roosevelt Revolution,* New York, 1933.

Mackenzie, Compton, *Mr. Roosevelt,* New York, 1944.

McIntire, Ross T., *White House Physician,* New York, 1946.

Mitchell, Broadus, *Depression Decade,* New York, 1947.

Moley, Raymond, *After Seven Years,* New York, 1939.

Nevins, Allan, *The New Deal and World Affairs,* New Haven, 1950.

Perkins, Frances, *The Roosevelt I Knew,* New York, 1946.

Rauch, Basil, *Roosevelt from Munich to Pearl Harbor,* New York, 1950.

———, *The History of the New Deal,* New York, 1944.

Reilly, Michael F., *Reilly of the White House,* New York, 1947.

Roosevelt, Eleanor, *This I Remember,* New York, 1949.

———, *This Is My Story,* New York, 1937.

Roosevelt, Elliot, *As He Saw It,* New York, 1946.

Roosevelt, Franklin D., *Government—Not Politics,* New York, 1932.

———, *His Personal Letters,* 4 vols., New York, 1947, 1948, 1950.

———, *Looking Forward,* New York, 1933.

——, *My Friends*, 28 History-Making Speeches, Buffalo, 1945.

——, *On My Way*, New York, 1934.

——, *Roosevelt's Foreign Policy, 1933–1941*, New York, 1942.

Roosevelt, Sara Delano, *My Boy Franklin*, New York, 1933.

Rosenman, Samuel I., ed., *The Public Papers and Addresses of Franklin D. Roosevelt*, 13 vols., New York, 1938, 1943, 1950.

——, *Working With Roosevelt*, New York, 1952.

Schlesinger, Arthur M., Jr., *The Age of Roosevelt*, 3 vols., Boston, 1957–1960.

Sherwood, Robert E., *Roosevelt and Hopkins: An Intimate History*, New York, 1948.

Stettinius, E. R., Jr., *Roosevelt and the Russians*, New York, 1949.

Stimson, Henry L., and McGeorge Bundy, *On Active Service in Peace and War*, New York, 1947.

Tully, Grace, *F. D. R., My Boss*, New York, 1949.

VII. GEORGE W. NORRIS: DYNAMIC DEMOCRAT

Bailey, Stephen K., and Howard D. Samuel, *Congress at Work*, New York, 1952.

Congressional Digest, May, 1930.

Coyle, David Cushman, *Land of Hope*, The Way of Life in the Tennessee Valley, Evanston, Ill., 1941.

Hodge, C. L., *The Tennessee Valley Authority*, A National Experiment in Regionalism, Washington, 1936.

Kirchway, Freda, "George W. Norris," *The Nation*, Sept. 9, 1944.

Lief, Alfred, *Democracy's Norris*, The Biography of a Lonely Crusade, New York, 1939.

Lilienthal, David E., "Senator Norris and the TVA," *The Nation*, Sept. 23, 1944.

——, *TVA, Democracy on the March*, New York, 1944.

Neuberger, Richard L., and S. B. Kahn, *Integrity*, The Life of George W. Norris, New York, 1937.

Norris, George W., "Electric Light Rates in Ontario, Canada," *Cong. Rec.*, Aug. 22, 1935.

——, *Fighting Liberal*, New York, 1945.

——, "The One-House Legislature," *Annals* of Am. Acad. of Pol. & Soc. Sci., Sept. 1935.

——, Peace Without Hate, Lincoln, Nebr., 1943.

——, "Progressives Unite!" *The New Republic*, Sept. 28, 1942.

——, "The Road to Permanent Peace," *The New Republic*, Jan. 17, 1944.

——, "TVA on the Jordan," *The Nation*, May 20, 1944.

——, "Why Henry Ford Wants Muscle Shoals," *The Nation*, Dec. 26, 1923.

Nye, Russell B., *Midwestern Progressive Politics*, East Lansing, Mich., 1951.

Pritchett, C. H., *The Tennessee Valley Authority*, A Study in Public Administration, Chapel Hill, 1943.

Selsnick, Philip, *TVA, The Grass Roots*, Berkeley, Calif., 1949.

Villard, O. G., "George W. Norris," *The Forum*, Apr. 1936.

——, *Prophets True and False*, New York, 1928.

White, William Allen, review of *Integrity* in *The Saturday Review of Literature*, Aug. 10, 1937.

VIII. HUGO L. BLACK, NEW DEAL JUSTICE

Anderson, Paul Y., Weekly column in *The Nation*, June 4, 1938.

Beard, Charles A., *The New Republic*, New York, 1940.

Black, Hugo, L., "I did Join the Klan," Radio speech, Oct. 1, 1937, *Vital Speeches*, Oct. 15, 1937.

——, "Inside a Senate Investigation," *Harper's Monthly Magazine*, Feb. 1936.

——, "Lobby Investigation," Radio speech, Aug. 8, 1935, *Vital Speeches*, Sept. 1, 1935.

——, "The Bill of Rights," James Madison Lecture, New York, 1960.

——, "The Shorter Work Week and Work Day," *Annals* of the Am. Acad. of Pol. and Soc. Sci., March 1936.

——, "The Wages and Hour Bill," Senate Speech, July 27, 1937, *Vital Speeches*, Aug. 15, 1937.

——, "To Win the War and the Peace," *The New Republic*, July 27, 1942.

Corwin, E. S., *Constitutional Revolution, Ltd.*, Claremont, Calif., 1941.

Curtis, Charles P., "How About Hugo Black?" *Atlantic Monthly*, May 1939.

——, *Lions Under the Throne*, Boston, 1947.

Engel, Irving M., "Justice Black After Seven Years," *The Nation*, Oct. 7, 1944.

Fairman, Charles, *American Constitutional Decisions*, New York, 1950.

——, "Does the Fourteenth Amendment Incorporate the Bill of Rights?" *Stanford Law Review*, Dec. 1949.

Frank, John P., *Mr. Justice Black*, New York, 1949.

——, and Robert F. Munro, "The Original Understanding of 'Equal Protection of the Laws,'" *Columbia Law Review*, Feb. 1950.

Freund, Paul A., *On Understanding the Supreme Court*, Boston, 1950.

Havighurst, H. C., "Mr. Justice Black," *Nat. Lawyers Guild Quarterly*, June 1938.

Konefsky, S. J., *Chief Justice Stone and the Supreme Court*, New York, 1946.

Lerner, Max, *Ideas for the Ice Age*, New York, 1941.

McCune, Wesley, *The Nine Young Men*, New York, 1947.

McLaughlin, Andrew C., "The Court, the Corporation, and Conkling," *Am. Hist. Rev.*, Oct. 1940.

Morrison, Stanley, "Does the Fourteenth Amendment Incorporate the Bill of Rights?" *Stanford Law Review*, Dec. 1949.

New Republic The (Editorial), "The Case of Mr. Justice Black," Sept. 29, 1937.

Pritchett, Herman C., *The Roosevelt Court*, A Study in Judicial Politics and Values, New York, 1948.

Rodell, Fred, "Black vs. Jackson," *Forum*, Aug. 1946.

——, "Justice Hugo Black," *American Mercury*, Aug. 1941.

Ryan, John A., "Due Process and Mr. Justice Black," *The Catholic World*, April 1940.

Schlesinger, A. M., Jr., "The Supreme Court: 1947," *Fortune*, Jan. 1947.

Swisher, Carl B., *The Supreme Court in Modern Role*, New York, 1958.

United States Reports, Cases Adjudged in the Supreme Court, 1937–1960, Vols. 302–360, Washington, D. C.

Williams, Charlotte, *Hugo Black*, A Study in Judicial Process, Baltimore, 1950.

IX. HARRY S. TRUMAN: THE NEW DEAL IN ECLIPSE

Abels, Jules, *Out of the Jaws of Victory*, New York, 1959.

Allen, Robert S., and William V. Shannon, *The Truman Merry-Go-Around*, New York, 1950.

Barth, Allan, *The Loyalty of Free Men*, New York, 1951.

Bundy, McGeorge, ed., *The Pattern of Responsibility*, Boston, 1952.

Byrnes, James F., *Speaking Frankly*, New York, 1947.

Coffin, Tris, *Missouri Compromise*, Boston, 1947.

Daniels, Jonathan, *The Man of Independence*, New York, 1950.

Douglas, William O., "The Black Silence of Fear," New York *Times Magazine*, January 1953.

Edwards, Robert V., *Truman's Inheritance*, Caldwell, Idaho, 1952.

Forrestal, James, *The Forrestal Diaries*, ed. by Walter Millis, New York, 1951.

Fuller, Helen, "Has Truman Lost the Left?" *The New Republic*, December 17, 1945.

Helm, William P. *Harry Truman*, New York, 1947.

Hillman, William, *Mr. President*, New York, 1952.

Leahy, William D., *I Was There*, New York, 1950.

Lowenthal, Max, *The Federal Bureau of Investigation*, New York, 1950.

Lubell, Samuel, *The Future of American Politics*, New York, 1952.

McCune, Wesley, and John R. Beal, "The Job that Made Truman President," *Harper's Magazine*, June 1945.

McNaughton, Frank, and Walter Hehmeyer, *This Man Truman*, New York, 1945.

McWilliams, Carey, *Witch Hunt*: The Revival of Heresy, Boston, 1950.

Nation, The, 1945–1953.

New Republic, The, 1945–1952.

New York *Times*, 1945–1952.

Rovere, R. H., "President Harry," *Harper's Magazine*, July, 1948.

Smith, A. Merriman, *Thank You, Mr. President*, New York, 1946.

Stimson, Henry L., and McGeorge Bundy, *On Active Service in Peace and War*, New York, 1948.

Stone, I. F., *The Truman Era*, New York, 1953.

Truman, Harry S., *The Economic Reports of the President*, New York, 1949.

——, *The Truman Program*, ed. by M. B. Schnapper, Washington, 1949.

——, *Memoirs*, 2 vols., Garden City, 1955–1956.

——, *Mr. Citizen*, New York, 1960.

——, *Truman Speaks*, New York, 1960.

Vandenberg, Arthur H., Jr., *The Private Papers of Senator Vandenberg*, Boston, 1952.

INDEX